WAR AND RURAL LIFE
IN THE EARLY
MODERN LOW COUNTRIES

Myron P. Gutmann

Princeton University Press
Princeton, New Jersey

This book has been composed in Garamond

Printed in The Netherlands by Van Gorcum, Assen.

To My Parents and
To Roy

Table of Contents

List of Illustrations –
Maps – Tables – Figures

Illustrations

Maps

Tables

Figures

Abbreviations Used in Notes and Bibliography

AEL	Archives de l'Etat à Liège
AEL C*de*J	Archives de l'Etat à Liège, Cours de Justice
AEL PdD	Archives de l'Etat à Liège, Cathédrale, Secrétariat, Protocoles des Directeurs.
AEL PR	Archives de l'Etat à Liège, Parish Register collection.
AEL CP	Archives de l'Etat à Liège, Conseil Privé.
BIAL	*Bulletin de l'Institut Archéologique Liégeois.*
BSAHL	*Bulletin de la Société d'Art et d'Histoire du Diocèse de Liège.*
BSSLL	*Bulletin de la Société Scientifique et Litteraire du Limbourg.*
CAPL	*Chronique Archéologique du Pays de Liège.*
Mém. Cour.	Academie Royale des Sciences, des Lettres et des Beaux-Arts de Belgique. Mémoires Couronnés et Autres Mémoires. Collection in-8°. (Collection in-4° referred to as Mém. Cour. in-4°.)
NOTICES	Daris, Joseph. *Notices sur les églises du diocèse de Liège,* 17 vols. Liège, 1867-1899.
RAL LVO	Rijksarchief in Limburg. Land van Overmaas.
RBPH	*Revue Belge de Philologie et d'Histoire.*
Vieux Liège	*Bulletin de la Société Royale "Le Vieux Liège".*

A Note on Measures and Moneys

Measures

The following measures were in use in the Basse-Meuse in the seventeenth and eighteenth centuries:

Measures of Capacity[1]

Measure	Number per Muid
Muid of Maastricht (560.16 liters)	1
Maldre	4
Setier, vat	24
Quarte, kop	96
Pognoux	384
Muid of Liège, Dalhem, Aachen (245.696 liters)	1
Setier, vat	8
Quarte, kop	32
Pognoux	128

Measures of Surface Area

Measure	Number per Bonnier
Bonnier (0.87178 hectare)	1
Journal	4
Grand Verge	20
Petite Verge	400

Moneys

The principal money of account in use in the early modern Basse-Meuse was the florin, but there were at least four different florins: those of Brabant, of Liège, of Brabant-Liège, and of Holland (also called guilders).[2] They are all related to subsidiary units of money as follows:

Unit	Number per Florin
Florin of Brabant	1
(and Florin of Brabant-Liège)	
Patard	20
Aidant, Liard	80

The value of these units of account varied tremendously, both in relation to one another and in relation to the common gold and silver coins of the era. Where money is represented in the text in terms of coins, I have also shown its value in Florins of Brabant-Liège (the predominant money of account in the Liégeois Basse-Meuse) in order to provide comparisons and according to this table of values.[3]

> 1 écu = 3 fl. (to 1660) or 4 fl. (1660-1750)
> 1 escalin = 7.5 patards (to 1660) or 10 patards (1660 to 1750)
> 1 patagon = 1 écu
> 1 daler = 1.625 florins (after 1660)
> 1 rixdaler = 3.25 florins (after 1660)

Acknowledgments

This book grew out of my Princeton University doctoral dissertation, written under the supervision of Professor Theodore K. Rabb. In the process of transforming it into its present form, I have been aided by several institutions and individuals, whom I would like to thank here. A number of colleagues have been kind enough to read all or part of the various drafts that went into this book, and to make helpful comments. They are Professor Rabb, Etienne Helin, J. W. Smit, Philip J. Benedict, Robert Darnton, Nancy Fitch, Christopher R. Friedrichs, Guy Fitch Lytle, Janet Meisel, M. Gwyn Morgan, Alberto Palloni, J. F. R. Philips, Richard Ryerson, William Sewell, R. Malcolm Smuts and J. M. Winter. I owe special thanks to Dr. J. C. G. M. Jansen of the Sociaal Historisch Centrum voor Limburg, because he not only read and commented upon several chapters, but also allowed me to make use of certain data that he had collected for his own work. Despite the invaluable contributions of these individuals, any errors of fact or judgment that remain are entirely my own.

This work could never have been completed without the kind assistance, on many occasions, of the staffs of three archives in Liège and Maastricht. The Archives de l'Etat à Liège, under the supervision of Dr. Georges Hansotte; the Stadsarchief en -bibliotheek te Maastricht, under H. H. E. Wouters; and the Rijksarchief in Limburg made this book possible. There is no way for an outsider to sufficiently thank these institutions and their staffs for their patience and dedication.

Several American institutions provided me with both moral and financial support along the way. The Princeton History Department was unfailing in its commitment to my work while I was a student. Their recommendation led me to Judith Rowe of the Social Science User Services office of the Princeton University Computer Center. The demographic and economic computations (and especially the family reconstitution of the parish of Wandre) which underlie this work could

never have been completed without the constant attention devoted to it by Mrs. Rowe. At Texas, the University Research Institute and the Population Research Center have helped me in additional ways, by supporting me, and this research, as it moved along. Jeannie Taylor and Donna Lynn Gotch, of the Center, typed this manuscript as it progressed. Finally, the American Council of Learned Societies, through its program of Grants-in-Aid to Recent Recipients of the Ph.D., financed a much-needed research trip to Europe in the summer of 1977.

Part of Table 4.2 appeared in "War, the Tithe and Agricultural Production: the Meuse Basin North of Liège, 1661-1740," in Herman van der Wee and Eddy van Cauwenberghe, eds., *Productivity of Land and Agricultural Innovation in the Low Countries (1250-1800)* (Leuven: Leuven University Press, 1978), pp. 65-76. I reprint the table here with the permission of the editors and publisher. Portions of Chapters VI, VII and VIII appeared in a preliminary form as "Putting Crises in Perspective: The Impact of War on Civilian Populations in the Seventeenth Century," *Annales de Démographie Historique* (1977), 101-128. That material, plus much of Chapter IX, also appeared as "Why They Stayed: The Problem of Wartime Population Loss," *Tijdschrift voor Geschiedenis*, 91 (1978), 407-428. I would like to thank the editors of these journals for permission to reprint portions of that material here.

To my wife, Barbara, goes the greatest thanks. Her faith in me and in this project over the past six years has been unfailing, and her contribution to its present form monumental. I could not work without her.

M.P.G.
Austin and Houston
January 1979

Part 1

The Background

Introduction:

War and Other Crises in Early Modern Life

In 1946 Jean Meuvret published a groundbreaking article titled "Les Crises de subsistance et la démographie de la France d'Ancien Régime."[1] In his article Meuvret pointed out that ancien régime France had been periodically and viciously hit by severe crises, and argued that these crises pushed a large portion of the population – people who were in any event only barely surviving – below the line of subsistence. In Meuvret's view, these crises were the cause of the stagnant French economy and population of the seventeenth century. It was a century characterized by repeated, severe, subsistence crises, which eliminated the potential for continued growth in French society. Finally, Meuvret delineated three varieties of crises: extreme food shortages, epidemic diseases, and war, which exhibited the characteristics of the other two in combination.

Young French historians eagerly took up Meuvret's construct. Subsistence crises became one of the ways to look at the seventeenth century. The single most important work to derive from it was Pierre Goubert's *Beauvais et le Beauvaisis de 1600 à 1730.*[2] Goubert outlined for his readers the complexity of French provincial society, and described the various social groups which felt subsistence crises acutely. In this and other works Goubert demonstrated that there was a fundamental dichotomy in the population of ancien régime France.[3] A minority of the population was "independent," i.e., they were able to support themselves by their own economic resources and were sufficiently resilient economically to weather most crises. But the majority of the population was economically "dependent." They worked as laborers for their more prosperous neighbors. Even if they had a farm, they had to borrow a plow-team from their wealthier neighbor, or depend on part-time farm or industrial jobs to supplement their income. This dependent majority lived very near the subsistence line; when a subsistence crisis struck, they might slip below the surface of survival, very likely never to reappear.

In addition to Goubert, a number of other scholars were at work on this group of subjects. By 1970, Goubert could call on sufficient other works to publish a "reappraisal" of the demographic significance of Meuvret's early work.[4] Even at that time, however, war had hardly been considered, because, while Meuvret regarded war as an important aspect of subsistence crises, he considered it a complex and not easily studied subject. Thus, while we have had numerous studies of famine and dearth, and even disease, war remained relatively unstudied. Very recent works continue to disregard or minimize it.[5] Although we know a great deal about the economic, social, and demographic consequences of the first two of Meuvret's crises, we know all too little about the consequences of the third — war — particularly in western Europe.

This is regrettable, because only when we understand war will we understand the other two causes of early modern hardship. Subsistence crises were not all alike, but rather a combination of a varying number of elements molded by internal structures like the local economy and population, and external forces like war, European markets, weather, and epidemic disease. Their impact was not always the same, but depended in intensity, frequency, and duration on both the internal structures and the external forces. I will add a refinement to Goubert's reinterpretation of the original hypothesis. He found that Meuvret's subsistence crises caused few deaths; they acted only in concert with epidemic disease. But Goubert underestimated: we will see that the only great periods of economic hardship and population loss occurred when more devastating combinations occurred. The great catastrophes of early modern Europe took place when war, harvest failure, and epidemic disease all came at once.

War is an important subject in the social, economic, and demographic history of early modern Europe, even without its role as one leg of the subsistence crisis tripod. For generations of European men, women, and children, war was an element of almost everyday experience. Surely it was frequent enough. George Clark wrote that there were "only seven complete calendar years [in the seventeenth century] in which there was no war between European states . . . ."[6] For those who survived its strains, war left an indelible mark on their lives. For those who perished of its rigors, we need now say very little. In early modern Europe, as today, war was one of the main shapers of men's lives. In spite of its importance, most early modern social historians have ignored its impact, probably because they have been concerned with the unchanging elemental structure of life. War's unpredictability

and repeated changes made it unsatisfactory for such an analysis. The only body of literature about war's social and economic impact is devoted to Germany in the Thirty Years' War; but that literature is for the most part dated and precedes the methodological revolution that has overtaken the study of European history in the last thirty years.[7]

Like the social historians, the military historians have ignored civilians in wartime. Although we know how armies fought battles in early modern Europe, we have only recently learned who provided those armies with money and supplies and how they functioned between battles, and we know very little about how civilians (outside the bureaucracies) participated in the process of supply, camp, and preparation.[8] Yet this subject is important. Without an understanding of war's impact on civilians, we will never understand European society, how people lived, or even war itself before the industrial revolution.

This book is about the wartime experiences of people who lived in the western European countryside in the seventeenth and eighteenth centuries. It will go beyond war's contribution to the debate on subsistence crises and look at two much broader questions in the history of early modern wars and warfare, and their relations with civilian life: first, how did war's impact change between 1620 and 1750? And, second, why did some regions suffer less than others from comparable military action?

To approach the problem of describing the relations that rural civilians developed with armies that visited their communities, and the impact of those visits on their lives, we will examine in turn three structural elements of early modern life. They are, first, the community's relationship with armies, and especially the problems of housing and feeding troops and meeting their demands for money and supplies; second, the economic consequences of military presence, especially in terms of agricultural production and the price of food; and, finally, war's demographic consequences. The objective will be not only to measure the material costs and benefits of war for civilians, but also to get some idea of how people perceived war's impact on their lives.

The relationship between war and civilians is a broad subject. In the absence of earlier works on the same problem, this type of study demands that we focus on a relatively limited geographical area over a limited number of years in order to isolate questions and formulate hypotheses on a broad range of subjects. This is especially important when assembling quantitative material. We will consider war's impact by examining largely annual data describing community finances,

agricultural production, prices, population, and vital events, and then comparing them to the chronology of war and other crises in a small region. We will focus on an area in eastern Belgium and the Netherlands, between and around the cities of Liège and Maastricht. It was called the Basse-Meuse in the local French dialect.[9] In its broadest frame, it can be said to have contained some forty or fifty administrative units, including small and large villages, and very small towns. In the mid-eighteenth century, it probably had a population of fewer than fifty thousand. Temporally, we will focus on the years 1620-1750 because they encompass the dramatic changes in warmaking and government that occurred between the beginning of the Thirty Years' War and the end of the War of the Austrian Succession in 1748. Perhaps unfortunately, the wars of the sixteenth century are not included here. Less military action took place in the Basse-Meuse then than later, and the documents necessary for the demographic, social, and economic study attempted below simply do not exist.

Because of the shortage of good series of quantitative data and of the time required to assemble them, we will rarely use all the farms, residents, villages, or parishes of the Basse-Meuse to measure population, production, and so on. Our data is a sample.[10] We have used all the years in the period considered, but we must recall that the number of wartime years in any one place, even in the bellicose seventeenth century, is also small. Despite the small number of cases and years involved, the evidence presented constitutes a valid sample, representative of war's impact in the Basse-Meuse. In the context of forty to fifty communities, population trends for twenty-two parishes, the tithe for fourteen villages, births and deaths in seven and six parishes, respectively, and price series for the two major markets constitute samples greater than the necessary minimum. They are significant proportions of such a small region. In a few instances I use a single case, such as the production of a single farm or the detailed demographic experiences of a single parish (obtained through family reconstitution), to illuminate very detailed points. Given the quality of quantitative information available, such a single-place approach is the one to use.

There are a number of reasons for studying the Basse-Meuse to understand the impact of war. The region has a long tradition of local historical study which has produced many useful monographs. Its archives are large and full of both public and private documents relatively undamaged by wars, despite the fact that the Basse-Meuse was

almost always involved in the thick of early modern wars. Finally, the Basse-Meuse offers an interesting perspective on the wars of the seventeenth and eighteenth centuries, because it was a rather prosperous region.[11] As we shall see, the region was located on the border between two of the most fertile agricultural zones in the eastern Low Countries. Its farmers were able to produce enviable amounts of grain, dairy produce, and vegetables. Its location near a busy river and the city of Liège, one of the earliest industrialized places in continental Europe, led to a wide range of opportunities for its residents, no matter what their status. Yet, the people of the Basse-Meuse felt the wars of the era in spite of the region's prosperity (the fact that the region was economically strong does not mean that all of its residents were prosperous). By examining the impact of wars on a prosperous and growing region, we will see both the basic impact of war and the ways that economic conditions changed that impact. Whether our conclusions will be representative of the Low Countries as a whole, or even all of Europe, must wait for additional local studies along the same lines as this. But it is my impression that our conclusions will hold generally for the Low Countries and specifically for the eastern Low Countries and the Rhineland.

The nature of the region in part determines the sort of wartime experiences its residents had. In fact, we will see that the economic structure and prosperity of the Basse-Meuse in large part controlled the way that military presence affected it. But that is not the point here. The Basse-Meuse felt war directly, through the presence of soldiers involved in marches, sieges, and battles, and stationed in camps. In this it was different from most regions in France and Spain, whose residents often felt war only through taxes and recruitment. That impact of war will involve a different study, one which focuses on the problems of the modern European state, and the costs of the growth of that state for its residents. Here, we are interested in those regions that suffered early modern wars directly.

* * *

If we agree on what we mean by the word *crisis*, it will be easier to understand war's impact on rural civilians, and to compare that impact to those of other phenomena. Just what was a crisis? The notion of a short-term crisis – the sense we will use in this work – has become muddied. People use it without thinking about its meaning. We can extrapolate from the work of Meuvret, Goubert, and others, to form a

classic, narrow definition of crisis as they applied it to demographic history. Their idea was essentially malthusian in nature: they saw a relationship between food supply and population, and hence thought of *subsistence crises*. A crisis, they might have said, was a change in the balance of vital demographic events (births and deaths) that turned population growth to stability or decline. In this way they explained that a structural system of periodic crises existed in early modern France. Regular if slow growth resulted in a malthusian structure where population exceeded food supplies. This situation, they hypothesized, was periodically reversed by a change in the balance of births and deaths (usually a great upsurge in deaths) so that the population no longer exceeded its material resources. Although not a strict dictionary definition, this was and is a workable definition of the word *crisis*.

Unfortunately, the meaning of the word crisis has grown beyond this narrow definition to encompass any form of extreme hardship, whether or not it upset the demographic balance, and whether it had as its base some change in the available supply of food or some other material aspect of life. If we agree on this broader definition, then we must say that much of the population lived in a state of perpetual crisis, because a large proportion of the early modern European population can be shown to have lived on the very edge of subsistence and hardship. Even though their resources were severely limited, and many lived near hardship, this notion of perpetual crisis probably gives an unnecessarily negative view of their lives, as well as rendering impossible any use of the word crisis to describe short-term changes.

In this book we will make use of a modified form of the original narrow definition of crisis. A crisis, according to this definition, will be any short-term (and thus terminable) series of events that was capable of producing a rapid shift away from the normal pattern of demographic events, either by increasing the number of deaths or by decreasing the number of children born. It is no doubt true, in theory at least, that bad weather will create these effects. When we look at the direct and indirect impact of weather on human experience, we will see that it did affect harvests, which affected prices, which in turn produced the crises we have spoken about. But the impact was attenuated by the indirect route which weather followed to play its role. War (and high prices and short food supplies, as agents acting alone) acted more directly and may have produced more immediate difficulty for the regions they affected. Here, as we shall see, we have the most devastating element in early modern civilization.

Chapter I

Magnet for Armies:
The Basse-Meuse Under the Ancien Régime

This study of the impact of early modern wars on rural life in the Low Countries has as its subject the region called the Basse-Meuse, which lies between and around the cities of Liège and Maastricht, near the Meuse River. Today, the Basse-Meuse is fully integrated into the modern Netherlands and Belgium, but in the seventeenth and eighteenth centuries that was not the case. The dominant characteristic of the Basse-Meuse in the ancien régime was its internal diversity. As late as 1789, political control was fragmented and still determined by the accidents and favors of medieval history. We will address questions of politics in greater detail later in this chapter, but this much is certain: the area was wholly a territory of borders, a series of frontiers between great states. In an era when borderlands were subject to the aggressions of ambitious statesmen, the Basse-Meuse became strategically central to the designs of Dutch *stadholders* and French kings.

Although the region was fragmented politically and divided linguistically (between speakers of Dutch and Walloon French),[1] it was quite uniform in the kind of life it offered its residents. Most of them were Roman Catholics, although Dutch Protestants appeared in Maastricht and some of the villages around it after the Dutch conquest in 1632.[2] And most of them were agricultural workers and farmers, engaged in the various farming tasks found in an area that divided two farming regions, the Hesbaye (large cereal farms) to the west, and the Pays de Herve (small dairy farms) to the east. Despite the emphasis on farming, the region's economy was, for its time, remarkably varied and relatively full of opportunities for work outside agriculture. The problem in defining the Basse-Meuse is not finding an area of sufficient uniformity to study, but rather in drawing the outside lines of such an area. I have chosen here to study the communities near the Meuse River; they are easy to identify and they should be fully representative of a larger region.

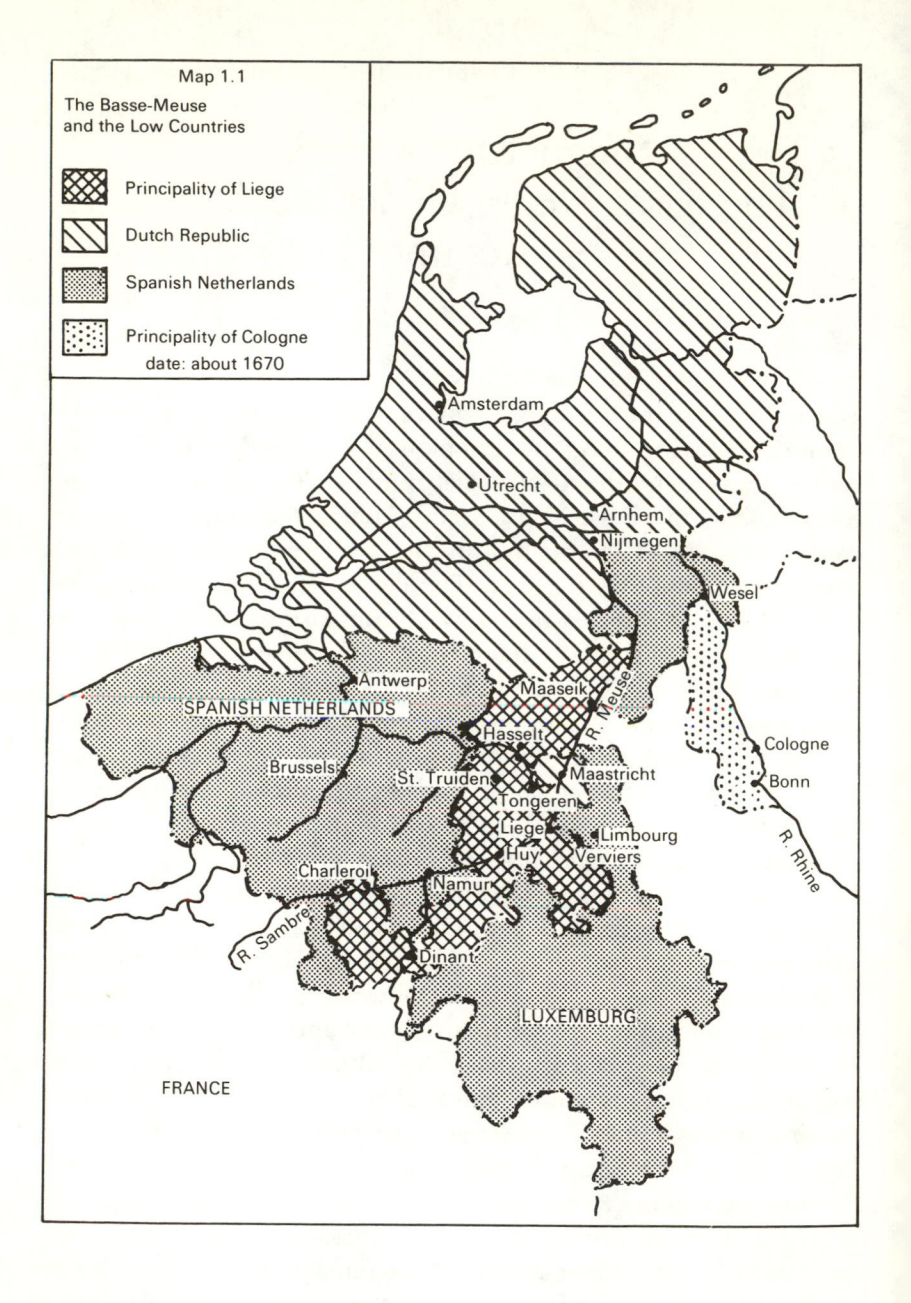

Map 1.1

The Basse-Meuse
and the Low Countries

- Principality of Liege
- Dutch Republic
- Spanish Netherlands
- Principality of Cologne
  date: about 1670

Amsterdam

Utrecht

Arnhem
Nijmegen

Wesel

Antwerp
SPANISH NETHERLANDS
Maaseik
R. Meuse
Hasselt
Cologne
Brussels
St. Truiden
Maastricht
Bonn
Tongeren
Liege
Limbourg
Huy
Verviers
R. Rhine
Charleroi
Namur
R. Sambre
Dinant
LUXEMBURG

FRANCE

I. Background: Government in the Basse-Meuse

The variety which characterized the Basse-Meuse was nowhere more evident than in its political structure, and it is this political structure which caused it to be dragged repeatedly into war. We will first examine that governmental structure before turning to the specific events and conditions that forced the people of the Basse-Meuse to experience so many wars. The basic question we must answer is: who were the sovereigns that divided the responsibility for governing the Basse-Meuse at the beginning of the period we are studying, in 1620? Then we can turn to the meaning of that sovereignty and the reasons why the Basse-Meuse saw so many armies in the seventeenth and eighteenth centuries, the fact which makes it so appropriate for a study of war's impact.

The Principality of Liège, which controlled more than half the area, was the dominant sovereign and power in the Basse-Meuse under the ancien régime. By the beginning of the seventeenth century, the principality had become something of an anomaly in the Low Countries. First, it was the only significant ecclesiastical principality remaining in the area. Also, within the borders of what are now Belgium, The Netherlands and Luxemburg, it was the only substantial governmental unit not incorporated into either the Dutch Republic or the Spanish Netherlands. Of those portions of the Low Countries which retained some allegiance to the Holy Roman Empire, Liège alone was a member of the administrative Circle of Westphalia; all of the others were members of the Circle of Burgundy.[3] Furthermore, only Liège was formally neutral in international disputes.

Two other sovereigns controlled portions of the Basse-Meuse in 1620 (see Map 1.2). In reality, the King of Spain ruled through two administrative units: one a conglomerate which consisted of the Duchy of Limbourg and the three "Lands Beyond the Meuse," and the other the Duchy of Brabant.[4] The Emperor stood as direct sovereign over several communities and remained in theory the ultimate suzerain over them all. The city of Maastricht was a special case, governed by a "condominium" of Liège and Brabant (Spain), which shared sovereignty and divided administrative and judicial responsibilities.[5] Defense of the city was left in the hands of the Spanish, who maintained a garrison there in the early seventeenth century.

After the settlement of the Thirty Years' War, yet a fourth sovereign entered the picture. The Dutch conquered Maastricht in 1632 and

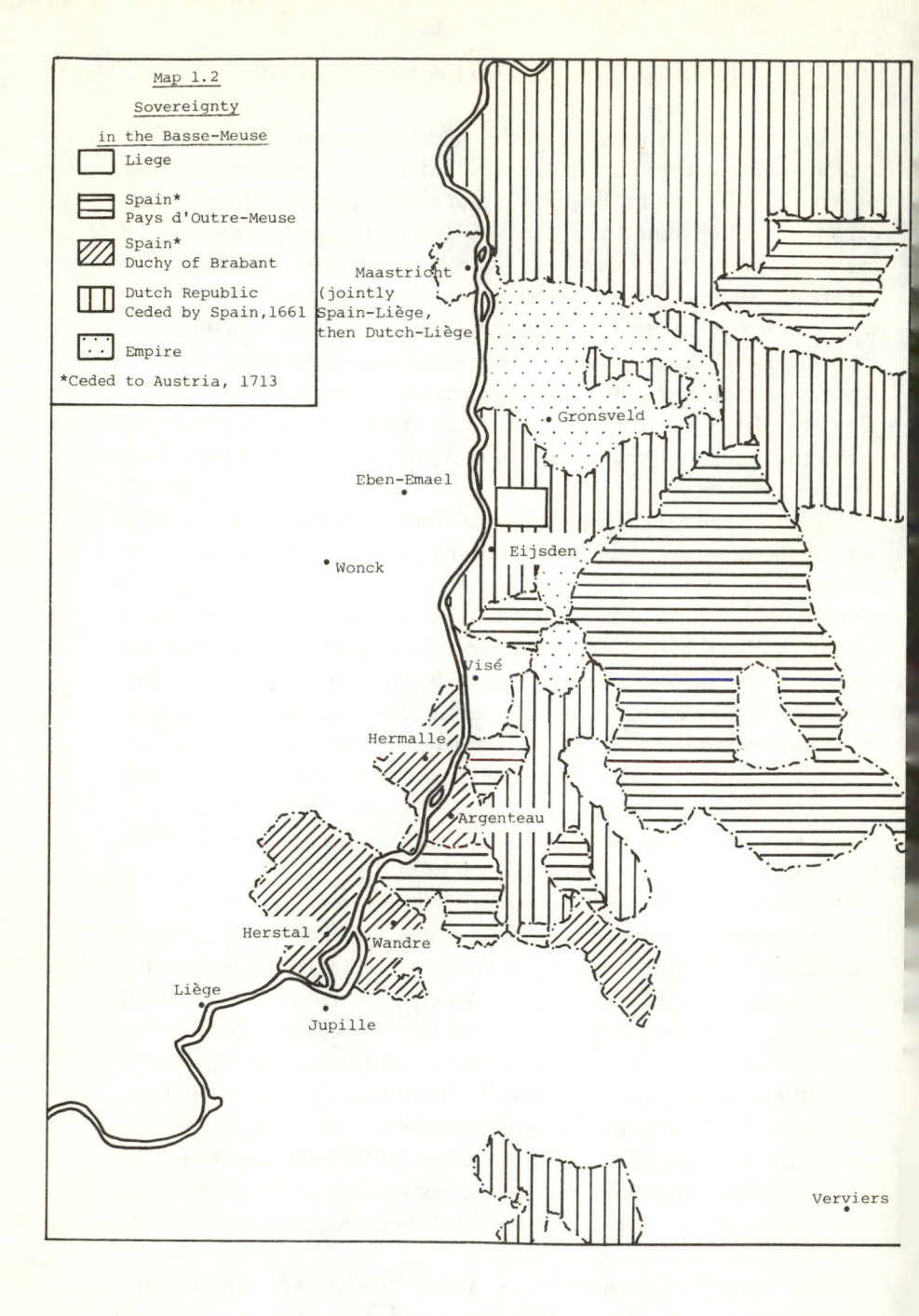

Map 1.2

Sovereignty
in the Basse-Meuse

☐ Liege

⊟ Spain*
Pays d'Outre-Meuse

▨ Spain*
Duchy of Brabant

▥ Dutch Republic
Ceded by Spain,1661

⋯ Empire

*Ceded to Austria, 1713

Maastricht (jointly Spain-Liège, then Dutch-Liège

Gronsveld

Eben-Emael

Eijsden

Wonck

Visé

Hermalle

Argenteau

Herstal

Wandre

Liège

Jupille

Verviers

occupied a portion of the Spanish "Lands Beyond the Meuse." The settlement of the war ultimately transferred to them sovereignty over some of the formerly Spanish Basse-Meuse.

What did this sovereignty mean? The various states that controlled the Basse-Meuse were technically in command of the lives of the area's residents. The Princes of the princely states — the Prince of Liège and the King of Spain (usually acting through a governor in Brussels) — or, later, the Estates General of the Dutch Republic (for the new Province of Dutch Limburg) — made laws and administered the higher levels of justice. They consulted with their estates, one representing the Principality of Liège, and others the Spanish "province" of the "Lands Beyond the Meuse" and the Dutch "province" of Limburg, who together with the prince determined taxes. Moreover, the sovereign (Prince or Estates General) had the right to determine foreign policy and otherwise carry on the affairs of government. Since the Principality of Liège was the major sovereign of the Basse-Meuse, we will, to a certain extent, concentrate on the history and experience of that Principality. Still, except for their relations with foreign powers in time of war, there was very little to distinguish between the citizens of one state or another. And, as we will see in later chapters, even in wartime little separated the experience of Spanish subjects, for example, from that of Liège's subjects.

One possible difference from sovereign to sovereign was law, but while distinct legal customs distinguished the areas of different sovereigns, they were not starkly dissimilar.[6] Nor did laws or borders constitute solid barriers to movement or to interaction among the citizens of the area. Local notaries often practiced under the laws of two or more sovereigns. Residents of Liégeois villages owned or leased land in villages subject to the King of Spain or the Dutch Republic, and actively farmed them. Being all borders, the region became all the more homogenous because the fragmentation of the political process removed governmental actions still farther from the lives of the mass of the people.

While they might appreciate the relative privileges offered by one sovereign over another, at least in terms of low taxes, political neutrality, or an agreeable religion, most citizens of the Basse-Meuse had little to do with sovereigns and central governments. If any government concerned them, it was that of their village or town. Before the reorganization of the 1790's, at the time of the French regime (1794-1815), most of the residents of the Basse-Meuse lived in small-

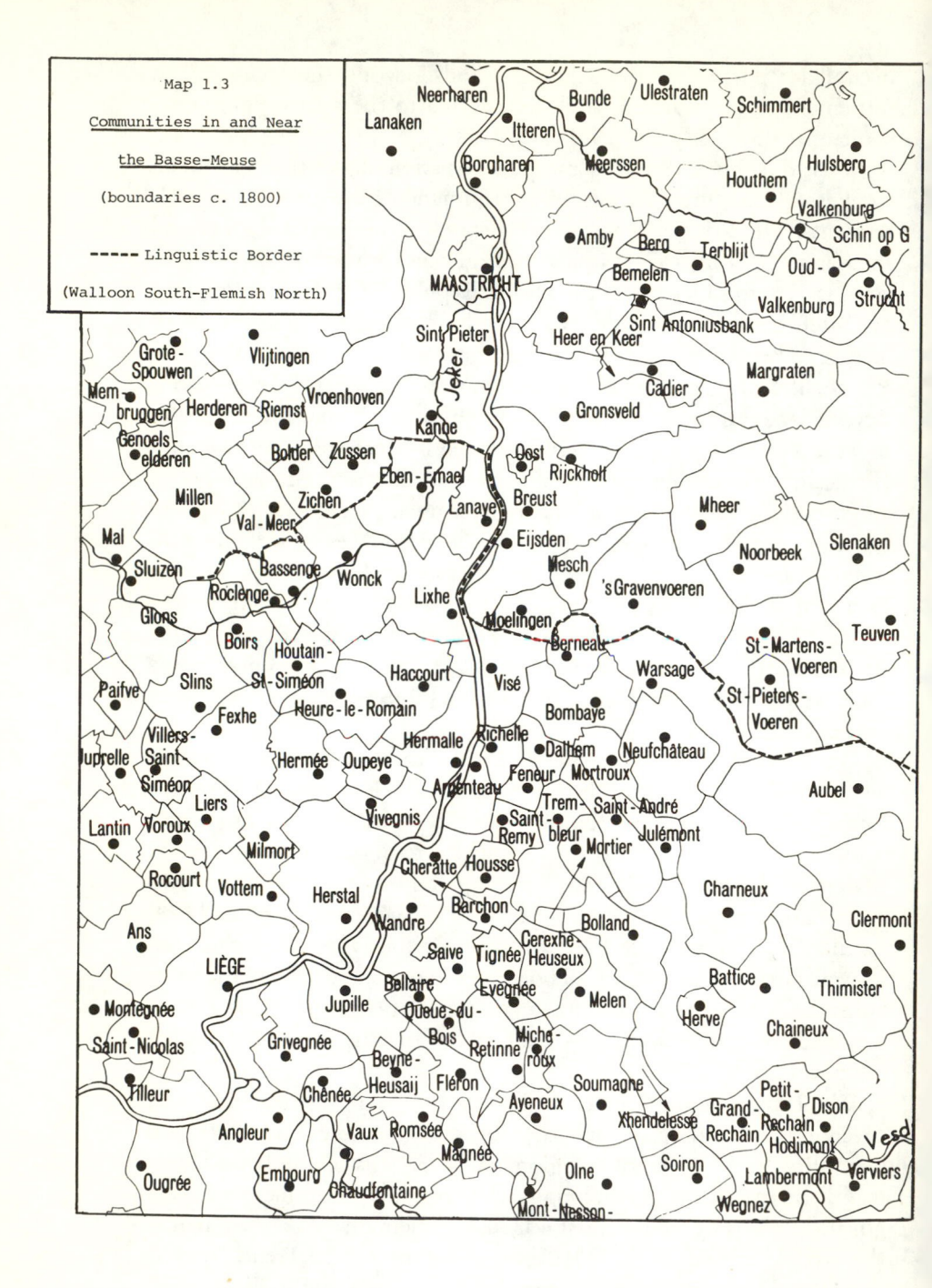

Map 1.3

Communities in and Near

the Basse-Meuse

(boundaries c. 1800)

----- Linguistic Border

(Walloon South-Flemish North)

14

to-medium-sized seigneurial villages. Only two communities, Dalhem and Visé, had their origins in ancien régime towns, with democratic constitutions, independent of a lord's control. Throughout the Basse-Meuse, however, local governments were remarkably uniform in their basic organization, no matter who their sovereign was, or whether they were a constituted town or merely a seigneurial village.[7]

The basic elements of local government in the ancien régime, as in the middle ages or today, were justice and taxes. Not all justice was administered at the local level. There were certain matters that were outside the jurisdiction of local courts, such as capital crimes and a variety of other criminal and civil matters. Such cases were handled by courts of appeal and higher instance, in accordance with the procedures of the larger judicial units established by each region's sovereign. In the seigneurial villages, justice was administered by a local court – usually consisting of seven members – appointed by the seigneur. Similar courts existed in the towns, but their prince appointed the members of the court.

Taxation was more important than justice. All the sovereigns except the Holy Roman Emperor raised taxes from their citizens. These taxes paid for the mechanisms of government administration, of defense and war, and of the princely entourage. Yet nowhere in the Basse-Meuse were taxes expecially high, at least if compared with those levied by France and Spain in the seventeenth century. The Principality of Liège had no army and until the eighteenth century very little government. Even the Spanish Netherlands were not heavily taxed, since they could rely on their formal administrative independence from Spain to withstand such demands. Only the Dutch Republic – a sovereign in the Basse-Meuse after 1660 – was a major military power in the second half of the seventeenth century. That might have called for high taxes, but it seems that the Dutch consciously under-taxed their newly acquired territory to compensate for the devastation of the Thirty Years' War.[8]

Still, some tax revenue had to be raised. Local estates divided the needs of the central government among clergy, nobility, and commons; then each group divided its share among its members, roughly according to wealth.[9] Finally, individual communities divided that burden, together with local needs, among their tax-paying citizens. They collected a variety of taxes, on property, on persons, and on consumption. In Chapter II, I will discuss some of the ways that more extensive taxes were raised to pay for the damage and demands of war.

This group of communities, with their variety of governments, saw

armies all too frequently in the turbulent years from 1620 to 1750. Too many things happened in those years to narrate here. Rather, important events, especially those of a military and political nature, are set out in a Chronological Table (Appendix A). To summarize, military action took place in the Basse-Meuse during every major war in the period – the Thirty Years' War (1618-1648, with important action in the Basse-Meuse during 1632-1638); the Dutch War (1672-1679); the War of the League of Augsburg (1688-1697); the War of the Spanish Succession (1701-1714); and the War of the Austrian Succession (1741-1748, in the Basse-Meuse, 1746-1748). Moreover, the region usually felt even minor wars, such as the Franco-Spanish continuation of the Thirty Years' War (1648-1659), the War of the Devolution (1667-1668), the War of the Reunions (1683-1684), and the War of the Polish Succession (1733-1735).

What brought armies to the Basse-Meuse in the seventeenth and eighteenth centuries? It was only infrequently to fight battles. The armies of the age met head-on only rarely.[10] Only two battles were fought in the Basse-Meuse itself (Haccourt, 1746, and Laeffelt, 1747), and only three or four within fifty kilometers. Generals preferred sieges and the occupation of fortresses and cities. The City of Liège had two fortresses, and, while it was technically neutral, foreign troops often occupied them during wartime. Maastricht was, as we shall see, even more of a prize. There were four major sieges of Maastricht between 1620 and 1750, each bringing a substantial army into the region to surround the town and prepare the siege.

Far more important than battles or sieges for the people of the Basse-Meuse were the less strategically formal reasons why armies came to visit. First, armies had to travel and the Basse-Meuse was a speedy route for armies travelling both north-south and east-west. Second, while armies in the seventeenth and eighteenth centuries did not fight in the winter, they no longer disbanded. Rather, at the end of the campaigning season, they attempted to find a place to make a winter camp. Armies in transit and winter camps, rather than battles and sieges, were the real scourge of the people of the Basse-Meuse.

Still, two characteristics of the region distinguished the Basse-Mosan people from others who lived near the line of march. First, the region was rich in both grain and the industrial goods necessary to supply armies. An army that camped near the City of Liège could usually count on being well fed and well equipped for its next campaign. Second, the region had no way to keep armies out. Although the Principality of

16

Liège was nominally neutral, it was no Switzerland. Flat, virtually unarmed, and riven by internal disputes, the Principality could not resist being crossed or occupied, frequently with dire consequences for its finances and its citizens.

These three reasons for the attractiveness of the Basse-Meuse and the larger Liégeois region will be the subject of the rest of this chapter. Because it follows from the preceding discussion of sovereignty and government, we will first address the issue of Liège's neutrality and the divisions in the Liégeois state. Then, we will explore geo-political considerations and the question of Maastricht. Finally, we will describe the economy of the Basse-Meuse and show how its relative richness contributed to the region's magnetic lure for the armies of the ancien régime.

II. *Liège's Neutrality and the Princes of Liège*

Liégeois neutrality originated in the fifteenth century.[11] As Burgundian power grew at the end of the middle ages, Liège resisted attempts to bring it under a Burgundian "protectorate."[12] Only after the sack of Liège by Burgundian troops in 1468 did the city give in. But Charles the Bold died in 1477, and his heirs could not hold Liège.

Relieved of Burgundian domination, the Liégeois Estates and the Prince-Biship declared their neutrality in international disputes. It was a declaration of weakness, designed to remove them from their continuing precarious position between France and Burgundy. Although the King of France and the Burgundian Duke of Brabant finally agreed to respect Liégeois neutrality in 1492,[13] that agreement was by no means definitive. The character of Liégeois neutrality developed over more than a century of difficult tests. It became especially strained during the Netherlands Revolution, when the Principality seemed to stand between an aggressive United Provinces and an angry Spain.[14] The ultimate test of Liégeois neutrality took place in the seventeenth century in a series of wars between the Dutch Republic, France, and the Habsburgs.

The neutrality of the Principality of Liège ought to have prevented the occupation of any Liégeois territory by any foreign army, prevented billeting, and prevented the kind of exactions by *contribution* that we will describe in Chapter II. Moreover, the mere crossing of Liégeois territory by an army was an abridgment of that neutrality unless the Prince of Liège gave his consent. Even when permission was granted,

17

foreign troops were supposed to reimburse the civilian population fully for all costs and destruction.[15]

Its neutrality born in weakness, the Principality of Liège never had the strength to protect itself. Given its strategic location, the great powers and their generals rarely thought it in their interests to respect Liégeois neutrality. Only force could keep them out. But Liège raised only one army of any significance. In the early 1690's, during the War of the League of Augsburg, she had perhaps 6,000 men under arms,[16] and that was grossly inadequate for protection. The roughly contemporary battle of Neerwinden, fought in 1693, brought together a combined total of 130,000 French and Allied troops.[17] Rural and urban militias, even with the occasional aid of Bavarian armies allied to the Prince of Liège, rarely succeeded in keeping foreign armies away. The all-too-frequent solution was to allow the foreign troops to enter the principality, and to hope they would leave soon.

Diplomacy was an alternative to force, but effective negotiation was frequently impossible. Besides the principality's weakness, there were the clashing interests of the Prince and his citizens. The Bishops of Liège were not only Prince and Bishop of the principality, but all too often allies, agents, and members of the great European families. In the seventeenth century, the principality was almost continuously ruled by a series of younger sons of the Bavarian Wittelsbachs, who usually also held the neighboring and more important archepiscopal electorate of Cologne, and who spent much of their time in Bonn or Cologne.[18] It is not surprising to discover that these Bishops of Liège ignored the interests of their subjects or, worse yet, attempted to use their position to advance personal or dynastic interests. Kings and Emperors courted their favor, attempting to convince the Bishops of Liège to come to their aid, if only by permitting troops to cross through the principality without opposition. The Princes were often persuaded by bribes, promises of advancement for their family, or simply by misplaced feelings of loyalty to the Emperor.[19] In the second half of the seventeenth century, three Liégeois Bishops entered wars, hopelessly compromising their neutrality.

The usefulness, even the survival, of Liégeois neutrality was also endangered by the internal tensions which constantly disrupted the principality and the city of Liège in the seventeenth century. At the heart of the dispute was not neutrality, but a conflict over who was going to govern the state. The city of Liège had a centuries-old tradition of popular democracy, a tradition that conflicted with the desires of its

often ambitious Princes. In the past, the city had cooperated with the Prince in the Estates of the principality and against the clergy, nobility and other towns, but the city's desire for self-government had a new birth in the late sixteenth century, following the democratic Dutch example, and under the strains of strongly pro-Spanish absentee bishops and the growing menace of the Duke of Alba and Spanish absolutist government in the Netherlands.[20]

During the Thirty Years' War (1618-1648), the principal cause for disagreement between the citizens of Liège and their Prince, Ferdinand of Bavaria (1612-1650), was the method by which the city's leadership was to be elected.[21] In 1613, Ferdinand restricted the franchise, allowing himself to dominate future elections and angering the citizens of Liège. When he and his opponents sought an international forum for the resolution of their dispute, the principality could not preserve its neutrality. Again and again, as the dispute flared into open insurrection, Ferdinand asked Spanish and Imperial armies to put military pressure on the City.[22] His urban opponents logically asked the other side for help. France and the Dutch were only too willing to "protect" the neutrality of Liège, if it would benefit them strategically and diplomatically. Thus, both the Prince and his citizens compromised Liégeois neutrality.

In the era of the Thirty Years' War, both the Prince and his enemies argued that they alone wished to preserve Liégeois neutrality, since the other side was willing to call in foreign intervention. Besides the troops that arrived as a result of these calls for aid, the internal disunity left the principality open to the constant passage of troops. Only in 1649, after the end of the war, did Ferdinand manage to reassert his authority through the use of military force. He finally and decisively instituted the regressive franchise law of 1613.[23]

During the first half of the seventeenth century, Ferdinand of Bavaria attempted to maintain his neutrality while relying on the Emperor, his nominal overlord, for aid. In the second half of the century, his Wittelsbach successors gave up the pretense of neutrality and shifted their allegiance to France. This contributed to an even greater military presence in the Liégeois region, including those areas not subject to the Prince of Liège. Maximilian Henry, Ferdinand's successor (1650-1688), participated in the opening phase of the Dutch War (1672-1678) by making a treaty with France and, in May of 1672, declaring war on the Dutch Republic. He went even further to aid his new allies by welcoming into the Principality a large French army

embarked on a Mosan offensive. The people of Liège viewed these acts as breaches of their neutrality; the civil conflict that resulted lasted until 1684.[24]

The pattern established by Maximilian Henry in the 1670's was repeated by the next Wittelsbach Prince of Liège, Joseph Clement (1694-1723), in the War of the Spanish Succession (1701-1714). Like his brother Maximilian Emanuel, the Governor of the Spanish Netherlands, Joseph Clement joined the French coalition at the outset of the war and welcomed French troops into his territories.[25]

Between Maximilian Henry and Joseph Clement of Bavaria, the Canons of the Cathedral of Liège briefly elected one of their own number to the bishopric, but even he could not avoid the internationalist behavior of the late-seventeenth century Liégeois Bishops. Soon after his election, Jean-Louis d'Elderen (1688-1694) entered the War of the League of Augsburg (1688-1697) on the Allied side. His action led to the bombardment and burning of the city of Liège in June, 1691. He even raised an army of six thousand men – probably, as we have seen, the largest Liégeois army before the French (and Liégeois) Revolution of 1789 – to fight alongside the English, Dutch, and Imperial armies.[26]

A Liégeois prince who allied himself with one side in a major European war, or who called on an army to aid him in his internal political squabbles, could not refuse his friends the right to camp in his territory in the winter, or to recruit for their armies from among his subjects. He certainly could not keep them out by declaring his neutrality. At the same time, if those armies got out of control and destroyed or stole property, or if the opponents of his friends took vengeance and exacted contributions throughout the territory, an unarmed state could do little but beg for better treatment. These were the consequences for the Principality of Liège of the actions of its princes in the seventeenth and eighteenth centuries. Rarely subject to sieges because of its neutrality, it still suffered the rigors of armed visitors.

III. Maastricht and the Mosan Military Corridor

We cannot blame all the consequences of war for the whole Basse-Meuse on the Princes of Liège or their opponents. There were strategic reasons why armies came to the region, the most important of these being the fortified city of Maastricht, a vital point on the Meuse River

20

III. 1. *Pillage and Burning of a Village*, by Jacques Callot (1633)

and, after the Dutch conquest in 1632, the farthest south and most exposed point in the Dutch Republic.

Vital for understanding Maastricht's role and the role of the Basse-Meuse in general was the military need to navigate and cross the Meuse. The river was a central route for troops; it connected France with the Spanish Netherlands and the Dutch Republic, and in the Thirty Years' War – when France was allied with the Dutch – it was part of the "Spanish Road" that served as a safe military route connecting Spain with its territories in the Low Countries.[27] Armies marched on roads and fields near the river, and artillery was floated down the river on barges. These capabilities gave the Meuse a vital role, when the Dutch fought first Spain (until 1648) and, later, France (after 1667).

The Basse-Meuse played an important role in east-west troop transport as well. The area was an ideal place to reach and then cross the river, for two reasons. First, both to the east and west, the land was relatively flat and bare of forests. Troops coming from Germany could easily cross the Pays de Herve and the Hesbaye to get to Brussels and points farther west and south. Once at the river, crossing was especially easy in the Basse-Meuse. There were bridges at Liège and Maastricht (there were no bridges over the Meuse north of Maastricht), and shallow water crossings at three points between them. At Visé, Argenteau, and Herstal, men, horses and wagons would cross the river quickly, safely, and conveniently without need for a bridge.[28]

Military planners in the seventeenth and eighteenth centuries recognized the strategic importance of Maastricht as a point of control for the Meuse. Four times in the period discussed here, major sieges were mounted before its fortifications, and three were successful. In 1632, the Dutch General Frederick Henry attacked then Spanish Maastricht and succeeded in bringing it under Dutch control. The Peace of Westphalia, in 1648, confirmed the Dutch in that possession.[29] With its transfer to Dutch control, and the new European alliances that made Spain and the Dutch Republic allies against France after 1659, Maastricht became a French strategic objective. In 1673, Louis XIV conquered Maastricht in the siege that took the life of the famous French soldier, d'Artagnan.[30] Three years later, Louis' army successfully withstood a Dutch attempt to reconquer the city;[31] the Treaty of Nijmegen, in 1679, returned Maastricht to the Dutch.[32] Yet one more siege was to follow before 1750; it was by France in 1748, at the end of the War of the Austrian Succession.[33]

IV. The Economy of the Basse-Meuse

Just as Liégeois neutrality does not fully explain military presence in the Basse-Meuse, the strategic importance of Maastricht and the Meuse does not complete the picture. Armies came to the Liégeois region, including the Basse-Meuse, for purely practical reasons, especially between campaigns. The region was rich in grain and other military supplies and, as we have seen, easy to occupy. A brief explanation of the nature of the land and economy of the Basse-Meuse will show why this was so, as well as provide background for our subsequent discussion of the ways that military presence affected the lives of the people of the Basse-Meuse.

Predictably, the economy of the rural Basse-Meuse was overwhelmingly agricultural. Although mining, handicraft manufacturing, and the river trades also flourished, these activities contributed much less than agriculture to the people's livelihood. Even the most industrial place in the Basse-Meuse, Herstal, had only 18 hectares of built-up land — out of a total area of over 1,500 hectares — as late as 1800.[34]

A. Agriculture: The Geographical Determinants

The Meuse River between Liège and Maastricht roughly divides the two most prosperous agricultural regions in eastern Belgium and the Netherlands: the Hesbaye region to the west and the Pays de Herve to the east. The farmers of the Basse-Meuse practiced a system of agriculture somewhere between the two neighboring regions' substantial differences in land, agricultural products, property ownership, and settlement patterns.[35]

The Hesbaye is a broad, dry plateau west of the Meuse River.[36] Covered by a rich alluvial soil of mixed sand and clay, it was a fertile cereal-farming region. Settlement was compact, with nucleated villages at fairly close intervals. Farms were large, frequently owned by urban clergy and leased in large units to prosperous peasant farmers who employed wage laborers to assist them.

The Pays de Herve, to the east of the Meuse, offers a substantial contrast to the Hesbaye. A rich, green, undulating landscape of small plateaus and shallow valleys, it has been a dairy farming region, known for the quality of its butter and cheese, since the sixteenth century. It begins a few kilometers east of the Meuse, leaving the area nearest the river with Hesbignon soil, but Hervian undulating terrain, and

stretches nearly to the present German border. Land ownership in the Pays de Herve also differed from that of the Hesbaye. Individual small family farms – or groups of a few farms – were scattered all through the countryside. Since farms were small and primarily devoted to dairy farming, it is unlikely that they produced all the food they ate. Farmers made regular trips to markets in villages near their homes, as well as to Liège, to trade their cheese and butter for grain from the Hesbaye (bread was the staple in everyone's diet) and for money.

Within the context of the Hesbaye and the Pays de Herve, the Basse-Meuse has its own special character. If we were to travel from west to east, we would proceed from a high plateau of fields on the west, down into a habitable and fertile river valley. The valley walls often supported vineyards in the past;[37] where they were too irregular for vines, they formed good natural pastures. The valley itself was covered with fields, except at its lowest points, where flood plains made excellent pastures. If we continue, we climb the steeper eastern walls of the valley to arrive on another highland, which differs from the plateau west of the Meuse by its more varied character. It is broken by streams moving to the river, by woods, and by natural pastures. North of Visé the river valley broadens to form a "Mosan plain." There, rather than moving up directly from the river to the precursers of the Hervian landscape, the river valley broadens out, and the valley's edge is at least two and one-half kilometers east of the river, creating fertile fields and lowland pastures.

Most Basse-Mosan farmers practiced a traditional three-year rotation of arable crops.[38] Communal restraints still governed their actions, and farmers usually employed a rotation of winter grains one year, summer grains the next, and finally fallow on their open, irregularly shaped fields. Local livestock provided a moderate amount of manure. The winter grains grown were spelt and rye, with some wheat; the summer grains were mostly oats and barley, supplemented by pulses (peas, beans, and oil-producing plants).

On the eastern edge of the Basse-Meuse, near the Pays de Herve, farmers in the seventeenth and eighteenth centuries were becoming dairymen. While in most Basse-Mosan communities in this period about 80 percent of all land was used for arable crops, on the eastern edge nearly half was devoted to pasture farming.[39] In 1685, farmers in Bombaye fed cattle on 44 percent of the village's land.[40] A century later, cattle fed on about 40 percent of the land of Housse, about 45 percent of the land of Neufchateau, and half of Cheratte.[41] The farmers of these

24

villages contributed their dairy products to the growing market for Hervian butter and cheese.

Their farms were not necessarily large. In the dairy-farming areas east of the Meuse, farms were especially small, in part because profitable dairy farming required very little land, and in part because the growing rural industries of the region were more prevalent east of the Meuse. Farmers with only a small plot of land could support themselves by spinning, weaving, or knitting and, as a result, the population grew and farms were divided.[42] In Richelle, for example, in 1722, more than 55 percent of all farmers worked less than one *bonnier* (about 0.87 hectare or 2.15 acres), and some 31 percent worked less than one-half *bonnier*, the absolute minimum needed to support a family by dairy farming.[43] The population of the Basse-Meuse was densest near the city of Liège, in the dairy-farming areas, and along the river, where there were the most opportunities for alternative employment (and thus the least need for a self-sufficient farm). Away from the thickly populated areas, the farmers were better off. In Emael, for example, 80 percent of all tax-paying farmers in 1717 had more than one *bonnier* of land, probably the minimum needed for self-sufficiency among traditional cereal farmers.[44] Farther west, towards the Hesbaye, farmers had even larger farms, many of them working twenty *bonniers* or more.

The very small farmers who lived and farmed in Richelle clearly survived on the margin of subsistence; even their somewhat more prosperous neighbors in Emael were not much better off. Many of the residents of the Basse-Meuse made up what Pierre Goubert has called the *dependent* majority of the population.[45] In a prosperous region like the Basse-Meuse, they might be comfortable. But, to reach that level, the large number of sub-subsistence farmers and the totally landless supplemented the produce of their small field or garden by working as farm laborers for the peasants who operated larger farms. In addition, many of them worked when they could in the part-time industrial jobs available in the area. Still others worked on the river or in the City of Liège and its *faubourgs*.[46]

In later chapters, we will see a number of ways in which war affected the people of the Basse-Meuse; it destroyed their property, took their food, money, and animals, enriched a few but drove many into debt, starved them, and even led to their deaths. War hit the dependent small farmers and laborers hardest. They had the smallest cushion against disaster. That cushion, when available at all, came from industrial employment, which they hoped would be adequate when war struck.

25

They worked in the very same industries that helped attract armies to the region around Liège. These armies came not only to be fed, but to be supplied with the machines of war.

B. *The Basse-Meuse and Liégeois Industry*

The region of the City of Liège has been known as a center of heavy industry for more than four centuries. It produced large quantities of coal and iron and manufactured metal products long before the industrial revolution.[47] Among these products, weapons stand out: Liège has long been one of the world's great centers for the manufacture of guns and other military equipment.[48] Thus, armies that came and camped around Liège could not only find full granaries, but could leave with all the new weapons they needed, provided by the obliging craftsmen and gun-merchants of Liège and its neighborhood.[49]

This mercantile and industrial function was largely fulfilled by the citizens of the city of Liège, with recourse to materials provided by a substantial hinterland. The Basse-Meuse played a significant role in this industry at every stage, from providing raw materials to manufacture and delivery, and for non-military industrial goods as well. The biggest contribution the Basse-Meuse made to the industries of Liège was coal production. The villages near the City of Liège were important mining centers, and Herstal and Wandre had especially sizable deposits.[50] From these two villages, the veins extended south into Saive, Jupille, and the City of Liège, and north at least as far as Cheratte, Dalhem, and Hermalle-Argenteau. The Basse-Mosan coal mines supplied markets not only in Liège, but in northern France and, most important, in Holland, the destination of one-third of its production.[51] In the seventeenth and early eighteenth centuries, little of this coal was used in the production of iron and steel. But the people of Liège used it to heat buildings and homes, which freed firewood for the armaments and other metal products produced in the region.[52]

Even in the direct production of weapons, the Basse-Meuse played a role. While forges were not numerous there, for lack of nearby iron, the manufacture of iron products did take place in the Basse-Meuse. Herstal, Saive, and other communities near the City of Liège were noted for their hardware industry, and Herstal has long been known for its manufacture of guns and other weapons.[53]

Other industries flourished as well in the Basse-Meuse. Clothwork, more than armaments, was its largest industry, spread throughout the countryside between the Meuse and Rhine rivers.[54] There were two

reasons for the prominence of clothwork in this region. First, fast-moving streams leading down to the Meuse and good local supplies of fuller's earth attracted fulling mills. Second, and probably more importantly, there was a ready supply of part-time and seasonal labor. In a census of industries made by Belgian officials in 1764, most of the villages along the right bank of the Basse-Meuse were producing cloth (it did not include the left bank, which was ruled by Liège, or those places on the right bank controlled by the Dutch).[55] Each place had one or more *fabricants* – manufacturers – with one or more looms each and a staff of spinners and weavers. In Cheratte, the factory belonging to Baston Squivée and Nicolas Belin supported eighty persons.[56]

*   *   *

Like Liégeois "neutrality" and its geographic situation, the healthy economy of the Basse-Meuse attracted armies. In succeeding chapters, we will both study how those armies and the civilians of the Basse-Meuse interacted and measure the economic and demographic consequences of military presence. Military incursions exacerbated weaknesses in the Basse-Mosan economy, such as the dependent villagers who could not support their families on their own land. But we should not assume that military occupation was always wholly destructive, nor that it inevitably had ill effects. The Basse-Mosan economy remained healthy, with only short adverse interludes, throughout the worst years of war and calamity of the seventeenth century. The region, as we will see, did not suffer severe losses of population. In many years, the agricultural and industrial workers of the area profitted from the presence of additional markets for their produce. Many Basse-Mosan peasants were financially independent agriculturalists. Of the rest, it seems, many found paying work in the region's industries. The result was a socially and economically healthy society that was capable of surviving the potential hardships associated with repeated and protracted military occupations.

Part 2

The Burden of Military Presence

Chapter II

"God Preserve us From Living Through Times of War"

Describing the events of 1673, Henri de Sonkeux, the bourgeois chronicler of Verviers in the late seventeenth century, wrote the following:

"On October 15th war was declared by Spain against France in the city of Brussels, to which the French responded in Paris on the 20th.

"It was because of this that the inhabitants of the Duchy of Limbourg hid their belongings, and all their animals, in Verviers as well as other cities with so much haste that one had to take pity on them . . ."[1]

De Sonkeux was not describing an isolated phenomenon. The mere declaration of war in early modern Europe caused a groundswell of anxiety and excitement, in both the cities and the countryside.[2] The immediate reaction was fearful preparation. For villagers like those of the Basse-Meuse, it was necessary to move valuables to what they thought was a safe haven and to prepare, on short notice, to take themselves, their livestock, and all the farm implements and domestic goods they could carry to some sort of refuge. For the authorities, it was also a time of hasty action, either to keep war from their territory or, if that was impossible, to arrange for generous treatment by occupying armies.

Everyone felt economic anxiety, since taxes and financial burdens increased in wartime, even beyond the inexorably rising cost of seventeenth-century government. The onset of war led people to assume the worst — that their lives, homes, and property would be damaged, with a safe return to normal life perhaps years away. A generation's work of accumulating property for the future could be easily wiped out by just a year or two of warfare.

The people of the Basse-Meuse dreaded war because it enveloped their lives. They feared the presence of troops who, whether friend or enemy, literally camped in the villages, fields, homes, and even the beds

31

of the peasants, and, in short, entered into all aspects of everyday existence. The disruption caused by their presence could be overwhelming and the financial drain occasioned by the need to feed them was a heavy burden for peasants, no matter how prosperous.

Military men expected civilians along the route of march to pay the cost of war. A French phrase, *le pays doit nourrir le soldat*, governed the military thought of the age. It was not the land, of course, that fed the soldier, but the people who lived on the land. As commanders in Germany learned in the Thirty Years' War, no soldier could live off the land once the people had been driven away.

Like every other institution under the ancien régime, the making of war was governed by old and established traditions, which determined much of what we will describe in this chapter and those that follow. Yet this period produces a powerful sense of change and development. The gradual emergence in the sixteenth century of the apparatus of the modern state, and the growing scale of all aspects of government, especially warfare, had made the traditional system of warmaking increasingly impracticable. Beginning slowly in the sixteenth century, both strategic and organizational aspects of military life underwent modification.[3]

The real transformation in military organization and warfare, especially as it affected civilians, took place in the seventeenth century, between 1600 and 1715; thereafter, advances of equal magnitude in organization and strategy had to await the French Revolution and the Napoleonic wars.[4] The impact of these changes on the everyday problems of feeding and housing troops, and the new mechanisms for raising money in the field, were felt by the people of the Basse-Meuse in some ways in 1650, and very much more so by 1700. This chapter will concentrate on the "traditional" system; Chapter III will focus on the developments that led to better conditions for civilians in wartime.

I. Popular Perceptions: Violent and Undisciplined Men

The people of seventeenth-century Europe have left us innumerable clues to explain why they were anxious at the approach of war. War, they knew, was a violent business, leading by its very definition to pain, loss, and death. Moreover, they accepted the inability, or unwillingness, of officers to control their soldiers. War was a trade carried on by violent and undisciplined men; it all too often spilled over into civilian life.

32

No social scientist can go back into the early seventeenth century and ask questions about people's perceptions of war. We are left, for better or worse, with their testimony as it has reached us. That testimony takes a number of forms. For the Basse-Meuse and the region of Liège, we have complaints made by civilians about the experience of war;[5] we have relatively "objective" chronicles in which educated men attempted to record what happened in the time and place they lived;[6] and we have a very few purely literary works, written in regional dialect and, therefore, designed for the edification of the peasants and townsmen.[7] To these local works we can add European-wide views such as H. J. C. von Grimmelshausen's novel, *Simplicissius Simplicissimus*, about the Thirty Years' War,[8] and some artistic reactions to the impact of war, most notably Jacques Callot's series of etchings, *The Miseries of War*, and the magnificent engravings by Romeyn de Hooghe that illustrate this book.[9]

These works accuse both officers and soldiers, especially in the first half of the seventeenth century, of serious crimes. They depict the commanders of armies as crass and uncaring about civilians, their troops as unpaid, ill-fed, and undisciplined. The result for civilians was invariably the theft of money and goods, violence towards individuals and animals, and the destruction of everything the soldiers could not take with them. Soldiers' actions read like a textbook outline of criminal practices: burning, looting, assault, rape, murder, thievery, and desecration of churches.[10] The written works almost always follow a pattern, and it is worthwhile to summarize their ritualized tale in order to illuminate the themes by which people perceived military presence in this first main wartime period, the era of the Thirty Years' War.

In most of these stories, there are relatively few main characters. A small number of soldiers and surprised civilians interact, producing a strong sense of individual experience; Simplicissimus does not even recognize soldiers when they accost him, thinking rather that they are wolves.[11] Weri Clabå, the main character in a Walloon dialogue about the Thirty Years' War, begins his story,

> It was Wednesday, at the dinner hour
> When a mass of Mansfeld's soldiers came.
> Not demanding lodging or food,
> They arrived, enraged, at the hearth
> To steal and sack
> Without saying a word, not even "to the death," or "on guard."[12]

Sometimes the villagers have been alerted of an army's approach and

arm themselves to defend their homes.[13] But such attempts rarely succeed, and the local militiamen are either killed or driven into hiding while the army goes about its business.

The pattern of behavior, once the soldiers establish themselves in the home or village, is similarly ritualized. Civilians left in the village try to get away if they can. When Simplicissimus brings his soldier-wolves home, he expects his parents to meet him at the door. But they " . . . came not: for they . . . had found the back-door open and would not wait for their guests."[14] Once in the house, while a few soldiers are sent to hunt for the missing villagers, the rest set to stealing. In Weri Clabå's tale,

> It was a game to see who could take the most
> And who could steal the best and the finest.
> One took the plates, another the platters . . . .[15]

Soldiers are organized thieves, if one believes the recitation of these poets and authors, or the visual evidence of Callot: few of his drawings are without a wagon in front of the door, piled high with the fruits of their theft (Illus. 1).[16]

The soldiers' thievery had less impact than the violence and destruction that were the next steps in their progress. Once they had found everything of value, they turned to the residents for sport and information about hidden valuables. In Callot's *Le Pillage* (Illus. 2), a man is being roasted over the fire, presumably to elicit the location of his valuables. Weri Clabå's father is killed and his sister raped.[17] In *Simplicissimus*, the men are tortured and the women abused before the soldiers destroy the household.[18] They burn wooden objects and eventually the house itself goes up in flames. The armies, disrespectful of all normal human values, seldom felt reverence for churches. In another Walloon dialogue, the villager Pascot reports their behavior:

> These fellows are the devil's friends,
> More vicious than dogs;
> Didn't they burn our church?
> They took everything and pillaged everything;
> The cross, the vase, the chalice.
> They respect nothing.
> They steal everything like the damned.
> They even vomit their filth
> On the altar of Our Lord.
> Good God![19]

The consequence, the stories and chronicles tell us, was that many people were driven from their homes by war, left to fend for themselves without family, property, or tradition. Simplicissimus was the perfect

wartime literary character, born as a result of one battle, orphaned by another, shuttling from army to army or living as a vagrant as the years passed. The residents of the Basse-Meuse certainly knew of civilian vagrants and bandits. The region's dialect included a specific word, *Harlaque*, which signified pillaging homeless peasants unsettled by military incursions.[20] Some displaced villagers sought protection in rustic havens, like the group from the village of Wonck who, in 1636 and again in 1747, fled to the rocky stone-cutting caves in the Mountain of St. Pierre under Emael, Eben, and Kanne.[21] More commonly, however, the citizens of the Basse-Meuse imposed on their neighbors in the cities, towns, and even villages of the region – in any place where they thought they would find food and avoid marauding troops. The published ordinances of the city of Liège suggest that it was considered a haven, if an unfriendly one, since foreigners were constantly to be sought out and deported. Not even the clergy were safe from the need to take refuge. In 1676, the Canons of the Collegiate Church of St. Hadelin in Visé packed up their archives and relics and moved into the city of Liège for the duration of the war.[22] They wished to avoid suffering like the monks in Callot's *Devastation of a Monastery* (Illus. 3).

Despite some literary exaggeration, there is clearly considerable truth in these descriptions. An old man, taught about the seventeenth-century wars by his centenarian aunt, was interviewed in the mid-nineteenth century. He pointed at the bayonet marks in the oak door to his seventeenth-century home and gravely told his audience, "God preserve us from living through times of war" (*Dieu nous preserve de vivre en temps de guerre*).[23] Yet we cannot assume that such experiences were normal in the Basse-Meuse. We shall see that very few civilians were murdered by soldiers during any of the wars. And we shall see that the region was not depopulated when soldiers took everyone's possessions and destroyed their homes, forcing them to go on the road as vagrants.

Nonetheless, the people of the Basse-Meuse suffered psychological hardships during wartime. They probably knew that they would not be attacked by soldiers but, understandably, they could never be sure. While they suffered material and financial damage, very few were driven from their villages. To understand the normal experience – that which happened to most – of the citizens of the Basse-Meuse during the wars of the seventeenth and eighteenth centuries, we will have to turn to more mundane matters. How did civilians and soldiers interact in this era? While violence was important and continued to be so (as it is today), we will see that there was a increasingly organized and

cash-oriented relationship in the provision of money, supplies, and services to the armies that visited the Basse-Meuse.

II. Housing an Army

The need to make camp was the first order of business for troops in the field. On the march, or for short stays of only a day or two, troops camped in the woods or fields, near rivers, or wherever there was sufficient room for them to stay.[24] Even such a short stay, at the periphery of the villages, could have a devastating impact on local communities. An army of moderate size, remaining for only a few days, could easily destroy part of an area's livelihood. Ten thousand men who camped on the fields of a village or two – an area that ordinarily supported five hundred or one thousand inhabitants – could devastate the villagers' agricultural production for that year. Land near roads was almost invariably rendered useless for the duration of any war.[25]

In 1672, following an eight-day camp by the French army, the Abbot of Val-Dieu observed that, "The rye which was ruined has been re-seeded in barley which has produced only a meager harvest. But the spelt and wheat have reappeared sufficiently well to produce what is estimated to be half a normal harvest."[26] This is an unusual case because the army of Louis XIV in the Low Countries in 1672 was very large (more than 100,000 men). But this quotation gives us an idea of the impact of an army's presence, even when it stayed only a few days and demanded little or nothing in direct payment.[27] If every farm was reduced to half its normal output by a week's stay, the villagers might starve the next winter. A longer stay could eliminate agricultural production for an entire year.

The traditional system of housing troops, moreover, would have brought them into the homes of the local population for anything longer than the shortest stay. When preparing for or defending against a siege, in garrison or winter quarters, or even while momentarily stopped to lick wounds after a siege or battle, troops lodged in the homes of civilians. Barracks hardly existed before 1600, and troops rarely carried tents with them.[28] Rather, if an army was going to be in one place for a week or more, especially in winter, soldiers slept in the homes (and probably barns) of the citizens.

The obligation to lodge a large number of troops was a crushing burden on the population of a single village or even a cluster of villages. A population of two thousand or less might have to support – and find

room for – ten thousand troops and their companions, since armies invariably travelled with women, children, and animals. When a company of infantry camped at Verviers in 1674, for example, it consisted of 100 armed men; along with them there travelled 20 women and 50 horses carrying baggage.[29]

Most residents could expect to lodge about the same number of soldiers as there were people in their household. In 1695, 35 cavalrymen and 5 women camped at Emael, a village of 50 to 60 households.[30] Such numbers probably represent the smallest lodging demands that could have been expected. The Priest of Emael had a more normal experience when he housed 2 officers of the Count of Anhalt in his little house in 1672.[31] In eighteenth-century occupations, the same rough equivalency between residents and lodgers operated. In the winter of 1746-1747, a Hessian army occupied part of the Basse-Meuse.[32] In Saint-Remy, "each household with any property had to house two or three or four soldiers, depending on its size."[33] The same was true in Jupille.[34] When 2 companies of Danish soldiers visited the Dutch village of St. Gertrude on 11 June 1736, a total of 215 men, 26 women, 15 children, and 17 horses were lodged by the villagers.[35] They were divided among 29 households. While the average number of soldiers per household was about 7, most residents housed 5 or fewer soldiers, and 8 had 10 or more. Thus, a few large houses or barns in St. Gertrude had a crowd of soldiers but, for most residents, lodging troops meant a doubling of household size, and not a situation where the soldiers outnumbered the normal members of the household.

Of course, dramatic crowding was always possible and did occur. In 1697, 4 battalions – perhaps 1,000 men – were lodged at Emael.[36] Truly extraordinary numbers could be lodged in a fortified chateau, such as the Dutch troops who stayed in the chateau of Nedercanne in 1632.[37] Large numbers continually lodged in Verviers during the Dutch War. On 25 October 1678, 20 companies of infantry and 8 of cavalry arrived, adding, one can assume, more than 3,000 men and a large number of women and horses to a city that normally contained only 6,500 inhabitants. Six days later, on November first, the French added 51 more companies of infantry, literally swamping the native population.[38] The implications for the health of all concerned were dramatic, as we will see.

Besides providing a roof over the heads of troops, the householder had other obligations. In addition to food, which we will discuss presently, he usually provided various supplies and services under the broad category of "utensils." What were these utensils? Obviously, they

varied according to time and place, depending on the strength of the army and its desire and ability to make demands. In Verviers, in 1678, de Sonkeux describes the minimum utensils as "wood, fire, pepper, vinegar, candles, bedding, a bowl (to eat from), and a cooking-pot."[39] Such demands could drive a poor man, and even a moderately prosperous one deprived of his earning power by war, into debt or out of his home. Furthermore, troop in long occupations seldom limited their demands to such small items. "After two weeks in the homes of their hosts," de Sonkeux continued, "they were to receive a pair of shoes, in addition to the pair of hose given as a welcoming present."[40] The soldiers' demands escalated during the months of occupation. By the end of their stay, the troops had received a complete new wardrobe.

It is difficult to assign a monetary value to the cost of lodging, and even the cost of utensils and other services provided, since they varied so greatly from one lodging experience to another, and often were combined with the cost of feeding troops. Later in this chapter, we will attempt to evaluate the cost of food and lodging together, as well as taxes paid by the villagers of the Basse-Meuse. Surely the cost of lodging, both to the community and to the individual householder, was high.[41] And any computation of the costs would have to include the amount of physical damage inflicted on the household and its contents, and the psychic damage to its residents, by the unruly behavior of ill-disciplined young soldiers.[42] Even if the community might eventually reimburse the householder for supplies, utensils, and repairs, the initial cash outlay and the anxiety were the exclusive responsibility of the householder himself.

III. Feeding an Army

An occupying army had to be fed. In theory, the army paid its troops in cash and they then bought their food – usually from the householder with whom they lodged – out of their pay.[43] That was the case in Verviers in the winter of 1674, when " . . . a bourgeois lodging a foot soldier gave two écus each month and utensils. For a cavalryman one gave three écus [twelve florins] each month, plus utensils and fodder for the horses. The money was given to the burgermasters, by the burgermasters to the captains, and by the captains (who kept an escalin [one-half florin] for each écu) to the soldiers. Most of the soldiers gave the money they received from the officers to their hosts in order to be fed whatever the family had in its kettle."[44]

Whether the army or the local citizenry paid for the cost of the food, the community always faced the immediate task of providing it; and a large number of troops and animals could call for vast amounts of bread and forage. In 1674, the citizens of Verviers contributed 50,000 pounds of bread each day to the Dutch army putting siege to Maastricht![45] They also supplied meat, 200 barrels of beer, and 400 bottles of wine. Verviers was already a small city in 1674, with about 6,500 residents, and so survived this imposition. For smaller places, such demands could be disastrous. The French requested 30,000 rations of bread from the 1,000 unprepared residents of Visé in September, 1746.[46] The 140 householders of Eysden in 1675 were unable to fulfill a request for 1,169 rations of forage, each weighing nearly 30 pounds.[47] Even if the army reimbursed the community for the commodities, finding and delivering large quantities of food could drain all the manpower resources of a village or small town, hopelessly distracting it from other tasks.

The cost of providing the food cannot be dismissed lightly. When armies took up winter quarters, we know that the communities in which they lodged provided the initial money to pay for the food.[48] Military leaders obviously felt that local citizens should pay for feeding the armies.[49] Because of changing circumstances from war to war and camp to camp, it is difficult to quantify the cost of feeding an army. We can make one estimate by examining the expenses of the tiny town of Dalhem while the French put siege to Maastricht, from 7 April to 7 May 1748. For this one month, Dalhem paid 2,500 florins, mostly for food. A normal year's tax revenues were less than 1,000 florins.[50] The late 1740's were years of relative moderate prices, but when the price of foodstuffs was high, the burden on the region could be astronomical. In 1680, as a consequence of the high prices of the 1670's, the burghers of Verviers paid three florins a day to lodge and feed a sergeant, and two florins for a foot-soldier. In 1749, in the War of the Austrian Succession, they paid only two sous, or one-twentieth as much.[51] It is not surprising that the wars of the late seventeenth century, which came at times of very high prices, forced villages and towns into debt.

IV. Pioneers and Wagons

The cost of war cannot always be measured in thousands of florins and cartloads of wheat. The people of the Basse-Meuse were called upon repeatedly in the wars of the seventeenth and eighteenth centuries to contribute their wagons, animals, and drivers to the task of carting

baggage and supplies from one camp to another, and to assist in the preparation of fortifications or sieges. Armies had tremendous, if transient, needs for manpower of a totally unskilled nature. When digging trenches to put siege to a city, when building a fortress, or tearing down the walls of a fortified city, those needs became monumental. As soon as the task was finished – and it might last only a few days – the manpower became superfluous to a fighting army; thus, it was supplied by calling up civilians. These civilians served as pioneers (trench-diggers) for the armies of the day.

Louis XIV reports in his memoirs that he called for 20,000 peasants to work on his siegeworks at Maastricht in 1673.[52] The practice was extremely common. In 1747, the village of Milmort contributed 142 man-days of service as pioneers and guides to the Austrian army, while the combined villages of Fexhe and Slins gave 202 days to the Dutch army.[53] While the number of days contributed does not seem to be excessive, they could come at inopportune times of year, and could take men far from their homes. In 1675, de Sonkeux tells us that the French siege of Limbourg (25 km. east of Liège) required peasants from as far away as the Hesbaye and the countryside of Jülich, in Germany.[54] This drain of manpower, he argued, helped cause the disastrous famine of that year.

The armies' need for cartage for its baggage and supplies placed a similar strain on the manpower and horsepower of the Basse-Meuse and nearby places.[55] In 1747, when Milmort and Fexhe-Slins devoted together 344 man-days to pioneering, they gave 981 man-days to carrying goods for the Austrian and Dutch armies.[56] At times, such demands for carriage could be well organized and efficiently provided. In May of 1675, the French army requested that Eysden provide fifteen wagons with horses and drivers (complete with their own food) for three days to haul grain from Aachen to Maastricht. When the French thought some of those wagons had not been provided, they fined the village 10 écus (40 florins) for each absent wagon.[57]

It is true that armies often paid pioneers and especially wagon-drivers for their services and that, for many of the poor people of the Basse-Meuse, this was welcome money. In 1748, at the French siege of Maastricht, pioneers were paid two escalins (one florin) a day.[58] There were two problems, despite the fact that farmers with wagons might find the work profitable. First, demands for wagons and drivers could come at the wrong time of the year, when wagons, animals, and drivers were needed for planting or harvest. And, second, even when the work

came at a welcome time of year, it could have unpredictable consequences. When the Austrian army evacuated their camp at Dalhem on 7 April 1748, they requisitioned baggage wagons which followed when the French drove the Austrians from their first new camp. The men of Dalhem did not return home for ten days and some lost their horses.[59]

V. Raising Money: Occupation and Contribution

According to ancien régime law, armies could use two justifications to raise money while in foreign territory. They used the first − the right of expropriation − when they actually occupied a territory.[60] Usually, the village, town, or region where the army camped was forced to feed the army, to contribute money, and perhaps to pay an indemnity to have the army leave its territory promptly. Sometimes, the occupying force acquired a kind of temporary sovereignty (which might be obtained permanently if the occupation resulted in cession of the territory at the end of the war), with the power to raise taxes as a sovereign right.

Armies used the second justification for raising money, the right to collect *contributions*, to obtain food and cash in those areas that were nearby, but not actually occupied.[61] Basically, an army could demand *contributions* from any community that was unable to resist its demands. This was simply an extension of the age-old practice of sending out foraging parties to gather the supplies an army needed; it derived its questionable legality from the idea that communities could ransom property which the army had a legal right, under the prevailing law of war, to loot and burn.[62] In the early seventeenth century, *contributions* arose out of two developments. First, armies grew so large that the old methods of raising money for the army at home and spending it in the field were no longer adequate. Second, a number of the belligerents in the Thirty Years' War were not major states capable of paying for their large armies. The Catholic League, the ex-King of Bohemia, and even the Holy Roman Emperor, to name the most prominent, could not raise large sums by taxation in their dominions. Their generals − the innovators were Mansfeld, Spinola, Tilly, and, of course, Wallenstein − instead developed the system of *contributions* to make the territories where war was waged pay for its costs.

The power to collect *contributions* is a clear example of might-makes-right; anything the army could get was deemed legal. Raiding parties entered nearby or unoccupied territory and made demands

punctuated by violence. Fire and kidnapping usually served as persuaders.[63] The troops might burn a house or two as a warning or kidnap a few men, to be ransomed by the village. In 1650, in the Principality of Looz, a section of the Principality of Liège to the northwest of the Basse-Meuse, Lorraine troops kidnapped women and children to hold for ransom.[64] In Saive, on Easter Sunday, 1677, a party seeking *contributions* found everyone in church in their best clothes. Seizing the opportunity, they stripped everyone naked and, besides appropriating all the clothes, took hostages to be held for ransom.[65]

In general, if the ransoms were not paid, the troops had the right either to kill those they had kidnapped or to burn the village.[66] If the villagers deserted their homes, hoping that, by being absent when the raiding party returned, they might be saved, open season was declared. The village would be burnt after everything of value had been stolen. In October, 1683, during the relatively minor War of the Reunions, a French force sacked the church in the village of Petit Rechain, because the villagers had evacuated to Verviers. This was the second time in less than two years that Petit Rechain felt the blow of retribution – called *exécution* in the language of the day. On 31 December 1681, the village had been attacked because "of some payment promised to some passing general during the wars, and they had not kept their promise."[67] In 1746, the town of Visé refused to provide 30,000 rations of bread to an allied army. The punishment was harsh and swift, as the town fathers reported the next day: "We have been squeezed dry; our gardens have been ravaged, our hops and their trellises pillaged and burnt, our fruit trees despoiled; the people are wiped out and in the last of their miseries. The plunderers have forced open and stolen from the houses. This was a night of unending theft."[68] Fear of this sort of retribution kept the peasants paying for the right to stay in their homes, to keep some of their goods, and to await the next visit from the ever-hungry armies.

Of course, these raiding parties did not limit themselves to a pleasant threat and warning and then wait until they were civilly paid. They stole everything that was at hand and then used the threat of *exécution* to find hidden valuables. Thus, in Saive on Easter Sunday, 1677, the troops took all the animals they could find, in addition to clothes and hostages. Later in that same year, on August 6, French troops from the garrison of Maastricht visited the village of Herve, a local center of pasture farming to the east of the Basse-Meuse.[69] They burned several houses and took all the cows, a terrible catastrophe for a community

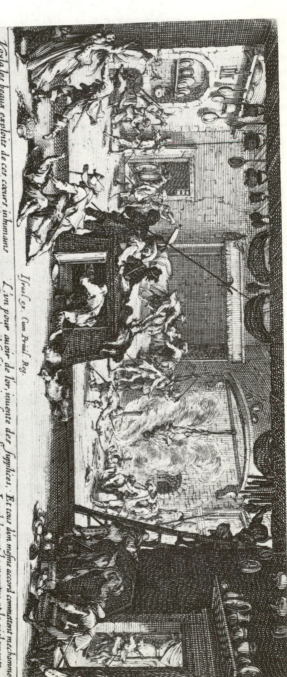

Voyla les beaux exploits de ces cœurs inhumains
Ils ravagent par tout rien n'eschappe à leurs mains
Israel cy. Cum Priuil. Reg.

L'un pour auoir de l'or, inuente des supplices,
L'autre à mil forfaicts anime ses complices ;
Et tout d'un mesme accord commettent meschamment
Le vol, le rapt, le meurtre, et le violement . 5

Ill. 2. The Pillage, by Jacques Callot (1633)

43

supported by its dairy herds. The villagers paid a large sum of money to ransom their cattle.

The process of collecting *contributions* was in a constant state of development in the seventeenth century, but by the 1660's it had reached a sort of ritual. The general or military governor seeking *contributions* sent out parties carrying written requests for grain, fodder, or money. By the 1670's, these notices were often printed forms, with only the date, the name of the community to pay, and the amount requested written in by hand.[70] The demand for *contributions* permitted the community a certain amount of time to produce, and sometimes the right to pay money instead of goods. The comunity's first response, of course, would be to send their most distinguished citizen to beg for a lighter *contribution*. Thus, in Visé, in 1689, when they received a request for *contributions* from the Intendant of Luxemburg, they sent Major de Heusen to see if he could arrange for a smaller payment.[71] Similarly, in 1675, when the village of Eysden received a request from Maastricht for 1169 rations of forage, they sent a letter to the Governor asking him for a reduction, because of their poverty.[72]

Very often, these attempts to reduce *contributions* involved bribery. At the minimum, the party delivering the request for contributions was treated well, given small gifts, and served refreshments.[73] The giving of gifts to officers for special treatment in time of war has a long history, well reported in the Basse-Meuse. In April of 1689, the Visé Town Council authorized a payment to the Governor of Maastricht to keep the town free of troops in passage.[74] On June 19th, they gave a Liégeois Captain five écus to take his troops and leave the town.[75] And if it was impossible to get troops to leave, once arrived, well-placed bribery might result in better treatment. On 23 April 1690, Visé paid five patacons (20 florins) to a lieutenant so he would keep order among his troops.[76] The same day they gave a present of a *muid* of oats to Cornet Blonet, so he would delay the arrival of some troops by two or three days.

Bribes paid to individual officers closely resemble official safeguards obtained for wider protection from armies or generals; often only the terminology was different. In 1674, the villagers of Serexhe-Heuseur placed all their grain in the church to protect it. When occupying troops arrived, they bribed those troops with some of the grain. They were followed by a representative of the French Governor of Maastricht whom the villagers paid to leave two safeguards (troops who stayed in the cemetery) to protect the church.[77] Of course, not all the proceeds of

these safeguards and bribes went directly into the pockets of officers. By the mid-seventeenth century, armies received a substantial amount of their revenue from the sale of safeguards.[78]

In the end, these attempts to secure better treatment did little good. In Serexhe-Heuseur, the French guards in the churchyard could not prevent German troops from pillaging many houses. The military commanders seldom reduced their demands, and even the best-intentioned officers had a hard time controlling their troops. The villages suffered the presence of armies and either produced the supplies requested (the demands were seldom for money, but more often for food), or bought them on the open market. This was because *contributions* were of great utility to an army. They could be demanded by a relatively small force, from a very large area, and yield large amounts of money, food, and other valuable goods.[79] They were especially useful to garrisons, which had large needs and relatively few men, yet could not occupy a large area with their camp.[80]

Contributions were an everyday and devastating expense in the Basse-Meuse, especially in the seventeenth century. In theory demanded only from enemy territory, they posed a dilemma to the villagers of the Basse-Meuse and, especially, to the residents of the supposedly neutral Principality of Liège. Rather than having one enemy demanding *contributions*, they invariably had two. When two great powers were at war – such as France and the United Provinces in the 1670's – it was likely that one of the armies would enter the principality and demand *contributions* or lodgings from the defenseless citizens. The inhabitants could only agree, since they had no army to enforce a refusal. But once they had paid one side in the war, they were fair game for the other side, who would claim that they had aided the enemy. Both the citizens of the Principality of Liège and their leaders had no choice under these circumstances but to beg forgiveness, plead poverty, and hope to get off as lightly as possible.[81]

Those portions of the Basse-Meuse and its neighbors that owed allegiance to one of the belligerents faced a similar problem. In the quotation on the first page of this chapter, de Sonkeux tells the story of the unfortunate inhabitants of the Duchy of Limbourg, part of the Spanish Netherlands' "Lands Beyond the Meuse." They were permitted to enter Verviers (Liégeois territory), but only on the condition that they help pay the *contributions* negotiated by Verviers with the French. He goes on to say: "The Count of Monterey [governor of the Spanish Netherlands] expressly forbad them to contribute, but the poor

communities suffered from both sides: they contributed to friends as well as enemies, because they could not resist military force."[82]

VI. Paying and Borrowing

A description of the practices of feeding and housing troops, and the legal theories under which armies collected food and money, ignores the reality that someone had to pay for those demands. Clearly, the residents of the communities or regions involved paid the cost of troops camped on or near their soil, but that end was reached by a variety of methods, depending on the circumstances.

While the final burden fell on the taxpayers, they rarely made direct payments to an army, although they did provide certain services to troops lodged in their homes. Rather, the direct financial burden was usually met by the communal organization or, sometimes, in seigneurial villages, by the lord of the manor. These procedures, which had certainly existed in the sixteenth century or earlier, were themselves something of an advance over a genuinely primitive system, under which the individual homeowner dealt directly with individual troops. By the seventeenth century, the community raised money and disbursed it, determined how many soldiers were to be lodged in each house, and in general acted as a buffer between individuals and the army.[83] When individual householders made out-of-pocket payments – as they might have done to feed troops or to provide the utensils described above – they were reimbursed as quickly as the community was able to do so. When lodging troops in his home, for example, the householder was entitled to a money payment from the community for each lodger for each day.[84] He presented a receipt of some kind to the communal authorities, documenting his expenses. The treasurer was then supposed to deduct the resident's tax obligations (everyone had to contribute some share to the cost of lodging, but that share might be smaller than his actual expense), and reimburse the rest. Of course, as we shall see, communities were frequently without any cash to make such payments and the householder might have had to wait months, if not years, to be repaid.

The community then had three methods of obtaining the necessary cash to meet its obligations: taxing its citizens, sharing the burden with neighboring communities or obtaining aid from the regional estates, and borrowing.

Extraordinary taxation was the obvious first response to the ex-

46

traordinary demands of war. It was best, no matter what the expense, to raise a single extraordinary tax, make the payment, and be done with it. Communities had recourse to the full range of taxation – taxes on property, capitation taxes, and taxes on consumption – to meet wartime demands, but they were limited by law to certain taxes for certain needs. In the Principality of Liège, for example, most of a community's wartime expenses – lodging and feeding troops, refreshment of parties, providing pioneers and guides – were paid from personal taxes, defined either as head-taxes or taxes on consumption or trade.[85] Only *contributions* could be paid with a tax on property. Residents of the Basse-Meuse considered this an important distinction, and the kinds of taxes and their use in wartime led to many disagreements and lawsuits.[86] This is because a personal tax fell only on the residents of the community, while a property tax was paid by all who had property there, whether resident or not. Obviously, the inhabitants of a community preferred the property tax, since it would spread the burden more widely. On the other side, property holders who lived outside the community resisted these taxes, arguing that they were not obligated to help meet the demands of war for any community but their own.

The village of Eysden in the late seventeenth and eighteenth centuries provides an example of the tax burden of war. From 1664 onward, we have three tax series, raised for different purposes (Table 2.1).[87] None of the series is complete, but they present unambiguous evidence of the cost of war and the way it was financed. The longest and most important series (62 years out of 76, from 1664 to 1739) is that of the capitation tax, based on the number of people in each household. The proceeds of this tax paid for communal expenses and most military obligations. The second series is a property tax, paid at the rate of so many florins per *bonnier* of land; it was used chiefly to pay the village's share of the taxes levied by the Dutch Republic, but, on occasion, to pay the interest on long-term debts incurred for village projects or to meet wartime expenses. The series is shorter (27 years out of 40 from 1691 to 1730) than that of the capitation tax. The third series is a short, but vital, record of the taxes raised to pay contributions to the French armies in ten years between 1690 and 1708.

Eysden's taxes will help us to understand the burden of wartime taxation. From the 1660's and the 1720's, we see that the community's peacetime tax revenues, drawn from the capitation tax, were about 500 florins a year. Wartime needs forced them to raise four, five, or even six times as much money. One need only look at the progression of tax

Table 2.1 Eysden Taxes (Dutch Guilders)

Year	Property Tax	Capitation Tax	French Contributions	Total
1664		805		
1665		735		
1666		532		
1667		529		
1668		464		
1669		468		
1670		620		
1671				
1672		2,333		
1673				
1674		1,628		
1675		1,809		
1676		2,026		
1677		2,138		
1678		2,027		
1679		1,184		
1680		910		
1681				
1682				
1683				
1684				
1685				
1686				
1687		606		
1688		324		
1689		768		
1690		1,104	1,664	
1691	2,491	1,392	1,664	5,547
1692		1,198		
1693	2,340	1,857	1,830	6,027
1694	2,454	2,485	1,830	6,769
1695				
1696	2,518	3,152	1,830	7,500
1697	1,893			
1698	2,288	2,277		4,565
1699	2,809			
1700	3,037	1,250		4,287
1701		1,101		
1702	3,432	3,158	1,331	7,941
1703		960		
1704	3,224	1,530		
1705	3,441	1,524	977	5,942

Table 2.1. (Continued)

Year	Property Tax	Capitation Tax	French Contributions	Total
1706	2,913		977	
1707	2,450	1,676	977	5,103
1708	3,016	1,316	977	5,309
1709		740		
1710				
1711		1,866		
1712		1,484		
1713		1,360		
1714		911		
1715		714		
1716		744		
1717		1,183		
1718	2,763	778		3,541
1719	2,870	994		3,864
1720	2,889	1,063		3,952
1721	2,473			
1722	2,584	866		3,450
1723	2,520	578		3,098
1724	2,816	580		3,394
1725	2,294	1,047		3,341
1726	2,426	450		2,876
1727	2,392	477		2,869
1728	2,800	521		3,321
1729	2,852	486		3,338
1730	2,860	652		3,512
1731		466		
1732		454		
1733		449		
1734		453		
1735		417		
1736		458		
1737		502		
1738		503		
1739		459		

revenues from 1688 to 1696 to see the taxes grow from 324 florins a year to more than 3,000 florins a year, as the burden on village revenues grew. The growth in wartime property taxes, mostly used to finance the central government, was not so dramatic. Only in the years 1702-1708, during the War of the Spanish Succession, did total property tax revenues rise, and this was to meet local, not central, government needs.

When we add the three types of taxes together we can see that, at least from 1690 onward, war doubled or tripled the normal tax burden. We can compare totals for 1693 (6,027 florins), 1696 (7,500 florins) or 1705 (5,942 florins), all war years, with 1728, a peacetime year when 3,321 florins were raised. The doubling or tripling of taxes in wartime cannot be called insignificant, and we must consider carefully what this tax burden meant. The easiest way to understand the situation is to compare this tax burden to the productive value of the land of Eysden. In the seventeenth and eighteenth centuries, there were 416 taxable *bonniers* of land in Eysden; thus, all taxes combined reflected about 14 florins per *bonnier* in 1693, about 18 in 1696, and about 8 in 1728.[88] Later, when we examine the impact of war on agriculture, we will see just what proportion of a farmer's profits such taxes represented.[89] But it is not premature to say that the increased taxes raised to pay for wartime expenses, when coupled with reduced production, made life very hard for the farmers of the Basse-Meuse.

Naturally, most villages and towns could not support a large number of foreign troops with their own immediate resources. They had to share the burden among a number of communities. During the lodgings in and near Verviers in the 1670's, many of the costs were shared by the four other units of the Marquisate of Franchimont.[90] The city of Liège often made similar arrangements with those villages very close to it (and including almost half of the Liégeois Basse-Meuse) which made up what was technically called the *banlieu* of the city.[91]

In the absence of cooperation among communities, the primary sources of relief were the estates of the Principality of Liège or one of the other sovereign units. Oppressed villages and towns always requested aid from the Estates when they were burdened by especially harsh demands for money, food, or lodging. This spread the burden of lodging troops over the whole Principality, an equitable approach. The Principality's Estates understood their responsibilities. In wartime, their actions were almost exclusively devoted to raising money (through special taxes) and keeping foreign troops out of the Principality.[92] But in the seventeenth century and earlier, the estates of the Principality were always impecunious. Even their decisions to levy taxes to pay for their own expenses and those of the Prince often had no results.[93] They rarely had any money to contribute to the expenses of their citizens.

All too often, the residents of the Basse-Meuse and nearby areas were forced to borrow money to meet their wartime needs. While they would have preferred to pay such costs from current tax receipts rather

than to saddle the community with debts, they had no choice. They simply could not raise enough taxes to pay expenses or, when they did impose taxes, the revenue could not be collected. It should go without saying that the disruption and new expenses that made the taxes necessary made it difficult for some individuals to pay the taxes.[94] So from the lowliest laborer and farmer to lords, towns and villages, and even provincial estates, everyone borrowed in time of war.

Both economic conditions and economic institutions in the Liégeois region permitted individuals and institutions to borrow when extreme need arose. The most significant economic condition, of course, was the continuing strength of the Liégeois economy, based on strong nearby agriculture, powerful incipient industry, and the city's role as a commercial center on a navigable river. Borrowing and lending always took place in the region, in order to pay for commercial ventures, finance industrial development, and build. The cost communities paid for money borrowed in wartime was remarkably moderate. While they sometimes had to pay as much as eight percent, their costs were usually limited to five or six percent per year.[95] The body of lenders included, among other important groups, a particularly numerous and wealthy group of clergy, always ready to lend excess cash until it was needed for their own building projects.[96]

The economic institution which permitted easy access to money was the notarial system of Liège and its suburbs. The notaries prepared the documents necessary for a loan under local laws and served the even more important function of middlemen and brokers. Their role should not be underestimated. In many, if not most, loans taken out at all times during the ancien régime, and certainly during wartime, the notary located the lender and his capital and brought lender and borrower together.[97]

Although there was not an enormous upsurge in total lending in wartime in the Basse-Meuse, it is nonetheless true that loans had to be sought to meet the extraordinary financial burdens that all individuals and institutions faced during wartime, and that these loans drew money away from other, more productive, fields of endeavor. Thus, in a survey of the lending activity organized by one Liégeois notary during the decade of the 1670's, Claude Desama has described the changing requirements for credit in a decade of war.[98] The years preceding the Dutch War had been a relatively long period of peace and growth in the Liégeois economy, but the outbreak of war in 1672 slowed the economy and the volume of loans decreased. During none of the two-year periods

after 1671 did the number of monetary transactions reach the level of the warless years, 1670-1671. But a significant number of new loans were made, even though there was a severe depression and very high prices in the middle of the decade. Loans for normal economic activity were replaced with loans to support the cost of war.

Measuring the impact of wartime borrowing, like measuring the impact of the cost of war on local and personal finance, is a complicated procedure, perhaps demanding a large-scale study of its own. It is possible, however, to speculate about the long-range consequences of the use of borrowed money to pay for the costs of troops in passage and the other military expenses that the rural communities incurred. Frequent military action in the Basse-Meuse in the seventeenth century, and the continual resort to credit, resulted in a steadily increasing indebtedness of the countryside. These debts were often not repaid for a decade or more; many communities were burdened with obligations incurred in the late seventeenth century until the second or third decade of the eighteenth century.[99] As a consequence, the economic resources of the villages and towns were drained into the cities, where the moneylenders lived. While the indebtedness may have created hardships in the countryside, it contributed to the continuing commercial and industrial prosperity of Liège, even in a century of wars.

The wealth of the countryside was also transferred to the cities by means other than the payment of interest. Some debtors defaulted or had to sell their property to prevent default. This happened to communities: after the village of Lixhe borrowed money to support the costs of the Dutch War, it requested permission from the prince-Bishop of Liège, in 1678, to alienate communal property in order to pay off some of the debts.[100] Individuals also lost their land. The wars of the seventeenth century caused some of the noble landowners in the Basse-Meuse to sell their land to the prosperous bourgeois of the cities.[101] The evidence is not quite so clear that the economic pressure of wars cost the region's peasants their land. The creation of a rural proletariat in the region seems to have been accomplished only with the first phase of industrialization in the second half of the eighteenth century.

VII. Toward a Monetarized Wartime Regime

The developing system of *contributions*, the incremental growth of taxation, and the continued use of credit to finance the costs of war in

the Basse-Meuse point to the direction of change in the traditional military system. Yet the traditional system persisted, certainly throughout the seventeenth century and well into the eighteenth. We have seen the evidence of that persistence: soldiers lived in the homes of civilians and, very often, ate at their tables. Even when they did not, it was the civilians who had to provide the food. Moreover, armies trampled fields and threatened to burn villages; the old, violent ways of war remained. We know that the traditional system persisted because the predominant characteristic of modern war, mass mobilization, could not yet happen to the villagers of the Basse-Meuse. Even in wartime, armies were a small, rather isolated enclave within society. The notion of a whole society mobilizing to make war (which began at the time of the French Revolution) was as alien to the Basse-Meuse in the seventeenth century as were the political ideals which finally brought the revolution, and mobilization, to the Basse-Meuse at the end of the eighteenth century.

But at the same time that the traditional ways continued, war, from the point of view of rural civilians, became more systematized and monetarized. *Contributions*, higher taxes, and more frequent loans were clues to what would come in the future. This new wartime regime permitted planning and a more flexible set of responses to the demands put on the Basse-Meuse by its frequent military visitors. By the early eighteenth century, those changes were to develop into a world where the burden of military occupation for the peasants of the Basse-Meuse was considerably lightened.

Chapter III

The Burden Lightens

"Despite the weight of requisitions, the occupation [1746-1748] was not too difficult to support. The sweetness of manners which was then spreading in France manifested itself by a method of warmaking that no longer adopted the pitiless brutality of Louvois." – Henri Pirenne, *Histoire de Belgique*, V, 224.

Fortunately for the villagers of the Basse-Meuse, the meaning of military presence changed considerably between the beginning of the seventeenth century and the beginning of the eighteenth. This change coincided with a significant transformation in the character of war itself. Armies grew enormously and the strain placed on the primitive mechanisms for supplying their needs led to much more efficient systems of provisioning. More numerous officers had more control over their troops, as the character of war changed from the anarchic medieval *mêlée* to the gentlemanly "chessboard" warfare of the eighteenth century.

That eighteenth century wars were less destructive of civilian life and property than those fought earlier is one of the fundamental historiographical truths of the relationship between war and society.[1] Improved provisioning and taxing systems spread the burden over broader areas. Rulers and generals saw that bilateral reductions in demands on civilians would preserve their own citizens' capacity to pay more taxes. With less desire to create enemies, they attempted consciously to reduce the immediate burden on civilians in the theater of war; with better control over their troops, they could achieve that end, first by bilateral diplomacy and then on the field.

Toynbee stated the argument for improved conditions: "Our eighteenth-century princes in the West are exceptional in the frankness with which they waged their wars as a private sport; yet it was no more possible for them than for other war-makers to ride rough-shod over the consciences of their fellow human beings; ... the players of their eighteenth century war-game found themselves constrained to be as

54

moderate in the conduct of their wars as they were cynical about the motives for which they made them."[2]

Not every historian agrees with Toynbee's perception of the eighteenth century. George Clark argues that any appearance of improvement in the wartime treatment of civilians in the eighteenth century was mere posturing by politicians, without real effect on the lives of civilians.[3] Clark's argument makes some sense. The most important single change in seventeenth-century warfare was the increase in the size and cost of armies, which led to greatly increased taxes and to an increased need for financial resources in the field. Though the good intentions of monarchs and generals helped to bring an end to examples of sudden, catastrophic violence, the increased costs of their enlarged armies imposed a more moderate but, nonetheless, perceptible and continuing burden on the peasantry.

Still, the case of the Basse-Meuse and, more generally, all of the Low Countries seems to support Toynbee, although not without ambiguities. From the very beginning of the seventeenth century changes were at work in the military world.[4] Discipline improved in the first half of the century; that improvement was coupled with a transformation in the provisioning system, the system of disbursing funds, and in general with an overhaul and centralization of military organization. Those improvements coincided with the last of certain older burdens that lay on civilians and troops. The Thirty Years' War saw the last civilian massacres, the end of catastrophic battlefield casualties, and, at least in the Basse-Meuse, the last private armies. After the Thirty Years' War, the main characteristic of military presence in the countryside became long-term financial drain.

In the second half of the century, new laws and bilateral diplomacy began to govern the conduct of armies in hostile territory; the financial drain was rationalized and moderated. A system of treaties of *contribution* largely replaced raiding parties no later than the 1660's. By the 1670's, an understanding between the French and Spanish further rationalized the demands for *contributions*. While these measures were obscured, delayed, and partially offset by skyrocketing costs of war and government, rural life became less disrupted in wartime, with a clear improvement in the eighteenth century.

I. Reforming Military Discipline

By the end of the seventeenth century, reforms in European armies

eliminated much of the random and unsanctioned violence that had characterized earlier wars by improving military discipline and military organization, and by ending sectarian religious warfare. The process that led to improved discipline resulted from strategic changes in European armies designed to make them more flexible and effective on the battlefield.[5] The Spanish pioneered these changes in the sixteenth century, and the Dutch General, Maurice of Nassau (1586-1625) and the Swedish King, Gustavus Adolphus (1611-1632), made further contributions. These innovators attempted to mold effective armies by breaking them into small, precise military units. They made military drill obligatory and increased the number of officers in proportion to the number of men. Better discipline was a logical result. Almost every army in Europe attempted to adopt these reforms by 1650.

Troops that were better-drilled and better-disciplined, with a higher proportion of officers to enlisted men, were less likely to engage in acts of unprovoked or unplanned violence. This became even more probable when, as we shall see, kings and generals began to feel that civilian populations should be treated as gently as possible. The better control exercised by military leadership over their charges meant that there was a good chance that these policies would result in truly better treatment of civilians.

As early as mid-century, in 1649, when Maximilian Henry, the Prince of Liège, quelled a revolt in the city of Liège, he acted on those assumptions. The chronicle of that year wrote about his actions after attaining success: "As it was difficult to prevent the troops from carrying out attacks and pillage, Maximilian charged Laurent de Mean [and others] . . . to assign camping locations to his troops and to prevent them from pillaging by furnishing their daily needs."[6] The great powers shared this feeling. In 1690, the Allies in the War of the League of Augsburg issued regulations that "severely organized the camps and instituted a sort of special police to stop marauders."[7]

The great innovation of the mid-seventeenth century was the development of strong civilian control over armies. Civilian control, which imposed bureaucratic administration and lines of communication from new ministers of war (such as le Tellier in France) to battlefield commanders, permitted the enforcement of a military code of conduct.[8] Although such codes surely existed prior to the seventeenth century, the reign of Louis XIV saw them become part of growing national legal systems. By 1680 France began the publication of all its laws for the army, a series that came, by 1706, to fifteen

volumes.[9] And in 1709 Sparre published his *Code militarie ou compilation des règlements et ordonnances de Louis XIV faites pour les gens de guerre . . .,* an officer's portable guide to the rules of conduct for himself and his men.[10] At the same time, military courts developed to enforce these rules. Military conduct and discipline, while hardly perfect after 1650, was surely better than in the past, especially if we consider the enormous growth in the size of armies that took place.

Paradoxically, the greed of military leaders was in part responsible for the growth of order, control, and discipline. Armies by the late seventeenth century were gargantuan organizations, needing vast amounts of food, money, and matériel. Their increasingly formalized structure demanded order and left little leeway for unaccounted troops to travel about Europe when they should have been fighting. Moreover, if troops stole things or disrupted economic affairs, the armies' normal demands would be more difficult to meet.

The same motivation led to the elimination of private armies by the middle of the seventeenth century. During the Thirty Years' War private armies maintained by small princes plagued the Basse-Meuse, roaming the countryside and living off the land.[11] Wallenstein was only the best known of the independent military leaders, active in Central Europe and Germany. For Western Europe, and for the Basse-Meuse, there were other freebooters, most notably Duke Charles IV of Lorraine, the Croatian troops of Jean de Weert, Count Mansfeld, General Salazar, and, briefly at mid-century, the Frenchman, the Prince of Condé.[12]

The population of the Low Countries feared the troops of these leaders more than any others in the first half of the seventeenth century – with reason. When the war shifted its focus decisively to the Low Countries in the 1630's, the troops of the Duke of Lorraine and Croatian troops camped in the Principality of Liège during virtually every winter from 1635 to 1654.[13] The people of the Basse-Meuse suffered particularly severely from 1649 to 1654, once the war slowed down and the Fronde prevented France's leaders from controlling their armies. The Duke of Lorraine finally withdrew his troops from the Principality of Liège in July, 1653, in return for a payment of 10,000 patacons (30,000 florins). Yet, he stayed away only six months, until January, 1654.[14]

Like their marauding and pillaging troops, these generals declined in importance with increased military centralization. By the middle of the seventeenth century they were too costly to maintain and too difficult

to control. The major European states could by then maintain centralized armies large enough to fight their wars. Spanish authorities arrested Charles IV of Lorraine in 1654, as a direct result of his devastation of the countryside in and near the Basse-Meuse and sent him to Spain, where he stayed until after France and Spain made peace.[15] Private armies such as his never reappeared in the Basse-Meuse.

II. Redefining Military Customs: Lodging and Feeding

Seventeenth-century reforms partially lifted the burden of lodging the troops off the backs of householders. The garrison of Maastricht constructed barracks in 1616,[16] and it is likely that the Citadel of Liège, constructed in the 1650's, also contained barracks, so that the troops residing there would not be a burden on the city's residents.

Furthermore, in the summers, the earlier trend towards the troops' camping outdoors in jerry-built shelters continued. This happened especially during sieges, which brought many more troops to the Basse-Meuse in the campaign season than did battles. When Frederick Henry's troops made camp for the siege of Maastricht in 1632, "The whole Leaguer [siege camp] was formed of Hutts of Strawe and some Tents, so that I could not imagine how it was possible that so much Strawe should be found about one Towne, and gathered in so few dayes."[17] Obviously, the construction of a discrete and defensible camp surrounding the fortification of Maastricht had strategic value, but it also kept troops out of the homes of nearby villagers.

New procedures only slowly changed the most serious housing problem, the winter camp. Still, armies made progress. Describing a winter camp established by the French around Richelle in 1701, the Curé of Hermalle-sous-Argenteau wrote: "On September 6, about seven or eight thousand French and Spanish came to camp at Argenteau and Richelle. They built a bridge below the chateau of Argenteau, at the place where one crosses the river by boat. Then, using all sorts of wood, they constructed barracks in the fields by building little houses covered by plastered straw, and built kitchens and stables for each company."[18] These camps were not universal by 1701, however. The French army, for example, made no systematic effort to keep troops out of civilian homes until the 1760's.[19]

To judge the improvement in housing requirements, the best approach will be to make a direct comparison between the conditions which operated in the wars of the seventeenth century and those of the

eighteenth century. Daniel Berlamont has made such a comparison for Verviers in 1678-1679 and 1746-1748; we can make use of his conclusions to illuminate the improvements that took place between the late seventeenth century and the mid-eighteenth century. In the matter of housing, the evidence is clear. A town like Verviers, even in 1746, still lodged troops in winter quarters in the homes of individuals. But the majority stayed in barracks. The conditions of lodging for householders had changed dramatically. They might find troops lodging in their homes, but the number of troops and the number of homes involved were smaller. According to Berlamont, "the lodgings of 1678 had been much more onerous [than those of 1746-1748] for a much shorter stay."[20]

Moreover, the organization of lodging in Verviers in the 1740's was more equitable, because the procedure was more carefully controlled and the city had more cash to meet the obligations that had also been paid for by the citizens seventy years earlier. In the 1670's, less than ten percent of the total cost of the occupation was available to the leadership of the city in cash from all sources: from loans, from advances paid by some bourgeois, and from the payments made by those who lodged no troops. In the occupation of the 1740's, on the other hand, the civic administration was able almost immediately to raise over ninety percent of the total cost from loans, taxes, and a contribution from the estates of Liège.[21] Finally, even the cost of borrowing money was lower in the eighteenth century. Verviers paid three percent for its loans in 1746-1748, because money was abundant; in 1678-1679, on the other hand, they had borrowed little because interest rates were over six percent, and lenders were hard to find.[22]

The armies made their greatest advances in the methods of feeding troops and supplying their clothing and arms. It was this improvement that really saved the residents of the Basse-Meuse. As early as the late sixteenth century, the Spanish army began to convey these supplies directly to the armies, in kind, rather than by payments to the troops, who were to make their own purchases. This had a practical purpose, from the point of view of effective military performance. Sixteenth-century armies were perenially impecunious. If they were unable to pay their troops, and the troops needed cash to buy food, all sorts of complications arose. Troops deserted, or they resorted to credit or to violence to obtain food; mutiny was common.[23] Unrest continually troubled the army maintained by the Spanish government in the Low Countries; in the years from 1572 to 1607, it suffered 45 mutinies, 21 of

them after 1596.[24] Poor pay and the consequent poor food and clothing surely helped cause these outbursts.

One solution was to supply each soldier with the clothing he needed, and with a daily ration of bread. According to Geoffrey Parker: "It was easier, more humane and far safer to run up debts to the merchants who supplied food and other munitions to the army than to leave the soldier unpaid and unprovided, and it was not difficult to supervise a small clique of entrepreneurs dealing in bulk and subject to contract. Bread, clothes, arms and shelter came to be provided directly by the Army. . . . By 1630, about half the soldier's wages were paid in kind".[25]

The Spanish army which Parker describes was at the forefront of the changes made by the early seventeenth century. At that time, in the midst of the Thirty Years' War, the movement toward paying in kind through a commissariat was restricted to western Europe, and perhaps only to Spain and the Netherlands. In Central Europe, in the German theater of the war, the traditional method of living off the peasants was still in full force.[26]

Contractors working for the government had the responsibility for providing bread rations. Sometimes with travelling ovens and supplies brought directly from the home country, but more often using the ovens of local bakers to bake grain and flour bought or requisitioned on the spot, the armies and their contractors fed the troops.[27] The process of moving from a situation where local populations met all the needs of the army to one where the army met those needs itself was slow. The greatest progress was made in armies on the march or prepared for battle. Slower progress attended the mounters and resisters of sieges. And, again, winter quarters changed slowest of all: essentially medieval practices survived into the eighteenth century.

By 1700, however, the witnesses living in the Basse-Meuse give clear evidence of improved provisioning. As we saw, the French constructed a sophisticated camp around Richelle in 1701. In that same year, de Sonkeux described two battalions that arrived from Richelle as "lodging peacefully at their own expense."[28] Later, when two regiments of French troops — 700 men — arrived to form a garrison, they required the Verviétois to provide them only with fire and shelter, much less than the complex demands for utensils and clothing made in the Dutch War some twenty years earlier.[29]

The origins of the changes just described, both in military discipline and in the housing and feeding of troops, lay more in the need for effective fighting units than in intentional efforts to ameliorate the burden on civilians who happened to be in or near the area of battle. It would be wrong to perceive humanitarian impulses or intentional goodwill in the actions of military leaders in the first half of the seventeenth century or earlier, even if they resulted in improved relations with civilians.

In the second half of the century, however, that order of priorities was reversed. Military leaders now made a conscious effort to act in a civilized manner toward occupied civilians and enemy territories.[30] Some authorities attribute the change of attitude to the end of sectarian religious warfare and the Thirty Years' War.[31] They argue that the extreme and often violent behavior toward civilians in the first half of the seventeenth century was religiously grounded; when the religious antagonism ended, military leaders had no more desire to oppress civilians. We have no evidence that this is true; it is more likely that better behavior and treatment emerged from the quest for absolute power and the need to muster all the productive energies of the countryside toward war.

Whatever the explanation, it is clear that from the mid-seventeenth century onward princes and generals became aware of an obligation toward civilians. We can see this attitude in the behavior of the Prince of Liège. When the Prince attempted to bring his citizens back under control in 1649, he burned parts of two villages. Yet, once he had achieved the goals of restoring his authority, the Prince changed his stance radically. His Journal of the events of 1649, published that year, reports that "... he provided the troops with supplies from the moment of their arrival [in the Basse-Meuse] and sent M. de Hautepenn [who was] ... charged with the daily task of procuring food and everything that the army needed, so that the people in the Principality would suffer as little as possible from the presence of the soldiers."[32] The Prince of Liège rarely made war, and this document may grossly overstate his concern for his subjects. Still, that he cared about public opinion enough to report it in his version of the events of 1649 signifies growing concern among European princes.

Far more significant for all the people of Europe was the attitude of Louis XIV, the preeminent monarch in the second half of the

seventeenth century. Louis held as benevolent an attitude toward the people whose territory he occupied, at least on paper, as the Prince of Liège. When he attacked the Dutch Republic in 1672, he distributed a document to all the communities he reached. In its first paragraph, he told them that: "His Majesty has been obliged, only with displeasure, to carry the War into the Lands possessed by the Dutch, and his design is only to punish those of the government, and not to ruin the populace, which have had no part of the evil conduct by which the government has been run. His Majesty has judged it appropriate to send the present ordinance in order to inform the people of the fashion by which he has resolved to support his armies and the order that he wishes to hold them to for their relief."[33]

In subsequent paragraphs Louis promised to pay his army punctually, to keep them in order, to have them feed themselves (except for forage), to allow civilians to take their animals and goods inside the protection of towns, and to provide those towns with inexpensive safeguards to protect them from any marauders. Louis' aims are admirable, even if we doubt that his armies performed as he told everyone he wanted them to. His attitude in 1672 signals the dramatic reforms that were on their way by that date. It offers a marked contrast to the behavior of some earlier leaders, and certainly those like Wallenstein and Charles of Lorraine, who openly built their power through exploitation of the countryside.

IV. Legal Reforms: The State Takes Over

Louis XIV, while at the forefront, was not alone. In the last three decades of the seventeenth century, and the first of the eighteenth, several states attempted to reduce wartime burdens on civilians in occupied areas. The first step was to reduce the burdens on territories subject to *contributions* by a system of treaties of *contribution*, which appeared, perhaps as early as the late 1640's, and certainly by the War of the Devolution in 1667. A sovereign granted permission under certain conditions to local authorities (at the level of a significant portion of a province) to negotiate with the enemy. A system evolved by which whole regions agreed to pay the enemy (each agreement was called a treaty of *contribution*), meet his demands, and avoid the violence of individual raiding parties seeking *contributions* from village to village. These payments could be deducted, at least in part, from normal tax obligations.[34]

62

In the Dutch War, however, the increasing demands for money spurred by enormous armies led to new problems. The French and the Spanish rulers of the Netherlands then attempted to achieve a bilateral reduction in *contributions* in the Low Countries. They met at Deynze, a village outside Ghent, between September, 1676, and February, 1678.[35] Although the Conference of Deynze produced no treaty, it affected the future conduct of war. In early 1677, Louis XIV decided unilaterally to adopt the principal conclusion of the meetings. By 1678, according to van Houtte, the Belgian historian who has studied the conference, the Spanish concurred although no treaty resulted.[36]

The unilateral decision taken by Louis XIV affected three aspects of the collection of *contributions*.[37] First, total *contributions* to be drawn from an area must not exceed the amount of taxes paid in a normal peacetime year to the legal sovereign of the territory. In Louis' regulation of 1677, the base year established for French troops demanding *contributions* from the enemy was 1669. The second major change confirmed the rule that armies must negotiate *contributions* with a whole province, or a significant portion thereof, rather than collect them from individual villages. The third area of change restricted the recourse to violence in the event *contributions* were negotiated but not paid. Prior to Deynze, armies made no distinction between the temporary inability to pay and the unwillingness to negotiate a treaty of *contribution*. As a consequence of Louis' decision, *exécution* by fire was forbidden unless a community deserted its homes. If the villagers stayed in place, their homes would be spared, but they could be forced to give up hostages and livestock.[38]

The civilizing influence of the atmosphere of the Conference of Deynze cannot be underestimated. Based on the foundation established by the rational collection of *contributions*, the legal principles ultimately established led to a significant reduction in civilian burdens in time of war. Territory subject to *contribution* had in the past been caught between two warring states. The understandings reached at Deynze rationalized and civilized those burdens, reduced the total collected to the level of peacetime taxation, divided and spread the burden among the residents of a fairly large area, and eliminated the danger of gratuitous violence in the event that the system partially broke down.

In the same way that the civilizing improvements in provisioning did not reach the Basse-Meuse until after 1700, the results of the Conference of Deynze had their first impact at the end of the Dutch War, in 1677. Their full repercussions were some time in coming. The

War of the Reunions, and the War of the League of Augsburg, in the 1680's and 1690's, were fought as though Deynze had never occurred.[39] Only in the War of the Spanish Succession, in the 1700's, does van Houtte see the implementation of the Deynze agreements. For one thing, he found virtually no *exécution* by fire after 1700. Furthermore, the tone of polite dealing on the part of opposing armies and generals when considering issues of *contribution* had triumphed completely by the War of the Spanish Succession.

While the impact of *contributions* lightened, lodging and feeding troops became less onerous, and military discipline improved, a further development took place: the state provided a more durable buffer between armies and civilians, permitting the civilians more opportunities to go about their normal business during wartime. The origins of this progress surely lie with the assumption by communities, for their residents, of the burdens of dealing with armies. The system of treaties of *contribution* and the results of the Conference of Deynze confirmed the same development. At the same time civilians gained control over armies. Now, civilian administrators began to accompany armies, arranging for recruitment, lodgings, food, and supplies. When civilian agents for armies dealt on a practical basis with civilians representing groups of communities in the path of march or the place of winter quarters, there was hope that civilians would not interact so violently with soldiers, nor suffer so much from their presence.

Once again, the Principality of Liège can provide us with an example of this process. Throughout most of the seventeenth century, armies which crossed or lodged in the principality dealt with individual communities or *ad hoc* agents of the Prince or Estates. In 1690, however, the Prince appointed Jean de Mont military commissioner for the principality, a position that continued to exist until the end of the Liégeois state, in 1794.[40] The Commisioner's responsibilities included dealing with foreign armies. He or his agent met them when they arrived in the principality and cooperated with their officers or civilian agents to make sure they were lodged and received what they needed without trouble from the citizens of Liège. He reported regularly to the Prince's *Conseil Privé*, and where necessary adjudicated disputes between armies and civilians.

The people of Liège clearly became accustomed to the state's acting as a buffer between them and the great armies. By the mid-eighteenth century they expected the state, or someone, to reimburse them for their expenses and any damage during military camps or occupations.

Ill. 3 *Devastation of a Monestary*, by Jacques Callot (1633)

As a consequence, the archives of the Liégeois *Conseil Privé* dealing with armies grow progressively richer for every decade of the seventeenth and eighteenth centuries.[41] There are very few documents for the whole Thirty Years' War; by the 1730's and 1740's, there are numerous dossiers, mostly containing summaries of the expenses of individual villages. We can see that the state became an effective buffer by turning again to Daniel Berlamont's study of Verviers. In the occupation of 1746-1748, the Estates of Liège provided nearly thirty percent of the total cost of lodging the French army in Verviers, whereas they had ignored requests for financial assistance during the occupation of 1678-1679. This distributed the cost of lodging over a much wider area: the whole Principality of Liège.[42]

The state helped its communities in another novel way in the 1740's. In the settlement of the War of the Austrian Succession, the French government agreed to reimburse the Principality of Liège for its citizens' costs attributable to the French presence and occupation of the principality. The Liégeois government called for an official accounting of the costs of the war, and received 36,750 individual requests for reimbursement.[43] Each village presented an accounting of its damages and contributions to the French army. And the French actually paid. Between 31 December 1746, and 11 July 1755, they paid two and one-half million florins, which were then divided among the villagers of the principality according to their individual losses.[44]

Some villages of the Basse-Meuse received substantial reimbursements under this program. While Oupeye received about 8,500 florins, and Saive only about 2,300, both Haccourt and Eben-Emael received nearly 25,000 florins.[45] Surely, this reduced the overall costs of war for the people of the Basse-Meuse. But we must not force our optimism too far. The French money could not reimburse all of the expenses of the villagers of the Principality of Liège; the Estates and Prince distributed it according to a formula that repaid only about two-fifths of the amounts claimed.[46] Admittedly, the 25,000 florin French reimbursement helped Haccourt and Eben-Emael. But they still had to wait nearly seven years to receive all of it and needed to raise the remaining 37,500 florins. By the mid-eighteenth century, the costs of war for the communities of the Basse-Meuse lightened, but hardly disappeared.

V. Measuring the Improvement

In subsequent chapters, we will examine a number of social, economic,

and demographic indicators of war's impact to see if it lightened outside the realm of housing, feeding, behavior, and community finance. We will see that, in spite of some ambiguity, war's demographic and economic costs lessened. Still, this analysis raises a problem: our use of demographic and economic variables to study war and its changing impact implies that all military events in the Basse-Meuse were comparable. But war was no monolith. Those events took place as much as a century apart, with armies of different sizes, led by different generals, staying different amounts of time, representing a number of states, and with different objectives. We should avoid as far as possible the temptation to treat war as a single independent variable which changed only by lessening its impact over time. It will not be enough to say that states were at war in a certain year, or that the people of the Basse-Meuse saw soldiers in the course of that year. War's impact varied, surely from season to season and year to year, if not in daily or weekly intervals. What determined the level of war's impact each time? There were a number of ways we might establish the character of military presence during a given year. (Because most of the variables we will use to measure war's impact — such as average annual prices or the total annual production of a farm or a village — are annual measures, our basic unit of time will be a year.)

The size of an army and the exact duration of its stay are obvious choices for the means to gauge war's impact. It is easy to predict that a large army should cause more damage (insofar as armies always caused damage) than a small one. But it is difficult to determine the exact size of an army. For most epochs, we know only battle strengths (which are themselves subject to considerable question), and not the size of forces while on the march or in camp; virtually all contact between civilians and soldiers, however, took place during sieges and between battles, when troops were camped in and around towns and villages. Even the most thorough search in many military archives, therefore, would not produce the figures needed for accurate computations. The same problem applies to the duration of an army's stay in a village, town, or region. It is very difficult to know the exact date when each unit arrived in each locale and the exact date they left.

Beyond the question of obtaining the evidence needed to judge size and duration, we should question whether, in fact, the impact of an army on a village, town, or region is, in fact, proportional to the product of the size of forces present and the number of days they are there. While there may be such a relationship, it is not very exact. Once

the number of troops increased beyond a certain point, it took an extremely large additional increase in the size of the army involved to alter its impact significantly. Similarly, after a certain point in time, a longer stay by an army made little difference. How many troops and how long a stay made a difference? It is difficult to say, but it is clear the numbers could not be very large since at least until the end of the seventeenth century (when the impact of occupations and winter camps began to lighten) even a modest military force exceeded in a very short time the resources of most Basse-Mosan villagers. The point I am trying to make is that there is not much sense in distinguishing between the Battle of Haccourt in 1746 and each of the sieges of Maastricht (1632, 1673, 1676, 1748) by the number of troops on each side or by the length of the siege, or in distinguishing between winter camps in various years of the 1690's according to the size of the force involved, etc. It is not clear that it makes a difference, and the data to give a valid answer are almost impossible to obtain. Finally, the dependent variables (like production or prices or population size) are often so imprecise that exact independent variables for military impact are unnecessary. Instead, we will use two basic components, the significance and duration of the war (in years instead of days) for the eastern Low Countries, and the kind of military activity involved, to establish the character of military presence during a given year. These characteristics are easy to obtain and in some crucial ways encompass size and duration as well as adding other important information.

When we consider the impact of a year's military events on the Basse-Meuse, the first question we must ask is whether the war was significant for the Low Countries, since it will be our working hypothesis that significance is directly related to the war's consequences for the population. A significant war, for our purposes, was one in which the Dutch Republic was a belligerent and which produced operations during more than two years. Why these two criteria? A warring Dutch Republic, unlike Spain, France or even the Principality of Liège, was a sure indication that *consequential* military activity would occur in the Basse-Meuse. The question of duration is important because war had a cumulative impact. As a long war stretched on, each succeeding year seems to have been more serious for the people of the Basse-Meuse than the last, all other things being equal. Reserves which might in good times last a year or two rarely survived the continuing demands of hard times and soldiers for three or more years. We can thus arrange the wars of the seventeenth and eighteenth centuries into two

68

groups. The Thirty Years' War, the Dutch War, the War of the League of Augsburg, and the Wars of Spanish and Austrian Succession surely had a more dramatic effect on the Basse-Meuse than the Franco-Spanish continuation of the Thirty Years' War (1648-1659), the War of the Devolution (1667-1668), the War of the Reunions (1683-1684), and the War of the Polish Succession (1735-1736), even though foreign troops entered the Basse-Meuse and did some damage in every one of the latter wars.

The wars of the seventeenth and eighteenth centuries brought armies to the Basse-Meuse for a variety of purposes. The nature of the activities in which the armies engaged determined, in part, the impact that military presence had on the lives of the people of the Basse-Meuse. This is our second criterion. Broadly speaking, we can identify three levels of military activity. The most intrusive was a major offensive or defensive action (such as a siege or battle) in or near the territory in question. These kinds of actions brought the densest and most desperate armies among the population. Troops in occupation or winter quarters were less intrusive. They were present for long periods of time and expected the civilian population to support them; the good sense of their officers, however, led them to be spread over many communities so that those communities could support the army for a long time without totally depleting community resources. The least intrusive military forces were those simply passing through. While these armies could be large, their brief stay (less than a week) made their overall impact lighter; there was only so much they could do in a few days, especially if they were primarily concerned with preparing for new activity elsewhere. Of course, they might use their brief layover to sweep through the region and gather supplies, and the marching path of a large army could be very destructive. But the press of time restricted the impact of troops in passage. If they stayed more than about a week, their presence became a form of occupation, and we should class it as such. During the balance of this book, I will use the significance of the war and the character of military activity to establish the character of war in an individual year. In that way we will learn whether we can distinguish between the impact of a siege and a winter camp, for example, and what the impact of each was.

We can now formulate an explanation of war's changing impact on various elements of community life in the seventeenth and eighteenth centuries. As we have seen in this chapter, the greatest wartime burden for Basse-Mosan communities, the expense and trouble associated with

military occupation and *contributions* began to ligthen after the middle of the seventeenth century. Although the progress of this development was slow at first, it was continuous and, by the mid-eighteenth century War of the Austrian Succession, the administrative mechanisms for dealing with visiting armies had changed dramatically. The change was part of the general development of European states in the seventeenth and eighteenth centuries. Rulers sought greater centralization of power in their hands, which led to more centralized, better-administered and better-disciplined armies. They eliminated, as far as possible, competing powers within the state who had in the past led private armies-for-hire. The growth of armies and the state increased costs, making them impossible to support completely through ad hoc contributions in kind. A monetarized army was the result. Perhaps surprisingly, the need to raise taxes to support these new cash-oriented administrative systems led to more equitable taxation and to a burden that, if not lighter, was at least less intrusive and less destructive of life and the productivity of the countryside.

When we examine the changing impact of war on the economic and demographic life of the community and on its social structure, we will find the change less direct and linear than it was for community functions. The demographic and economic consequences of simple military presence and military occupation surely lightened. Troops stole less, demanded less, destroyed less, and cost fewer Basse-Mosan residents their lives. The same was not true for the major military events of the age, sieges and battles. When armies came to the Basse-Meuse to destroy each other, they continued to destroy the lives of civilians. Although administrative changes helped, they were not enough; the economic and demographic consequences of the brief War of the Austrian Succession were as intense as the worst years of the Thirty Years' War or the Dutch War.

Why do we require this complex model of change? Why were changes in the several areas of military impact not direct, linear, and simultaneous with the expressed desire of the military powers to change? Essentially, the explanation must be that countervailing forces operated: war changed, but in a number of ways. First, warfare expanded, tremendously increasing the number of troops and the cost of each soldier. Second, the direct impact of the burden of war on civilians lightened, because of new institutions, better organization, and new attitudes. The interaction of these two forces renders vain our hope for a simple, linear, simultaneous development.

70

In the late seventeenth century, means were proposed to lighten the burden on civilians, but they were counteracted, and temporarily reversed, by the growth of armies and the increasing cost of keeping each man in the field. This accounts for the slow early development of changes in the ways communities handled military occupation and contributions. Only about 1700 did the balance tip toward lighter obligations for rural civilians. The improved administration of *contributions* and occupation meant that occupation also had a lighter impact on the population and the economy.

While the slow development of administrative reforms worked to lighten the weight of most forms of military presence, it only slightly affected the problems associated with major military events. There, the improvement of military technique and the growth of army size continued to weigh heavily on the economic and demographic affairs of the people of the Basse-Meuse. The only improvement possible occurred because wars in the first half of the eighteenth century were far less frequent than in the seventeenth century. Villages, towns, cities, provinces, principalities, even national governments, all had more resources in reserve by the 1740's, after nearly three decades of peace and prosperity, than they had had for any of the wars of the seventeenth century. By the middle of the eighteenth century, the tide had at least partially turned. The war of the Austrian Succession was still disastrous for the people of the Basse-Meuse, but it presented fewer problems to them than had war for their grandfathers seventy-five years earlier, and the people of the region were able to recover their momentum much more quickly.

Part 3

War and the Economy

Chapter IV

The Farmers: Short-Circuiting Agricultural Production

When the village of Herstal divided its share of the French reparations paid after the War of the Austrian Succession, Jean Binon reported the damage French soldiers inflicted on his farm. In 1746 they stole grain worth 760 florins, and destroyed a garden worth an additional 200 florins. In the following year, they prevented him from harvesting anything. They stole or destroyed crops that stood in his fields, such as the three *bonniers* and five *verges* planted in rye (worth 650 florins), or the five *verges* planted in wheat (worth 75 florins). His total loss of 1,240 florins in that year must reflect nearly all the potential revenue of his farm.[1]

One of the certainties in our discussion of war's impact on rural people has been that it disrupted their lives. In this, Jean Binon's experience is characteristic. It disturbed the normal and peaceful fabric of everyday existence, forcing people to search for new resources, to refigure their budgets, to see their property destroyed or their familiar church desecrated, and sometimes to lose their loved ones. As we saw in Chapters II and III, war constantly put stress on the economic fabric of peoples' lives. Villages had to raise extra money and find extra food; troops sometimes camped on and often destroyed their crops, homes, and farms; and warfare drained manpower from the fields.

In this chapter we will explore the ways that warfare disturbed the economic system of the Basse-Meuse. War had both temporary and much more far-reaching effects on the economy of the Basse-Meuse. Temporary, because the major wars of the seventeenth and eighteenth century (the Thirty Years' War, the Dutch War, and the War of the Austrian Succession) shut down the whole system for a year or more. Farmers lost production and income, landlords lost rents, the church lost tithe revenue and the state lost taxes. Fortunately, the region was heavily populated; as soon as residents could, they returned to their fields, pastures, looms, forges, and mines.

These temporary breakdowns, at least in the agricultural sector, accumulated into long-term agricultural stagnation in the late seventeenth century. The Basse-Meuse sunk into an agricultural depression, which began around 1670 and lasted until nearly 1700. While production stayed near normal in all but the worst years, farmers lost part of their revenues, went into debt, and could not pay their bills. The quality of life deteriorated, and, as we will see later, the population stopped growing. Nevertheless, at the end of the seventeenth century all this changed. With the War of the League of Augsburg, in the 1690's, war turned from a time of catastrophe to one of modest prosperity for most farmers. The region's industries continued to prosper. By the first decade of the eighteenth century, in agriculture as well as in industry, production and profitability were beginning an upward climb.

In Chapter I we presented an outline of the Basse-Mosan economy. Agriculture dominated it, split between a traditional grain-growing sector and a more progressive dairy farming sector. Workers from the agricultural communities supplemented their incomes by finding employment in expanding rural manufacturing and the area's coal mines. How did war influence this economy? The producers and consumers of the Basse-Meuse seldom went out of their way to leave a written description of war's impact on their fortunes. Still, we have their complaints to governmental officials. Moreover, ecclesiastical records provide rich testimony of war's impact on the economic life of the region.

The best of these documents are those maintained by the Cathedral Chapter of Liège and called the *Protocoles des Directeurs*.[2] The Cathedral of Liège was among the richest churches in northern Europe.[3] Its holdings were so large that the chapter appointed a full-time committee of three to five canons to "direct" its economic affairs. They in turn recruited ad hoc assistants from among the members of the Chapter and the other clergy of the Diocese.[4] The directors met several times each week to consider the reports of their agents and to lease property, collect money, and make arrangements with creditors and debtors. They received requests from tenants and debtors for permission to pay less than they owed the Church for tithe, ground rent, or mortgage. The canons often responded by granting a "grace" or remission for part of the obligation. Their minutes, the *Protocoles des Directeurs*, reflect the kinds of damage and loss that they accepted as requiring the remittance of money or grain owed. These records thus provide us with an

invaluable source for the character of wartime economic losses.[5]

I. The Character of Wartime Economic Losses

War, according to our documents, produced losses for farmers: loss of tools, buildings, animals, crops, and savings. Unfortunately, the documents seldom state precisely how these losses occurred, or what farmers actually lost. For the eighteenth century, statements such as Jean Binon's record the items lost, but even he did not relate what had happened to his farm. In the seventeenth century the documentation is sketchier. We must reconstruct the character of wartime economic losses from partial evidence; then we can attempt to measure the quantity of those losses.

The evidence presented by the documents of church and state leads us to two basic conclusions. First, the farmers and industrial workers of the Basse-Meuse did not respond to war by changing the *way* they farmed or otherwise earned their living. They might have changed the way they allocated manpower, or the amount produced, or even the routes taken by goods in transit, but they seldom modified the essential techniques of economic activity under the influence of war. The second conclusion involves the losses we can identify. The canons and the Prince's Council recognized two ways that armies caused economic losses to their citizens, tenants and debtors: destruction and theft. Consequently, we will first describe the kinds of destruction and theft that harmed agriculture and other economic activities in the Basse-Meuse in wartime.

War led to the *destruction* of crops and farmers' resources in two significant ways. First, some armies destroyed property inadvertently, or through the necessary undertakings of war. For example, troops who marched through a region, stopped overnight, or built a camp destroyed growing crops. We need only imagine the destructive force of ten to fifty thousand men marching through fields and meadows and then camping wherever they could find room. They probably left nothing standing.[6] Also, the construction of lines of fortification and siegeworks had the same result because the armies needed a clear view of their surroundings and the approach of any potential enemies.[7] Finally, inadvertence had a number of unexpected consequences, such as the destruction of livestock by the spread of disease among them.[8]

Armies also destroyed valuable rural property purposefully and

maliciously. Communities which angered an army seeking *contributions* were subject to *exécution*, which until the 1690's was usually by fire. Fire was the most common form of wanton destruction, and caused the greatest damage to animals, buildings, and tools. Without these no farmer could go about his business. For example, Jean de Lours of the parish of St. Walburge (at the northern border of the City of Liège), "had his house, barn, stable, and all his possessions and sheep, along with all his grain and forage and a horse, consumed by the fire... caused by the Dutch" in the fall of 1678.[9]

While wartime destruction was significant, the *theft* of standing crops, stored grain, animals, trees, and equipment by foraging soldiers seems to have caused the greatest losses. Certainly, theft caused the most complaints. This was in addition to the normal process, discussed earlier, of providing rations and *contributions* to armies. De Sonkeux reported in 1675 that "for the past few years, the only reapers in our fields have been soldiers."[10] Despite the important advances made in the economic relations between soldiers and civilians, foraging and pillaging parties still existed at the time of the War of the Austrian Succession, during the mid-eighteenth century.[11] Hungry soldiers cut standing crops, turned their horses loose in the fields, or simply raided barns and stables for what they needed. Improvements in the conduct of war had occurred, but they had not eliminated this aspect of its unpleasantness.

We can describe only a few of the many examples to give a sense of farmers' losses to theft and foraging. In the War of the League of Augsburg, and especially in 1693-1694, the tenants and debtors of the Cathedral of Liège complained that they had suffered a *fouragement general*. Soldiers had taken everything they could find. Many tenants received a grace remitting half of their obligations for those years.[12] In 1674, the Cathedral granted a 50 percent remission to the tithe-collectors of Visé, who had seen the French and Imperial armies either cut or eat all the winter-sowed grains (wheat, rye, and spelt) in the tithe district.[13] Similarly, Jacques Conegracht, who lived in Herstal, requested aid from the estates of Liège because in 1746 and 1747 the French and the allies "totally foraged" his farm, taking not only the crops from the fields but also the grain stored in his barn. The estates (his landlord) had even attempted to evict him because he was unable to pay his rent.[14] These losses, and the terrible problems they caused for the farmers of the region, are repeated again and again in the records of church and state.[15]

Armies also stole timber and animals. Many fruit trees grew in the Basse-Meuse, and armies always considered their lumber useful. In 1632 the lord of Eysden lost 100 of them at the time of the Dutch siege; more than a century later, in 1746, pandours and hussards (probably from the Austrian army) similarly cut fruit trees in Kanne.[16] Probably more important than the loss of trees were the losses of animals. Draft animals, dairy cattle, pigs, and sheep were easy prey. In 1678 the garrison of Hasselt attacked a farm in Voroux, killing nineteen large pigs and all the farmer's chickens.[17] In the 1670's, the canons of the Liège Cathedral gave many graces to farmers like the resident of Lanthin whose two horses were taken by the Dutch.[18] Once again, these complaints characterize the eighteenth as well as the seventeenth century. After the Battle of Laeffelt (1747), allied troops occupied Kanne and Nedercanne, and took "sheep, pigs, cows, and honey bees." While we must question what the troops did with the honey bees and, in general, assume that these claims are exaggerated, we can believe that some villagers were left so poor that those with any animals remaining were forced to sell them in order to buy bread.[19]

Destruction of crops and property, and theft above and beyond already high taxes and contributions, were not the only ways that people in the Basse-Meuse lost agricultural productivity in wartime. They also lost working time. Farmers feared the potential violence associated with military action, and stayed out of their fields. Troops seeking *contributions*, vagrant civilians, or leaderless soldiers could appear out of nowhere and attack a lone farmer, taking him hostage, harming him physically, or stealing his precious draft animals, tools, or clothing. The demands of armies for pioneers and wagons also diverted manpower, as the community of Wonck learned in the summer and fall of 1747. "During this time," they wrote in a request for aid to the estates of Liège, "it has been impossible to brew [an important autumn task], both because the troops have occupied our houses and because of the pioneers and wagons that this community must provide for the use of the army for moving the sick to their hospitals, for carrying fascines and palisades, and for going to search for forage for their horses and wood for their kitchens . . . thus the peasants and brewers have not been able to brew or slaughter [another autumn task] during the long stay of the armies."[20]

Because they were less exposed, the non-agricultural economic activities of the Basse-Meuse seem to have suffered less than farming in wartime. The farmers and laborers of the region were usually able to

find employment in the region's mines, cloth trade, and on the river. Only in the most catastrophic years, such as 1675, when military activity combined with an economic crisis, did de Sonkeux report that spinners and weavers could find no work in Verviers.[21] Still, there is considerable evidence that war created economic problems for farmers and non-farmers alike. Transportation was most affected. Armies obstructed roads, making trade more difficult for the region's export oriented industries.[22] They impeded the river trades as well. The Cathedral, for example, leased the right to fish, to run water-mills, and to ferry people across the river, for its riverside villages, to prosperous farmers and rural businessmen. The lessees ran into frequent problems, such as fishing seines that were deserted in the 1670's, mills that were underutilized because of the shortage of grain or villagers' fears, or monopolized by armies to the exclusion of local users, or ferryboats that were taken or destroyed by armies.[23]

On the other hand, it seems that the major income-producing operations – clothwork, metalwork, and the mines – continued operating. The archives of the Cathedral and of independent notaries contain mining business at a seemingly uninterrupted pace in the 1670's and 1690's.[24] The Cathedral owned land over many productive coal mines, yet their records show that no mines closed because of war in the 1670's; rather, they continued the process of granting permission to mine throughout the Dutch War. Similarly, when de Sonkeux reports on the events of 1674, he does not lament the closing of the town's spinning and weaving business that year, but only that "merchandise exported by our merchants had to be escorted [under guard] out of the area."[25] While the total volume of business probably declined at the height of the military crisis, war had only a modest negative impact on the mining and clothwork part of the Basse-Mosan economy.[26] And it must have pushed the iron-working and weapons-making parts of that economy from quiet prosperity to booming growth.

These subjective accounts of war's economic impact are extremely useful, but they provide only incomplete answers to our questions about the agricultural effects of war. To know that war frequently reduced the productivity of agriculture and harmed farmers is worthwhile and important. But other phenomena besides war influenced the size of the harvest. Farmers complained of (and received graces for) a number of natural causes of reduced production: dry summers, hail storms, flooding, high winds, heavy rains, sterile soil, and crops eaten by mice and ground snails.[27] Historians, like contemporary

observers, have blamed bad weather and praised good weather for their effect on crops. In this they are no doubt correct; weather, like general economic conditions (for example, prices or demand), offers an alternative to war as an explanation of the conditions described in this chapter. Goubert's description of subsistence crises, for example, attributes them to cold, wet, summer weather, which reduces the size of harvests and, even more important, destroys stored grain.[28] Other historians have explained the agricultural problems of the seventeenth century, not in terms of weather (of short duration), but in terms of changing climate (of long duration). Early modern Europe, they assert, experienced a "Little Ice Age," which shortened the growing season and reduced production in comparison with that of the late middle ages and modern times (since 1850).[29] Between 1550 and 1850 glaciers advanced, reaching two of their peaks in the seventeenth century. Some authors have concluded that the colder climate caused the so-called "crisis" of the seventeenth century.[30] Since we will be interested in relatively short-term changes, climate will not be a major concern here. The impact of the "Little Ice Age" was probably more or less uniform throughout the period we are considering. We are not considering agriculture over many centuries. But we must concern ourselves with short-term changes in weather.

How does weather affect agricultural production? For historical crops (modern wheat, for example, is quite different from seventeenth-century wheat because of selective breeding), the usual interpretation places most of the stress on precipitation, rather than on temperature.[31] Most crops could survive within a fairly broad range of temperatures. Thus a cold winter or an unusually hot summer, while unpleasant for humans and animals, often increased production. Unusually warm winters, on the other hand, were not productive. Of course, extreme weather, such as a very cold winter or a late spring frost, could ruin crops; fortunately for farmers, such occurrences were quite rare. Rainfall had a much more dramatic influence on agricultural production than did temperature. Too much rainfall, especially in the winter or the late summer, as harvest-time approached, was much more dangerous for production than was too little rainfall. And a wet summer following a wet fall and winter could be especially disastrous. Seed did not germinate properly and vital nutrients were leached out of the soil. Remarkably, the only time too little rainfall hurt crops was when drought came in late spring and early summer, when water is needed for growth.

We have two sources of weather data for the Basse-Meuse. While neither is perfect, both are at least as credible as our information on military activity. The first source, published by Vanderlinden in 1925, is a compendium of all the available subjective descriptions of the weather of the southern Low Countries.[32] Because Vanderlinden relied on the chronicle literature, it is possible that his data are incomplete (some chroniclers may have paid more attention to bad weather than to good), and difficult to use in determining climatic trends. Nevertheless, his summary permits us easily to identify years in which there were hard winters; mild winters; cold, rainy summers; hot, dry summers; and early or late frosts. Our second source will be mean winter temperatures (for November, December, and January) in the northern Low Countries, which have been estimated and compiled by Professor Jan de Vries.[33] The two sources reinforce each other: de Vries' winter temperatures correlate strongly with Vanderlinden's descriptions of winter weather conditions.[34] Unfortunately, they offer entirely too little information about rainfall during the various seasons. Still, both will prove useful when we compare war's impact on agriculture with that of the weather. What we will see when we make that comparison is that, important as weather factors were, nevertheless war was responsible for the distinctive characteristics of Basse-Mosan agricultural experience, especially in the late seventeenth century.

II. Measuring Destruction and Disruption

We cannot count the number of days of fieldwork missed by Basse-Mosan farmers in wartime. Moreover, farmers rarely recorded the proportion of a normal crop that soldiers or bad weather destroyed. We can, however, begin our analysis of war's impact on agriculture by examining the tithe, in order to understand how much Basse-Mosan farmers produced. Many historians have used the tithe to indicate long-term trends in agricultural production and productivity.[35] Here, while we will examine trends of some length, we will focus on short-term movements.[36] We will use the proceeds of the tithe to represent the immediate consequences of war and of natural phenomena. Then, we can see the relationship between war, weather, and production.

Farmers in the largely Catholic Basse-Meuse owed a tithe, roughly ten percent of their produce, to the Church, which was often collected by an urban collegiate church, and not by the local parish. In theory, the tithe, as a fixed proportion of production, is a perfect measure of

Ill. 4. The Cruelties Committed by the French, No. 7, by Romeyn de Hooghe (1673)

agricultural output. There are, however, limitations on the use of church records of the tithe. As happened with many other tithes in Europe, the canons of the chapters which owned tithes in the Basse-Meuse rarely collected it themselves; rather, they contracted with a "tithe-farmer" who agreed before the harvest to pay the church a fixed sum. The tithe farmer's profit was the difference between what he collected from individual farmers and what he paid to the church.

Obviously, if the tithe-farmer's profit stayed fairly constant over time, the amount he turned over to the church (ecclesiastical accounts recorded only the amounts owed to and received by the church), the tithe remains a reasonably good measure of agricultural production. This is especially the case when tithe contracts were auctioned annually, after planting, and to the highest bidder, so that they represented an educated guess as to the amount of the harvest. Our estimate of production becomes even more accurate if we use, not the contracted-for value of the tithe (nominal receipts), but the amount the church actually received from the tithe contractor (net receipts). This is because even when contracts were made in June or July, the harvest was sometimes unexpectedly worse than might have been predicted just two months before. The use of net receipts eliminates this problem. The tithe contractor might have made an agreement with the tithe-owner to permit him to pay less than the nominal value of his contract, he might have received a grace, or he might simply have defaulted. Net tithe receipts represent the actual amount collected by the chapter in the months or years after the harvest. They should thus be an excellent gauge of year-to-year changes in agricultural production.

In this discussion we will study eight series of Basse-Mosan tithe records, five near Maastricht (representing eleven villages) owned by the Maastricht Cathedral Chapter, and three nearer Liège owned by the Cathedral Chapter of Liège. Although the tithe-farmers usually contracted to pay their obligations in money or grain, our figures reflect the full range of Basse-Mosan agricultural production. They include the proceeds of both the "large tithe," collected on grains, as well as the "small tithe," which included virtually everything else. For example, when they farmed out the small tithe for Milmort in 1681, the Canons of the Liège Cathedral Chapter stated that it specifically included the following items: lambs, wool, hogs, chickens, turnips, apples, pears, and any other fruit or hay they may have produced.[37] Table 4.1 presents net tithe receipts for five tithe series in and around Maastricht.[38] The units expressed are *pares*, a mixture of rye, oats, and sometimes barley.[39]

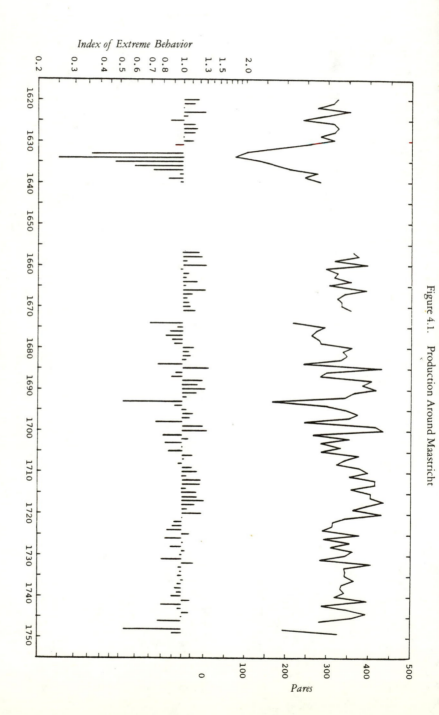

Figure 4.1.   Production Around Maastricht

Table 4.1 Production Around Maastricht
Five Tithe Series – Net Receipts

Year	Net Receipts (pares)	Index of Extreme Behavior	Year	Net Receipts (pares)	Index of Extreme Behavior
1620	323.6	1.18	1661	298.2	0.98
1621	312.9	1.13	1662	324.3	1.06
1622	277.9	1.00	1663	317.7	1.04
1623	351.4	1.27	1664	357.7	1.17
1624	290.8	1.05	1665	314.8	1.03
1625	241.9	0.87	1666	392.4	1.28
1626	315.6	1.13	1667	340.8	1.11
1627	327.0	1.17	1668	323.0	1.05
1628	318.9	1.14	1669	332.8	1.07
1629	280.7	1.00	1670	334.3	1.08
1630	315.6	1.12	1671	357.5	1.15
1631	257.8	0.91	1672	Incomplete	
1632	Incomplete data		1673	data	
1633	101.4	0.36	1674	218.6	0.70
1634	72.6	0.25	1675	294.0	0.94
1635	133.7	0.47	1676	275.0	0.87
1636	169.9	0.59	1677	262.2	0.83
1637	206.6	0.72	1678	280.1	0.89
1638	277.2	0.96	1679	287.7	0.91
1639	244.1	0.85	1680	357.8	1.13
1640	280.7	0.97	1681	338.8	1.07
1641			1682	348.3	1.09
1642			1683	332.4	1.04
1643			1684	244.1	0.76
1644			1685	429.6	1.34
1645	Incomplete		1686	299.1	0.93
1646	data		1687	288.3	0.89
1647			1688	404.5	1.25
1648			1689	382.9	1.18
1649			1690	417.2	1.29
1650			1691	362.9	1.17
1651			1692	341.1	1.05
1652	Incomplete		1693	168.4	0.52
1653	data		1694	300.0	0.92
1654			1695	345.6	1.05
1655			1696	372.2	1.13
1656			1697	355.3	1.08
1657	360.5	1.20	1698	246.2	0.75
1658	374.3	1.24	1699	414.2	1.25
1659	318.1	1.05	1700	432.6	1.31
1660	395.5	1.30	1701	268.1	0.81

Table 4.1 (continued)

Year	Net Receipts (pares)	Index of Extreme Behavior	Year	Net Receipts (pares)	Index of Extreme Behavior
1702	355.8	1.07	1726	290.5	0.83
1703	279.1	0.84	1727	354.9	1.01
1704	332.1	1.00	1728	310.4	0.88
1705	287.6	0.86	1729	361.7	1.03
1706	375.8	1.12	1730	344.3	0.98
1707	341.5	1.02	1731	282.9	0.80
1708	322.6	0.96	1732	403.7	1.14
1709	378.5	1.12	1733	342.4	0.97
1710	397.8	1.18	1734	346.4	0.98
1711	357.4	1.05	1735	343.2	0.96
1712	417.3	1.23	1736	365.5	1.02
1713	414.6	1.22	1737	337.7	0.95
1714	359.2	1.05	1738	332.4	0.93
1715	403.3	1.18	1739	340.8	0.95
1716	403.7	1.18	1740	319.5	0.89
1717	436.8	1.27	1741	397.1	1.10
1718	395.5	1.15	1742	289.6	0.80
1719	363.9	1.06	1743	346.4	0.96
1720	430.0	1.24	1744	390.9	1.08
1721	346.7	1.00	1745	359.9	0.99
1722	317.4	0.92	1746	281.2	0.77
1723	311.7	0.90	1747	Incomplete data	
1724	395.3	0.85	1748	192.9	0.53
1725	378.6	1.09	1749	328.3	0.90

Regression equation: Slope = 0.70086   Y-Intercept = −860.043
Parishes: Maastricht, Hees, Vlijtingen, Heer, Cadier, Sichen, Sussen, Bolder, Berg, Terblijt, Vilt
Source: J. C. G. M. Jansen, *Landbouw en Economische Golfbeweging in Zuid-Limburg 1250-1800: Een Analyse van de Opbrengst van Tienden* (Assen: Van Gorcum, 1979).

The long-term trend in the data presented in Table 4.1 shows that production may have been increasing through the first half of the seventeenth century, although the significant break in the data between 1640 and 1657 makes this conclusion far from certain. We do know that farmers produced more in the 1660's than in the 1620's, and much more than during the war-ravaged 1630's. They did not exceed the level they reached in the 1660's (at least in terms of decennial averages) until after 1710.[40] From 1660 until the end of the first decade of the eighteenth century, with the single exception of the 1670's, production

averaged around 335 *pares* per year. Only after 1710 did production again increase, producing two good decades in the teens and twenties of the eighteenth century. But after 1730 (and one might date the change as early as 1726), production fell back to its late seventeenth-century level, probably as a result of falling demand and lower prices.

Table 4.1 also presents an Index of Extreme Behavior, explained in detail in Appendix B, which removes the influence of linear trend from the data and makes them convenient for comparison. Thus an index value of 0.85 for tithe receipts suggests that agricultural production in that year was fifteen percent less than normal. Similarly, a value of 1.25 implies a harvest 25 percent larger than normal. A large index value generally means a good harvest, while a small value means a bad one.

As one might predict, bad weather reduced production in the Basse-Meuse, although its modest contribution to lost production will be something of a surprise. In 1625, 1684, 1698, and 1741, production was significantly less than normal, in each case during a year when weather was notoriously bad. We should not exaggerate this conclusion, however. In a statistical test of the impact of six weather conditions (hard winters; mild winters; cold, rainy summers; hot, dry summers; early or late frosts; and winter temperatures), only hot, dry summers significantly affected Maastricht-area production.[41] Given the relationship between crops and weather discussed above, this probably means that a very dry spring and early summer occurred, with hardly any rain, or else a dry season followed a very wet fall the previous year. As we will see, even this one weather condition was no more serious than severe war. Moreover, with only one exception, when bad weather caused serious production losses, the losses lasted only a single year, and not for extended periods. When we consider, in later chapters, the causes of the much-discussed subsistence crises that are said to have plagued Europe in the seventeenth century, we cannot hold long series of poor local harvests caused by bad weather exclusively responsible for high prices and consequent hard times in the cities and countryside.

War, on the other hand, could dramatically reduce agricultural production in the Basse-Meuse. In the 1630's, when the Thirty Years' War was most severe in the Basse-Meuse, production fell 64 percent in 1633 and 75 percent in 1634. For 1632, when Maastricht fell to a siege, we have no data, but surely very little was produced that year. Similarly, in the wartime years in the 1670's for which we have data, production again fell, although not as dramatically as during the earlier war. Between 1674 and 1678 (again, we have no data for the two worst years,

1672 and 1673), production averaged 85 percent of normal. The experiences we can measure for the 1670's reflect war's overall impact. We have data for 30 years of major wartime activity, in the 1630's, the 1670's, 1690's, 1700's, and 1740's.[42] The mean index value for those years is 0.86, suggesting that wartime production was 14 percent less than normal. Such losses were significant, but not catastrophic. They suggest that while in many years the people of the Basse-Meuse suffered extensive losses of production, in other wartime years production was near or even above normal.

We can also focus only on the years in which losses were most serious, and on periods of extended crises. There are five groups of wartime years (23 in all) in which two or more below-normal years follow each other, in one of which production was less than the mean crisis level of 0.86.[43] For those years the mean index value is 0.76, a loss of nearly one-fourth of normal production. Even if we include the four years for which we have no data, and assume no production at all in those years, the mean falls only to 0.65. Since it was these periods of bad years that represent the extreme case of war's consequences, we can say that, when one considers a number of communities, war's average effect was to reduce production at least fifteen percent, and rarely more than forty percent. In individual years, on the other hand, production could fall much lower, to one-fourth or less of normal. And individual farmers and villages may have been completely wiped out for a single year.

As we predicted, some wars were more serious than others for the farmers near Maastricht. The data show that more agricultural production was lost in the wars of the 1630's and 1670's (even if we ignore the years that were so bad that no data are available, 1632 and 1672-1673) than during later wars, both because of greater single-year losses and because of periods of agricultural crisis that lasted longer. The mild losses that coincided with the Wars of the League of Augsburg (1689-1697) and of the Spanish Succession (1701-1714; 1701-1706 in the Basse-Meuse) are consonant with the hypothesis suggested in Chapter III that, at the very end of the seventeenth century, the impact of war on civilian life began to diminish. Moreover, the evidence for the War of the Austrian Succession (1746-1748 in the Basse-Meuse), when production losses were very severe, confirms the idea that this war, with its continuous major military action in the Basse-Meuse, cannot reflect the amelioration of war's impact. Nevertheless, the brevity of that war for the Basse-Meuse, and the nearly forty years of peace that preceded it, meant that total losses attributable to 1746-1748 were less than those of

the seventeenth-century wars, and the recovery from those losses was probably much quicker.

The Liégeois net tithe receipts, presented in the first two columns of Table 4.2, show again that war's impact was moderate, but could drive production as low as 40 percent of normal.[44] Moreover, the wars of the seventeenth century were more severe, in terms of lost production, than the wars of the eighteenth century; and bad weather did not produce the same long series of reduced production as warfare. All this appears in the Liège net tithe receipts in spite of the fact that the Liégeois data are not as complete or precise as the Maastricht data. In Liège, unlike Maastricht, yearly tithe contracts were not used before 1700. Before then, the canons made them first for nine years, in the early seventeenth century, and later, (after about 1660), for three years at a time.[45] Moreover, the canons seldom auctioned these multi-year contracts to the highest bidder; rather, they let them to a small group of well-connected and prosperous peasants and merchants. We must be cautious about relying on even net tithe receipts from these series, since no one can predict the size of an individual harvest more than a few months in advance. The contracted values of the tithe for these three- to nine-year contracts depended on a safe minimum level of expected production, rather than on a maximum that changed from year to year.

Table 4.2   Production Around Liège

Year	Net Tithe Receipts (in muids Spelt)	Index of Extreme Behavior	Proportion Paid by Tithe Farmers		
			Milmort	Visé	Vottem
1661	335.9	0.85	84	43	97
1662	150.0	0.38	0	0	100
1663	Incomplete data		Incomplete data		100
1664	480.0	1.19	100	100	100
1665	455.8	1.13	100	100	98
1666	527.8	1.30	100	100	99
1667	528.8	1.29	100	100	99
1668	524.0	1.27	100	97	100
1669	430.1	1.04	87	68	99
1670	452.4	1.09	87	74	100
1671	473.0	1.13	79	87	100
1672	329.0	0.78	51	86	92
1673	379.8	0.90	76	93	84
1674	197.9	0.47	46	37	39

Table 4.2 (continued)

Year	Net Tithe Receipts (in muids Spelt)	Index of Extreme Behavior	Proportion Paid by Tithe Farmers		
			Milmort	Visé	Vottem
1675			46	22	
1676			c	23	
1677			c	c*	
1678			c	c	
1679					
1680					
1681					
1682					
1683					
1684					c
1685					c
1686					c
1687					67
1688					99
1689	Incomplete		Incomplete		94
1690	data		data		56
1691					49
1692					88
1693					0
1694					c
1695					c
1696					c
1697					76
1698					73
1699					91
1700					100
1701	551.3	1.13	94	98	100
1702	369.2	0.75	63	100	39
1703	418.6	0.85	25	98	65
1704	590.3	1.19	82	85	75
1705	340.2	0.69	100	78	64
1706	562.5	1.13	88	94	59
1707	316.6	0.63	88	67	47
1708	357.8	0.71	43	100	71
1709	404.8	0.81	94	92	87
1710	673.9	1.33	98	86	58
1711	Incomplete data		14		84
1712	626.0	1.22	82	100	91
1713	690.7	1.34	98	100	92

* 'c' indicates a collection contract.

Table 4.2 (continued)

Year	Net Tithe Receipts (in muids Spelt)	Index of Extreme Behavior	Proportion Paid by Tithe Farmers		
			Milmort	Visé	Vottem
1714	323.0	0.62	87	19	40
1715	499.2	0.96	68	27	95
1716	239.3	0.46	37	9	74
1717	664.7	1.27	79	83	88
1718	668.5	1.27	60	99	85
1719	603.0	1.14	99	87	75
1720	782.1	1.47	99	100	100
1721	403.5	0.76	45	c	100
1722	574.8	1.07	100	100	100
1723	641.7	1.19	100	100	100
1724	482.3	0.89	96	100	93
1725	616.2	1.14	88	82	100
1726	590.8	1.08	97	97	97
1727	731.2	1.34	100	100	100
1728	644.4	1.17	100	100	100
1729	691.5	1.25	100	79	100
1730	541.5	0.98	100	100	100
1731	473.2	0.85	96	97	100
1732	762.8	1.37	92	97	99
1733	569.2	1.01	100	77	100
1734	466.2	0.83	49	79	100
1735	582.2	1.03	93	100	99
1736	628.0	1.11	98	99	99
1737	508.7	0.89	100	c	100
1738	544.2	0.95	100	100	100
1739	605.1	1.05	100	100	100
1740	652.1	1.13	97	98	100
1741	591.8	1.02	92	97	100
1742	660.0	1.13	94	92	100
1743	519.7	0.89	56	91	100
1744	495.0	0.84	94	100	100
1745	607.4	1.03	67	100	100
1746	473.0	0.80	46	89	100
1747	193.2	0.33	84	100	100
1748	521.8	0.88	69	73	100
1749	692.6	1.16	75	100	100
1750	605.4	1.01	100	65	100

Regression equation: Slope = 2.3079   Y-Intercept = −3438.53.

We can reduce the importance of this difficulty for the Liégeois tithe series by examining net tithe receipts in another way. Since the Liégeois canons were willing to forgive a certain amount of the tithe-farmer's obligation, the ratio of the total amount paid by the contractors to the total amount they owed roughly equals the relationship of the year's harvest to a normal harvest. (See the last three columns of Table 4.2.)[46] By this measure the three Liégeois tithe series lost about 20 percent of a normal harvest in 1672 and 1673, more than 50 percent in 1674, and two-thirds or more in 1675 and 1676. After 1676, the normally enterprising tithe-farmers were no longer willing to shoulder the risk associated with their regular contracts (even if those contracts were at minimum values) and forced the churches owning the tithe to assume that risk, by paying its contractors a fixed sum to collect the tithe irrespective of the total value of the tithe that year. They did not return to normal contracting procedures until the 1680's.[47]

III. An Individual Farmer's Experience

Tithe receipts, the basic materials with which we can study agricultural production, are aggregate data. They represent the experiences of a single community or a number of communities, and their reflection of many farms makes them accurate. Although we should remember that the impact of war on production varied considerably, the Maastricht and Liège tithe data show war's modest impact on large areas in most wartime years, and its extreme impact in a few of those years. Aggregate data like the tithe, however, conceal a tremendous amount of individual variation, from farmer to farmer and from village to village. How may we understand the impact of the wars of the seventeenth and eighteenth century on the region's individual farmers?

The easiest way will be to study the production of an individual farm. We can do this for the Louwberg farm, which was located about five kilometers southwest of the center of Maastricht in the village of Vroenhoven (now part of Maastricht).[48] We have data for Louwberg because, from 1660 until the end of the ancien régime, it was sharecropped.[49] Each year, its owner received one-half of the farm's produce as rent. As a consequence, both landlord and tenant kept accurate accounts of the farm's production; and each year they recorded the total amount of each grain produced on the farm.

Table 4.3 gives the annual production of the Louwberg farm. Two representations of that production are made. They are first, the cash

equivalent, in florins, of the produce of a *bonnier* of land, and the same value represented as a quantity of grain, in effect deflating for changing prices.[50] I used the price of a *muid* of barley in Maastricht as a deflator, because barley is a valuable commodity (more valuable than oats or spelt), yet not quite as sensitive to changing harvest conditions as rye or wheat. In addition, I computed the index of extreme behavior for both the value of production in florins, and the deflated value of production in muids of barley.

Table 4.3   Production on the Louwberg Farm, 1660-1749

Year	Volume of Production (muids barley/bonnier)	Index of Extreme Behavior	Value of Production (florins/bonnier)	Index of Extreme Behavior
1660	5.6	1.86	168.3	1.63
1661	4.6	1.50	253.2	2.44
1662	3.1	1.00	103.5	0.99
1663	3.3	1.05	79.1	0.76
1664	3.8	1.19	96.1	0.92
1665	5.1	1.58	128.6	1.22
1666	4.1	1.25	108.8	1.03
1667	3.5	1.05	91.1	0.86
1668	3.1	0.92	75.7	0.71
1669	5.0	1.46	157.3	1.47
1670	3.4	0.98	88.9	0.83
1671	0.5	0.14	20.5	0.19
1672	1.4	0.39	43.6	0.40
1673	0.3	0.08	11.9	0.11
1674	2.0	0.55	111.1	1.02
1675	2.2	0.60	84.5	0.77
1676	-0-	-0-	-0-	-0-
1677	3.1	0.82	84.5	0.77
1678	2.1	0.55	76.4	0.69
1679	1.9	0.49	52.0	0.47
1680	4.4	1.13	119.8	1.07
1681	3.5	0.89	83.9	0.75
1682	4.2	1.05	93.2	0.83
1683	3.3	0.82	76.0	0.67
1684	1.7	0.42	68.0	0.60
1685	3.3	0.80	63.4	0.56
1686	2.6	0.62	67.6	0.59
1687	3.1	0.74	57.3	0.50
1688	4.0	0.94	81.8	0.71
1689	5.5	1.28	121.6	1.06

Table 4.3 (continued)

Year	Volume of Production (muids barley/bonnier)	Index of Extreme Behavier	Value of Production (florins/bonnier)	Index of Extreme Behavier
1690	3.4	0.78	83.2	0.72
1691	6.3	1.44	189.3	1.63
1692	3.7	0.84	135.4	1.16
1693	2.9	0.65	121.7	1.04
1694	6.4	1.42	161.8	1.38
1695	6.8	1.49	178.4	1.52
1696	4.3	0.93	138.8	1.18
1697	4.9	1.05	176.9	1.49
1698	6.1	1.30	365.7	3.08
1699	4.9	1.03	127.8	1.07
1700	7.5	1.57	197.4	1.65
1701	4.0	0.83	122.7	1.02
1702	5.9	1.21	161.5	1.34
1703	6.4	1.30	173.1	1.43
1704	4.3	0.87	99.1	0.82
1705	5.7	1.14	125.3	1.03
1706	6.0	1.19	126.8	1.04
1707	5.1	1.00	113.6	0.93
1708	4.6	0.90	187.2	1.52
1709	13.0	2.51	354.2	2.87
1710	6.0	1.15	138.1	1.11
1711	4.4	0.84	94.0	0.76
1712	7.8	1.47	189.0	1.52
1713	4.9	0.91	149.3	1.19
1714	6.8	1.26	136.4	1.09
1715	6.6	1.21	118.8	0.94
1716	7.1	1.29	136.2	1.08
1717	5.4	0.98	93.0	0.73
1718	6.9	1.24	139.8	1.10
1719	3.5	0.62	89.6	0.70
1720	6.5	1.15	118.5	0.93
1721	7.2	1.26	101.2	0.79
1722	7.9	1.37	119.4	0.93
1723	5.0	0.86	80.1	0.62
1724	6.3	1.08	177.5	1.37
1725	6.3	1.07	115.1	0.88
1726	5.1	0.86	112.4	0.86
1727	5.8	0.97	134.4	1.03
1728			Incomplete data	
1729	7.4	1.22	119.8	0.91

Table 4.3 (continued)

Year	Volume of Production (muids barley/bonnier)	Index of Extreme Behavier	Value of Production (florins/bonnier)	Index of Extreme Behavier
1730	5.0	0.82	110.3	0.83
1731	5.6	0.91	89.7	0.68
1732	5.5	0.89	89.1	0.67
1733	5.6	0.90	118.8	0.89
1734	5.3	0.84	74.4	0.56
1735	7.6	1.20	91.6	0.68
1736	8.4	1.32	117.6	0.87
1737	6.0	0.93	121.2	0.89
1738	6.5	1.01	144.1	1.06
1739	6.9	1.06	249.7	1.84
1740	8.8	1.34	211.4	1.55
1741	7.6	1.15	160.5	1.17
1742	1.8	0.27	55.3	0.40
1743	4.9	0.73	79.7	0.58
1744	8.6	1.28	146.7	1.06
1745	6.1	0.90	135.1	0.98
1746	5.7	0.84	166.3	1.20
1747	1.9	0.27	55.4	0.40
1748	4.1	0.59	99.5	0.71
1749	7.0	1.01	196.5	1.40

Regression equations: Slope = 0.042087   Slope = 0.414165
                        Y-Intercept = −70.3724 Y-Intercept = −584.338

Source: Louwberg farm worksheets, Archives of the Sociaal Historisch Centrum Maastricht. I appreciate the courtesy of Dr. J. C. G. M. Jansen, who was kind enough to provide me with these data.

As we should expect, the production data for Louwberg suggest the same conclusions as the tithe data for the Maastricht region, while the experience of individual years is more extreme. First, both the physical amount produced and the value of that production was greater in the first half of the eighteenth century than it had been in the last half of the seventeenth century, in spite of continually falling prices. Second, we can see in the Louwberg data just how seriously war could erode a farm's production. Expressed in *muids* of barley, production fell more than 50 percent below normal in five years of the nine from 1671 to 1679. In 1676 the farm produced nothing. In none of those nine years was production at or above normal. Finally, we can see the changing

96

Figure 4.2   Production on the Louwberg Farm

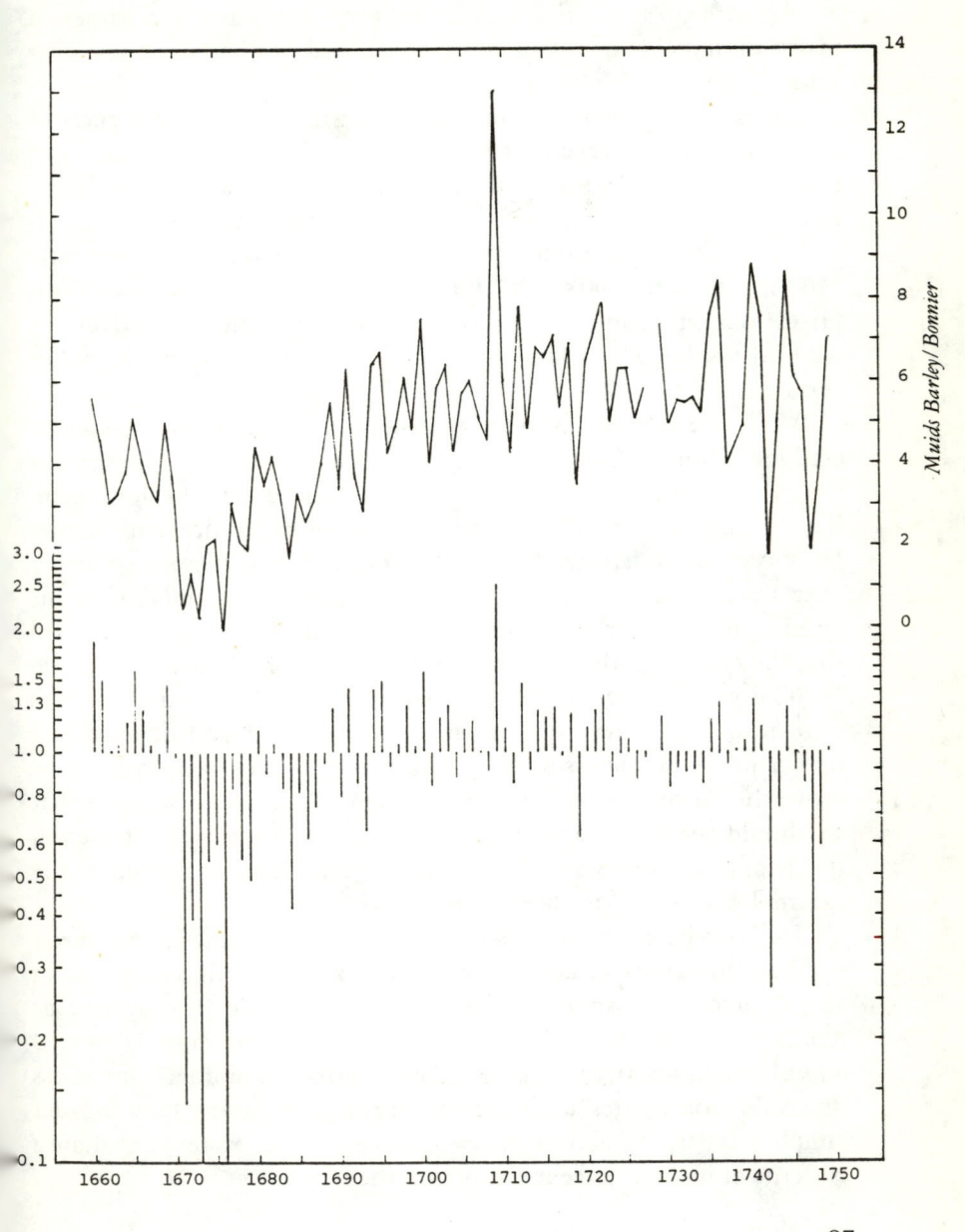

impact of war over time. The wars of the League of Augsburg and of the Spanish Succession were less destructive of production than the earlier Dutch War for the Louwberg farmer, and apparently less destructive than the later and much shorter War of the Austrian Succession. As indicated earlier, the War of the Austrian Succession struck the Basse-Meuse with great severity because in every year the region witnessed major military actions, something which had not happened in earlier wars.

We can draw one new conclusion, as well, from the experiences of the Louwberg farmer, and it speaks eloquently about his behavior in response to changing external conditions. Traditional periods of high prices, which should reflect declining production, often appear as periods of increased production at Louwberg. If we look at the early 1660's, at the late 1690's, at 1708-1709, or 1739-1740 – all periods when prices were high, and which should be associated with bad harvests – we find the Louwberg farmer making extraordinary profits. How can this be so?

While the relations between prices and production will be considered more fully in Chapter V, it appears that the Louwberg farmer saw prices rising, and increased his production in order to profit from them. Rather than being a victim of bad weather or high prices, this farmer (or succession of farmers, because the same behavior appears repeatedly over ninety years) was a conscious economic actor, modifying his farming to suit economic conditions. It should be no surprise to find that the farmers of the Basse-Meuse did fairly well in wartime from the 1690's onward, once the external conditions that destroyed their crops were restricted. They could then respond to increased demand and higher prices by increasing their production. It would be difficult to prove this pattern of behavior. But it seems likely, and it suggests that we should be very cautious about assuming that war simply acted upon the people of the Basse-Meuse; they also succeeded in making the external world bend to their needs and wishes.

The Louwberg farm will also permit us to consider the impact of war on the profitability of farming. Admittedly, this is only a single farm, and therefore no sample of the region as a whole. It may not be representative at all. Moreover, it was a rather large farm (about 12 *bonniers*, or 26 acres), and was owned by an urban landlord. Nevertheless its production figures and some of the things we know for a broader sample of Basse-Mosan farms, will permit us to examine changing patterns of income and expenditure in the face of war.

98

Table 4.4   Farming Income and Expenditures Under Changing Conditions

1. Normal Production (122 florins/bonnier)[1]

	Sharecropper (50%)	Tenant	Owner
Expenses:			
Rent/Landlord's share	61 florins	26 florins[2]	0
Seed[3]	12	12	12 florins
Taxes[4]	8	8	8
Tithe	12	12	12
Total Expenses	93 florins	58 florins	32 florins
Profit:[5]	29 florins (25%)	64 florins (55%)	90 florins (74%)

2. Production at 76% of normal (93 florins/bonnier)

Expenses:			
Rent/Landlord's share	46 florins	26 florins	0
Seed	12	12	12 florins
Taxes	8	8	8
Tithe	9	9	9
Total Expenses	75 florins	55 florins	29 florins
Profit:	18 florins (19%)	38 florins (41%)	64 florins (69%)

3. Reduced profits if taxes increased by 10 florins/bonnier[6]

Profits:	8 florins (9%)	28 florins (30%)	54 florins (58%)

[1] The figure of 122 florins per bonnier is based on the mean value of production at the Louwberg farm from 1660 to 1749. See Table 4.3.

[2] The rent figure is based on the rather low rent charged by the major churches of the city of Liège. They collected around three *muids* (Liège) of spelt per *bonnier* of normal land. That converts to 1.32 *muids* (Maastricht) per *bonnier*. At a price of spelt in Maastricht of about 20 florins per *muid*, the rent for a *bonnier* of land would be roughly 1.3 x 20, or 26 florins per *bonnier*. This is, as the discussion shows, a very generous rent, far below that charged by sharecropping landlords or private landlords who rented their land but who were more profit-hungry than the churchmen of Liège.

[3] The amount of seed used is based on a 1:10 yield ratio, based on normal production. The amount of seed changes little when production increases or decreases. See Jansen, "Agrarian Development and Exploitation in South Limburg," p. 259.

[4] Based on Eysden taxes. See Chapter II, pp. 47-50.

[5] From this profit must come the cost of living, a return on capital invested, the provision of new capital, and, especially on large farms like Louwberg, the salaries of wage laborers. The Louwberg farmer only paid one-third of his labor costs, while tenants and owners paid all of theirs. These are impossible to determine with present knowledge.

[6] See note 4.

99

Under normal conditions, the Louwberg farmer could support his family. He earned, in an average year, about 29 florins per *bonnier*, or roughly 25 percent of his annual revenue. While he would have to pay part of the wages of laborers (the landlord paid two-thirds) and feed animals, and possibly invest in equipment out of his roughly 350 florin profit, he surely could live decently from what he earned. Had his farm been smaller, he would have had more difficulty. To earn roughly the annual wage of a Basse-Mosan coalminer (who earned 15-20 patards a day working about three days a week, or about 100 florins a year), a sharecropper like the Louwberg farmer needed roughly four *bonniers* of land. Conditions were much easier for farmers who paid rent to institutional landlords, like the Cathedral Chapter of Liège (which still collected the same rents in the eighteenth century it had collected in the fifteenth): they earned roughly 64 florins per *bonnier* (although they paid 100 percent of their labor costs), and could probably survive on two *bonniers*. Of course, those farmers who owned their land did even better. For them, in moderately good years, one *bonnier* was probably enough.[51]

How did war reduce these profits? For the sharecropper paying fifty percent of his revenue to a landlord, the loss could be dramatic; and for the others, while they would be in better shape, the loss would be noticeable. Let us consider the tenant farmer with two *bonniers*. In good times, he earned 64 florins per *bonnier*, or 128 florins total. It is not much (in Verviers, it would buy roughly one loaf of bread a day), but it provided him with enough to survive. If war reduced his gross revenue by 24 percent (the mean loss for serious years), his profits would be reduced by 40 percent, down to 76 florins for the two *bonniers*. (See Table 4.4.) And if military presence led to the sort of extraordinary taxes levied in Eysden in the 1690's, his profits would fall to less than one-half of their original level. He then needed twice as much land to keep his family secure. The sharecropper, of course, would suffer much more than the tenant, since he paid a larger proportion of his revenue as rent. With reduced production and heavier taxes, only a farm as large as Louwberg would guarantee such a man food throughout the year. The small land owner, of course, was in better shape, and could weather many of these storms on the *bonnier* or two he owned.

For all but the most prosperous tenant farmers and owners, the ability to survive and to hold onto their property and possessions depended completely on how much they had been able to save in the past. Those who had little in reserve quickly sank deeply into debt,

especially in decades like the 1670's, when year followed year of reduced production and extraordinary taxes. Those frugal farmers who had built a substantial nest egg might live off those resources, while still meeting their obligations for rent, taxes, and tithe. No doubt they hoped the crisis would end quickly, so they could rebuild their savings. Families with less saved would survive, but probably could not pay rent, or tithe, or taxes, or all three. They rapidly became debtors, even if they managed to stay healthy. They became saddled, after a year or two of reduced revenue and high expenses, with a burden of debt that might take years to remove. Land owners might have to mortgage their land. Or they might send their children out to work as wage laborers, if they could find any work. At the very bottom of the social ladder were those, without savings and possibly already in debt, who did not even have enough saved to eat, even though they rented a small house and garden. Possibly they ate their seed, and borrowed the next year to plant again. Surely, it is these marginal farmers who died in the alarming numbers recorded in the wartime parish registers of the Basse-Meuse.

IV. Abandoned Farms and the Late-Seventeenth Century Agricultural Depression

Some farmers did not survive: war could and did drive farmers in the Basse-Meuse and neighboring areas out of the farming business and out of the region altogether. In 1681, for example, the citizens of the village of Latinne made a request to their Lord, the Cathedral of Liège.[52] They explained that some of their neighbors had abandoned the village, and no one paid taxes on the deserted land. Without this revenue the community suffered. Could they lease these abandoned farms and use the proceeds to contribute to their taxes? The Cathedral granted them permission. This is one example of the most severe form of wartime abandonment, by which property owners gave up their land. Such land could remain uncultivated (as it probably had in Latinne since the mid-1670's) until the legal problems associated with its ownership were resolved.

There were two other less extreme ways in which land stayed uncultivated. The first was the temporary failure of a farmer to cultivate a farm or field for a year or two. Thus, when the Cathedral granted graces to Jacques and Guilheaume Henry of Herstal in 1678, the canons noted that the brothers had not cultivated the farm at all in 1674.[53] The final source of idle farmland was more severe than a year or two of abandoned

tillage, but less severe than desertion by property owners. It involved the desertion or renunciation of leased land. Some tenants simply disappeared, but if they had some stake in the community they asked their landlord for permission to abandon the land. In 1697, for example, the heirs of the late Wathieu delle Haye of Oupeye requested permission to abandon a piece of land.[54] In another case, Simon Beaupere requested permission in 1675 from the Cathedral Chapter of Liège to renounce his lease for their farm at Ponceau, because he could not manage and the Chapter would not assist him.[55] In the event of such a renunciation, the landlord either had to come to terms with the tenant or else be forced to look for a new one in the middle of a war. How long land abandoned like this might remain uncultivated depended on the landlord. The churches of Liège charged low rents and kept a careful eye on their properties.[56] They were not afraid to evict non-paying tenants, even in wartime, and look for new ones.[57]

All our sources suggest that after war the farmers of the Basse-Meuse attempted to return their farms to normal productivity as quickly as possible. They repaired tools and buildings, acquired new animals if necessary, and replanted their fields.[58] While ongoing war may have prevented planting, as it did in 1673 for Henry Prevenaire of Mont St. André, we must imagine that many farmers worked in the fields even during wartime, attempting to get as much as possible from their land.[59] In 1691, the *intendant* of Hainaut wrote that, "even in the thick of war they work their land, although they should be sure that they will not be able to harvest, because of foraging troops."[60] After the war, we can be sure they were hard at work in their fields.

We have concentrated thus far on the short-term impact of war and of weather on farming. Did war and weather also lead to longer-term changes? There is some reason to believe that they did; together, man and the elements caused a downturn in Basse-Mosan agriculture during the last third of the seventeenth century. The farmers of the Basse-Meuse had a difficult time recovering from the Dutch War of the 1670's. During the 1680's they struggled to return to normal farming and normal profits, only to suffer a new setback in the War of the League of Augsburg. At the same time, bad weather caused a number of bad harvests and average winter temperatures were significantly lower during the years 1670-1699 than they had been previously or were to be in the first half of the eighteenth century.[61] Production figures for the Louwberg farm show that it consistently produced less than normal in the 1680's. Similarly, the farms administered by the Directors of the

102

Cathedral of Liège were clearly rebuilding depleted stocks and capital in the 1680's, as we will see below. Only the Maastricht tithe data are about normal in those years.

The problem we face, having suggested an agricultural depression in the Basse-Meuse at the end of the seventeenth century, is to isolate and understand its causes. To what extent did military action cause the difficulties encountered by the farmer of Louwberg and other farmers? What role did a temporary worsening of the climate, or a general European economic downswing, play? The Basse-Mosan agricultural depression in the second half of the seventeenth century was not unique. Such a downturn, although dated differently in different places, is part of the accepted interpretation of early modern agricultural history. The idea of a "General Crisis of the Seventeenth Century," although now stated with many reservations, had as its base the idea of agricultural shortages.[62] This idea is present in the work of Meuvret, who related agricultural problems to population; in that of Mousnier and Hobsbawn in their early discussions of the General Crisis; and in Slicher van Bath's *Agrarian History of Western Europe*, where it forms a major part of the chronological organization.[63] A large number of local studies have confirmed those general works. The widespread acceptance of the idea of a seventeenth-century depression should lead us to reconsider the causes of the depression in the Basse-Meuse. If other areas experienced downturns in the seventeenth century, even without war, it might seem necessary to modify, or even to abandon, our original assertion that war played an important role for the Basse-Meuse. Two considerations show that our hypothesis can stand.

First, let us look again at the experiences of the Basse-Meuse. Farmers prospered in the 1660's, suffered in the 1670's, and rebuilt in the 1680's and 1690's, despite new wartime pressures after 1688. Whereas in England and elsewhere the crisis is generally considered to have taken place at mid-century, the key decade in the Basse-Meuse is the 1670's, when the problems began, and the difficulties farmers experienced then must have been caused, in the first instance, by war. No bad weather or poor market conditions could possibly have caused that much production to be lost. This is not to say, of course, that poor weather or general European economic conditions did not retard the recovery. But war played a key role in starting the crisis.

We can see war's role in the Basse-Mosan agricultural depression in a second way, by looking at other European regions and seeing whether the specific causes and chronologies of their agricultural difficulties

were similar to that of the Basse-Meuse. If we look at some regions which experienced little or no warfare, like England, much of France, and the northern half of the Dutch Republic, the conclusions we draw will carry even more weight.

England will be our starting point. The agricultural history of England is varied according to region and soil type, but the following chronology seems to be valid: in the early seventeenth century, English agriculture slowed down from a very rapid sixteenth-century rate of growth, and was still inhibited during the revolutionary period (1640-1660).[64] After 1660, however, growth resumed. This is the era when English agricultural productions seems genuinely to accelerate, first meeting local demand and then exporting to other urbanizing countries. Problems developed in the early eighteenth century. Harvests remained quite variable, and farmers were extremely sensitive to persistent low prices. A period of genuine agricultural depression developed between 1730 and 1750, characterized by low prices and low profits, so that farmers could not pay rents and taxes.[65] Although depression is too strong a term, a similar period of reduced prices and production struck the Basse-Meuse and much of the Low Countries in the same years.

When we turn from England to the Northern Low Countries, yet another chronology appears. Recent monographic studies of Northern Holland and Friesland, regions relatively untouched by late seventeenth-century wars,[66] show a depression lasting nearly a century, from roughly 1650 to roughly 1750. These regions experienced population decline, less intensive agriculture and thus less production, and general economic hardship. The causes were independent of traditional "crises" and seem to be falling demand and increased costs which squeezed profits. The worst years of this extended economic depression for North Holland, as for England, were in the first half of the eighteenth century. "It all culminated," van der Woude writes, "between about 1730 and 1755 in the most serious crisis so far known to us in the history of Dutch agriculture."[67] In France, so a number of studies of agricultural production have indicated, the first half of the reign of Louis XIV (from the 1660's until the 1680's) was a period of unusual agricultural profitability,[68] and there were no nation-wide famines. From the late 1680's until after the agricultural crisis of 1709, however, that progress was reversed. It is likely that some parts of present-day Belgium experienced the same conditions.[69] Here we have the key to the Basse-Mosan experience. As happened in France and the rest of

Ill. 5. The Cruelties Committed by the French, No. 6, by Romeyn de Hooghe (1673)

Belgium, the 1660's brought prosperity to the Basse-Meuse. But while those other regions continued to prosper in the 1670's and 1680's, the Basse-Meuse suffered. Then, in the last decade of the seventeenth century and the first of the eighteenth, the Basse-Meuse was able to hold its own (perhaps because of high prices caused by war and universal shortage), in preparation for more growth in the eighteenth century.

The similarities and differences between the experiences of the Basse-Meuse and other regions thus become clear. Like England and France, the Basse-Meuse entered a period of prosperity in the 1660's. What distinguishes the Basse-Meuse is that the prosperity ended quite suddenly in the early 1670's and growth did not resume in any dramatic way in the 1680's.[70] Acceleration came again only in the second decade of the eighteenth century. Then, like England and the Northern Netherlands, the Basse-Meuse felt the impact of changing patterns of prices and prosperity in the 1730's and 1740's, although the farmers of the Basse-Meuse cannot be said to have fared as badly as those of the other regions.

We can begin now to explain the roles played in the Basse-Mosan long-term trends by local and European-wide phenomena. First, general phenomena were very important. Good climatic conditions probably caused the growth that began in the Basse-Meuse in the 1660's and in the 1710's. The long period of bad weather at the end of the seventeenth century probably contributed to the lack of growth there in the 1690's. And low prices and slack demand meant more extensive farming and lower production in the 1730's and 1740's. But the evidence also reveals war's very special contribution to the development of Basse-Mosan farming in the seventeenth and eighteenth centuries. War was the force that turned growth into decline in the 1670's, and it was war again which prevented the area from sharing in the general upswing and from reaching new heights in the 1680's.

In short, it is entirely reasonable to maintain, first, that war was responsible for the hardships of the 1670's; and, second, that, while severe winters and hot continental summers played some small part, war had a great deal to do with the slow, then aborted, recovery of the 1680's. We can see this in the *Protocoles des Directeurs* of the Cathedral of Liège. During the wartime years of the 1670's, the canons of the Cathedral seldom pursued actively tenants and debtors delinquent in their payments; rather, the Directors simply attempted to insure that they and their colleagues had sufficient revenue to support their per-

sonal needs and generate money for taxes and contributions in order to avoid, if possible, the destruction of ecclesiastical property in the countryside.[71] As soon as the war ended in 1678, however, the Chapter turned to settling accounts. According to their minutes for 1678 and 1679, the Directors devoted most of their time to granting remissions for money owed for the 1670's, and less to writing new leases for tenants who may have ended the war with an expired lease continued by virtue of a clause that guaranteed tacit renewal.[72]

The process of settling accounts moved slowly. If global production was nearly normal in the 1680's, the *Protocoles* reveal that many farmers probably used their revenues to rebuild their savings and replenish their stocks and tools rather than pay off rents and debts from the 1670's.[73] In 1681, the *Protocoles* include two angry statements about the unwillingness of the Chapter's debtors to come forward and pay, or even meet with representatives of the Chapter to make a settlement.[74] Moreover, total income in the Liège Cathedral Chapter was down in the 1680's.[75] The Directors continued to proceed slowly toward collecting what was owed them. When the War of the League of Augsburg broke out in 1688, they were still actively granting remissions for payments originally owed in the 1670's. Then, the process stopped again, while another war raged around them.

Only after the end of the War of the League of Augsburg, in the years from 1698 to 1702, do the church's records show the culmination of the thirty-year agricultural depression introduced by the Dutch War. This is dramatically clear in the writing of new leases. Often, the church would not renew a lease until the tenant had made an agreement to pay off part of his or her debt.[76] For many properties owned by the Cathedral Chapter of Liège, no new leases were written between 1670 and 1700, in spite of a normal practice of writing regular six or nine year leases for farmland.[77] In 1702 the Chapter finally brought its accounts up to date for the previous three decades. To avoid a repetition of the recent catastrophe, they instituted a strict new system that called for prompt payment with few opportunities for their tenants and debtors to complain. The canons could then watch as their tenants, debtors, and neighbors aggressively rebuilt for a more prosperous eighteenth century.

The agricultural downturn that occurred in the Basse-Meuse in the late seventeenth century is thus easily explained: in the 1670's, the region suffered very severely during the Dutch War, witnessing not only direct agricultural losses, such as crops and animals, but also the

destruction of buildings, farm equipment, and capital investment in general. The destruction of property and capital and the creation of debts in the 1670's meant that the 1680's were spent accumulating new investment and recovering slowly from the wartime losses. The recovery was not yet complete by the beginning of the War of the League of Augsburg. Thus, the final recovery was delayed until after 1700, giving the whole period from 1670 until 1700 a depressed character.

V. Changing Patterns of Landownership

Although there was a long downturn in agricultural fortunes in this period, there does not seem to have been a simultaneous wholesale deterioration of peasant landownership. This is something of a surprise, because two important recent works, Jacquart's study of the Ile-de-France at the time of the Wars of Religion and the Frondes and Cabourdin's study of Lorraine in the late sixteenth and early seventeenth centuries, have found that war and economic deterioration tended to reduce peasant landownership in a two-step process.[78] First, wartime circumstances forced peasants to borrow money, either to pay taxes or contributions, or to survive in the face of economic losses. Then, after the war, their profits were insufficient to repay their loans, and the subsequent foreclosures and sales led to the accumulation of land in the hands of a much smaller number of landowners, and in the hands of city-dwelling landlords.

While a process similar to this occurred in the Basse-Meuse, it did not cause a dramatic change and was limited by the region's particular economic conditions. To the extent that the countryside became indebted to the moneylenders of Liège and Maastricht (which surely happened) and property changed hands, the first victims were the lesser nobility rather than the peasants.[79] They were the victims of unpayable wartime debts. The bourgeois of Liège and Maastricht, to the extent that they acquired land in the countryside, were primarily interested in larger units: small peasant farms rarely seemed their goal except when a number could be acquired to build a single large farm. A Maastricht merchant created the Louwberg farm in the 1590's by purchasing a small farm and a number of additional parcels.[80] The farm remained unchanged for a long time thereafter because it became part of the endowment of an old peoples' home. For the most part, however, the transfer of rural property to urban landlords in the seventeenth century restricted itself to relatively large farms. In the early eighteenth century,

peasants still owned most of the small- and medium-sized farms.[81] They had avoided the loss of their land, at least during the wartime crisis of the late seventeenth century. Total urban domination of the countryside, and the consequent proletarization of the villages of the Basse-Meuse, came only with rapid population growth and the first wave of modern industrialization at the end of the eighteenth century.[82]

We can identify three reasons for the absence of large-scale turnover of the land of the countryside to urban owners in the seventeenth century Basse-Meuse. The first is simply a characteristic of the region's economy. By the late seventeenth century much of the eastern Basse-Meuse was simply not suitable for the kind of profit-making large-scale agriculture that might attract urban investors. The rolling Pays de Herve, ideally suited to small dairy farms, did not lend itself to large-scale arable farming. Consequently, in 1722, seventy-seven different residents of Richelle, on the east side of the Meuse, controlled land, most of the properties being very small. Nearly 80 percent of them included less than two *bonniers*, and only one farm, owned by a distant religious order, included more than ten *bonniers*. The second reason why peasant landownership in the Basse-Meuse did not disintegrate in the late seventeenth century was the existence of better investment opportunities elsewhere for potential urban investors in the countryside. These men could draw much better profits from trade or manufacturing than they could from purchasing peasant farms. This does not mean that they did not buy land in the countryside to ensure the world's perception of their wealth and status; but they bought extant, large farms that had belonged to impoverished gentry. In this fashion, the prominent Liégeois trading and manufacturing family, the Curtius, bought the Seigneurie of Oupeye. Relatively few townsmen made the effort to accumulate a significant number of small rural properties.

The persistence of industries in the countryside provides the final explanation for the ability of the Basse-Mosan peasants to hold onto their land despite the agricultural crisis of the late seventeenth century. The clothwork industries, the mines, and the river trades permitted the people of the region to earn money, either to pay off debts incurred in wartime, or to supplement the income derived from their land. These opportunities for employment in a classic proto-industrial situation contributed dramatically to the resilience of the area's economy in the early modern period.

In this chapter we examined ways that war influenced production in the essentially agricultural Basse-Mosan economy. The conclusions we must draw from this study are not complex. Nearly every aspect of warfare led to destruction and loss in the countryside, at least before the 1690's: troops in passage, military camps, and foraging parties, each led either to the destruction or theft of crops in the fields or to the theft of standing crops or reserves saved up for sale, seed, or food, and to the theft or destruction of animals, and tools and equipment such as wagons or boats. Only after 1690 is there any indication that war turned from a burden to a benefit. With the War of the League of Augsburg and the War of the Spanish Succession, if not with the brief but devastating War of the Austrian Succession, and as long as soldiers stole and destroyed relatively little, the farmers of the Basse-Meuse profited from increased wartime demand.

Even in the most serious years of wartime loss, the region does not seem to have lost the majority of its agricultural production. Individual farmers, of course, often lost their whole crop in wartime. But from the data that are available, we can say that wartime losses could be as low as fifteen percent and as high as forty percent for the region as a whole.

Possibly the most interesting conclusion we can draw comes from comparing war-related impact with that of natural phenomena. War's losses year after year could accumulate, especially after nearly a decade of continual loss (the 1630's or 1670's), into an extended period of economic stagnation, while farmers slowly paid off their debts and saved and replaced lost capital. While natural phenomena such as dry, hot summers could reduce production, the losses were not very severe, and they never accumulated into multi-year disaster. The idea that bad weather, or sequences of years of bad weather, can be held responsible for periodically upsetting the precarious balance of seventeenth-century demography is not confirmed by these data. When we come to an examination of demographic hardship in the early modern Basse-Meuse, we will have to look elsewhere for an explanation.

Chapter V

Prices and the Liégeois Food
Supply in Time of War

When war or weather temporarily shut down the agricultural system of the Basse-Meuse, people did not give up eating. Large numbers neither died of starvation nor emigrated to places with better food supplies. Rather, they stayed at home and survived as best they could, eating the food they had grown, saved, or could buy. Food could always be obtained from elsewhere in Europe; local food shortages simply meant that merchants imported food, and prices rose temporarily.

The price of bread grain – the principal component of most peoples' diet – was primarily established for all the region of Liège (including Maastricht and both cities' hinterlands) in the market of Liège.[1] The market in Amsterdam, the principal entrepôt of northwest continental Europe, dominated Liège in turn. In time of shortage we might expect that market conditions in Amsterdam, limitations on trade from there to Liège, and subsequent distribution problems within the region around Liège affected the local food market in Liège and its hinterland (for the rest of this chapter, Liège will be taken to mean the entire area where Liège's market was dominant). Yet the forces acting on the market could differ in wartime from those acting when bad weather caused harvest failure. This chapter will describe the mechanism of food supply for Liège and show how war affected that mechanism.

While early modern villagers and townsmen ate a large variety of foods, the principal items in the diet of the Basse-Meuse and neighboring areas were bread and beer. Both came from grain: the bread was usually made of rye and the beer of barley, but consumers very probably mixed the ubiquitous and inexpensive spelt, a primitive relative of wheat, with both. City dwellers consumed bread almost exclusively; in the countryside, particularly when fresh fruits and vegetables were available, people ate a number of supplements, especially a sort of vegetable porridge.[2] For the purposes of our discussion of food, however, we shall concentrate on the supply of rye: it was the

most widely used bread grain in continental Europe, and officials everywhere recorded its price, making it easy to study.

The market for foodstuffs was one of the most important economic meeting-grounds for city-dwellers and villagers in the ancien régime. All cities depended on imported grain. Furthermore, a monetarized economic system existed in most rural areas in the early modern Low Countries. In the Liégeois hinterland, villagers constantly traded in the marketplace. The dairy farmers of the Pays de Herve traded their butter and cheese for grain and flour. Moreover, in the largely grain-growing areas of the Basse-Meuse the dense and intermingled population of subsistence farmers, day laborers, handicraft workers, and miners needed more food than their small gardens could produce.

They bought their supplies from more prosperous farmers, who traded their surpluses for other commodities and for cash to pay rents and taxes. In normal times, then, the buyers came from many categories: city dwellers, dairy farmers, laborers, handicraft workers, and miners. The sellers were the producers of grain, from the Hesbaye, the Condroz (another grain-growing region south of Liège) and the operators of larger farms in the transitional Basse-Meuse.

I. Harvest Failure and the Marketplace

What happened to that marketplace when a harvest failed? First, the number of sellers (i.e., supply) declined as the number of farmers with surpluses decreased. Second, the number of buyers (i.e., demand) increased, not only because shortage forced otherwise self-sufficient farmers to purchase grain, but also because hoarders proliferated in time of shortage, buying supplies against future need and higher prices. Finally, any armies in the area further increased demand. The ultimate result was higher prices.

Still, a single harvest failure did not by itself cause very severe repercussions in the food market centered at Liège. One such bad harvest could be absorbed and cushioned by a thoroughly monetarized and widely trading European economy. Harvest failure in one region in one year could be compensated for (at relatively high prices) by excess production elsewhere. But if a total harvest failure followed a mediocre harvest, or if two failures followed each other, or if the harvest failure spread over Europe, a true crisis developed. No excess supplies would be left anywhere, because demand had totally overwhelmed supply. Prices

skyrocketed in a matter of months, starvation and disease spread, and three or four years of very hard times were at hand for all but the wealthiest peasants and townsmen.

When such large differences between supply and demand occurred, the merchants of Liège met them by going outside their own region to find food. The first and natural sources were other nearby cities, especially Sint Truiden, the main town of the Hesbaye.[3] It was there that the authorities of Liège bought grain to feed a hungry population during the shortages of 1531 and 1546. After Sint Truiden, the merchants tried Huy, Dinant, and Hasselt first; then they went farther, to Aachen, Namur, Cologne, or the Mosan cities below Liège, such as Roermond and Venlo.[4] Only if these sources were not fruitful would merchants buy grain in Amsterdam or the other Atlantic ports of entry for Baltic supplies. That was the case in the devastating shortage of the 1560's, and consistently in the seventeenth and eighteenth centuries.

The most convenient route for transporting imported grain, in terms of rapid carriage and low shipping costs, was up the Meuse from Dordrecht to Liège, and then trans-shipment there for Maastricht and other locations in the region.[5] Unfortunately, the Mosan route, which would bring goods from Dutch into Liégeois territory, also passed through Spanish territory on the river. Toll-stations existed at Venlo and Roermond, in the Spanish province of Gelderland, and at Navagne, next to Visé, between Liège and Maastricht.[6] Defeated by the free-trading Dutch in the first half of the seventeenth century, and having lost Maastricht, the Spanish were hardly sympathetic to free trade through their territory. Dutch villagers even complained, in 1632, that after the Spanish lost Maastricht they closed off access to the low-water *passage* across the Meuse at Navagne.[7] Moreover, the Principality of Liège collected duty at both Liège and Maaseik, its largest ports on the Meuse. Trade along the Meuse in the seventeenth century became heavily taxed, very costly, and sometimes closed.

The Spanish and Liégeois collected duties high enough to make land transport from Amsterdam competitive with the river route from Dordrecht. It may have been slower, but it could largely confine itself to Dutch territory, and avoid both the expense and the delays of the tariff-stations on the Meuse. In the late seventeenth century, land transport, even of heavy articles, was one-third to one-half cheaper than river transportation.[8] Moreover, the land route, with its multitude of obscure and ill-patroled roads, lent itself to profitable smuggling, thus avoiding the entry and exit duties at the Liégeois border.

II. Impediments to the Grain Trade: Problems of War and Harvest Failure

The impediments to trade the Spanish erected along the Meuse were characteristic of seventeenth-century thinking about free trade. In the era of mercantilism, trade became the servant of national policy. Thus, the supply of food to Liège and to points farther up the Meuse was not conditioned simply on the three linked variables of supply, demand, and price.

In times of shortage, every sovereign and local government worked to restrict the trade of foodstuffs: they attempted to ensure the importation of sufficient inexpensive food to provide for their population, while preventing anything from leaving to seek higher prices elsewhere.[9] When food shortage struck, the Principality of Liège forbade the export of grain and other articles of everyday consumption, and severely regulated their trade within the principality's borders. Every other state in Europe behaved the same way, because an ensured food supply severely reduced the possibility of domestic unrest.[10] In truly European-wide crises, even normal exporters of grain, like the Dutch and the Baltic states, forbade their merchants to send food out of the country.[11] They placed the desires of merchants and landlords for profits on the international market below the need to feed the population at home.

To the extent that war caused localized harvest failures, authorities responded to war in the same way they responded to shortages caused by bad weather; they closed off exports and encouraged imports in order to feed their population. The churchmen of Liège even contributed money to this effort. In December, 1625, the clergy of Liège contributed 10,000 florins to buy grain for free distribution to the population; in 1709, the Cathedral Chapter lent 20,000 florins, free of interest, for the purchase of grain in Holland.[12] Moreover, the edicts of the Principality of Liège show continuous concern to limit trade and encourage imports on a number of occasions in the seventeenth and eighteenth centuries.[13]

Military considerations also impeded trade in early modern Europe. A country at war ordinarily prohibited trade with the enemy.[14] Residents of occupied territory or territory subject to *contributions* had their mobility greatly reduced: even when they obtained a safeguard for their town or village, they were subject to imprisonment if they ventured outside it. No one could strictly enforce this system.

Merchants circumvented or ignored trade prohibitions. Since armies needed to be fed, their officers always gave some civilian provisioners (called *licentes*) permission to move freely. Even the movement of non-trading civilians was only half-heartedly restricted. A system of passports, granted by an officer in return for a fee, constituted a major loophole.

Like many other military issues, limitations on trade in wartime changed after 1660. At first, armies restricted the rather easily obtained permission to trade with the enemy as a *licente*. The general growth in military activity and its administration that coincided with Louis XIV's assumption of power called for better regulation. So passports, heretofore necessary for personal travel, began to govern the movement of commodities. They facilitated control over the movement of goods as well as providing armies with a handy source of additional income. Finally, we can detect in trade evidence of the lessening military grip on civilians. In 1675, France and Spain reached an agreement, the Treaty of Freyr, that reduced wartime trade restrictions. Trade in time of war became subject only to those regulations in force in peacetime.[15]

In addition to official efforts to close or open trade, other factors influenced the food supply of Liège. The same raiding parties that went in search of contributions could easily discover a cargo of grain en route. Troops frequently failed to honor passports. Moreover, the general disturbance of the countryside provided hazards for merchants shipping food into a war-torn area. In 1675, Louis Burton, who had contracted to collect the tithe for the village of Monfrin, reported that he had not been able to bring the grain he collected into Liège. The roads were too dangerous, he reported, after soldiers confiscated two of his loaded wagons on the road from Dinant.[16] The merchants of Verviers met the same problem with a different, if common, solution. In 1674, de Sonkeux reported that " . . . during this disturbed time one had to purchase grain in Liège and return with a strong escort for the wagons."[17] We must presume that, while smuggling and armed escorts increased the food supply, they could not compensate for the supplies that became unavailable through the closing of normal channels.

The impact of war and weather on the trade into and out of Liège can be documented, at least in part, by looking at prices in Liège and Maastricht, and relating them to those at Amsterdam. While it would be desirable to use a full market-basket of food, as well as prices of industrial commodities, our study of prices will be limited to bread grains and mostly to rye.[18] To put this analysis in perspective, we can

examine the long-term price trends in Liège, Maastricht, and Amsterdam from the end of the sixteenth century until the middle of the eighteenth century.[19] Figure 5.1 presents 21-year moving means (chosen to show long-term price trends) of the price of rye in Maastricht and Amsterdam, and of spelt in Liège, while Figure 5.2 presents annual prices and the value of the index of extreme behavior for the price of rye in Liège.

In the sixteenth century, Liège, Maastricht, and Amsterdam, like the rest of Europe, experienced a long period of price inflation. By the 1580's, that upward trend had begun to stabilize, with little new inflation until after 1610.[20] Beginning then, prices rose again, continuing until the 1640's or 1650's. Thereafter, prices drifted downward, except for renewed inflation in the 1670's and again in the 1690's. There are distinct periods of slowly declining prices in the 1650's and 1660's, in the 1680's, and in the early eighteenth century. In the late 1730's and 1740's, prices began again to rise.[21]

The similar chronology of long-term change for prices in Liège and in Amsterdam suggests that the two markets were closely linked. This conclusion is supported by the results of a statistical study of correlations between short-term price movements in Liège, Maastricht, and Amsterdam. Table 5.1 presents correlation coefficients for rye prices between Amsterdam and four other cities: Liège, Maastricht, Utrecht, and Arnhem.[22] The figures for Utrecht and Arnhem, computed by Walter Achilles, provide us with both a ''control'' and a point of comparision to Achilles' important work on the relationship between prices in different markets and the development of price-relationships between markets in the sixteenth and seventeenth centuries. As Achilles suggested, the relationship between prices in Amsterdam, Liège, and (although to a lesser extent) Maastricht grew closer in the seventeenth and eighteenth centuries. In each forty- or fifty-year period considered, the correlation coefficient is higher than in the previous period. This was the result of more efficient markets and probably better means of transportation as well. We should reach another conclusion. The coefficients for Liège and Maastricht are lower than those for Utrecht and Arnhem. This is probably due to the greater distance and tariff barriers that existed between the Basse-Meuse and Amsterdam, relative to those between the other Dutch cities and Amsterdam.[23] Still, the correlation coefficients for Liège and Maastricht are very high. Year-to-year changes in prices in Liège and Maastricht usually followed the pattern established in Amsterdam.

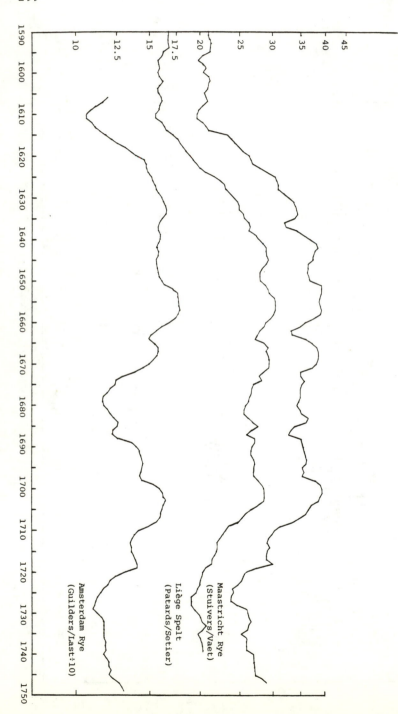

Figure 5.1　Long-Term Price Movements in Liège, Maastricht and Amsterdam 21-Year Moving Means

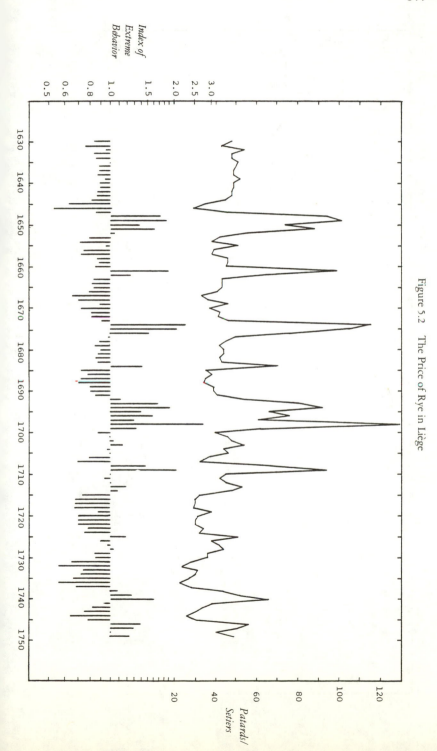

Figure 5.2 The Price of Rye in Liège

Table 5.1   Correlations Between Rye Prices in Various Markets

	Amsterdam with			
	Utrecht	Arnhem	Maastricht	Liège
First half of seventeenth century	0.953 (1601-1644)	0.886 (1601-1650)	0.573 (1620-1659)	0.611 (1620-1659)
Second half of seventeenth century		0.872 (1651-1700)	0.776 (1660-1699)	0.798 (1660-1699)
1620-1699			0.692	0.730
First half of eighteenth century			0.631 (1700-1749)	0.814 (1700-1749)
1620-1749			0.715	0.790

All coefficients are at a significance level of 0.001.

We can establish the same conclusion by showing that local production was not primarily responsible for determining prices in the Basse-Meuse. Here, we need to correlate the index of extreme behavior for production for a given harvest, with the index for the annual prices during and after that harvest. This can be done by comparing production for the harvest year ending in September of a given year, with the prices that begin that same month and run for a year. The relationship is significant, but not strong enough by itself to determine prices. The strongest relationship is between the Maastricht tithe series and Maastricht rye prices; the correlation there is −.319, suggesting, first, that higher production led to lower prices, but also that production accounted for about ten percent of the annual change in prices.[24] When we correlate Maastricht production with Liège prices, the relationship is weaker, and when we correlate the single-farm production of the Louwberg farm with these prices, there is no significant relationship at all.[25] What do these results show? First, the production of a single farm, like Louwberg, has no impact on prices, although the combined production of many farms near Maastricht has a significant, if not decisive, impact on local prices. Although local production influenced prices, it contributed far less than the European-wide phenomena measured by the Amsterdam market.

We must draw the conclusion that, even if the Liégeois region was agriculturally self-sufficient in normal times, it was not self-contained.

Prices in the market were not determined simply by local supply and demand, with occasional recourse to more distant markets when there was a local surplus or shortage. The Liégeois marketplace established prices in Liège, but only as local variations on the conditions in the grain market in Amsterdam, dominant for all of northwest continental Europe.[26]

The implications of this finding contribute to our study of the impact of war on prices and the marketplace. Close and continuous commercial ties throughout the Low Countries caused Amsterdam to dominate prices in Liège. Furthermore, weather was super-regional. Bad weather and shortage in Liège often coincided with bad weather and shortage elsewhere, in Amsterdam and even in the Baltic grain growing regions that supplied Amsterdam.

But war could be a local problem. The destruction of a vital harvest by conscious governmental policy or by excessive numbers of troops could strike Liège and be unnoticed in Amsterdam. Limitations on trade between Amsterdam and Liège that forced prices upward in Liège had no effect on prices in Amsterdam. By comparing the short-term movement of prices in the three cities — with special references to the extreme behavior of prices in time of harvest failure and war — we can isolate the impact of localized military action on prices in Liège, and the market structure that determined them.

One benchmark we will establish is the short-term movement in the price of rye at Amsterdam. If Amsterdam represents general market conditions, it represents most of the impact of weather on prices. With trade relatively free and unencumbered in the absence of war, even very local harvest failures (such as a localized hailstorm at a crucial moment before the harvest) fed into a large regional price picture. If that hailstorm occurred near Liège, the Liégeois food market would have bought food elsewhere — perhaps in Amsterdam itself — raising demand for the whole larger region and probably raising prices everywhere. While the absolute change in prices as a result of bad weather (such as the hailstorm mentioned above) might differ in Amsterdam and Liège, the relative change in prices would have been similar.

*　　*　　*

At least eight times between 1620 and 1749, in 1625, 1649, 1661, 1674, 1693-1694, 1698, 1708-1709, and 1739-1740, the price of grain in Liège

reached an extremely high short-term peak. Bad weather, war, or a combination of the two caused all these periods of high prices, either directly or indirectly. In the following pages, we will separate the periods of high prices caused simply by war from those caused by weather and consequent low production, and those caused by a combination of the two. Did war increase prices? To answer that, our first task will be to separate war's indirect influence on prices through production from its direct impact on prices.

To the extent that war damaged harvests but did not restrict trade, it had the same effect on prices as weather-caused harvest failure. When an army wiped out production near Liège, or if an army created so much additional demand that local stocks were depleted, obtaining an adequate food supply necessitated going to Amsterdam. In that case, demand for the large region would have increased relative to supply, and relative price increases would have remained the same in Amsterdam and Liège.

But if military action disrupted the trade in food stocks, or if profiteers drove prices up to capitalize on a captive military market, a different phenomenon should have occurred. If grain available in Amsterdam could not reach Liège, the price of grain available in Liège should have risen much higher, relatively, than the price in Amsterdam. Similarly, profiteering like that forbidden by the Visé Council in 1701 (when brewers, beer-sellers, bakers, and all other merchants who sold human foodstuffs became subject to a fine if they sold their products to soldiers for more than the price they charged citizens of Visé) was localized.[27] We can test the influence of these forces on the market by comparing the relative change in the annual price of rye in the two cities. Unfortunately, we cannot make comparisons at less than yearly intervals because the Liégeois price archives were destroyed by bombing in the Second World War. We will rely, then, on annual changes, measured by the index of extreme behavior. The annual index values and prices for rye sold at Amsterdam, Liège and Maastricht, and spelt sold at Liège, for the years 1620 to 1749, are given in Appendix C.

Although a complete description of the sources and nature of the various series of prices examined here is not necessary, I should add a word about the three series of prices that will be the principal source for the rest of this chapter. First, all three prices reflect harvest-years. For the year 1663, for example, the price given reflects prices in effect from roughly September 1, 1663, through August 31, 1664. The prices given for Liège and Amsterdam are arithmetic means of weekly prices during

that harvest year. The price of rye at Maastricht, however, is more of an indicative price: it reflects the arithmetic mean of two weekly prices in the second half of June. Thus, the Maastricht price given for the harvest year of 1663 actually represents the price of rye in June, 1664. There is sense in this; prices listed for 1663 reflect the conditions of the harvest in that year, and any impact that season's military campaign might have had. Finally, while the prices recorded for Liège and Maastricht are retail prices, the price of rye at Amsterdam is given in the relatively large units in which it was sold at *wholesale* to bakers and retailers.[28] Nevertheless, we can reasonably assume that proportional changes in wholesale and retail prices were sufficiently equivalent that we can rely on them.

We must keep in mind that these are prices for unmilled rye, while the food that was purchased in most cities was bread, the result of two intermediate operations, milling and baking. Unmilled grain was probably the basic commodity in the countryside, but we must still recall that these prices reflect an annual mean, which disguises fluctuations within the year. Fortunately, de Sonkeux periodically reported the price of bread in Verviers in 1675-1676, a period of extreme shortage.[29] Consumers faced enormous price increases. The normal price of grain in Verviers was seven or eight patards for a loaf weighing seven pounds. After the bad harvest of 1674, that price had begun to rise, reaching about twice its normal level in late winter or early spring, 1675. De Sonkeux reports a price of eighteen patards in February, 1675, and fifteen patards in April.

Once the military season began, however, the price skyrocketed. By mid-June, 1675, the price ranged from three to ten times normal, from 25 to 80 patards for a loaf of bread. Furthermore, de Sonkeux adds, there was very little work for wage laborers in 1675. The harvest of 1675 must have been much better than its predecessor: by January, 1676, the price of bread had sunk to 17 patards, bringing great joy to the population. By June, 1676, a year after it had reached its peak, it was down to 10 to 12 patards, fifty percent higher than normal. While the harvest of 1676 must have also improved, stocks needed to be replenished. Annual prices returned to normal only in 1677.

Obviously, annual mean prices of grain cannot properly reflect the prices paid by people buying bread in town, or even those buying flour or grain in the countryside. The annual prices of rye in Liège show a price roughly twice normal in 1674 and 1675; yet in the worst months following the bad harvest of 1675, prices probably tripled, and many people must have paid four, five, or even eight times the normal price of

bread, just to feed their families. Our grain prices, then, only show the minimum amount of price change, and the minimum level of misery caused by those higher prices.

III. War as a Cause of High Prices

We can test war's impact on prices by returning to the correlation coefficients computed for rye prices in Amsterdam, Liège and Maastricht. The statistical correlations between those prices were strong. If, however, we remove wartime years from those computations, the relationships become even stronger.[30] Why is this so? Literally, these coefficients mean that in wartime price movements in the three cities tended to be less uniform than in all years. In peacetime, price movements were more uniform than in all years. As we will see when we look at the actual differences between index values, prices in Liège and Maastricht went up more in wartime than did those at Amsterdam. The difference in correlation coefficients and the higher index values at Liège and Maastricht confirm war's impact on prices. The measurable impact was not very great because the price differences between Amsterdam and the Basse-Meuse reflect only trade limitations and profiteering, and not all of war's impact, such as increased demand or damaged crops in the absence of trade restrictions. We will reach the same conclusion, that war raised prices, within limits, when we look at the raw data themselves.

Before we can consider those raw prices and the index computed from them, we must first consider a fundamental question: What level of higher-than-normal annual prices caused a subsistence crisis? How much more than normal could people pay before they began to eat less, or lost the ability to function normally? Any definition of the threshold of a crisis is arbitrary, not least because the definition varied from social group to social group among the people of the Basse-Meuse. For some, any increase in prices would sink them even further below the subsistence line; for others, at the opposite end of the scale, price increases made little difference. The internal divisions in the data presented in Appendix C can give us some hints about a definition of high prices. In the index of extreme behavior, a value of 1.0 represents normal. There are many index values that fall around 1.0 and below, and even as high as 1.2, a price twenty percent higher than normal. In one or two periods, the peak reached thirty percent higher than normal, but otherwise peak values rarely fell between 1.2 and 1.6.[31] The eight peaks mentioned

above are all periods where the year of highest prices had a value roughly 60 percent higher than normal, an index value of 1.6, or greater. For the purposes of this discussion, we will consider a crisis any group of years characterized by a number of years when the index value went above 1.0, including at least one year when the value exceeded 1.6. Even then, we must not ignore the years when prices swelled to only twenty or thirty percent higher than normal. For Liège and Amsterdam, these are mean prices recording a whole year's experience. When the price rose only thirty percent above normal for the annual mean, it may have doubled normal in the worst weeks or months of the year.

To establish whether it was war, bad weather, reduced production, or a combination of these which caused high prices, we can compare the eight periods of high prices in Amsterdam, Maastricht, and Liège. War could not have caused four of these periods of high prices, those with peaks in 1661, 1698, 1708-1709, and 1739-1740 (we will refer to whole periods by these peak years). There was no major military action in the Basse-Meuse in any of these years, so war is not to blame.[32] These periods of high prices share two other characteristics. First, all four show relatively similar intensities in Liège, Maastricht, and Amsterdam (Figure 5.3), confirming the earlier assertion that, in the absence of wartime trade limitations, prices would rise by about the same amount in all three markets. Second, all four occurred during years of well-known, European-wide high prices, presumably caused by bad weather and limited production. While weather was bad in three of the four periods (cold, wet summers, the sign of a coming subsistence crisis), production was not necessarily reduced.[33] Maastricht tithe receipts fell dramatically below normal only once among these four periods, in 1698. In the other three, they were about normal. But if bad weather did not affect production in the Basse-Meuse, how did it influence prices? First, it might have caused reduced production somewhere else, driving those people into the international marketplace in search of supplies, and thus raising prices. The price of grain was not very elastic. A small shortage might lead to a substantial increase in prices. Moreover, it is possible that a rainy summer, even if it scarcely reduced the harvest, made storage of older supplies more difficult. We might speculate that a second, psychological, factor is involved as well. Prices were not wholly established by supply and demand. A cold, wet summer made people feel insecure. They feared the food supply would deteriorate. Merchants began to hoard against higher prices and, predictably, prices began to rise, even before the harvest. Citizens of

early modern cities felt that the merchants, not the weather or the harvest, were responsible for high prices. In the Basse-Meuse, at least, they were right. Prices reflected what merchants, especially those in Amsterdam, felt they should be, based on their reading of weather conditions and the marketplace. They raised prices if there was a significant shortage anywhere in their trading domain. For the people of the Basse-Meuse, this was a self-fulfilling prophecy. Despite an adequate local harvest, the many people who bought their food in the market found the supplies available to them and, thus, their diet greatly diminished because prices were so high.

Figure 5.3   Relative Intensity of Eight Crises

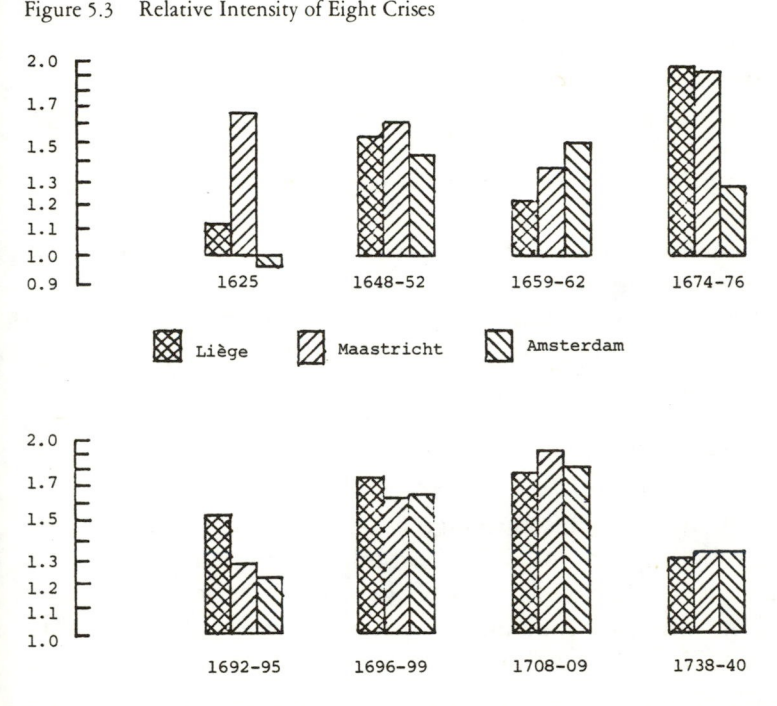

Value represented graphically is the mean of the index of extreme behavior for the years shown for each city.

Value for Liège in 1625 is for spelt. All other values are the index for the price of rye.

While war could not have affected prices in four of the eight periods of high prices, it surely had an impact on the other four, those with peaks in 1625, 1649, 1674, and 1693-1694. In all these instances, moreover, prices were higher in Liège or Maastricht than in

Amsterdam, confirming war's influence. We must not, however, attribute the entire price rise in these years to the impact of war. Weather was bad in these years, too, and, except for 1625, prices in Amsterdam were well above normal. War was able to inflate prices, but it rarely caused a subsistence crisis through food prices by itself. When combined with bad weather, however, war could be catastrophic for the people of the Basse-Meuse. Thus, military activity in the Basse-Meuse could provide the difference between rather high prices and a genuine crisis.

The mid-1670's and the early 1690's make clear war's additive impact on top of already high prices. These are periods of combined catastrophe, war, and general high prices caused by bad weather in much of northwestern Europe. How much did war contribute? The change in prices shown in the index of extreme behavior for the two periods is two to three times as high in Liège and Maastricht as in Amsterdam, if one considers the peak, and about twice as high if we consider the mean change in price over the three-year duration of the two crises (Figure 5.3).[34] If the difference between the Mosan cities and Amsterdam is entirely due to wartime restrictions on trade, then at the end of the seventeenth century, wartime restrictions had a great impact, turning otherwise bad harvests from a moderate shortage to a genuine and extreme crisis, with a full doubling of prices in the 1670's and as much as a 90 percent gain in the early 1690's.

Even when acting alone, war had an inflationary impact. The years around 1635, and those around 1684, provide good examples of its effect. Here again, war increased prices that were already higher than normal. War's contribution to high prices was rather modest, increasing them by fifty percent or less (probably 25 to 30 percent) on an annual basis. In the worst weeks of the year, it might briefly double prices. Only when war combined with extremely bad market conditions and already high prices did the conditions of life for consumers become truly dire.

IV. Prices and the Amelioration of War's Impact in the Late Seventeenth Century

Did prices respond to the lessening of military destruction at the end of the seventeenth century? The thought is an attractive one. We saw in Chapter III that the financial demands made by armies began to decline noticeably at the end of the seventeenth century. Earlier in this chapter,

126

we showed that, by the late seventeenth century, similar forces helped open trade between belligerents (it is helpful to recall that Liège was a belligerent in all of Louis XIV's major wars). These forces would lead one to believe that prices should have been less sensitive to war by the end of the seventeenth century.

To the suggestive evidence of diplomatic intent coupled with military and political practices, we can add knowledge about the quality of European food supplies and their relationship to demand between 1600 and 1750. J. A. Faber has studied the relationship between declining imports from the Baltic into Amsterdam and increased domestic food supplies coupled with reduced European demand.[35] Imports of Baltic grain into Amsterdam declined dramatically; in the fifty-year period 1700-1749, shippers brought in less than half that of the period 1600-1649, a century earlier. According to Faber, increased food production in western and southern Europe, and a smaller or stable seventeenth century population, caused that decline. Declining imports, increased home production, and a stagnant population about to grow again suggest that in the second half of the seventeenth century and certainly in the early eighteenth century Europeans had an increasingly secure food supply. From the security it offered came larger food stocks and less severe reactions to bad harvests or the other effects of war or bad weather.

We can test the hypothesis that war's impact lightened by looking at the index values for prices in the late seventeenth and eighteenth centuries, and comparing them with those for earlier wars. The hypothesis is only partially proved. While the people of the Basse-Meuse paid high prices for grain during the wartime years 1674-1676, and 1692-1695, those prices were the result of the combination of bad weather and war. In the eighteenth century, both wartime periods we examined, 1701-1706 and 1746-1748, saw only modest price increases, with peaks at about 25 percent greater than normal. The situation in the eighteenth century, then, was no better than that in the early 1630's, and 1671-1673, other times when there was war without simultaneous bad weather. We must again draw the conclusion that war as a single cause raised the price of even very sensitive commodities like rye very slightly; the seventeenth-century changes in wartime customs were not sufficiently powerful to make those increases smaller still.

*　　*　　*

The marketplace of Liège and its region brought together a wide variety of buyers and sellers. Large and small farmers, marginal rural laborers, industrial workers, merchants, and city dwellers met to barter their money or goods and supply their needs. It was, very probably, a self-sufficient system for providing food to the area's residents, and it is likely that the thriving long-distance trade into and out of Liège was restricted, in normal times, to industrial raw materials and finished industrial goods. All the same, good communications linked the food supply of Liège to the food market in Amsterdam, the dominant market of northwest continental Europe, and the maker of price-trends for Liège and the rest of a very large region. Liégeois merchants went to Amsterdam and the other Atlantic ports to buy food for their city when local supplies were inadequate as a result of war or bad weather.

The destruction of crops, the disruption of farming activities, and the increased demand, all caused by military incursions into the Liégeois region in the seventeenth century, certainly contributed to higher prices. But the integration of the markets of the Low Countries spread those higher prices all through the region, and certainly to the dominant market in Amsterdam. To the extent that trade was permitted to operate freely, and that those harvest failures were limited to a single year, war had only a limited impact. In these limited circumstances, war caused no crises for the consumer, even though, as we have seen in earlier chapters, it caused hardships for farmers whose earnings it reduced.

Only when trade was significantly disrupted did war lead to major crises for consumers. We have measured these crises by the short-term price increases in Liège and Maastricht relative to those at Amsterdam. The circumstances when war had such an impact were an already disrupted harvest, such as those of the mid-1670's or early 1690's, coupled with an active war fought in the Low Countries. Then, war clearly inflated prices in the Basse-Meuse far beyond their increase in Amsterdam. War alone seems to have increased prices by one-fourth to one-third on an annual basis, suggesting that, at times during a year of wartime experiences, the people of the Basse-Meuse paid twice the normal price for their grain. When war combined with bad weather, annual prices could double, and it is likely that the peak within the year reached four or five times the normal price of grain. Despite any imprecision in these figures, one can say with conviction that war always increased prices perceptibly, and, when natural setbacks also occurred, the increase was dramatic indeed.

128

Ill. 6. The Cruelties Committed by the French, No. 4, by Romeyn de Hooghe (1673)

The people of the Basse-Meuse felt these higher prices in a variety of ways, according to their role in the community. For consumers, and especially for subsistence-level consumers who earned wages and had to purchase their food, war surely caused a personal crisis of limited food. The story of Servais Ernotte is a case in point. In March, 1674, he retired and turned over a substantial part of his property to his son-in-law in return for an annual payment of 30 *dallers*, on which he would live.[36] Unfortunately, prices began almost immediately to rise. By May, 1675, Ernotte and his son-in-law returned to the notary to draft a new agreement. The earlier agreement "was not sufficient to provide for his food and unkeep, because of the present shortage of food . . ." Servais then turned over all the rest of his property in return for a guarantee that his son-in-law would provide for him for as long as he lived, no matter how much it cost.

The experience of Servais Ernotte differed dramatically from the opposite class of consumers, the nobility, *rentiers*, and clergy of the countryside. For them, war's impact on prices was a slight annoyance. A few months, or even a year or more, of higher prices would hardly have bothered them.

The substantial farmers of the Basse-Meuse, those who made their living by producing for and selling on the market, must, on the other hand, have profitted handily from the higher prices caused by war. As we have seen, by the 1690's, they were often able to avoid any loss of production during wartime; and, if the farmer of Louwberg is a valid example, they may have tried to increase their production to take advantage of higher prices. The producers of the Basse-Meuse benefitted from the combination of higher prices and a slowly improving situation in wartime that gave them at least normal, if not increased, production to sell to merchants and armies.

War's economic impact was never wholly negative in the Basse-Meuse. The region frequently prospered, even in trying times for other places, and thus the wars of the seventeenth and eighteenth century may have brought population to the region, rather than driving it away. The meaning of the interaction of war and economic development on the personal lives of the people of the Basse-Meuse will appear much more clearly as we discuss war's demographic consequences in the next three chapters.

Part 4

Victims and Survivors

The Specter of Depopulation

"The Brabant countryside was a distressing sight. As soon as one went beyond the land surrounding the towns, the fields were wild and neglected. Dikes were broken, and the polders around Antwerp, which had been so fertile, had been reduced to a desert. Most farms, owned by the institutions of Antwerp, Lier, Herentals, Malines, Hoogstraten, and Brussels in Kempen and in Central Brabant, were in ruins. Cattle had practically disappeared. Most of the farmers and their families were dead. Large packs of wolves roamed over the deserted country. In most villages the peasant population had fallen to a third or half and lived in the most miserable conditions. The situation was equally gloomy in Flanders. . . . Between Roeselare and Ypres the countryside was almost completely deserted. As late as 1 August 1597 the States of Flanders were informed that the parishes of *Ghelevelt, Gidts, Staeden, Rosebeke and Passendaele* in the Castellany of Ypres were still uninhabited. The economic vitality and financial strength of the agricultural population were utterly broken."[1]

In this passage Herman van der Wee, a modern historian, describes the condition of the countryside of the southern Low Countries in the late 1580's, after the worst Spanish excesses of the Dutch Revolt. The countryside was nearly deserted and almost destroyed. In *Simplicissimus*, much the same happened after the soldiers attacked Simplicissimus' family and community. His village, it seems, completely disappeared, his family and neighbors were killed or driven off; afterwards he lived in the woods with his friend the hermit.[2] From Simplicissimus' time to ours, observers have perceived early modern wars as deadly to civilians and their communities. Historians, poets, artists, and novelists have portrayed the Thirty Years' War and the wars of Louis XIV as leading almost inevitably to rural depopulation. To what extent was that true? For the Basse-Meuse, as we will see, it was not true. With the exception of a few hard years at the end of the seventeenth century, the Basse-Meuse never lost its prosperity, nor a significant part of its population.

But the experience of the Basse-Meuse may be unusual, if the

quotation from van der Wee and Simplicissimus' experience are accurate. The histories of other regions have taught us that depopulation must be the starting point for any analysis of war's demographic effects. Relying on the subjective but compelling storytelling of *Simplicissimus* and Freytag's *Pictures of German Life,* but also on the more academically objective versions of modern historians, we have come to equate depopulation and extraordinary personal losses with military action in the sixteenth and seventeenth centuries.[3]

The modern historical literature about early modern Europe is rich in examples of population loss associated with war. Germany is the classic case, and the best recent scholarship tells us that the cities in Germany lost a third of their population during the Thirty Years' War.[4] War struck the countryside even harder, eliminating 40 percent of the rural population. Since wars were not fought uniformly over Germany, it is obvious that large areas must have been left virtually without civilians. Armies repeatedly crossed Brandenburg, for example, which suffered very severely.[5]

War seemed enough of a catastrophe to be elevated into the pantheon of destruction created by Jean Meuvret in his hypothesis that subsistence crises ruled the demographic behavior of early modern France.[6] War, Meuvret said, was one of the three forces producing subsistence crises, the other two being famine and epidemic disease. There are French examples to support his assertion. Western France was especially hard-hit during the Wars of Religion at the end of the sixteenth century; and the region around Paris, according to Jacquart, lost population, although not catastrophically, at the time of the Frondes in the middle of the seventeenth century.[7]

The French and German examples are not the only well-known cases documenting the destructiveness of early modern wars. Other regions also suffered. Geoffrey Parker collected the experiences of a number of towns in Flanders and Brabant during the Netherlands revolt at the end of the sixteenth century.[8] He reports on fifteen towns, of which twelve lost half or more of their population between 1570 and 1600; all but one lost at least one-fourth. And, according to Parker, rural areas fared worse: in one example he cites, there was a 99 percent population loss in southern Flanders in the 1580's.

During the Thirty Years' War, many of the Rhenish borderlands between France and the Empire suffered large population losses. Roupnel has described large losses in the traditional Duchy of Burgundy; an army virtually swept the region clean of civilians.[9] Humm

has identified a dozen communities in Lower Alsace that disappeared as a result of war.[10] Similarly, historians have identified large population losses in Luxemburg and Lorraine.[11] And the as-yet-unwritten demographic history of the Principality of Liège would show areas ranging from south of Namur to just south of Liège devoid, or almost devoid, of residents during the Thirty Years' War.[12]

Unlike these other regions, the villages and rural towns of the Basse-Meuse were in no sense depopulated by the wars that raged around them between 1620 and 1750. This chapter will present the evidence which shows the dynamic nature of the Basse-Mosan population in wartime. This, of course, raises a fundamental question, whether the Basse-Meuse represents the true historical situation and whether our picture of the other areas has been distorted by stereotypical exaggeration. So far as I can tell, the truth lies somewhere in between. In other words, the Thirty Years' War and the Dutch Revolt certainly had a more serious effect on Germany and the Netherlands, respectively, than did wars fought in the Basse-Meuse on that region during the seventeenth and eighteenth centuries. But it seems unlikely that the damage was quite as severe as some authors have led us to believe. If anything near depopulation occurred, it lasted only a very short time. On the other hand, the Basse-Meuse itself may have fared much better than we might otherwise have expected, but that in itself demonstrates the need for caution in assessing the effects of any war fought in Europe during the period with which we are concerned.

Prior to the unification imposed on the Basse-Meuse in the 1790's by the French, the area's political diversity prevented any standardized taxes, censuses, or other record keeping. None of the states which controlled the Basse-Meuse was a great record keeper like the French, and the peculiar limitations and ancient customs imposed on the Spanish/Austrian and Dutch possessions such as local estates, further inhibited uniform and regular record keeping. As a result, our study of population size must turn, not to uniform and broad-based censuses or tax records, but to taxation and seigneurial records peculiar to individual communities, or to records of the church.

Only one series of documents will permit us to examine the population of the Basse-Meuse as a whole. Periodically, the ecclesiastical officials of the Diocese of Liège visited each parish; among the data they collected were the normal number of communicants (between 60 and 75 percent of the population).[13] These data are available for twenty-two Basse-Mosan parishes, for various years in the seventeenth and

eighteenth centuries.[14] Using a procedure described in E. le Roy Ladurie's *Paysans de Languedoc*, these stated number of communicants can be reduced to an index, the value of which in a given year roughly represents the number of communicants that year as a percentage of the highest number of communicants for any year.[15] Table 6.1 presents these data.

Table 6.1   *Index of Communicants in the Basse-Meuse, 1624-1763*

Year	Index Value
1624	70
1658	79
1699	77
1700	80
1712	92
1763	99

(For meaning of index see above).

The index of communicants presents a picture of overall population growth, temporarily checked in the late seventeenth century. These data do not give us a precise chronology of changing population size because of the widely spaced years in which the diocese conducted complete visitations. Still, the index of communicants indicates the pattern of changes in the Basse-Mosan population. Between 1624 and 1658 (the Thirty Years' War), the population grew by more than 10 percent in spite of repeated military occupation and the successful Dutch siege of Maastricht.

After the visitation year of 1658, growth stopped. The index value, 79 in 1658, slipped to 77 in 1699, and rose to 80 in 1700, evidence that the forces pushing population size upward in the first half of the century had lost their strength after 1658. The last third of the seventeenth century, beginning with the Dutch War in 1672, and ending with bad weather and terrible harvests after 1698, was the most serious concentrated period of military activity and harvest failure in the seventeenth century. Although the index of communicants does not permit us to identify precisely the moment when stagnation began and growth stopped, it does show the general chronology of seventeenth-century population developments in the Basse-Meuse, and their relationship to crises.

The population of the Basse-Meuse, while stagnant at the end of the seventeenth century, increased in the eighteenth century. By 1712, the index of communicants was 15 percent larger than it had been in 1700.

And by 1763, the population seems to have increased by a healthy 25 percent over its numbers two-thirds of a century earlier.

We now have a general working chronology of the relationship between crises and the population of the Basse-Meuse: growth in the seventeenth century was interrupted after mid-century, probably by repeated invasion, siege, and military occupation coupled with harvest failures. After the intensity and frequency of war lessened in the eighteenth century, the population grew again. Only in one extended period, then, did the characteristic growth of the Basse-Meuse slow. But these indications are crude; we should plot the population changes of the Basse-Meuse more carefully by examining data that are available for small segments of the region on an annual or nearly-annual basis.

The Seigneurie of Herstal, the largest communal unit in the ancien régime Basse-Meuse, included the modern villages of Herstal and Wandre, plus part of the Coronmeuse section of present-day Liège.[16] Its residents constituted a large segment of the Basse-Mosan population; in 1754 5,000 people lived in the parish of Herstal alone.[17] As a consequence, the history of its population will provide us with a good idea of the history of the whole Basse-Mosan population.

Residents of the Seigneurie could attain the status of "bourgeois," or formal residence. This status entitled them to certain privileges, most notably the imperial protections included in the fourteenth-century document known as the *bulle d'or* (golden bull), which prevented their arrest and prosecution outside their own territory.[18] For the rights of bourgeoisie they paid a tax to the seigneur, and it is the records of this tax that will permit us to follow the development of the population of Herstal.[19]

Who were the bourgeois of Herstal? To become a bourgeois, one had to be an established member of the community, of good character, and able and willing to pay the tax. The formal requirements demanded the possession of a hearth and *crama* (a device for suspending a pot over a fire). After a suitable length of residency (five to ten years), one made an application, and after an inquiry into the applicant's character, the seigneurial court certified his acceptability. A simple ceremony and payment of the tax each year confirmed his status. For the sons of the bourgeois and men who married their daughters the procedure was even simpler: they became bourgeois by inheritance soon after their marriage. Widows of bourgeois retained their husband's former status, but paid half the normal tax.

These customs indicate that the lists yield a population of house-

holds, rather than individuals. Furthermore, it is a population of established households rather than all households, because the residency requirement eliminated the transient population. Therefore, the lists of bourgeois minimize year-to-year fluctuations, while presenting mid- to long-term population development. Also, it is not quite a complete population. Certain local officials, soldiers, militiamen, and holders of feudal property were exempt from payment. All these groups were likely to have been small. Finally, some bourgeois may have been too poor to pay in certain years and some residents may have been too poor to become bourgeois. This would have varied according to economic conditions, but the tax could not have been the principal differentiating factor. The tax was ten patards in Herstal and thirteen in Wandre. That was less each year than the daily salary earned by a local coal miner, or a family's daily food budget.[20] Clearly, with the exception of a small minority living in extreme poverty, anyone who met the residency requirements and wanted to become a bourgeois, could do so. And in the seventeenth century, at least, it seems most of them wanted this status.

Like the records of ecclesiastical visitations, the annual numbers of Herstal bourgeois (presented in Table 6.2 and Figures 6.1 and 6.2) suggest strong population growth in the seventeenth century with a somewhat surprising spurt at its end and slower growth in the eighteenth century. Over the whole period, 1620-1750, the number of bourgeois in the seigneurie tripled, from about 325 in 1629 to a peak of nearly 1,000 in the good years of the early 1730's. The tripling of the number of bourgeois was not the reflection of uninterrupted growth, however. Between 1629, the first year for which we have figures, and 1672, the year of the outbreak of the Dutch War, the number of bourgeois soared, virtually doubling from 332 to 625. During the next 25 years, the population stayed nearly static: before 1697, the total never exceeded 650.

At that time, the end of the War of the League of Augsburg in 1697, the number of bourgeois increased dramatically, to 840, an increase of more than a third. The next year, 1698, it increased an additional ten percent to 930. From that year onward, the number of bourgeois stayed nearly constant until the 1730's. In the 1740's the number of bourgeois declined because the Estates of the Principality of Liège acquired the seigneurie, and the residents either perceived less value in becoming bourgeois, or the new owners were less diligent than their predecessors in collecting their fees.

Table 6.2   Herstal Bourgeois

Year	Left Bank (Herstal)	Right Bank (Wandre)	Total	Year	Left Bank (Herstal)	Right Bank (Wandre)	Total
1629	197	125	322	1696	396	221	617
1631	226	131	357	1697	568	272	840
1632	225	139	364	1698	659	271	930
1633	247	136	383	1701	591	278	869
1642	255	122	377	1702	598	259	857
1644	273	147	420	1703	570	258	828
1648	298	140	438	1704	625	257	882
1656	332	194	526	1706	662	295	917
1659	302	172	474	1708	640	295	935
1662	348	184	532	1709	643	307	950
1663	341	179	520	1710	633	293	926
1664	330	175	505	1711	612	274	886
1665	331	176	507	1712	655	278	933
1668	355	200	555	1713	645	251	896
1672	394	231	625	1731	662	332	994
1673	391	202	593	1737	631	315	946
1674	392	212	604	1738	635	311	946
1675	370	179	549	1739	624	319	943
1676	386	179	565	1740	638	285	923
1677	364	190	554	1741	629	226	855
1678	350	185	535	1742	612	224	836
1680	394	198	592	1743	601	218	819
1684	386	208	594	1744	599	241	840
1685	356	189	545	1745	601	256	857
1687	352	200	552	1746	584	244	828
1688	354	196	550	1747	586	219	805
1690	382	213	595	1748	576	214	790
1692	388	214	602	1749	570	224	794
1693	406	237	643	1750	569	199	768
1695	397	220	617				

The increases of the 1690's are clearly not instances of sudden natural population growth. What happened? The answer will give us some insight into the behavior of the population of Herstal-Wandre during wartime. We can understand the large growth of the late 1690's if we examine the register of bourgeois, and compare the portion of it listing the bourgeois of Wandre with the reconstituted population of the parish of Wandre.[21] How did the register's list grow? Each year, the prior year's list was recopied, leaving out those who had died and adding the year's new bourgeois. Most of the bourgeois were men who

Figure 6.1   Population: Three Basse-Mosan Communities

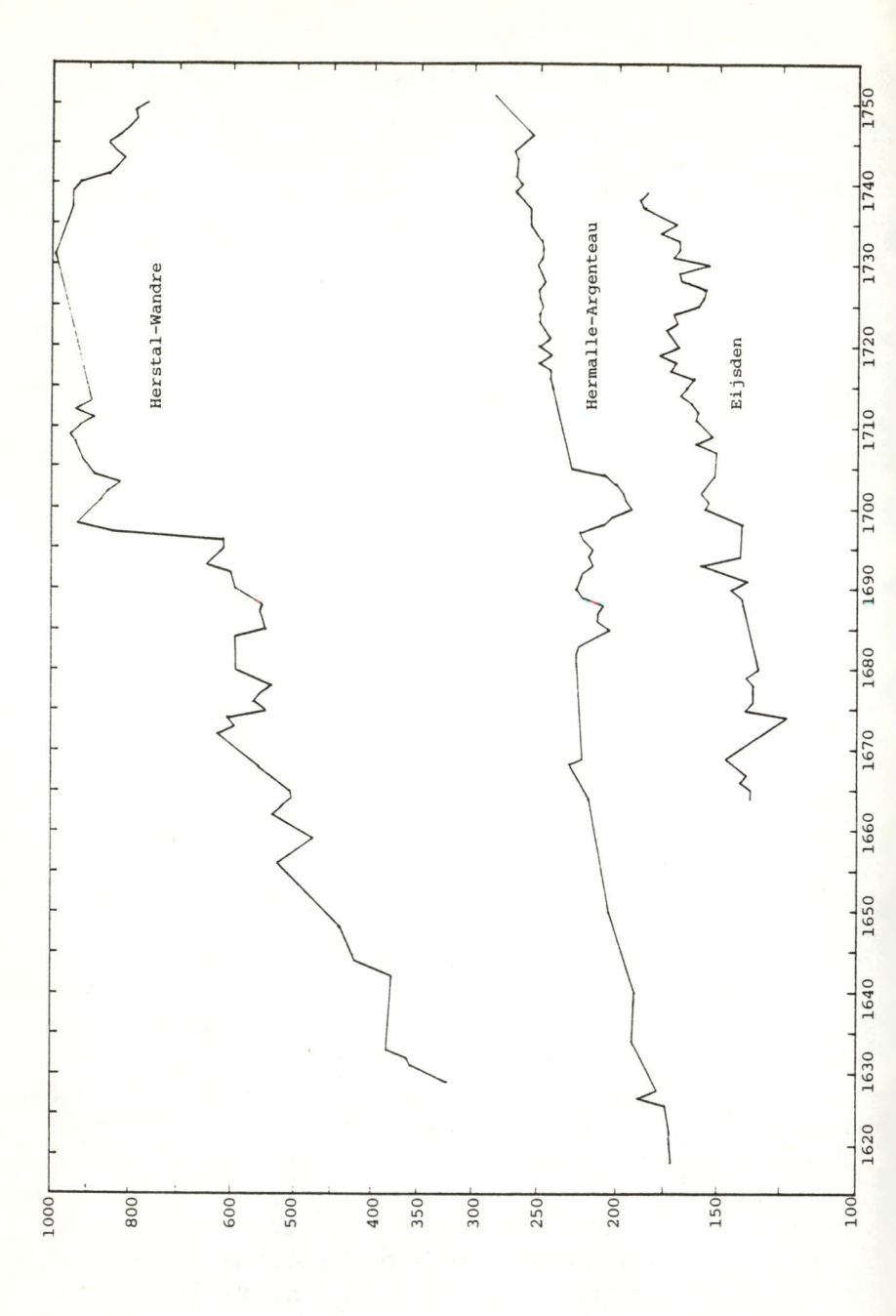

Figure 6.2   Short-Term Changes in the Herstal Bourgeois: Two Crisis Decades

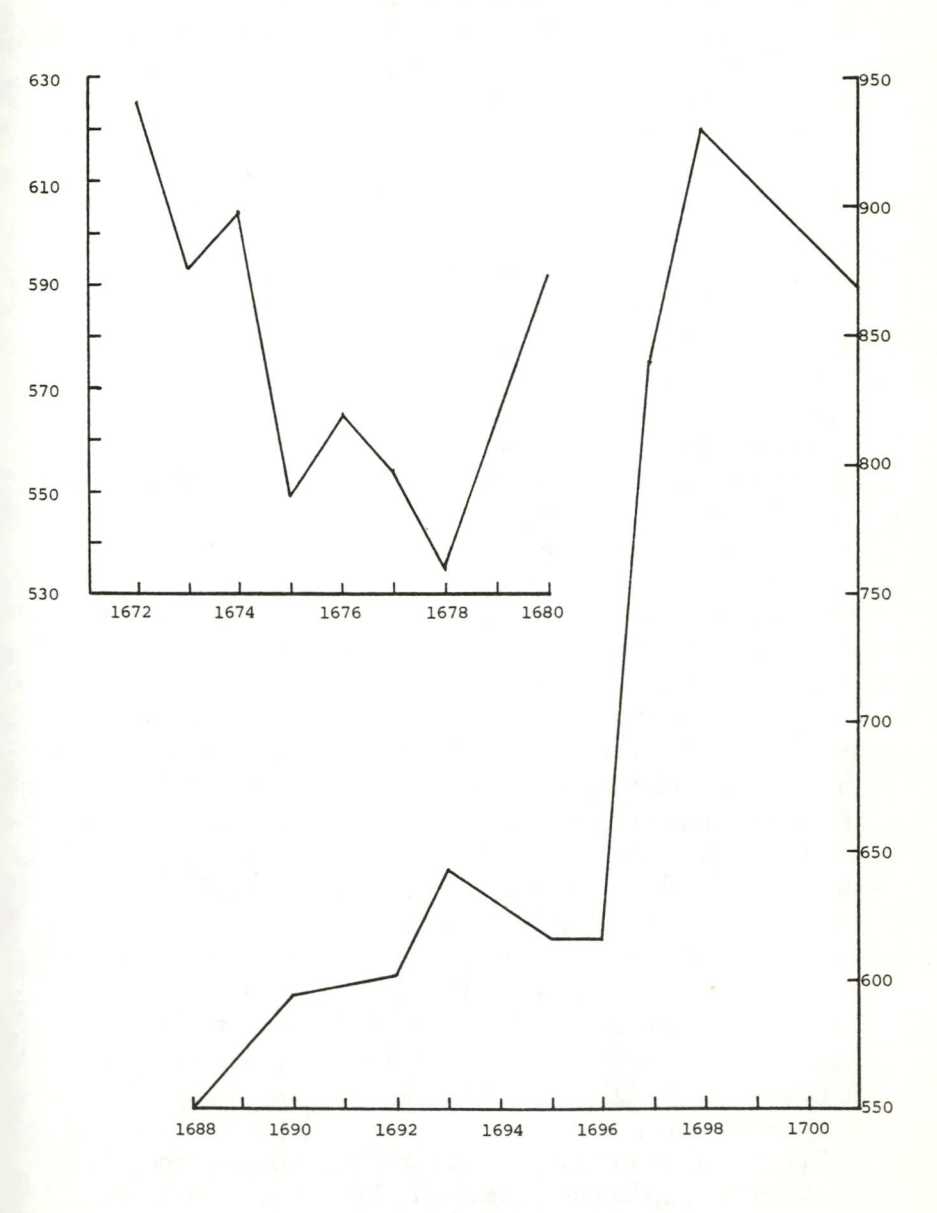

had recently married and established their own households. Entry into the company of bourgeois was not immediate, however. A time-lag often separated marriage and entry, even for the sons of bourgeois. Leonard Blanche, for example, married in May, 1691, but first appears in the list of bourgeois in 1697; similarly, Nicolas Darpion married in 1690, but appears only in the 1695 list of bourgeois. We might explain this delay as waiting to establish a household, or as waiting for the community to consider their candidacy.

The circumstances of 1697-1698 reflect both the economic and demographic forces at work in entry into the bourgeoisie. First, 60 Wandre residents married in the years 1695 to 1698, 20 more than the 40 who married from 1691 to 1694. These 20 explain two-fifths of the fifty additional Wandre bourgeois added in 1697 and 1698. In addition, the time-lag between marriage and entry into the bourgeoisie increased before 1697, because war and a major harvest failure disrupted the Basse-Meuse in the early 1690's.

The static number of bourgeois through much of the 1690's masks the beginning of renewed growth in the number of economically viable households. But that mask covers only some of the short-term changes that affected the population. Figure 6.2 shows the short-term adjustments in the number of bourgeois in the 1670's and 1690's. We can attribute the growth of 1697-1698 to accumulated new marriages waiting to enter the list of bourgeois; after 1698 another subsistence crisis struck. As a short-term consequence of that event, the number of bourgeois dropped from its high of 930 in 1698 to 869 in 1701.

The same short-term sensitivity appeared in the Herstal-Wandre population of bourgeois in the 1670's. During those wartime years the villages lost some population, but made it up very quickly afterwards. There were 625 bourgeois in Herstal-Wandre in 1672, the first year of the Dutch War. The war and the harvest failure that occurred in the middle of the decade had a dramatic impact on the number of bourgeois, which never again reached 625 in the decade. Although the pattern of population loss does not show a steady annual drop, the number of bourgeois shrank to 535 men and women in 1678, a loss of about 14 percent. After the war ended, however, the number of bourgeois grew, to 592 in 1680 and 594 in 1684, suggesting that the long-term loss caused by the Dutch War was about 5 percent, a loss that was not made up until the 1690's.

The conclusion we must draw is that the population of households of Herstal-Wandre responded to the combined negative economic and

142

demographic conditions that occurred in wartime. All the same, war hardly depopulated the community; rather, its strong earlier growth was retarded. Once the long period of economic malaise associated with the last three decades of the seventeenth century ended, the number of economically viable households increased.

Herstal-Wandre was only one administrative unit out of many that we might include within the Basse-Meuse. Yet its demographic development parallels that of other communities. The seigneurie of

Table 6.3   *Argenteau Landholders*

Year	Number of Landholders	Year	Number of Landholders
1619	172	1703	201
1622	173	1704	207
1623	173	1705	228
1626	174	1716	243
1627	188	1717	243
1628	179	1718	250
1634	192	1719	242
1640	190	1720	250
1649	203	1721	243
1650	205	1722	247
1664	217	1723	250
1668	229	1724	250
1669	221	1725	248
1682	225	1726	250
1683	225	1727	250
1684	224	1728	246
1685	205	1729	249
1686	212	1730	251
1687	212	1731	248
1688	208	1732	248
1689	221	1733	249
1690	225	1734	254
1692	222	1735	256
1693	215	1736	257
1694	217	1737	256
1695	215	1738	261
1696	220	1739	267
1697	223	1740	263
1698	209	1741	267
1699	204	1743	266
1700	193	1744	269
1701	196	1746	255
1702	198	1751	284

Argenteau also spanned both sides of the Meuse, north of Herstal-Wandre. It consisted of the villages of Argenteau, on the east bank of the Meuse, and Hermalle-sous-Argenteau, on the west side. Each *manant*, or landholder, of the seigneurie was obliged to pay a small tax each year; the proceeds of this tax are our source for the seigneurie's changing population size.[22] Simple residency determined landholder status in Argenteau, rather than the strict requirements facing potential bourgeois in Herstal. As a consequence, the number of landholders, as shown in Table 6.3 and Figure 6.1, was subject to more short-term fluctuation than the Herstal bourgeois.

The number of landholders of Argenteau, like that of bourgeois in Herstal, grew in the seventeenth and eighteenth centuries. From 1619 to 1751 they increased from 172 to 284, a gain of 65 percent. This is less than the spectacular growth of the Herstal bourgeois, and is probably explained by Herstal's greater proximity to the City of Liège, which made Herstal part of that growing city's suburban sprawl.[23] But, like Herstal-Wandre and the index of communicants, Argenteau stopped growing in the last third of the seventeenth century. In 1668, the number of landholders reached 229. The next year, probably as a result of the plague epidemic that struck the Basse-Meuse in 1668, only 221 paid the tax. The community returned to its 1668 population of landholders only in 1705, after the end of the disastrous epoch of wars and harvest failure at the close of the seventeenth century. What is especially dramatic about the landholders of Argenteau is their growth after 1700. Between 1670 and 1700 they had suffered a net loss, from 221 to 193. But between 1700 and 1720 they grew by 25 percent, reaching and then exceeding their former maximum. Their remarkable growth in those years is another confirmation of the resilience of the Basse-Mosan population, and of the lightened burdens on it after 1700.

Our picture of strong population movements in the Basse-Meuse in the seventeenth and eighteenth centuries can be completed by examining one further series of population figures, for the community of Eysden, at the northern end of the Basse-Meuse, just south of Maastricht.[24] The figures for Eysden (Table 6.4, Figure 6.1) represent the number of households paying the personal tax collected by the community after 1663, when the Dutch took possession once and for all.

The taxpaying population of Eysden showed strong growth in the second half of the seventeenth century and the first half of the eighteenth, a nearly 40 percent growth over 75 years (from 137 in 1664

144

Table 6.4   Eysden Personal Taxpayers

Year	Number of Households Paying Tax	Year	Number of Households Paying Tax
1664	137	1712	160
1665	137	1713	163
1666	141	1714	168
1667	138	1715	165
1669	147	1716	162
1674	123	1717	173
1675	139	1718	170
1676	136	1719	178
1677	136	1720	169
1678	136	1722	175
1679	138	1723	170
1680	134	1724	172
1688	140	1725	165
1689	141	1726	163
1690	145	1727	162
1691	138	1728	168
1693	158	1729	169
1694	141	1730	155
1698	141	1731	172
1700	157	1732	169
1701	155	1733	169
1702	158	1734	178
1704	152	1735	170
1707	151	1737	187
1708	161	1738	189
1709	153	1739	185
1711	161		

to a peak of 189 in 1738). This growth roughly equals that experienced in Hermalle-Argenteau in the same period, but falls behind the experience of Herstal. The community was able to preserve its population in spite of the rigors of war and of harvest failure between 1670 and 1700. From a peak household population of 147 in 1669, it briefly declined and then seemed to stabilize around 140 during the last three decades of the seventeenth century. But by 1700 Eysden was on its way to the same sort of strong eighteenth-century growth that characterized the Basse-Meuse as a whole.

Although some differences persist in the local data examined, it is not difficult to draw a general picture of population change in the Basse-Meuse. In the seventeenth century the Basse-Meuse grew quickly until the disasters that began, along with the Dutch War, after 1670.

The population of Herstal-Wandre probably doubled in the first seventy years of the century, and there was growth, but at a reduced pace, in neighboring communities and in the region as a whole. After 1670, however, the population temporarily stopped growing. Repeated military action and economic distress caused by high prices and harvest failures stymied population growth by frustrating the formation of new households, killing off the heads of existing ones, and making the area economically unstable and unattractive for migrants.

In the eighteenth century, the population of the Basse-Meuse began to grow again, although at a slower pace than before 1670. In the first half of the century, the index of communicants shows a 25 percent increase, sizeable in the context of Europe in that age. Other indicators show that the region quickly recovered in the first two decades of the eighteenth century from the stagnation of the late seventeenth century. Then, the growth slowed as the region gathered its resources for the tremendous growth that took place in the second half of the eighteenth century.

The pattern of demographic change in the Basse-Meuse – a period of stability or decline between two periods of growth – is similar to the development of agriculture and the economy discussed in Chapter IV. We should raise the same question here that we raised there: is war really to blame? Does the region share enough experiences with other, warless regions to suggest that war had little or no impact? In part the question is premature, because in two subsequent chapters we will break down population change and reconsider this issue in more detail. But it is worth considering the question in crude terms, because the question is one of great importance. Let us look at the trend of population development in other parts of northern Europe. In places very near the Basse-Meuse, the trend is almost identical to the region we have studied. In rural Brabant, for example, which had a chronology of war and epidemic very similar to that of the Basse-Meuse, population trends were almost identical.[25] The population grew before 1670 and after about 1700, with a period of stagnation or decline in between those years. The scholar who studied Brabant attributes the cause of this pattern to essentially the same processes as we will identify in Chapters VII and VIII.

What about other regions? In the northern Netherlands, and especially Friesland and North Holland, the pattern of demographic change echoed the agricultural changes.[26] Between 1650 and 1750 the population declined, primarily in response to reduced demand for

certain commodities and declining agricultural activity. In the more southerly and easterly parts of the Dutch Republic, the chronology was rather different. In three regions that have been studied – Overijssel, the Veluwe and the area of Bois-le-Duc – fighting was severe during the Eighty Years' War of Dutch Independence, 1568-1648, and this kept the population stagnant and caused it to decline in some places.[27] After the end of the war, these territories expanded, although we do not have a very precise chronology. For them, the period from the middle of the seventeenth until the middle of the eighteenth century was one of growth, especially because only the area of Bois-le-Duc was involved in the wars of Louis XIV.[28]

We can turn, finally, to the experiences of France in the seventeenth and eighteenth centuries. As happened in parts of the Dutch Republic, demographic developments in northern France mirrored the development of the economy.[29] The years from 1660 until the late 1680's were good years, and the population grew slowly, recovering some of the population lost during the Thirty Years' War and the Fronde. From 1690 until at least 1717, population growth turned around again. Struck by the last great wave of famines and by epidemics, the population of the northern half of France shrunk below its seventeenth-century minimum. The great growth of the eighteenth century began only in the 1720's.

Like northern France and the parts of the Dutch Republic that had been damaged by the Eighty Years' War, the Basse-Meuse was ready for growth in the 1660's. But, unlike those areas, the growth came to an abrupt end after 1670. Why did the growth end then? The proximate cause, as we will see in Chapter VII, was a tremendous increase in mortality from epidemic disease. Those epidemics did not happen in a vacuum, however. Rather than European-wide outbreaks like the Bubonic plague, they were diseases of sanitation like dysentery, spread among a war-weakened and war-impoverished population by soldiers and bad food and water. Some of the epidemics might well have occurred without the military activity, but then they would never have been as severe as they were. Others, such as those of 1672 and 1673, probably would not have occurred at all. The military action of the 1670's led to the abrupt, early end of Basse-Mosan growth. That growth might have stopped a decade or two later, in the face of the famine of 1693, for example, but that is beside the point here. The wars were crucial to what happened in the Basse-Meuse. Events there are not the mere reflection of general trends in northern Europe, or of the local

occurrence of some "General Crisis of the Seventeenth Century."

Before we turn to the components of population change, we must consider one final question raised by our general discussion of population movements, and especially by the fact that the renewed eighteenth-century growth began by 1700. Did the War of the Spanish Succession have little or no impact on the population of the Basse-Meuse, unlike earlier wars? And what about the War of the Austrian Succession, in the 1740's? I suggested in previous chapters that at the end of the seventeenth century there was a definite amelioration of war's impact on the lives of the people of the Basse-Meuse, at least in terms of the nature of their relations with visiting armies, and perhaps in the impact of those armies on economic life. Does that hold true for the demographic effects as well? The data discussed in this chapter suggest that it does. We have seen that, after thirty years of stagnation, the index of communicants jumped 15 percent between 1700 and 1712; that the landholders of Argenteau regained their pre-1670 numbers between 1700 and 1705, and then grew another 10 percent by 1716; and that the experience of the Herstal bourgeois and Eysden personal taxpayers suggests the same conclusion.

We cannot easily identify the cause of this growth in the face of military action; perhaps it was the accumulated need to grow after thirty years of population stability. There should be no question, however, that it occurred, and that it means that the War of the Spanish Succession, unlike the War of the League of Augsburg and the Dutch War, was unable to hold back population growth in the Basse-Meuse. Our data for the War of the Austrian Succession, which reached the Basse-Meuse in 1746-1748, are less complete, but the experience of the Argenteau landholders suggests a loss of 5 percent in 1746, and probably a further loss of population in the following two years. There is no question that war could still reduce the population in the 1740's, but because the war was short and came after thirty peaceful years, recovery followed immediately.

The most important conclusion we can draw from the overall population experience of the Basse-Meuse in the seventeenth and eighteenth centuries is the resilience of its population in the face of war. Unlike the populations of areas of the Netherlands and France in the wars of the late sixteenth century, or of sections of Germany, Lorraine, Luxemburg, and the Duchy of Burgundy in the Thirty Years' War, the Basse-Meuse did not lose a significant part of its population in wartime. The population stabilized, and in Herstal in the mid-1670's the popu-

lation declined very briefly by about fifteen percent before recovering in half a decade. This was not depopulation.

Why does the Basse-Meuse appear to have had a different experience from the other regions in wartime? The reasons should not be exclusively demographic, since the purely demographic consequences of war should be general, and not vary greatly from region to region. Rather, the differences are related to social and economic conditions. The population of the Basse-Meuse did not decline dramatically in the wars of the seventeenth century because the people of the Basse-Meuse managed to preserve a sense of community and thus a population: people stayed, making do under trying circumstances. Moreover, the region seemed sufficiently prosperous and safe to attract migrants.

The great historical demographer, Roger Mols, hinted at the mechanisms of population stability when he suggested that wartime depopulation is not the result of temporary migratory flight, but the failure of the population to rebuild itself: deaths increase and births and marriages decline, so that the dead are not replaced.[30] Mols was only partly correct. Migration does play a role, because a population that is strong enough to rebuild by natural increase after a catastrophe will probably attract migrants also, while a community that cannot rebuild also cannot prevent people from leaving. There is then a strong economic component to the survival of communities in wartime. The communities Humm identifies in Lower Alsace that disappeared as a result of war were already sinking before the war began; war may only have accelerated their demise.[31] Similarly, the places in Flanders and Brabant discussed by van der Wee and Parker and mentioned at the beginning of this chapter were all part of an essentially prosperous Low Countries economy; even if we believe the potentially exaggerated reports on which van der Wee relied, these communities rebuilt extremely quickly, repopulated by migrants and returning residents in less than a decade.[32]

This implies that the demographic strength of the Basse-Meuse, like the demographic fate of all communities in wartime, had a strong independent economic determinant. That economic force produced a group of influences that determined whether the population would restore itself after a crisis through marriage and migration. For individuals to marry and commit their new families to life in a community, and for new migrants to be attracted and possible emigrants to be discouraged, a community must offer them a future. They must expect to be able to earn a living and have neighbors. Those

expectations are probably more important than short-term hardship.

Before returning to the role of the economy in war's impact on society, we must understand the basic elements of war's role in demographic change: more deaths and fewer births. These are the building blocks of population change, together with migration and marriage. In Chapter VII we will focus on the victims of war's presence in the Basse-Meuse, by looking at wartime mortality. In Chapter VIII, the survivors will be our subject, those people staying and arriving, marrying and having children. These are the people whose confidence in the region preserved the Basse-Meuse in spite of early modern wars.

Chapter VII

The Victims: Death and Military Action

Our common notion of war's impact on population is that it led abruptly to depopulation, either by killing civilians or by driving them away. While the supposed final result, depopulation, seems somehow extreme for the Basse-Meuse, this notion is at least in part correct. Military action did lead to civilian deaths, but while it may also have led to some temporary migration away from the scene of action, migration was seldom the principal cause of war-induced population loss. The reasons for this are largely economic. In the countryside, peasants had the misfortune to find troops in close proximity in wartime, living in their houses or barns, or camping in their fields. This was surely something to be avoided, but to run and hide led almost inevitably to total loss. Fields needed to be tended. Vacant farmhouses and un-protected barns might be destroyed, and armies, which were mostly interested in extracting money from civilians in the path of march, looked with disfavor on those who took their possessions and fled. In other words, while there is ample evidence that people moved around during wartime, temporary or permanent migration left only a small mark on the population of the Basse-Meuse. To explain how war may have reduced the Basse-Mosan population, we will have to look at mortality.

The number of deaths occurring monthly in nine Catholic Basse-Mosan parishes with good surviving parish registration will serve as our basic data for the analysis of war's impact on mortality.[1] Unfortunately, none of the nine parish registers series is complete for all the years from 1620 to 1749, and so we will examine two combinations designed to provide the best aggregate information while incorporating as few corrections as possible for incomplete data.[2] Table 7.1 presents the experience of four parishes for the years 1628 to 1660, providing annual numbers of calendar-year deaths and the index of extreme behavior for those numbers of deaths.[3] Table 7.2 presents six parishes for the years

1661 to 1749. In addition, Figures 7.1 and 7.2 show the index graphically.

Table 7.1 Deaths in the Basse-Meuse, 1628-1660: Calendar Year Deaths

Year	Deaths	Index of Extreme Behavior	Year	Deaths	Index of Extreme Behavior
1628	25	0.51	1645	29	0.64
1629	49	1.00	1646		
1630	51	1.04	1647	Incomplete Data	
1631	56	1.15	1648		
1632	37	0.76	1649	42	0.94
1633	68	1.41	1650	43	0.97
1634	89	1.85	1651	26	0.59
1635	43	0.90	1652	35	0.80
1636	78	1.64	1653	51	1.17
1637	Incomplete Data		1654	59	1.36
1638			1655	47	1.09
1939	50	1.07	1656	57	1.33
1640	25	0.54	1657	46	1.08
1641	42	0.90	1658	40	0.94
1642	35	0.76	1659	41	0.97
1643	30	0.65	1660	49	1.16
1644	38	0.83			

Parishes: Hermalle-Sous-Argenteau, Cheratte, Dalhem, Haccourt
Regression Equation: Slope = -0.2304; Y-intercept = 424.58

I. The Crises

The data show that when serious military events took place in the context of a continuing series of military actions in the Basse-Meuse, the number of civilian deaths skyrocketed. The best examples are the 1630's and 1670's. Both periods saw intense military action in the Basse-Meuse, with successful sieges of Maastricht and efforts by the losers to retake that city and hold their ground in nearby villages. As a result, the number of deaths per year peak in both 1633-1636 and 1673-1678. The first coincides, it is true, with one of the last great outbreaks of Bubonic Plague in northern Europe.[4] In 1635, 1636 and 1637, plague seemed to strike everywhere in the Low Countries, northern France, and Germany. But this alone is insufficient to explain large number of deaths. We need to bear in mind also that 1633-1636 saw the aftereffects of the taking of Maastricht by the Dutch, the actions of their new garrison in that city, the attempts by the Spanish to retake Maastricht, and the repeated strategic maneuverings in the small

152

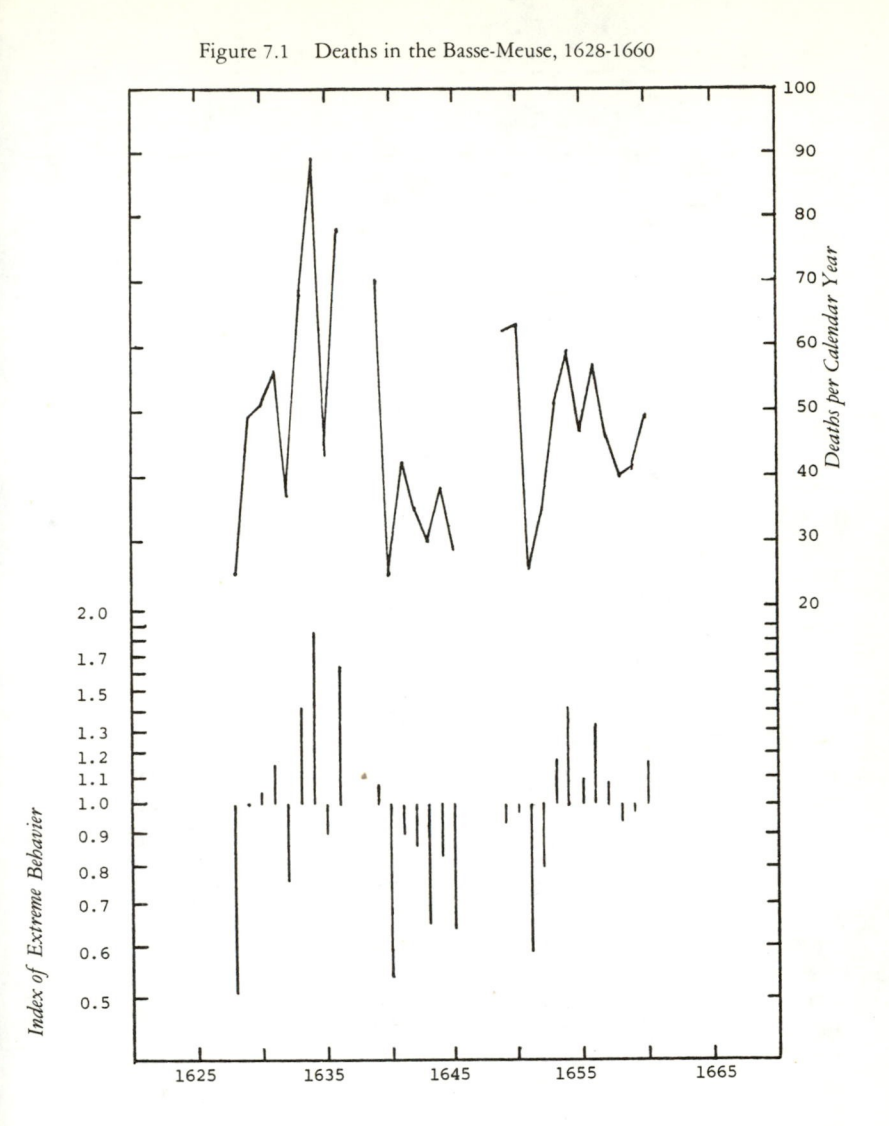

Figure 7.1   Deaths in the Basse-Meuse, 1628-1660

Basse-Mosan forts at Argenteau, Dalhem, and Navagne. The crisis of the 1670's coincides with Louis XIV's entry into Mosan affairs, his seizure of Maastricht, and the attempts by the Dutch to recoup that loss. The events of 1675-1676 brought military action to both Liège and Maastricht. The epidemic of dysentery, almost certainly spread by soldiers, that broke out at the same time caused the greatest peak of deaths in the Basse-Meuse in the seventeenth century, 223 in 1676, nearly two and one-half times the normal level for the six parishes.

153

Table 7.2 Deaths in the Basse-Meuse, 1661-1749: Calendar Year Deaths

Year	Deaths	Index of Extreme Behavior	Year	Deaths	Index of Extreme Behavior
1661	100	1.20	1704	74	0.67
1662	88	1.05	1705	66	0.59
1663	70	0.83	1706	75	0.67
1664	52	0.61	1707	85	0.75
1665	56	0.65	1708	90	0.79
1666	87	1.01	1709	91	0.80
1667	89	1.02	1710	96	0.84
1668	143	1.63	1711	107	0.93
1669	111	1.26	1712	113	0.97
1670	81	0.91	1713	91	0.78
1671	69	0.77	1714	97	0.83
1672	65	0.72	1715	103	0.87
1673	115	1.26	1716	121	1.02
1674	145	1.58	1717	91	0.76
1675	103	1.17	1718	102	0.85
1676	223	2.40	1719	111	0.92
1677	80	0.86	1720	156	1.29
1678	106	1.13	1721	136	1.12
1679	111	1.17	1722	111	0.91
1680	87	0.91	1723	101	0.82
1681	75	0.78	1724	150	1.21
1682	92	0.95	1725	107	0.86
1683	116	1.19	1726	132	1.05
1684	81	0.83	1727	155	1.23
1685	118	1.20	1728	172	1.36
1686	81	0.82	1729	235	1.85
1687	74	0.74	1730	141	1.10
1688	94	0.93	1731	126	0.98
1689	71	0.70	1932	127	0.98
1690	65	0.64	1733	123	0.95
1691	126	1.23	1734	96	0.79
1692	109	1.06	1735	116	0.89
1693	144	1.39	1736	118	0.90
1694	196	1.88	1737	115	0.87
1695	122	1.16	1738	102	0.77
1696	57	0.54	1739	111	0.83
1697	57	0.54	1740	115	0.86
1698	85	0.79	1741	218	1.62
1699	120	1.11	1742	173	1.28
1700	125	1.15	1743	134	0.98
1701	71	0.65	1744	91	0.67
1702	124	1.13	1745	91	0.66
1703	92	0.83	1746	176	1.27

Table 7.2 *(continued)*:

Year	Deaths	Index of Extreme Behavior	Year	Deaths	Index of Extreme Behavior
1747	259	1.87	1749	97	0.69
1748	160	1.15			

Regression Equation: Slope = 0.64576; Y-intercept = -989.416
Parishes: Herstal, Wandre, Hermalle-sous-Argenteau, Cheratte, Dalhem, Haccourt

Figure 7.2   Deaths in the Basse-Meuse, 1661-1749

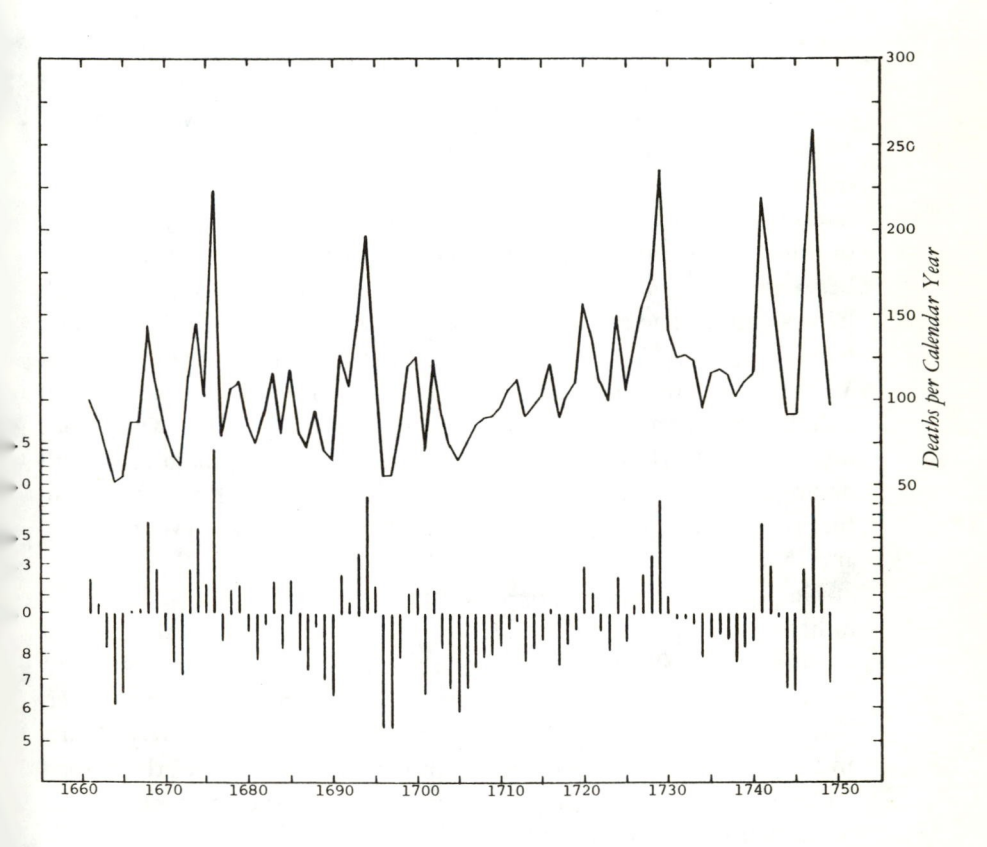

Later in this chapter we will attempt to identify those who died, but we must make clear at once that these total numbers of deaths per year include adults, and very few children. Parish registers in the Basse-Meuse, as in most of the Diocese of Liège, seldom included the deaths of children before the mid-eighteenth century; on the whole, register keepers rarely recorded the deaths of live-born children who died before confirmation.[5] In the parish of Wandre, the priest entered no more than ten children's deaths as regular funeral masses in the death register in the years from 1666 to 1759, even though registration in the Liègeois area improved in the early part of the eighteenth century. Thus, the deaths which occurred in wartime were not simply an upsurge in infants' and children's deaths, but the deaths of adults, whose lives war shortened considerably.

In earlier chapters, we considered the need to differentiate among three kinds of crises, those caused by military action, those caused by bad weather (and consequent harvest failure), and the two combined. In this chapter and the next, we will continue to study the relative importance of different causal factors, but we will group them differently, and add epidemic disease (such as European-wide plague outbreaks) to our consideration. Previously, we have distinguished between war as a direct force in rural life, war as a force acting through harvest failure, and bad weather as a cause of harvest failure. For the two remaining chapters, we will continue the analysis introduced in Chapter V, when we discussed prices. War's influence on the population through harvest acted only through the food supply. Thus, we will not distinguish here between the various causes of harvest failure; we will distinguish only between the direct impact of war on the population, that of harvest failure (collapse of the food supply), whatever its cause, and that of epidemic disease.

Despite the excessive mortality military presence provoked, years of military activity in the Basse-Meuse did not coincide with the greatest mortality crises. That dubious honor belonged, in the ancien régime, to the combination of war with a harvest failure caused by bad weather. Thus, when we rank the three varieties of crises — war, harvest failure, and epidemic disease — and their combinations, in terms of their effect on mortality, we will arrive at the following order: most serious, combination of war and bad weather; second, war alone; third, plague or other epidemic; and, fourth, harvest failure caused by bad weather.

The highest index values shown in Tables 7.1 and 7.2 are associated with combination crises, those for 1676 and 1694. The year 1676 is an

Ill. 7. The Cruelties Committed by the French, No. 5, by Romeyn de Hooghe (1673)

example of the kinds of circumstances that combined to kill the most people. The weather was bad. The previous year, 1675, saw a cold, wet summer, making it difficult to harvest a dry crop and even more difficult to store it dry. Little food was left. In 1676, the reverse happened: the summer was hot and dry. While that was not necessarily disastrous for crops, the hot weather lowered the water table and made access to fresh water more difficult. The stagnant, low water remaining in streams and wells deteriorated quickly.[6] The situation was ripe for dysentery and the other endemic gastrointestinal diseases of poor hygiene that went by that name. The situation was compounded by the large number of troops in the area. The French removed their garrison from the Citadel of Liège, concentrating their forces at Maastricht, where they were attacked by the Dutch in an unsuccessful siege that lasted from 6 July until 26 August. Dysentery, spurred by climatic conditions and spread by the presence of soldiers, raced through the population, producing an index valve for deaths in 1676 of 2.40; nearly two and one-half times the normal number of people died.

The year 1694 was similar to 1676. Although weather was not especially bad in the Basse-Meuse in 1693, it was bad elsewhere in Europe, causing prices to rise. In 1694, the summer was again hot and dry. To this hot, dry weather we can add the presence of at least two substantial armies. The allied army attacked the French Garrison at Huy, south of Liège, in September and defeated it. After the siege, Liégeois and allied troops took winter quarters throughout the Basse-Meuse. Once again, a gastrointestinal epidemic spread through the population, raising mortality 88 percent higher than normal.

War alone was less deadly than combined crises. In 1632-1634, for example, military action and a regional epidemic preceded the bad weather, which did not peak until 1635-1636.[7] Three further examples in which both military action and a large number of deaths preceded a harvest crisis were the siege of Maastricht, and follow-up, in 1673-1674, the attack on the city of Liège in 1691, and the battles and siege at the end of the War of the Austrian Succession, in 1746-1748. In 1674, the index of extreme behavior reached a peak at 1.58, an increase of nearly 60 percent; in 1691, it showed a rise of 23 percent above normal, to 1.23; and, in 1747, it soared to nearly double normal, an index value of 1.87.

Plague seems roughly equal to war in its severity, even though there is only one clear case in the series of index computations. The years 1668-1669 show remarkably high mortality — an index value of 1.63 in 1668 — without evidence of major warfare or bad weather. The last

outbreak of bubonic plague near Liège explains this high mortality; it caused roughly the same level of mortality as the wartime crisis of 1674.[8]

We can order mortality crises as follows: combined catastrophies were the most severe, war and plague were less severe, and harvest failure was the least severe. More people died in the wartime crisis of 1633-1634 than in the agricultural crisis (felt throughout Europe) of the mid-1620's;[9] similarly, the century's worst mortality crisis, in the mid-1670's, far exceeded the harvest failure of 1659-1661; the military or combination crises of 1691 and 1694 caused more deaths than the harvest failures of the later period, the mid-1680's, 1698-1700, and 1709-1711; and the last wartime crisis, 1746-1748, was more deadly than the harvest failure that peaked in 1741. This ranking also appears in general statistical evidence. By comparing correlation coefficients (Appendix D) computed for years of major warfare and for the price of rye in Liège (indicative of harvest failure) with annual mortality, we see that war produced a much higher correlation coefficient with harvest-year deaths (0.323) than did rye prices (0.167). While the figures are not wholly comparable, they do show the different relationships between war, harvest failure, and mortality, and the order of magnitude that separates them.

Why do the various causes of excessive mortality rank themselves this way? The answer, as we will see, lies in the mechanism by which epidemic disease spread in rural populations, and the influence of food supply on health and mortality. Before we consider this in more detail, we should examine additional data. We have seen how deaths distribute themselves through the years from 1628 to 1750. Next, we will examine the distribution of deaths through the year, and the causes of these excessive deaths. Then it will be possible to understand why war, epidemic, and harvest failure had the impact they did on mortality in the Basse-Meuse.

The seasonal distribution of deaths follows a relatively constant pattern in most pre-industrial European populations. The number of people dying rises sharply from a minimum in June and July to a yearly high in the fall, in September, October, and November; stays relatively high for the rest of the winter; and then begins to drop in April or May to return to the lowest levels in June or July.[10] The monthly distribution of more than 13,000 deaths in the nine Basse-Meuse parishes is given in Table 7.3, and shown graphically in Figure 7.3.[11]

159

Table 7.3 Monthly Distribution of Deaths (Harvest Years)

	AUG	SEP	OCT	NOV	DEC	JAN	FEB	MAR	APR	MAY	JUN	JUL	TOTAL
All Years													
Number	995	1,335	1,462	1,233	1,173	1,284	1,092	1,268	1,191	967	835	805	13,640
Proportion	.073	.098	.107	.090	.086	.094	.080	.093	.087	.071	.061	.059	
Years of High Mortality*													
Number	226	480	555	405	319	360	257	288	302	227	190	204	3,813
Proportion	.070	.126	.146	.106	.084	.094	.067	.076	.079	.060	.050	.054	
Years of Normal Mortality													
Number	769	855	907	828	854	924	835	980	889	740	645	601	9,827
Proportion	.078	.087	.092	.084	.087	.094	.085	.100	.090	.075	.066	.061	

* Years included: 1632-1636, 1668-1669, 1673-1676, 1691-1694, 1727-1729, 1740-1741, 1746-1747

Note: These figures have not been corrected to show the impact of months which have different numbers of days. Such a correction would only slightly change the values presented, and would not affect the analysis here.

Figure 7.3   Monthly Distribution of Deaths

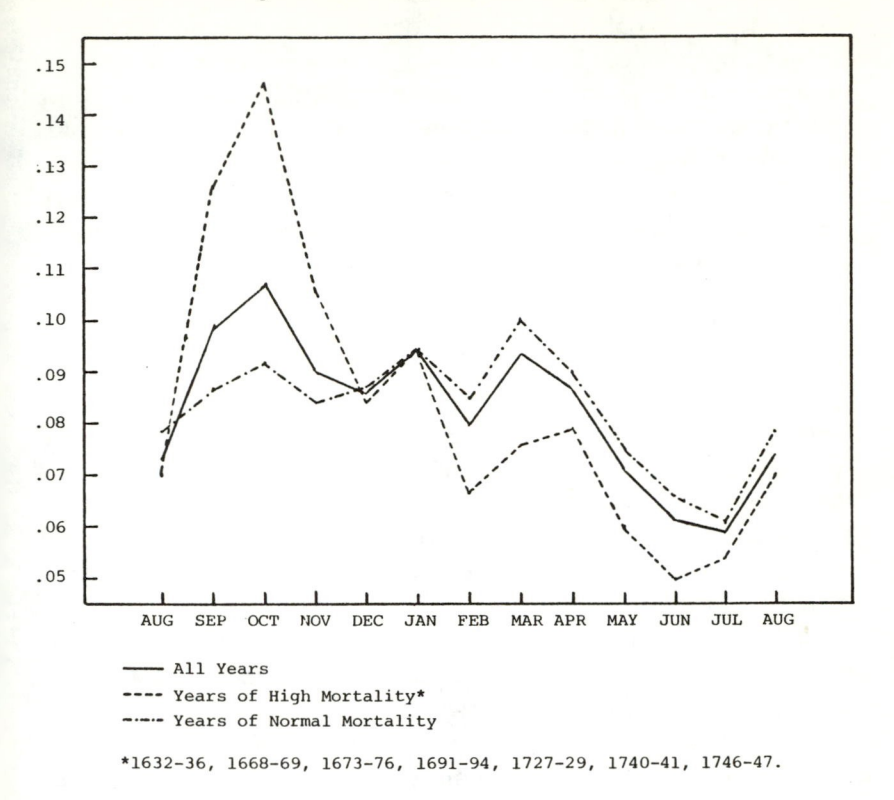

AUG   SEP   OCT   NOV   DEC   JAN   FEB   MAR APR   MAY   JUN   JUL   AUG

——— All Years
- - - - Years of High Mortality*
-·-··- Years of Normal Mortality

*1632–36, 1668–69, 1673–76, 1691–94, 1727–29, 1740–41, 1746–47.

For all the years under consideration, mortality in the Basse-Meuse reflects seasonal weather and harvest conditions and the peculiar seasonal preferences of the epidemic diseases of the era. The summer months with their yearly minimum number of deaths reflect good weather conditions, the first fruits and vegetables, and relatively easy summer communications and transport. But the good fortune of the summer did not last long. The July and August heat spoiled food supplies, and bubonic plague, when it came, struck its first victims in August. The late summer and fall brought the epidemics, with the peak number of plague victims dying between August and October, and the peak number of dysentery victims almost always succumbing in October.[12] To the seasonal characteristics of diseases were added the problems of the harvest. Hot weather, an always inadequate diet, and the strenuous physical demands of the harvest weakened the adult population. The year following a bad harvest was especially serious; in

that case the food left from the previous years ran out before the new harvest, forcing people to eat spoiled food, food that was not yet ripe, or even garbage or grass. Even when a good harvest followed a bad one, the time it took to gather, thresh, and mill the grain could create extreme shortages in September and October. The population was vulnerable to the diseases of the season, and people died in the autumn. The plateau across the rest of the winter months, although lower than the autumnal peak, represents a continuation of fall conditions, ameliorated when cold weather killed disease carriers. The number of deaths declined when the weather first broke and new food supplies became available in May. Their maximum production in June and July completes the cycle.

When we divide all years into those characterized by very high mortality and those *not* characterized by very high mortality, the annual pattern changes. We see that the autumnal maximum merely reflects the extraordinary influence of a few years of extremely high mortality. It is very exaggerated in those years (nearly three times as many deaths in October as there are in June), and not present in the years of normal mortality. In the years of normal mortality, the parishes of the Basse-Meuse show another, more modern, pattern: deaths are spread evenly throughout the year, with a slight peak in March and April, the peak months of non-epidemic mortality.[13]

Crisis mortality was caused by epidemics that struck the Basse-Meuse in September, October, and November. But we should not assume that all epidemic mortality occurred in those months. Unpredictable events caused high mortality too; their very unpredictability provides reason enough to understand why the peaks might change from year to year, or why, instead of a single peak, the number of deaths stayed high throughout the year. For one thing, epidemic disease, while normally striking hardest in September, October, and November, was not unknown in other months. In Hermalle-sous-Argenteau, the priest identified *peste* (probably bubonic pague) as killing an unusual number of people in June 1630.[14] In April of 1623, he wrote that a *contagion* caused an unusually large number of deaths.[15] In June 1634, the curé of Emael wrote the following: "At the beginning of the month, a contagious malady broke out at Emael. In a single house, six persons succumbed in the space of two weeks."[16] Overall, he reported seventeen deaths in the months of June and July, an extremely large number for that parish. And a classic case of the effects of a mortality crisis on a family occurred in the parish of Wandre in February, March, and April of 1674: on 24

February, a service was held for the daughter, Isabeau Bicket; on March first, five days later, her mother, Catharine Malaise, died; finally, after a month, their husband and father, Wathieu Bicket, succumbed.[17] Summertime and late winter could be just as hard on the population as the autumn epidemic season.

II. Causes of Death

What caused these excess deaths in times of war or harvest failure? Violence associated directly with war occurred, but soldiers killed very few residents of the Basse-Meuse. For example, on 27 September 1644, Dutch troops who had recently retaken Dalhem from the Spanish killed Hendricqs Gappar, a resident of the town.[18] Nearly thirty years later, on 15 June 1674, troops from the Spanish-controlled Duchy of Limbourg, fighting in the Dutch War, intercepted the riverboat that travelled regularly from Maastricht to Liège. According to the parish register of Herstal, they killed five people; four of them were civilians, and one was a young girl.[19]

Soldiers, however, rarely murdered civilians, except when provoked. They acted violently, needless to say, but they directed their violence more towards property than lives. The burning of the village of Lixhe in 1672 and the pillage of Herstal in 1676 are more representative examples of violence.[20] Troops burnt homes, stole or killed animals, carted off or destroyed grain, straw, forage, and anything else of value, but they seldom murdered civilians. Most often, one imagines, the civilians ran off too quickly to be caught by troops more interested in booty. We know, of course, that civilians sometimes stayed and fought back, organized into militia to fight off the potentially demanding troops; in those cases, soldiers sometimes killed citizens of the Basse-Meuse. However, the people of the Basse-Meuse only rarely responded to armies in this way, and their efforts never produced many fatalities.[21]

Nor is it likely that the deaths of many soldiers, killed either in battle, skirmish, or camp, crept into the parish register. Their own commanders and chaplains hardly knew the names of those who died on the march, in battle, or, more often, of disease in camp, and it is most unlikely that anyone informed local priests of their deaths.[22] The deaths of garrisoned soldiers occasionally appear in the parish registers of small fortified places, such as Dalhem in the 1620's and 1640's, but our counts exclude them.[23]

We should mention one final category of soldier-deaths. Residents of

the Basse-Meuse served as soldiers and officers in all the major and minor European armies.[24] Sometimes, when they died in service, their families were notified, a mass recited, and the death entered in the home-parish register. Such instances are rare and, like the deaths of garrisoned troops, we have excluded them from our figures.[25]

Disease was the real cause of the excess deaths in times of crisis in the Basse-Meuse. The monthly distribution of deaths showed that most of the excessive deaths occurred in large clusters in the epidemic-disease months of September, October, and November. Lumped together in this fashion, the authors of the parish registers frequently described them as *contagion, dysentery,* or *peste*. During these epidemics, from what we can guess, people died of epidemic gastrointestinal or pulmonary disease (probably influenza, typhus and dysentery), sometimes plague and, less frequently before the eighteenth century, smallpox.[26] They often coincided with the years of intense military activity. In Herstal, the parish register reports disease in September and October, 1633; in March through July, 1634; and again in the fall of 1636.[27] In Haccourt, the priest reported dysentery (which may just have been epidemic diarrhea) in October and November, 1634, and in July, 1636.[28] In Hermalle-sous-Argenteau, the priest wrote about dysentery in his register in the fall of 1633, and *peste* in October, 1635.[29] Melchior Crahay, the chronicler of the village of Sart, east of Liège, described a *coreuse discenterie* that was "so contagious that it raced everywhere like a fire. It carried many people of all ages and sexes to the Other World."[30] Later, in August and September of 1676, the priest of Cheratte blamed dysentery for the 21 deaths in his parish in those months, more than half the people who died in Cheratte during all of 1676.[31]

We should note that, while the keepers of parish registers attributed deaths to various infectious diseases, they never blamed starvation for these deaths. While the apparent similarity of symptoms between death by starvation and amoebic dysentery may have confused them, it is not likely.[32] There is, nevertheless, a significant statistical relationship between food supply, as indicated by agricultural production, and mortality, and a possible relationship between prices as an indication of food supply and mortality.[33] This does not necessarily suggest that people died of starvation, but, rather, as the distribution of deaths through the year showed, that the population's health was very closely tied to the availability of food. When food was in short supply, people became weak and much easier victims of the infectious diseases that lived in their environment. Despite the hardships visited upon the Basse-Meuse

by war and famine, we have little reason to believe that its residents let their neighbors starve. We must believe the testimony of the priests and other observors that infectious disease, and not starvation, killed unusually large numbers of people from time to time.

Contemporary observers, chroniclers, and historians saw the connection between disease and the presence of armies in the vicinity of the Basse-Meuse. In June, 1676, de Sonkeux wrote, "the pestilential hot fevers began to abate after having nearly depopulated Verviers. They had originated at the siege of the city of Limbourg."[34] Later that same summer, he attributed a *mechante dissenterie* (wicked dysentery) to a French pillaging expedition.[35] In August of that year, an epidemic broke out in Sittard, near Maastricht. Chroniclers attributed it to injured soldiers.[36]

Still more examples occurred in the 1690's. After the battle of Landen-Neerwinden, fought by the French and the Allies on 29 July 1693, in an area about 40 kilometers west of Liège on the main road to Louvain, "the great number of dead bodies around Neerwinden caused dangerous maladies that infected the Hesbaye and were felt all the way to Liège."[37] Even after the French left in mid-August, the disease, called "hot fever" (*fievre chaude,* the same disease de Sonkeux mentioned) persisted, killing, nearly half the population of the Quarter of Montenacken, a unit of the Principality of Liège roughly midway between the Basse-Meuse and the Landen-Neerwinden area.[38] Nor was the eighteenth century different. The intense military action of the 1740's again brought disease to the region. In 1746, following a four-week French camp, the residents of Kanne and Nedercanne wrote, "after the troops left the illness reigned among us so well that seventy died, including 35 heads of families."[39] And the priest of Wandre identified the cause of death in the epidemic of 1747 as, "dysentery when the allied army was camped from Housse to Maastricht."[40]

When the authorities recognized the connection between military action and epidemics, they moved to prevent the spread of disease. The Liégeois authorities shut down the annual fair of Sint Truiden (to the west of the Basse-Meuse), in 1630, recognizing the difficulties, "in these times of war, of shortage of grain, of contagious disease, and of misery."[41] While 1630 was not a year of major new military action, it was one of great brigandage and disruption, caused by dispossessed citizens and soldiers garrisoned at Maastricht and throughout the Mosan region. Besides closing the fair at Sint Truiden, the Liégeois authorities also issued at least eight other edicts dealing with disruption

and civil unrest and the need to suppress and evict soldiers, vagabonds, and other evil-doers.[42].

*   *   *

What we have learned about the distribution of deaths throughout the year and the causes of the excessive deaths that periodically struck the Basse-Meuse will help us to understand why combined crises caused the most severe mortality there, and why war was more deadly than simple harvest failure. As we saw, most excess deaths in the Basse-Meuse resulted from epidemic infectious diseases, which predominantly struck in September, October, and November. No one died of starvation. How did these diseases spread, and why did they kill people at that time of year? The spread of crisis diseases in the Basse-Meuse depended on two factors. The more important of the two was the presence of the disease; it had to be in close proximity (or spreading wildly) for people to catch it. The second factor was susceptibility. Epidemic disease spreads more easily in a weakened population. These factors provide at least a partial explanation for our ranking of the various kinds of crisis mortality.

Armies caused crisis mortality in the countryside by bringing disease to civilians. Military life in the seventeenth century was a rural activity. The large armies that moved around, fighting occasional battles and threatening and setting siege to strategic fortresses, rarely lodged in cities. More often, their vast size, and the ability of walled cities to keep them out, forced them to lodge in villages and camp in the fields. The garrisons maintained in fortified cities were small, never more than a few thousand men, and much smaller than the armies that camped outside their walls, trying to defeat them. For example, the peacetime garrison of Liège in the 1650's was 2,000 infantry and 200 cavalry; in the 1670's, the Dutch garrison of Maastricht contained more than 10,000 men, a small force compared to the French army attacking it.[43] The large, closely packed and disease-ridden armies in the countryside brought disease and death to the villagers with whom they came in contact.[44]

War brought disease to the rural civilians of the Basse-Meuse, but the clear seasonal pattern of deaths in wartime years shows that the mere presence of an army caused few epidemics. Most of the excess deaths associated with war occurred in the autumn, but armies appeared in the Basse-Meuse in an almost uniform distribution throughout the year.

166

The season of greatest military presence would not have been September through November, but the time of winter quarters, from late November until March.

Armies contributed more than disease to Basse-Mosan mortality. They brought hardship and reduced food supplies. The peak in deaths in September, October, and November suggests a strong relationship between war, the failure of the harvest, and deaths. We saw in Chapter IV how war severely reduced harvests. Bad harvests and high prices reduced the food supply for the people of the Basse-Meuse. Poor nutrition weakened their resistance to disease. The years of extraordinarily high prices combined with military action, like 1676, saw the most severe mortality of the seventeenth century. But war reduced the resources of the population even when food supplies were adequate and prices not stratospheric; people succumbed because all their grain or money had gone to the armies, and they could not buy food, no matter what its price. A simple harvest failure offered a much less complex situation. The absence of an external source of disease made the impact of harvest failure much lighter than that of war.

Before drawing some final generalizations about the impact of various forces on mortality, we should reconsider war's role. In a work such as this, which is focused on war, there is a persistent danger of blaming everything on war. Before we attribute high mortality to the impact of military presence, we must ask whether the epidemics would have broken out at all without the presence of an army. Our answer should be mixed. On the basis of events in other nearby regions, such as Brabant, it is likely that some epidemics would have come to the Basse-Meuse anyway, although many of them are directly attributable to either the conditions caused by armies, or to their transmission of disease. If these epidemics might have come to the Basse-Meuse even in the absence of military activity, we can ask another question: would the same number of people have died? The answer is no. Without the hardship and potential for transmission associated with armies, the number who died would have been considerably smaller.

We can now propose a general model of the impact of wars, epidemics, harvest failures, and their various combinations, on mortality, for the Basse-Meuse. It should account for the ranking of mortality crises determined earlier in this chapter. The three mechanisms through which these forces operated were the presence of disease, shortage of food, and general hardship. Area-wide epidemics (even without war) and war itself brought disease into the region, explaining

their roughly equal contribution to crisis mortality. To the extent that war may have been slightly more deadly, it was because long, severe wars also created economic hardship, depriving people of resources and making it difficult for them to obtain food, even when prices were reasonable. Harvest failure caused by bad weather had the weakest impact because it influenced only the availability of food, through local production and prices. It was less severe than war, because war's hardships lasted so much longer. Only when the two combined, as they did in the 1670's, did weather contribute to genuine crisis mortality.

III. The Victims

We have until now ignored the identity of the people who died in such numbers in the Basse-Meuse, except to say that our figures are for adults. It is very hard to answer the question, "who died?" The quality of registration regarding deaths is at best weak, especially when it comes to identifying and differentiating the population by age, sex, or marital or economic status. Without a time-consuming attempt to link up the evidence from a large number of sources – not only the parish registers for births, marriages, and deaths, but also the records of notaries, of the civil registers of contracts, and of the courts, as well as tax and seigneurial accounts – it will be impossible to know very much about the people who died at any time, and especially about the excess dead. The weakest members of the community – the old and the young, the sick and certainly the poor – died first and most often, relative to their numbers in the population. Yet these are the people about whose lives it is hardest to learn anything, even with the most thorough searching through the whole range of early modern sources.

We may legitimately assume that, as elsewhere, excess deaths in the Basse-Meuse struck the most fragile members of the community first and heaviest.[45] Aside from infants and young children, about whom we will speak presently, the very old must have died at the greatest rate. Of course, more of the very poor, those who were closest to the subsistence line, died than did their more prosperous neigbours. And finally, we can project that those struck by repeated events – first, loss of property, then the need to take refuge, and finally by starvation or epidemic in their place of refuge – would have been most vulnerable to hunger and disease.

De Sonkeux made this report about the extreme mortality in Verviers during the worst years of the Dutch War. It gives an idea who

it was that died; moreover, the anonymity of the people to de Sonkeux, an interested observer, suggests their low status and transient role in the community: "Many persons of both sexes died in the years 1676, 1677, and 1678, whose names I did not know. The rue de Hodimont was very depopulated by great pestilential fevers which killed seven or eight each day. But the great mortality was in the year 1676. On 12 February 1676, twelve persons of both sexes, whose names I did not know, died, mostly poor and indigent folk."[46]. Of course, while the poor, the old, and the already ill died in the largest proportions, the wealthy of the Basse-Meuse were by no means immune. Catherine de Hodeige, widow of Charles Boesmanq, an important lawyer at the Liégois courts, and three of her five children all died of plague between November, 1636, and February, 1637.[47]

IV. Infant Mortality – the Problem of Survival

The discussion of mortality, and excess mortality in time of war, concentrated exclusively on adult mortality. Yet it is important to understand the mortality of infants and young children, who were probably the weakest members of the community. The reason we have avoided this subject until now is that the study of infant and childhood mortality, in its usual terms, is virtually impossible for the Basse-Meuse, because the parish registers rarely recorded the deaths of infants or children. To circumvent this dilemma, we will examine an index that represents the proportion of legitimate children born each year who survived to adolescence, for the reconstituted population of the parish of Wandre. Such a proportion surviving is also the proportion *not dying*, so that a low proportion surviving implies high mortality up until adolescence, and a high proportion surviving implies a lower mortality. If we cannot know the number of infants and children who died in wartime or during other crises, perhaps the proportion surviving to adolescence will provide clues to the problem of mortality for infants and children in times of high adult mortality.

Unfortunately, the proportion of those born each year who survive will obscure the effects of mortality for given wartime years, for the determination is delayed until the survivor reached his or her teens or even later. His survival cannot be described only as avoiding death during the year he was born, or even that year and the next year, but over several years, when the general mortality experience was quite varied. We do know however, from sources such as the Coale-Demeny

West model life tables, that out of a cohort born in a given year, more than 55 percent of those who died by age fifteen died in the first year of life.[48] While still leaving us with the need for caution when using the proportion surviving as a substitute for infant mortality, most of the mortality reflected in the years up to age fifteen did occur in the year of baptism and the first year or two that followed. Even then we must conclude that the measure is a minimum, since there were very probably children born who did survive but who do not appear to have survived, either because they left the parish before they married, or married elsewhere, or never married.[49]

Figure 7.4 shows results of the study of survival for men and women combined, for the years 1666-1710. It was necessary to exclude the years after 1710 owing to defects in the Wandre parish register data, the result in turn of a change in the quality of registration which took place after 1740. This change in the nature of registration would unrealistically lower the proportion surviving who were born after 1710, since the poor quality of registration made it impossible to reconstruct some marriages, thus excluding individuals who really survived.

The conclusion that one must draw from the index of survival is that infant mortality appears to have responded only to the most serious of those conditions which produced periods of high adult mortality. Overall, the mean proportion surviving was about 55 percent of the legitimate children born; the standard deviation is .087. In only two years did the proportion surviving drop significantly below the mean, less one standard deviation (about 0.46), for those children born in 1667 and 1674. Not surprisingly, these years coincide with two periods of extremely high adult mortality, the plague epidemic of 1667-1668 and the combined military crisis and harvest failure of the mid-1670's. In the very serious crisis of the 1690's, the proportion surviving does not show any dramatic decline. This suggests that the survival of legitimate children, and by extension infant mortality, may not have been as sensitive to war and other crises as adult mortality.

In part, this lower sensitivity can be attributed to two factors. First, and very important, is the role played by reduced births. In Chapter VIII we will discuss the role of war in reducing the number of births, but it can be stated here that war and other crises lowered fertility. Either as a result of reduced fertility or increased pregnancy loss, fewer children were conceived and born in times of war or harvest crisis than during other, more normal, times. It is possible that the more vulnerable elements of the community lost more births than their more

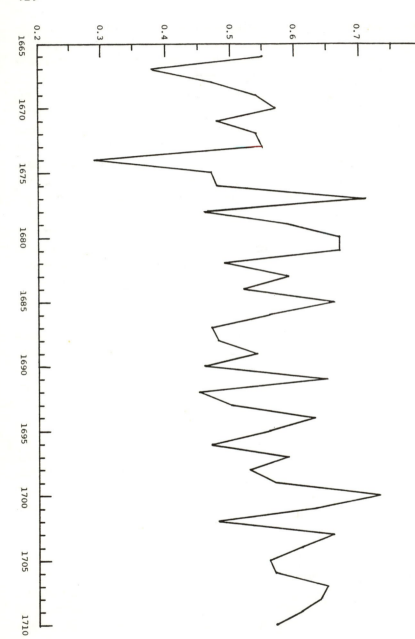

Figure 7.4   Proportion Surviving, Wandre Legitimate Births Men and Women Combined

prosperous neighbors. Thus, those infants who were subject to the greatest risk of death in the first two years of life were never conceived or, if conceived, were never born. In terms of absolute numbers, fewer children survived in many years of crisis. But fewer were born, too, and the proportion surviving remained at, or near, its normal level.

A second explanation is offered by the possibility that the severity of war and its effects on food supplies may have declined. In Chapter V, I suggest that food supplies increased in western Europe by the first half of the eighteenth century, at the same time that the major military powers attempted to reduce the impact of their troops on civilians. Infant and childhood mortality may have been much more sensitive to food supplies than was adult mortality. It is thus possible that any improvements that occurred in the supply of food might have been an important cause of improved rates of childhood survival in the Wandre population.

*　*　*

Despite any bright spots, like childhood survival, our entire discussion of war and mortality considers communities subject to very high mortality. Compared with those in modern industrialized nations, and even in a number of less-developed countries today, death rates were very high. Even if we treat the proportion surviving to adulthood as a minimum, it is unlikely that more than 60 percent of all children born survived to their teens. And on this basis, the Coale-Demeny West model life tables indicate an expectation of life at birth of not quite 35 years. Even those surviving to age fifteen could not expect to live much beyond age 55.

The effect of war on this already high level of mortality was to wipe out much of the population growth the Basse-Meuse might have experienced. How much did war and epidemics cost the Basse-Meuse in terms of mortality? There are 24 years in Tables 7.1 and 7.2 when the index value for deaths exceeds 1.19. If we look only at those years when mortality was very high, we find a mean index value for mortality in times of crisis of 1.48. Forty-eight percent more people than normal died in these times. The death rate nearly doubled and the average expectation of life fell by at least a third, to the range of twenty to twenty-five years. War significantly reduced the lifetimes of the people of the Basse-Meuse.

We can see the impact of these increases in an illustrative if not

scientifically representative example. In the three wartime years, 1674, 1675, and 1676, 202 children were born in the parish of Herstal, while 137 adults died. To account for the absence of infants' and children's deaths in the death figures, we can multiply the number born by 0.6 (the proportion surviving), making roughly 120 who survived. In those three years, the parish of Herstal suffered a net population loss of 15 to 20. For comparison, we can take three peacetime years, after the Dutch War, of relatively low mortality, 1679 through 1681. One hundred seventy children were born in Herstal in those years, which, when reduced by a survival rate of 0.6, makes 102. On the other hand, 98 adults died, a net population gain of less than five.

Admittedly, these net gains and losses are not large in the context of a parish with a population of more than 3,000. But what they show is that very modest gains were providing population *growth* in the seventeenth century. In the final years of the seventeenth century, repeated years of high adult mortality, coupled with slightly higher infant mortality, negated any possible growth.

We must stress one final conclusion. At one time, historians attributed much of the excessive mortality that reduced population growth in pre-industrial Europe to bad weather and bad harvests, which they labeled "subsistence crises". That hypothesis has been subject to constant revision.[50] The evidence presented in this chapter confirms the work of others which shows that the idea of subsistence crises controlling population growth is far too simple. Poor food supply surely contributed to ill health, but the most important factor causing the periodic increases in the number of deaths was the presence of disease, spread either by a self-generating epidemic or an army. Moreover, bad harvests and bad weather did little that directly caused high mortality. In a region where trade was effective, distant markets controlled by merchants, not the weather, most strongly influenced the food supply. When they made prices high, and war or epidemic brought disease to the Basse-Meuse, many people died.

The Survivors: Childbearing and Marriage

While war's demographic impact damaged the Basse-Meuse, it did not destroy the region or any of its communities. Despite the financial and personal hardships of military occupation, and the losses to temporarily excessive mortality, none of the area's villages disappeared, even for a few days or weeks. The most serious consequences we can find are large numbers of dead and the momentary abandonment of a few farms by farmers extremely hard hit by war's ravages.

How did the communities of the Basse-Meuse preserve their populations in the face of wartime losses? Who took the places of the many who died and the few who left? Children born to couples who survived or who married during and after the crisis, and immigrants, replaced them. The reason the Basse-Meuse could prosper and stay populous, in a relative sense, is that it remained attractive to migrants and to the marriageable. It offered opportunity for those who wished to become members of the community either by marrying and establishing households, or by moving in to make a new place or to assume the place of someone who died.

In this chapter we will explore two elements of replacement, childbearing and marriage. While both contributed to the stability and growth of the region, both also were subject to impediments raised by war and other crises. We will begin by examining those impediments; once we understand them, we can turn to the question of how the forces of replacement helped rebuild the population of the Basse-Meuse and kept it growing during and after the wars of the seventeenth century.

Childbearing is the first key to understanding the rebuilding process and the impediments that hampered it. While we easily foresaw war's impact on mortality, we cannot easily predict its impact on childbearing. We might reasonably assume that war reduced childbearing, but we will see that its impact was not direct. Rather, war disrupted marriage and limited food supplies, and they in turn reduced

childbearing. It is on childbearing, we will find, that the classic subsistence crises of early modern Europe operated.

Our measure of childbearing will be the number of baptisms. Ancien régime governments saw little need to record births, and left the task to the clergy, who were concerned only about their sacraments. When we refer to reduced childbearing we will concern ourselves with the number of children the priests of the Basse-Meuse baptised. We will call the difference between the normal number of baptisms and the actual number that took place *lost baptisms,* those which might have occurred but did not because of unusual conditions. It is these lost baptisms that we must identify and explain.

Figure 8.1 and Table 8.1 present the number of baptisms each year for seven Basse-Mosan parishes during the calendar years, 1665-1749.[1] The index of extreme behavior is included in Table 8.1 and shown graphically in Figure 8.2. Fortunately, the priests of the Basse-Meuse did a good job recording baptisms. They insisted that most baptisms take place within 24 hours of birth, insuring that virtually all live births resulted in baptisms.[2] On the few occasions that baptisms could not take place within 24 hours of birth, the priest noted the delay when he actually baptised the child; such notes are rare in the parish registers of the Basse-Meuse.[3]

Table 8.1   Baptisms in the Basse-Meuse

Year	Number of Baptisms	Index of Extreme Behavior	Year	Number of Baptisms	Index of Extreme Behavior
1665	230	1.01	1681	238	0.99
1666	270	1.18	1682	229	0.95
1667	237	1.04	1683	288	1.19
1668	236	1.03	1684	254	1.05
1669	279	1.21	1685	235	0.97
1670	261	1.13	1686	257	1.05
1671	247	1.07	1687	283	1.16
1672	246	1.06	1688	259	1.06
1673	203	0.87	1689	279	1.13
1674	186	0.79	1690	274	1.11
1675	223	0.95	1691	276	1.12
1676	155	0.66	1692	270	1.09
1677	172	0.73	1693	215	0.86
1678	225	0.95	1694	178	0.71
1679	203	0.85	1695	229	0.91
1680	237	0.99	1696	283	1.13

Table 8.1 (continued)

Year	Number of Baptisms	Index of Extreme Behavior	Year	Number of Baptisms	Index of Extreme Behavior
1697	265	1.05	1724	290	1.06
1698	255	1.01	1725	273	1.00
1699	187	0.74	1726	256	0.93
1700	215	0.84	1727	279	1.01
1701	274	1.07	1728	266	0.96
1702	221	0.86	1729	262	0.94
1703	212	0.83	1730	253	0.91
1704	245	0.95	1731	289	1.04
1705	242	0.94	1732	259	0.93
1706	260	1.00	1733	259	0.92
1707	286	1.10	1734	286	1.02
1708	285	1.09	1735	298	1.06
1709	268	1.02	1736	298	1.05
1710	232	0.88	1737	314	1.11
1711	262	1.00	1738	289	1.02
1712	301	1.14	1739	343	1.20
1713	275	1.04	1740	288	1.01
1714	286	1.08	1741	204	0.71
1715	269	1.01	1742	289	1.01
1716	285	1.07	1743	293	1.02
1717	315	1.18	1744	280	0.97
1718	322	1.20	1745	285	0.98
1719	330	1.22	1746	310	1.07
1720	248	0.92	1747	235	0.81
1721	284	1.05	1748	248	0.85
1722	271	1.00	1749	328	1.12
1723	281	1.03			

Regression Equation: Slope = 0.78467; Y-Intercept = -1079.36
Parishes: Herstal, Wandre, Vivegnis, Hermalle-sous-Argenteau, Dalhem, Haccourt, and Heure-le-Romain.

I. The Crises

Figure 8.1 and the data presented in Table 8.1 leave little doubt that baptisms, like deaths, responded sharply to the negative influences that disrupted life in the Basse-Meuse. During the 1670's, twice during the 1690's, and again in 1741, the number of baptisms per year plummeted. Less significant declines occurred in 1685, in 1702-1703, in 1710, and in 1747-1748. In general, most of the years in which the region ex-

Figure 8.1   Baptisms in the Basse-Meuse

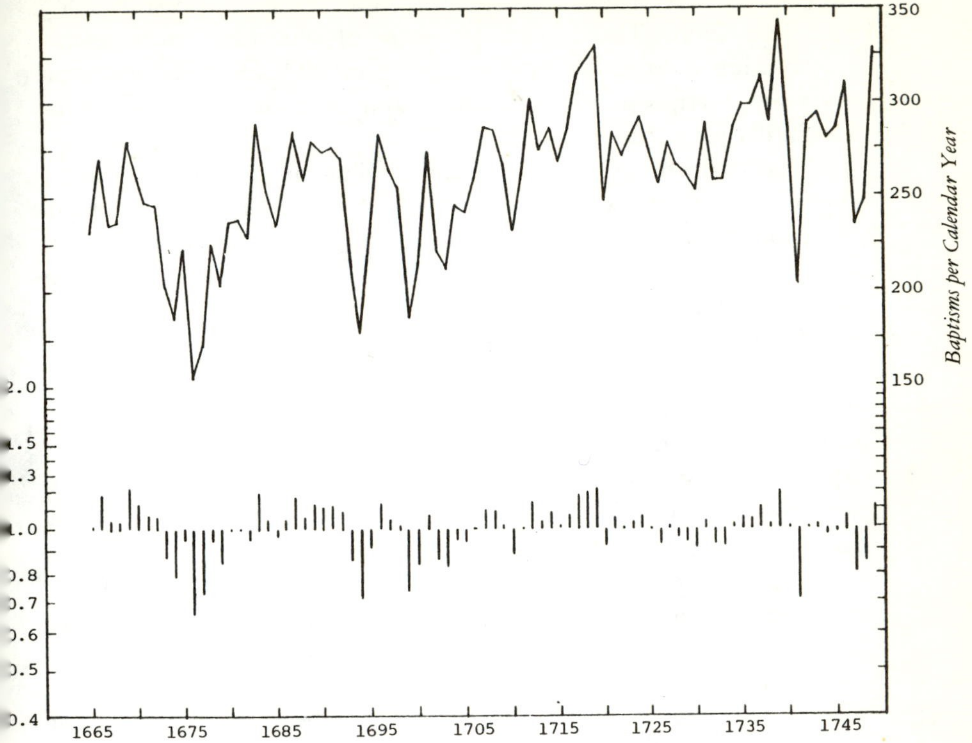

perienced a sharp increase in the number of deaths show a diminished number of baptisms.

Yet childbearing was never as severely reduced as mortality was increased. While the deadliest years, 1676, 1694, or 1747, cost twice the normal number of people their lives, the worst birth losses were about one third in 1676 (to an index value of 0.66) and less than 30 percent in 1694, 1699, and 1741. Since the direction of change differed – a crisis causes more deaths but fewer births – it would take a loss of 50 percent of normal births roughly to equal a doubling of deaths. The crises of the late seventeenth and eighteenth century never reduced childbearing by that amount.[4]

As we have done for production, prices, and mortality, so we can order the periods of reduced childbearing by severity and cause. The pattern we see in childbearing is different from that of mortality. Harvest failure appears to have been more important than war as a force reducing births. Obviously, the two great combination crises, with

177

their peaks in the Dutch War (1676) and the War of the League of Augsburg (1694), maintained their position as the great destroyers of the population. They constitute two of the four most severe childbearing crises in the years beginning in 1665. However, we must order simple crises, war, harvest failure, and epidemic disease differently for childbearing than for death.

The contrast between war and harvest failure, in demographic terms, appears when we examine the 1690's and 1700's. If we look at childbearing first, we see that the worst childbearing losses occurred in 1694 and 1699. Although war and harvest failure combined to cause one, and a simple harvest failure caused the other, they were of roughly equal severity. In the next decade, the two periods of reduced childbearing, 1703 and 1710, also had different causes but both reached the same order of magnitude. When we consider mortality, we see that the parity no longer exists. The worst mortality coincided with the combined catastrophe of 1691-1695; the harvest failure of 1699 and the war of 1701-1706 had less, but roughly equal severity; and the harvest failure of 1710 caused no excess deaths at all.

The conclusions drawn for the complex years from 1690 to 1710 can be reached again by considering the 1740's. In that decade, the greatest mortality occurred at the end of the decade, when the events of the War of the Austrian Succession overwhelmed the Basse-Meuse. Childbearing behaved otherwise. The most severe loss of baptisms took place not at the end of the decade, at the time of the war, but at the beginning of the decade, in 1741, when prices were high and food supplies short.

Our general conclusion must be this: combined war and inadequate food supplies reduced childbearing the most; reduced food supplies alone were second; war was third in rank; and epidemic disease, like the plague epidemic of 1667-1670, hardly affected childbearing at all.

The fact that the smallest number of baptisms, in 1699, followed the worst harvest of the seventeenth century, when prices were at their highest in Liège, confirms the relationship between childbearing and changes in the food supply. We can test this hypothesis by studying the statistical relationship between baptisms and deaths on the one hand, and the price of rye on the other. There should be a positive relationship between prices and the number of deaths, and a negative relationship between prices and the number of baptisms.[5] We use prices here, rather than production, because prices are a better indicator of the amount of food available for consumption.

As Table 8.2 indicated, a better food supply clearly reduced deaths

Ill. 8. The Cruelties Committed by the French, No. 1, by Romeyn de Hooghe (1673)

and increased births. The important relationship appears when we compare the magnitude of the absolute value of the correlation coefficients. The relationship between baptisms and prices is much stronger than the relationship between deaths and prices. If we correlate, not baptisms, but conceptions with prices, the relationship between prices and childbearing is even stronger.[6]

Table 8.2   Correlations Between Childbearing, Mortality and The Price of Rye in Liège*

Deaths	(Harvest Year)	.1672	(.037)
Baptisms	(Harvest Year)	-.4847	(.001)
Conceptions	(Harvest Year)	-.5749	(.001)

* Figures are Pearson correlation coefficients computed for annual index values for the variables shown. Data may be found in Tables 7.1, 7.2, 8.1 and Appendix C. The figures in parenthesis are significance levels.

The significance of these correlations is not that war failed to reduce childbearing, but that it acted primarily by restricting available food supplies. The differences between childbearing and mortality, and their susceptibility to different kinds of external forces, reflect the complex processes controlling each, and the peculiar characteristics of war. It should not surprise us that disease associated with armies should have a profound impact on the number of civilian deaths during years of military action and occupation, and that the same force (other than the role of war in reducing food supplies) would not reduce childbearing as dramatically or as unidirectionally. The impact of war on childbearing, far more than its impact on mortality, was indirect.

We can confirm the strong relationship between childbearing and food supplies by examining the distribution of baptisms and conceptions through the year (Figure 8.3 and Table 8.3). The distribution shows that it is conceptions that best reflect the year's seasonal conditions. The distribution of conceptions essentially reverses the yearly distribution of deaths.[7] Each year, the annual peak in conceptions took place in June, after building up in April and May. In July it began to fall, resuming the April level, and by August the number of conceptions had nearly reached the floor it assumed until the next spring. The year's low point in terms of conceptions occurred in September, October, and November, and is about ten percent less than the level of the late summer and winter months, August and December through March. The annual peak in conceptions, in May through July, coincides with the low point for deaths. Likewise, the months of fewest concep-

180

Table 8.3   *Monthly Distribution of Childbearing (Calendar Year Baptisms)*

	Month of Baptism												
	JAN	FEB	MAR	APR	MAY	JUN	JUL	AUG	SEP	OCT	NOV	DEC	TOTAL
All Years 1620-1749													
Number	2,958	3,076	3,578	2,956	2,557	2,258	2,208	2,205	2,414	2,423	2,402	2,375	31,410
Proportion	.094	.098	.114	.094	.081	.072	.070	.070	0.77	0.77	.076	.076	
19 Years of Low Childbearing*													
Number	461	460	597	477	401	338	311	345	377	351	363	354	4,853
Proportion	.095	.095	.123	.099	.083	.070	.064	.071	.078	.073	.075	.073	
	APR	MAY	JUN	JUL	AUG	SEP	OCT	NOV	DEC	JAN	FEB	MAR	
	Month of Conception												

* 1673-1679, 1693-1695, 1699, 1700, 1702-1705, 1741, 1747-1748

Figure 8.2   Monthly Distribution of Childbearing

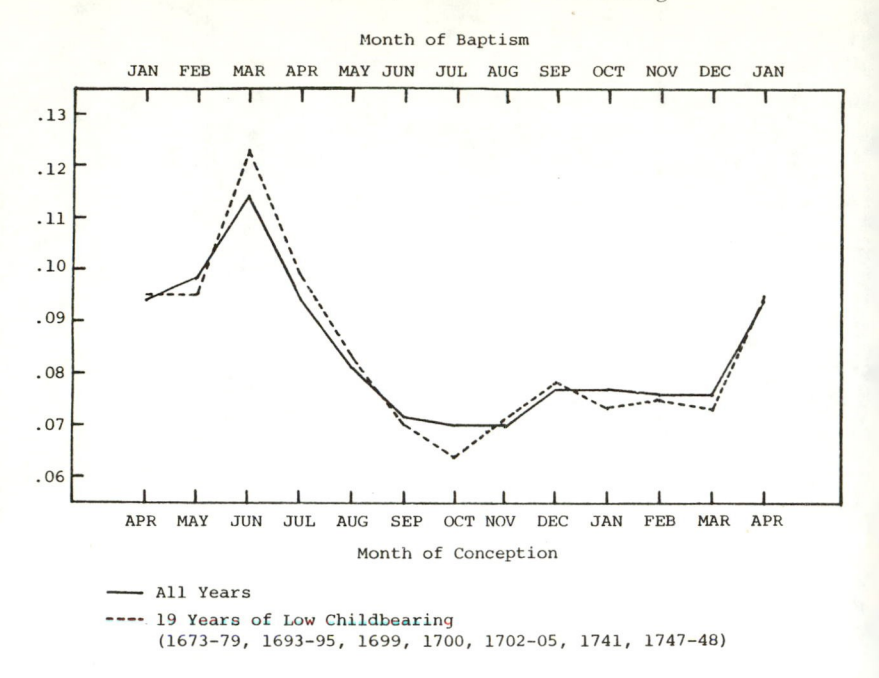

Month of Baptism

Month of Conception

—— All Years

---- 19 Years of Low Childbearing
(1673–79, 1693–95, 1699, 1700, 1702–05, 1741, 1747–48)

tions, September through November, coincide with the months of greatest mortality.

Surprisingly, the pattern described above changed little in years of reduced childbearing. Table 8.2 also includes the seasonal distribution of baptisms and conceptions for nineteen years when Basse-Mosan mothers gave birth to relatively few children.[8] The pattern experienced in those years differed insignificantly from the pattern for all years. The slight difference suggests that although harvest failure and war disrupted the normal pattern of conception and birth, the disruption distributed itself more or less evenly throughout the year.

Breakdowns in the chain of food supply and war (although to a much lesser extent) periodically reduced childbearing in the Basse-Meuse. Through what mechanisms did harvest failure and war reduce the number of baptisms in some years? Why did war reduce childbearing less than did harvest failure? Three likely mechanisms show what reduced baptisms. They are delayed births (or prolonged inter-birth intervals); the indirect consequences of mortality; and delayed marriages. Each contributed to lost baptisms, although hardly equally.

II. Delayed Later Births

Delayed later (or non-first) births made the largest contribution to reduced childbearing in the Basse-Meuse. These are births which actually took place, but only after a longer than normal interval. The interval between births is a crucial component of a non-contracepting population's reproductive behavior; in such a population, a family's total fertility (the number of children ultimately born) directly relates to the duration of the marriage (the time between marriage and either menopause or the death of one spouse, whichever comes earlier) and the interval between births. For two marriages that last twenty years, where one has five children in ten years, and the other four, the first family will have ten children, the second eight. Yet the difference in mean intervals is only one-half year. First intervals, those between marriage and first births, rather than between two births, are usually much shorter than later intervals, and are related to other factors. We will consider them together with marriage, later in this chapter.

For later births, in years of low childbearing, the mean interval should have been longer than in all years or in all normal years, if some births or conceptions were delayed. Since it is likely that conceptions were delayed, the year following each period of low childbearing is also included, to find the intervals ending with births conceived during the last year of each period of low childbearing. The data for this study of interbirth intervals will be derived from the reconstitution results for the population of the parish of Wandre.[9]

To make the problem concrete, we can construct a convenient, if somewhat oversimplified, case. We can imagine a couple married in January, 1686. They had their first child after one year, in January, 1687, and then later children every 30 months.[10] Their second child would have been born in July, 1689, and their third in January, 1692. After their third child, however, the crisis of the mid-1690's developed and for reasons we need not yet discuss, their fourth child was born, not after an interval of 30 months, but after 42 months. Rather than being born in July, 1694, as we might have expected, it was born in July, 1695. This would reduce by one the total births for the 1694 calendar year; had this occurrence been repeated for many couples, as is likely, it would partially explain the drop in the number of baptisms observed in the Basse-Mosan parishes.

We can bring this example to life with two Wandre couples, Henry Charle and his wife Anne Thompson (women in the Basse-Meuse kept

their maiden names after marriage), and Leonard Bader and his wife Isabelle Cocquette. Both couples had their first child in 1687, and proceeded thereafter to have children on a more-or-less regular basis. Henry Charle and his wife had their next three children an average of eighteen months apart, while the Baders had their next three an average of twenty months apart. Each was due to have a child in 1693-1694. Yet they did not: the Charles had theirs in 1695, after a four-year wait, and the Baders delayed even longer, waiting 64 months, until 1697. Their experiences, which unequivocally show how war and other catastrophes delayed births, are presented in Table 8.4.

Table 8.4   Two Examples of Delayed Births

Birth No.	Henry Charle and Anne Thompson			Leonard Bader and Isabelle Cocquette		
	Year of Birth	Interval (Months)	Age of Mother	Year of Birth	Interval (Months)	Age of Mother
1	1687	10	31.2	1687	0*	28.4
2	1688	13	32.2	1688	15	29.7
3	1690	24	34.2	1690	20	31.3
4	1691	18	35.7	1692	24	33.4
5	1695	48	39.8	1697	64	38.7
6	1699	40	43.1	1701	44	42.3
7				1704	36	45.3

*First children (twins) born ten days after marriage

Date of Marriage: 2 May 1686
Age of Bride: 30 years
Age of Groom: 28 years

Date of Marriage: 10 May 1687
Age of Bride: 28 years
Age of Groom: 35 years

The evidence from reconstituted Wandre tends to confirm the hypothesis; delayed conceptions or births caused temporary declines in baptisms in years of crisis, as evidenced by prolonged birth intervals. In the period 1670-1759, we have intervals for 2,314 later (that is, not first) baptisms for complete families in Wandre; the mean interval length was 2.62 years or about 31.5 months.[11] We can consider the intervals ending in 25 years of low childbearing, in or after the mid 1670's, the early and late 1690's, 1702-1705, 1741-1742, and 1747-1749.[12] For those 25 years (there are 558 intervals) the mean interval was 2.81 years (nearly 34 months), 3 months longer than the mean for all the normal

184

years – defining normal as being any year not included in the 25 years here defined as having low numbers of baptisms.[13] For those 65 years of normal childbearing, the mean interval was 2.56 years or slightly less than 31 months.[14]

The significance of this 3-month mean delay will be more obvious if we recall that it is a *mean* delay; that it can be conceived of as a delay of 6 months among half the intervals, or one year among one-fourth. Such a delay is extremely large when we repeat that the greatest loss of baptisms was only about 35 percent, and that there are other causes of reduced childbearing besides delayed births.[15]

We can conclude from these data that for all births after the first, the mean interval increased at least 2.5 months in years of low childbearing. Delayed births account for a large proportion of the reduced childbearing in periods of crisis surrounding military activity and harvest failure. Moreover, we can add that this conclusion is not essentially changed when we consider each interval rank (second children, third children, and so on), or when we consider women's age. Delays took place among nearly all women.

III. Explaining Delayed Baptisms

What caused delayed baptisms? The answer to this question will help to explain how harvest crises influenced childbearing, and why war had less of an impact. The answer will be at best complex and contradictory. For one thing, explaining something in its absence is a difficult task. Seventeenth-century priests, the authors of parish registers, had little or no understanding of patterns of childbearing. They could not judge changing fertility patterns, as they could excess deaths.

Most conceptions were delayed, not by human choice, nor by the direct influence of wartime disruption, but by physiological imperatives. As a result of biological responses discovered in recent research, we know that nutrition has a powerful impact on childbearing: many women were physically infertile in time of famine.[16] Moreover, miscarriages would have been more common among women who were poorly fed, further reducing childbearing.[17]

Famine infertility is the result of the inability of women to ovulate when the amount of fat in their bodies drops below a certain level. That would have happened to the women of the Basse-Meuse when, as we saw in earlier chapters, agriculture was disrupted, food prices skyrocketed, and troops took their resources, in money and food. Most of

the historical research that led to the identification and verification of this phenomenon relied on the fertility experience of European women during the two World Wars of this century. In twentieth-century Europe, famine has been associated only with the extraordinary disruption and destruction of wartime; otherwise, harvest failure so severe that large populations are hungry is impossible. In the seventeenth century that was not the case. Many people were chronically hungry. Harvests frequently failed and when several followed repeatedly, the number hungry and the suffering of the chronically hungry increased. When war added its murderous disruption to even moderate harvest failure (as it did in the mid-1670's), the worst combinations of death, starvation, and loss of fertility coincided to deplete the population.

Inadequate nutrition not only prevented conceptions, it also reduced childbearing by causing miscarriages. Stated simply, a full-term pregnancy requires a substantial amount of energy (provided by food), to support the development of the fetus. When severe food shortages occur, many initially viable conceptions are lost to miscarriages and spontaneous abortions. Thus, we can explain at least some delayed baptisms as lost pregnancies rather than delayed conceptions. The interval between a stillbirth or miscarriage and a live birth is almost always shorter than the interval between two live births; thus, we might confuse the occurrence of two conceptions, one of which ended prematurely and without a baptism, with a single delayed conception.

Amenorrhea of famine and increased miscarriages were by no means the only causes of reduced childbearing in time of crisis in the seventeenth century. However, they suggest simple physical explanations for the reduction in childbearing that accompanied food shortages. If we add to that the general disruption of life, the price people paid in terms of uncertainty and anxiety, as well as in deprivation of their lives and property, we need not wonder that they conceived and bore as many as one-third fewer children in combined war and food shortage or in times of extremely severe harvest failure alone.

It would be wrong, however, to exclude any discussion of other possible explanations for delayed births. In particular we must address the issue of conscious contraception. Did it play a role in limiting conceptions during crises in the Basse-Meuse? People limit the size of their family when they recognize that they will benefit from having fewer children, through the ability to concentrate their resources on a smaller number of children. In general, this motivation, the necessary element for family limitation, is not known to have reached the western

European peasantry before French peasants began to limit the size of their families at the end of the eighteenth century.[18] We have no evidence that the citizens of the Basse-Meuse chose to limit their fertility in the seventeenth and eighteenth centuries. It is unlikely that they saw high prices or military occupations as so extraordinary that they should limit their families. By the time a child conceived in the midst of a crisis was born, the crisis would very likely have been over, and the material situation much improved. Given our knowledge of seventeenth-century attitudes toward children, once the crisis was over, an additional child would have been considered a benefit, rather than a liability.[19]

Another unlikely cause of reduced conceptions is a significant loss of husbands, away at war while their wives stayed behind. In general, and except for those areas in Europe, like Switzerland, known to have sent large numbers of men to war, the modern conception of wartime mobilization, with a severely reduced supply of adult males, did not operate before the French Revolution. A few men of the Basse-Meuse were soldiers, but they were either men without families, or men who took their families with them. Few would have departed temporarily, leaving a family behind.

While war took few men away from their homes, and cost the people of the Basse-Meuse fewer lost baptisms than harvest failure, it was not without some effect. One way it may have acted was through the indirect consequences of mortality on childbearing.[20] When birth rates are constant or even declining (as they were when intervals increased and conceptions were delayed) childbearing is related directly to the number of married women in the childbearing ages within the community. When war reduced the number of married women in the childbearing ages, they bore fewer children.

The role of mortality as an indirect brake on childbearing is subject to several limitations. The deaths of married adults reduced the number of conceptions at the height of the crisis. But the recovery from that decline would have been rather slow, as widows and widowers remarried, and new men and women reached marriageable and childbearing ages. However, reductions in childbearing were less severe than increases in adult mortality, and recovery from those reductions was quicker. Furthermore, we can contradict a hypothesis of a strong influence of mortality on childbearing by looking at the plague epidemic of 1668-1669. The plague epidemic caused severe mortality and it cannot be confused with a subsistence crisis caused by war or bad

weather. Food was not in short supply. If fertility was indirectly tied to all mortality crises, childbearing in the years 1668 to 1670 should have been significantly reduced. In none of those three years, however, did the number of children baptized decrease significantly.[21] Nor, if we look at monthly or quarterly totals, did the months of catastrophic mortality, September, 1668, to January, 1669, coincide with a major shortage of conceptions. We must see mortality's indirect impact on fertility as marginal.

IV. Marriages and First Births

While war's impact may have been marginal or ambiguous in other areas, our examination of marriage will show one sure way that war acted to limit childbearing. War delayed marriage, but it did not altogether stop the people of the Basse-Meuse from marrying. If they put off marriage during the rigors of wartime, their confidence in the region and their futures brought them to the altar in surprisingly large numbers as soon as the wars ended.

In earlier chapters we discussed the disruption and dislocation that struck Basse-Mosan life whenever war occurred. Given that disruption and the regular reversal of economic fortunes we can easily understand that marriage might be delayed until more secure times returned, so that the young people could support themselves and their soon-to-arrive children. Elsewhere in this chapter we argued that families, once formed, lacked the motivation necessary to limit family size consciously. That absence of motivation is not evident when dealing with marriage; the late ages at which people in the Basse-Meuse married for the first time, and the fairly high occurrence of premarital conceptions, suggest that marriages were probably postponed until people could form a viable economic household. The economic hardships which coincided with early modern demographic crises, and especially war, provided precisely the kind of conditions that made the creation of a viable household temporarily impossible.

Although Basse-Mosan marriage registers offer special problems, we can get an idea of the ways war delayed marriage by examining marriage in Wandre. We can count all the marriages of residents of Wandre, even though some of those marriages took place in other parishes. Table 8.5 presents the annual number of marriages in the Wandre register from the beginning of marriage registration, in 1679, until 1759.

188

Table 8.5   Wandre Marriages (Calendar Years)

Year	Marriages	Year	Marriages	Year	Marriages
1679	9	1706	14	1733	15
1680	10	1707	15	1734	9
1681	13	1708	12	1735	15
1682	14	1709	6	1736	18
1683	19	1710	16	1737	12
1684	12	1711	17	1738	16
1685	10	1712	12	1739	12
1686	13	1713	14	1740	6
1687	11	1714	16	1741	10
1688	5	1715	20	1742	17
1689	15	1716	21	1743	15
1690	15	1717	15	1744	10
1691	14	1718	21	1745	7
1692	9	1719	12	1746	7
1693	8	1720	14	1747	7
1694	9	1721	12	1748	15
1695	22	1722	8	1749	27
1696	16	1723	18	1750	15
1697	7	1724	15	1751	11
1698	15	1725	9	1752	13
1699	9	1726	15	1753	13
1700	12	1727	19	1754	10
1701	15	1728	11	1755	19
1702	11	1729	14	1756	17
1703	12	1730	9	1757	11
1704	13	1731	16	1758	11
1705	12	1732	17	1759	13

Source: AEL PR Wandre, 3,4

The Wandre marriages, because of their small numbers, provide only limited information about the relationship between war, economic hardship, and delayed marriages. But there are relatively small numbers of marriages (less than ten per year for several years) in 1692-1694 and in 1745-1747, when we would expect war's impact to have been the most serious. Two other conclusions can be drawn from these data. First, the marriages that did not take place at the height of the crisis were simply being delayed, since the two periods of marriage depression were followed immediately by the years when most marriages took place. Those individuals who postponed their marriages during 1692-1694 married in 1695, and those who postponed in 1745-1747 married in 1748 and 1749. When we compute the mean number of marriages by

decade, all the decades but one have a mean between 12 and 13 marriages per year. This confirms the existence of a regular pattern of marriage which was sometimes delayed. Even the one decade that differed, 1711-1720, adds to our understanding. In the first true decade of prosperity after four decades of wars and other hardships, an average of 16 marriages took place each year. Clearly better times temporarily increased the opportunities for marriage.

The second conclusion concerns the relationship between marriage and European-wide harvest failures. While the well-known periods of high prices and poor production coincided with relatively small numbers of marriages (see 1699, 1709, and 1740), they did not contribute as many delayed marriages as war or the combination of the two. As we saw earlier when we considered production and mortality, the economic and human consequences of high prices were not nearly as severe as those of war, nor as severe as some historians have led us to believe.

We will better understand the delays that marriage underwent if we examine the ages at which men and women married at Wandre. Everyone in the Basse-Meuse married late in life. The mean age at first marriage for all Wandre marriages from the first register entry in 1678 until the end of 1739 was 28.05 years for men. Women were only slightly younger when they married: 27.99 years. In general, it appears that those ages were increasing as the eighteenth century progressed, although the trend for men is not without some ambivalence. These data, in the form of decennial means, are presented in Figure 8.4 and Table 8.6.

Table 8.6   Ages at Marriage and Birth of First Child (By Decade)

| Years | Mean Ages at First Marriage | | Mean Ages of Women at the Birth of Their First Child (First Marriages Only) |
	Men	Women	Age
1680-1689	27.65 (43)	26.98 (40)	27.90 (33)
1690-1699	28.38 (56)	28.46 (49)	29.22 (43)
1700-1709	27.46 (48)	27.95 (62)	28.50 (47)
1710-1719	28.66 (75)	28.01 (90)	27.81 (75)
1720-1729	27.64 (62)	27.99 (79)	28.16 (62)
1730-1739	28.31 (67)	28.19 (67)	29.18 (66)
1678-1739	28.054 (353)	27.994 (388)	28.449 (326)

Figures in parenthesis are the number of ages on which the mean is based.

190

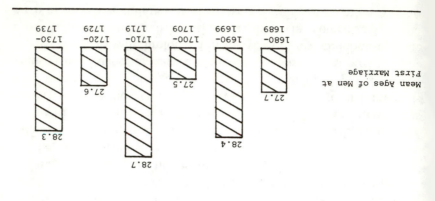

Mean Ages of Men at
First Marriage

1680- 1690- 1700- 1710- 1720- 1730-
1689 -1699 1709 1719 1729 1739

27.7 28.4 27.5 28.7 27.6 28.3

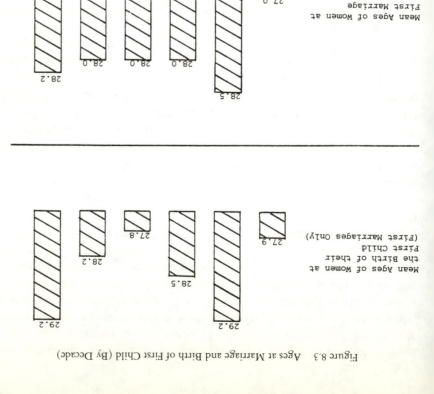

Mean Ages of Women at
First Marriage

27.0 28.5 28.0 28.0 28.0 28.2

Mean Ages of Women at
the Birth of their
First Child
(First Marriages Only)

27.9 29.2 28.5 27.8 28.2 29.2

Figure 8.3   Ages at Marriage and Birth of First Child (By Decade)

Decennial mean ages at marriage indicate the extent of delayed marriage in times of hardship. The worst conditions of any decade considered occurred during 1690-1699. In the middle of the decade, warfare and food shortage combined and at the end of the decade a severe food shortage occurred. Responding to those conditions the decade 1690-1699 presents very high ages at marriage for both men and women, at least one-half year later than the following decade, 1700-1709.[22] War and other causes of economic hardship surely caused delays in marriage, although the delays were not excessive. Marriages were not eliminated, only postponed.

In addition to our direct interest in delayed marriages as a measure of disruption in the Basse-Meuse in wartime, they are also of interest because delayed marriages contributed in a very direct way to reduced childbearing. If people delayed marriage in times of economic distress, the first children born to those marriages would have been delayed. First children constituted more than twenty percent of all children born to complete families in Wandre.[23] The delay of a significant portion of all the first children expected in a given year thus contributed significantly to all lost baptisms.

While the delay in ages of marriage indicates the extent to which delayed marriage reduced childbearing, we can see the same phenomenon by examining the age at which women gave birth to their first child. For all complete families in which the wife was not previously married, and where the first child was born prior to 1740 (the data after 1740 are problematic and make analysis difficult), the mean age of mothers was 28.45 years. For the decade of the 1690's, it was at least three-fourths of a year higher, 29.22 years, and significantly higher than any decade except 1730-1739 (see Figure 8.4 and Table 8.6). If we look at the age at first birth for fourteen years of low childbearing, again the figure is relatively high, 29.02 years, 0.57 years later than the mean age of women for first births in all years.[24]

The age of women at the birth of their first child is, of course, influenced by both the age of the woman at her marriage, and the interval between marriage and the birth. The first birth interval was subject to delay independent of marriage delays. If first birth intervals were significantly prolonged in times of low childbearing, that would reduce the influence of delayed marriages on delayed first births.

First intervals were prolonged in the years of low childbearing, but those delays account for little of the delay shown by women's ages at the birth of their first children. Women were roughly seven months (0.56

years) older at the birth of their first child in the years of reduced childbearing than they were in all years. First intervals (not including only children), on the other hand, grew by less than two months (0.15 years) in those years, from an average for all years from 1678 to 1759 of 1.16 years to one for nineteen years of low childbearing of 1.31.[25] Prolonged first intervals explain roughly one-fourth of the delay in an woman's age at the birth of her first child; this confirms our conclusion that delayed marriages caused most delayed first births.

*   *   *

We have conclusive evidence of major childbearing losses in the Basse-Meuse, just as we saw mortality increase. Childbearing and mortality, however, each responded differently. For mortality, all of Meuvret's three categories of crisis — war, harvest failure, and epidemic disease — affected the demographic process.[26] When two combined (as they did in the 1670's), the population was severely depleted.

Childbearing, however, was less sensitive to war than to harvest failure, and hardly felt epidemic disease. The delay in conceptions, largely caused by women's inability to ovulate under starvation conditions, accounts for most of the gap between the actual number of baptisms in years of low childbearing, and the normal number of baptisms. That is why harvest conditions had such a tremendous effect on childbearing. War's impact on childbearing was indirect, either by disrupting the food supply, or by creating such difficult economic conditions that people delayed getting married. Delayed marriages contributed less to lost childbearing, yet their impact was not inconsiderable. Of Meuvret's crises, only the secondary consequences of mortality seem to have had little or no effect on childbearing.

Taken together, the responses of mortality and childbearing to war, famine, and epidemic slowed population growth in the early modern Basse-Meuse — a growth that was certainly possible under the prevailing economic conditions. We can measure the pace of population loss in these years of crisis. We established in Chapter VII that the average mortality was 48 percent greater than normal in the worst years we measured. We can do the same for childbearing. There are eleven years between 1665 and 1749 in which the index fell below 0.86; of these, the mean value is 0.77, suggesting a 23 percent drop in childbearing. While we must keep in mind that these conclusions are only approximate (because they are based on rather small numbers of cases) we can still

draw an important conclusion. The losses we have attributed to severe mortality and reduced childbearing are considerable, but they are not the kind that led to depopulation.

Given normal ancien régime western European crude birth and death rates (deaths slightly above 30/1,000, and births around 35/1,000, with a normal net gain of 3 to 5/1,000), the crises experienced by the Basse-Meuse would lead to a net population loss of 2 percent per year or less.[27] This rate of population loss would take 20 years to equal the composite German population loss in the Thirty Years' War, for example (40 percent). Even in the worst possible cases, such as the combined Basse-Mosan crises of 1676 or 1694, the net population loss was only about 4 percent per year, calling for 10 years of catastrophic losses to equal the German experience. The conditions needed to create such a consistent loss of population over a long period of time simply did not exist in the Basse-Meuse in the seventeenth century. Crises lasted a year or two or three – in the worst period, the 1690's, six years out of a decade – but then they were over, and the population rebuilt. We will return to the reasons why the Basse-Meuse suffered such moderate losses, relative to other war-torn regions, in the final chapter. For now, a simple comment on what the losses meant for the region itself will suffice.

The range of losses suffered by the Basse-Meuse in wartime or when harvests failed convincingly explain the demographic downturn the region suffered between 1670 and 1700. We saw in Chapter VI how the region's early seventeenth-century growth slacked off around 1670. The region experienced a general stability characterized by rapid oscillations between slight declines and modest gains. The 1670's and 1690's were periods of losses, on the whole, while the 1680's saw a modest recovery. These changes can easily be explained by alternating periods of the modest losses (2 to 4 percent per year) which characterized the Basse-Meuse in times of hardship, with the very slight gains (under 1 percent per year) that the region experienced in normal times). There were enough bad years for the region to slow down its growth to zero between 1670 and 1700, but not enough to keep it from growing again rather dramatically after 1700.

After 1700, as we might expect, the consequences of war and other crises seem to have lessened. The War of the Spanish Succession, fought in the first few years of the eighteenth century, left only a very slight mark on the Basse-Meuse. Childbearing decreased and mortality increased, but only by small amounts. By this time, the destructive impact

194

of war, at least, seems to have been lessened as we expected. While the later War of the Austrian Succession was more destructive, it was very brief; hostilities ended in the Basse-Meuse, as in the other theaters of the war, before any long-term damage could be done. The eighteenth century, unlike the seventeenth century, was essentially a century of growth, relatively unhindered by the dramatic consequences of war and other catastrophes.

Chapter IX

The Impact of War in Perspective

"This year, we have been tested in an astonishing fashion by sickness, war, famine, and fire. First, a violent plague struck the village during the months of June and July, taking seventeen victims. Immediately afterwards, war unexpectedly came to us. The army of the King of Spain commanded by the Marquis of Aytona constructed a fort at Navagne, near the Meuse. Then, when it appeared they were going to put siege to Maastricht, they camped, some at Montenaken, others at Lanaeken, and a large part of the army here at Emael. The Marquis of Salada lodged here with three legions or regiments, one of infantry and two of cavalry. They behaved worse than barbarously: they destroyed everything; they cut trees, completely demolished many houses, and trampled whatever grain they could not steal, not even leaving enough to appease the hunger of the poor farmers. For that reason, we did not collect the tithe this year.

"My house, situated beside the cemetery, suffered an equally terrible destruction. I, Antoine Henrice, curé of Emael, had hardly recovered from the contagious malady that had struck me a short time before. I was not even able to leave the house without exposing myself to great danger, nor flee the impertinent Spanish soldiers as I would have wished. They hunted everywhere for food, straw, and other materials in order to construct their barracks. I was belatedly aided by one of their chaplains; together we chased them away as best we could. I offered lodging in my house to some soldiers, but it was in vain: they were afraid they would catch my illness. In the end, several who were more adventuresome did so, bringing their horses and coming to stay in my house, which they treated like their own and preserved from harm.

"I began my sickness on 20 July; the Spanish arrived at Emael on 2 August and retired on 8 September, the feast of the birth of the Holy Virgin, which fell on a Friday."[1]

The curé of Emael, writing in his diary in 1634, tells us of the four horsemen of his seventeenth-century apocalypse: sickness, war, famine, and fire. He was not wrong to believe that his parishioners in that one year felt virtually all the disruptive forces that his era had to offer; we know of little more they could have suffered. In earlier chapters I

evaluated the overall consequences of one of these scourges – war – in a variety of contexts. Here, I want to put war's impact in perspective, by showing its importance for the region's economic structure and prosperity.

I. War and Other Crises

Historians have long considered war one of the causes of the demographic and economic crises that they said periodically struck European communities, especially in the seventeenth century. And indeed many of the forces associated with military action in the Basse-Meuse had symptoms similar to the other two crisis-producing agents that were at work in the ancien régime: bad weather (which led to bad harvests) and epidemic disease. How was war different? I will begin by eliminating epidemics from our discussion, because major outbreaks of disease not caused by war or intensified by poor food supplies were almost unknown in the Basse-Meuse after 1600. To distinguish between the remaining two, I will compare the periods of hardship in the Basse-Meuse with an exemplar, in this case Pierre Goubert's description of the seventeenth-century French subsistence crisis:

"The true demographic crisis, as studied principally in northern, eastern, and central France, where the population is densest and grain is the standard crop, stems from a series of climatic accidents (usually high summer rainfall) in a given socio-economic context. Successive harvests have been poor and have not stored well; provisions have given out; the price of grain, and therefore of bread – the basic foodstuffs – has gone on rising, generally doubling, often tripling and quadrupling. Owing far more to the high cost than to the scarcity of food, the shortage seems to trigger off "mortality" and its companion phenomena, so that these seem to derive from rocketing prices, and do in fact derive from them to a great extent. Most people's incomes have not followed prices – quite the contrary – and the common people have turned hungrily to inferior or contaminated foodstuffs (dubious kinds of flour, rotten meat, grass, etc.). Epidemic diseases of the digestive system break out and are spread by beggars, pedlars, soldiers, and vermin. The incidence of starvation is far higher than was once thought."[2]

Many of the processes Goubert describes were at work in the Basse-Meuse. Prices rose more than the actual food supply warranted, and contributed more than the food supply to the demographic crisis. Nevertheless, the Basse-Mosan experience differed in other ways. Wet weather had little negative influence on agricultural and demographic processes, although it did affect prices. Hot, dry weather was a far more

197

potent force. Goubert also understimates the direct impact of food shortages on childbearing: high prices reduced the number of children born without the intervening action of high mortality. War's impact itself makes the Basse-Mosan experience significant and different. The presence of soldiers could set off an epidemic despite adequate food supplies and not excessive prices. These wartime epidemics killed considerably more people than the crises associated with harvest failure or high prices.

War and bad weather affected the people of the Basse-Meuse differently by the *intensity* and the *duration* of the hardships they caused. They differed in intensity in this fashion: while both war and reduced food supplies inflated prices, food supply problems caused greater inflation. Similarly, while war led to more adult deaths than did harvest failure, the situation was reversed for childbearing. Food supplies and poor economic conditions, not military action, restricted the number of children born. One might claim that war and bad weather produced equivalent crises, differing only in intensity, and that one of them was always more intense. That was not the case: the hardships differed in many ways. Nevertheless, one way to understand the differences is to consider whether war or bad weather affected each of the economic and demographic areas of life studied in this book more intensely. Table 9.1 demonstrates that intensity alone does not permit us conclusively to rank the two main causes of hardship.

Table 9.1   *War and Bad Weather: Relative Intensity of their Impact*

War Greater on	Equal Impact on	Bad Weather* Greater on
Mortality	Agricultural Production	Childbearing
Marriage		Prices
Rural Industry		
Agricultural Investment		

* or consequent poor food supplies

On the other hand, the duration of war unequivocally shows just how serious it was for the lives of the people of the Basse-Meuse. Seldom did the effects of bad weather last more than two years without some recovery. In the mid-1670's, or 1739-1740, bad weather wore itself out in about two years; in the 1690's there were two periods of bad

198

weather, centered on 1693-1694 and 1698-1699, but even then a few years of relatively good weather slipped in between. Military presence allowed no such respite. The intense military action that struck the Basse-Meuse in the 1630's brought continued hardship from 1632 to 1638; in the Dutch War of the 1670's, the French occupation lasted from 1672 to 1679. The War of the League of Augsburg seriously affected the region from 1689 to at least 1694. Such long-lasting difficulties, with year after year of loss and deprivation, depleted both the personal and material resources of the people of the Basse-Meuse.

The intensity of harvest failure and the long duration of military action sometimes combined to create the greatest hardships for the people of the Basse-Meuse. This is among my most dramatic findings: the people suffered most when war combined with bad weather sufficiently severe to reduce agricultural production. Their farms ceased to be productive. The price of food skyrocketed. People died in greater numbers and reproduced themselves at reduced rates. Thus, the greatest catastophes of the seventeenth and early eighteenth centuries took place in the mid-1670's and early 1690's, when both war and bad weather conspired to devastate the lives of the people of the Basse-Meuse. One such juncture following another, even after an interval of nearly two decades, significantly retarded the process of recovery.

People's perceptions of hardship also show war's great impact. While there is a considerable literature of climatic lament and amazement, it is not nearly as emotional or as extensive as that pertaining to war. There are no novels about hot or rainy summers to equal *Simplicissimus,* there are no paintings of floods or hailstorms to equal Callot's *Misères et Malheurs de la Guerre* or the other illustrations in this book. War was feared by all, like the great plagues of the late middle ages; dread and a feeling of powerlessness must have overtaken everyone.

Finally, only wartime crises, with their incredible duration, could modify the region's pattern of economic and demographic growth. Only war could produce the one extended halt in Basse-Mosan prosperity, between 1670 and 1700. Epidemics and bad weather might produce a year or two of difficulties, and a few years of recovery, but they could not turn around the region's generally favorable economic and demographic climate.[3] The dynamic mixed economy of the region around Liège probably explains this phenomenon. A bad harvest caused by bad weather might tip the balance in a locale with a poor or single-product economy; it could not do so in the Basse-Meuse.

War had a far more significant impact on the lives of the people of

the Basse-Meuse than did simple epidemics and harvest failures. However, I wish now to turn to why war in the Basse-Meuse and other regions produced such different results. We will see that war was itself less important than certain structural and secular characteristics of the Basse-Mosan society and economy. The character of crises did not determine the state of the economy, as Meuvret thought when he wrote in 1946 that repeated subsistence crises caused the French downturn in the seventeenth century. Rather, the state of the economy determined the character of the crises. We can turn the original notion of early modern subsistence crises on its head.

II. Why They Stayed

The experiences of the Basse-Meuse differed from those of other regions which were frequently fought over in the sixteenth, seventeenth, and eighteenth centuries. This was especially the case for overall demographic consequences. While other places, most notably Germany, lost population in wartime, the Basse-Meuse merely stopped growing. And while the agricultural sector of the economy stabilized along with the population, the growth of the heavy industrial sector (which boomed in wartime) compensated for this slowdown, at least in part. It will be worthwhile to explain why conditions in the Basse-Meuse differed from those in Germany and elsewhere. I will argue that those different conditions reflected the character of the different regions, as much as or more than they reflected the particular wartime conditions that produced them. Just as the impact of crises in general depended on the region in which they occurred, so does the overall impact of war.

The first point I should establish is that the experience of the Basse-Meuse was comparable to the regions more seriously depopulated during the wars of the sixteenth and seventeenth centuries. While others might argue that the Basse-Meuse and Germany experienced two different Thirty Years' Wars, I will simply repeat that the Basse-Meuse lies less than fifty kilometers from sections of Germany which lost 25 to 30 percent of their population.[4] Moreover, since the Basse-Meuse suffered most in the late seventeenth century, when armies were very large, it is even possible that its military experience was more extensive than that of many regions in Germany in the Thirty Years' War, when armies were smaller.

A further variant in war's impact on the countryside is the character

200

Ill. 9. The Cruelties Committed by the French, No. 3, by Romeyn de Hooghe (1673)

of military leaders and their ability and desire to control the behavior of their troops. Historians have attributed much of the destruction in Germany in the Thirty Years' War to Wallenstein's conscious effort to dominate the countryside and to support his troops through its total victimization and subjugation. In the same years, however, several semi-independent armies made the Basse-Meuse their resting place and abused the countryside to support their troops and enrich their treasuries. While these men are less well known and were less powerful than Wallenstein, they were no more careful to preserve their surroundings. Later in the seventeenth century the Basse-Meuse, like the entire Meuse basin, was a prime target for the French and their brutal military leader, Louvois.[5] These were the armies that did the most damage to the region, more than those of the Thirty Years' War.

Unlike varying levels of military strength or the nature of commanders, the changing character of war probably contributed to the particular level of destruction suffered by the Basse-Meuse. War changed considerably from the first phase of the Dutch Revolt, at the end of the sixteenth century, through the Thirty Years' War, which ravaged Germany in the first half of the seventeenth century, to the wars of Louis XIV, which damaged the Basse-Meuse between 1670 and 1700. Larger armies combined with better military behavior to bring a change in war's impact on the Basse-Meuse by 1700. The region may have felt these changes in the economic and demographic impact of war before the beginning of the eighteenth century. It is possible, though hardly proven, that they moderated the loss of growth experienced by the Basse-Meuse at the end of the seventeenth century.

It might also be suggested that the basic demographic phenomena characteristic of wartime differed from region to region, so that we cannot compare the wartime demographic experiences of the Basse-Meuse (even at their most severe) with those of other regions. This is a point which is difficult to resolve without comparable studies of changing mortality and childbearing conditions. For now, I would like to assume that the experiences of the Basse-Meuse are representative of those communities not totally annihilated by warfare (the overwhelming majority of places, even in Germany during the Thirty Year's War). What may have been unrepresentative about the Basse-Meuse was the region's marriage and migration experience. The regions which lost population must have experienced tremendous emigration. This was not the case in the Basse-Meuse. Moreover, serious economic problems may have made marriage and the establishment of new households even

more difficult in regions which lost population than in the Basse-Meuse.

While I have discussed war's impact on marriage, it has not been possible to say very much about migration, because the stu ly of migration before modern record-keeping systems is very difficult. For the Basse-Meuse, the best sources are the registers of entry into bourgeois status, for both the cities and the villages. Still, such records are difficult to interpret without equivalent documents from other regions. I did examine the registers of new bourgeois for Maastricht and Herstal-Wandre compiled in the late seventeenth century.[6] Both suggest that there was continued migration from places outside the immediate neighborhood, during and after the wars of the seventeenth century. The exact quantity of migration at different times is impossible now to ascertain. If anything, war seems to have reduced (but not eliminated) the movement of population from the Basse-Meuse to its main migratory destination, the industrial villages immediately surrounding the City of Liège. This would be in line with my conclusions above about the failure of the Herstal-Wandre population to grow until the end of the War of the League of Augsburg. Moreover, it would support, in a general way, the argument I am making here about the persistence of the Basse-Mosan population in time of war. Deprived of their principal migratory destination, the people of the Basse-Meuse had more reason to stay where they were until conditions quieted down.

Despite difficulties in their study, I think marriage and migration probably explain why the Basse-Mosan population experience differed from other places. In part, this is because they are all that is left. If more deaths and fewer births do not explain the different pattern of population loss, then a different pattern of family formation and migration, one which favored the Basse-Meuse in comparison with other regions, must be the key. Why did people stay in the Basse-Meuse, so that it did not lose population? There can be no contravening the fact that times were bad during early modern wars. Why, for example, did the curé of Emael not pack up and go elsewhere in 1634?

I will argue here that people stayed because they perceived that they had an investment in the land and the community and that present and future opportunities existed which were better than those offered elsewhere. The sense of community and some confidence about personal and economic futures gave the social organism that was rural society the resilience and the will to rebuild. These are largely specu-

lations, but they should provide us with a list of conditions that, when present, caused the population to stay and, when absent, encouraged it to disperse and, thus, decline. Their presence or absence in other societies will permit us to judge whether they were crucial to keep a population in place during a crisis, or simply icing on the prosperous Basse-Mosan cake.

A. Peasant Status, Social Structure, and Peasant Landholding

Absolutely fundamental to any model of what kept a rural population in place during wartime is its status; that is to say, the constraints that bound people to the land and, even more basically, their economic investment in the community. One of the constants of European civilization has been the existence of peasant populations, but by the seventeenth century there existed fundamental differences between the status of peasants in various European regions. A continuum existed, ranging from the nearly enslaved peasants of eastern and parts of central Europe who were tied to land or lord and owed heavy labor services, to the essentially free men of France, England, and the Low Countries who could move around and either purchase land with only nominal feudal dues or lease land at a reasonable rent.[7] Moreover, the social structure and division of land in individual communities varied tremendously from place to place in early modern Europe, with peasants in some places doomed to lives of wage or serf labor, while others leased land from a monopolistic landlord and still others divided the land in their community among themselves.

These conditions of peasant status, social structure, and peasant landholding delineate variations that I will call peasant investment in their community. Varying patterns of inheritance, while not studied in this book, also contribute. A peasant who was essentially enslaved in serfdom, who owned no land, and who owed large labor obligations to his lord had little economic investment in his community. If the disruption of war offered him an opportunity, he may well have packed up his few belongings and his family and gone looking for better opportunities elsewhere. Those who owned land, however, must surely have felt an investment in place, possessions, neighbors, and property. That investment gave them good reason to stay in their communities in times of difficulty, and to make every effort to rebuild after the danger ended. By staying home, they risked their persons and moveable property, while offering some protection to their farms and real

204

property. Even when they left briefly to avoid a single military incursion, they returned quickly to protect their investment. These peasants were willing to invest personally and economically in their community in spite of the dangers of repeated war and to borrow, in times of need, to carry them into the next period of plenty. Among these groups were the free peasants of the Basse-Meuse, who had a considerable stake in their communities. Farm land was relatively widely distributed among the population, although the dense population in the dairy farming villages east of the Meuse lived on rather small farms. Despite the small farms, their owners were investors in their communities; those investments kept them on their farms during and after wartime hardships.

B. Present and Future Opportunity

While relatively free status and access to land was a necessary part of the propensity of Basse-Mosan peasants to stay in their villages, it was not sufficient. They not only needed land and investment, but also to perceive that opportunities to survive and prosper, and to be a part of a community of families, existed and would continue to exist in the future. This was especially necessary in the Basse-Meuse, where many peasants owned small farms and, thus needed access to salaried employment and a market for foodstuffs. Put in more general terms, the likelihood that a civilian would stay in his home region during wartime difficulties varied according to his perception of present and future economic opportunities. Those perceived opportunities included general economic prosperity, available untilled land, ready access to credit, and substantial agricultural and non-agricultural employment.

At the heart of the economic reasons why people stayed in the Basse-Meuse was the pervasive prosperity of the region around Liège from the sixteenth century onward. This region included both fertile agricultural districts and some of the most concentrated sites of early heavy industry in continental Europe. The coal and iron industry of Liège, and the manufacturing industries which drew their supplies from it, generated a significant export market for unprocessed coal and iron as well as arms, munitions, and hardware. Moreover, the neutrality of the Principality of Liège, although insufficient to prevent military occupation, permitted the merchants and manufacturers of Liège to do business everywhere in Europe. This economic prosperity and political independence saved the region from hardship in the late sixteenth century, when the rest of the Low Countries suffered, and kept it vital

in the seventeenth century, when it, like the Dutch Republic, had only a very brief depression. But, unlike those of the Dutch Republic, Liège's resource base and incipient industries kept the region prosperous and growing even in the eighteenth century. This prosperity served to keep the people of the Basse-Meuse in their homes, even during hard times, confident that the region's continuing good fortune would serve them well.

The essential contribution made by Liègeois prosperity was to provide a sure supply of agricultural and non-agricultural employment to the residents of the Basse-Meuse. Many Basse-Mosan inhabitants owned or operated small farms and many of those farms were near the minimum size needed to support a family. Especially in time of economic difficulty, when the weather was bad, when crops were destroyed, or when taxes were very high, those farmers had need of employment for wages to carry them through the year.

Besides opportunities for employment, the Basse-Meuse offered its residents fairly easy access to credit, another element of economic opportunity. The availability of credit served two purposes: it provided cash to pay for war, and it permitted investment capital to carry on business during war and to reconstruct afterwards. By the seventeenth century, war-making became progressively more dependent on money, and the civilians that experienced occupation needed increasing quantities of cash to meet the obligation put on them by armies. Yet, individuals and communities in the countryside were often short of specie. The availability of credit permitted them to make payments without sacrificing their valuable and very real investments in land, buildings, tools, livestock and seed. Moreover, the availability of credit in the countryside at moderate rates of interest (5-7 percent) provided a continuing supply of investment capital with which the aspiring farmers of the Basse-Meuse could improve or rebuild their farms.

Opportunities existed in the Basse-Meuse, engendered by a general sense of prosperity, encouraged by the opportunity to own land, and paid for by the salaried labor of the region's residents in fields, mines, forges, and cottages, and by borrowed florins. The Basse-Meuse did not offer every possible opportunity, however. Because the region's population was dense and did not decline during the wars, little untilled land was available for immigrants or natives expanding their holdings. Thus, a major category of opportunity was unavailable; the availability of land was the sort of opportunity that could create a viable, youthful community out of nothing. The prompt migratory response to avail-

able land in many sections of Germany after the Thirty Years' War, and in the regions of Flanders and Brabant, temporarily depopulated during the Dutch Revolt, led to the very prompt recovery of population in those regions.

III. Wartime Population Stability

It is appropriate now to recapitulate the forces which maintained population stability in some wartime populations, and which in their absence permitted population loss. A demographic imbalance of too many deaths and too few births plays a central role in this model, because its persistence may cause population loss. I have suggested that there are general laws of demographic behavior associated with wars and that, if the experience of the Basse-Meuse is representative of conditions elsewhere in the seventeenth century, the usual loss of population due to a demographic imbalance in wartime is about two percent per year. In a few years of very extreme conditions, when war occurs simultaneoulsy with a very bad harvest, a population might lose four percent of its members, but those experiences were infrequent and never sustained. Over a long war, if a rural community were occupied and terrorized year after year, the two percent per year is realistic and, even then, it is unlikely that such a rate of population loss could be sustained for a decade without a total breakdown in (and desertion of) the community. These general rules of wartime demographic behavior make it likely that large-scale population losses, like those attributed to the Low Countries during the Dutch Revolt, and to Germany during the Thirty Years' War, were not the result of simple demographic imbalance.

I wish to suggest here that there were a number of other forces at work in the Basse-Meuse that led to population stability. When they were present, many families stayed in a region, in spite of hardships. When they were absent, the population would decline, because new households would not be formed by marriage, because new immigrants would not be drawn to replace residents who died, and because the old population would emigrate to places that offered more for the future. While war's impact changed over time, the most important phenomena that produced population stability are closely related to the socio-political structure of the region and, especially, to its economic structure and strength. I have called them investment and opportunity.

Investment consists of two elements. The first is the status of

peasants and the general social structure. It works in this way: a society with relatively free peasants, who have the opportunity to own property and farm on their own is more likely to survive a wartime crisis than a society where peasants are unfree (in the sense of serfdom) and restricted to a life as tenants or laborers. The second element is actual peasant landownership. If land is widely held, and not restricted to a few landlords, so that peasants either own land or can expect to have a farm before establishing a family, once again population stability will result.

Opportunity is a more diverse characteristic. Its importance is drawn from the likelihood that, if an individual or family senses present or future opportunity to live and possibly prosper in the community, they will stay. If not, they will leave. Opportunity, here, is more than simply owning land or the right to own land. I have suggested four main elements of opportunity. The first element is the general economic strength and prosperity of the region; the second is the availability of untilled land that can be occupied by poor natives or immigrants; the third is the opportunity poorer farmers have of supplementing their income by working at non-agricultural employment, or agricultural wage-labor; and the fourth is the availability of credit, which permitted farmers and non-farmers to finance the extreme short-term costs of war without selling off their farms and tools. Three of these elements of opportunity existed in the Basse-Meuse in the seventeenth century – economic strength, wage labor, and credit – and they contributed to the general resilience of the population in times of crisis.

Appendixes

Appendix A

A Chronology of Military and Political Events in the Basse-Meuse*

Year	Local Military Events	Other Events
1620		Weather: hard winter
1621		End of 12-year truce between Spain and Dutch
		Weather: hard winter; cold, wet summer
1622	SPANISH troops	
	Generals: Marquis de Spinola	
	Comte de Salazar	
	Locale: Wonck	
	Purpose: to join Maastricht garrison	
1623		Epidemics: contagious malady at Paris, Liège, Huy, Maastricht
1624		Epidemics: plague at Liège
		Weather: hot, dry summer
1625		Grain shortage
		Weather: mild winter; cold, wet summer
1626	SAXON Troops	
	General: Comte de Peer	
	Date: October	
	Locale: Pays de Liège	
1627	SPANISH Troops	Weather: cold, wet summer
	1) Locale: Saive	
	Date: June	
	2) General: Comte de Salazar	
	Locale: Pays de Liège	
1628	SPANISH (BRABANCON) Troops	Weather: cold, wet summer
	Origin: Maastricht garrison	
	Action: placed at Herstal	
	Date: January	
	IMPERIAL Troops	
	General: Tilly	
	Action: winter quarters	

* See page 230.

Year	Local Military Events	Other Events
1628, *cont.*	Locale: Pays de Liège PRINCE'S Troops Generals: Crunitz, Blanckart	
1629	IMPERIAL Troops (2 regiments) General: Tilly (stayed, at Prince's request, until October, to punish city's actions) SPANISH (BRABANÇON) Troops General: Count Henry van den Berg Number: 1 *corps d'armée* Locale: pays de Liège, banlieu & faubourgs of city Date: about October 14 MAASTRICHT garrison Governor: Seigneur de Lanoy de la Moterie Various destructive actions by his troops	Weather: hard winter; hot, dry summer General European harvest crisis, 1629-1631
1630	MAASTRICHT garrison Repeated actions in Hesbaye and along the Meuse	Epidemics: contagion at Liège (August)
1631	SPANISH Troops General: Salazar Number: 10,000 foot; 1,500 horse; 16 cannon Date: December Wanted to take winter quarters, but did not because of armed local opposition	July 7, 1631: Edict by Prince of Liège regarding behavior of foreign troops on Liégeois soil Weather: hard winter; cold, wet summer
1632	*SIEGE OF MAASTRICHT* Attacker: DUTCH Troops General: Frederick Henry of Nassau Date: June; capitulation to Dutch August 22 Counter-attackers: SPANISH Troops General: Count Henry van den Berg Number: 2 *corps d'armée* Date: June until capitulation IMPERIAL Troops	Weather: hot, dry summer Epidemics: plague at Liège (August to end of year)

212

Year	Local Military Events	Other Events
1632, *cont.*	General: Pappenheim Number: 1 *corps d'armée* PALATINE Troops DUTCH Army (other actions) General: de Frentz 1) took Argenteau 2) left a garrison in the City of Limbourg	
1633	DUTCH Troops (with Swedish cavalry) Generals: Henry of Nassau; Prince of Orange Date: October Locale: Visé	Weather: mild winter; hot, dry sum- mer Epidemics: plague at Liège
1634	SPANISH Troops General: Marquis d'Aytona Action: attempted to retake Maastricht; built fort at Navagne, and left a garrison there; retook Argenteau and left a garrison there Date: June to September	Weather: hot, dry summer Epidemics: plague at Visé, Liège
1635	FRENCH Troops 25,000 French troops travelled north along the Meuse. Met similar DUTCH force at Gronsveld; combined army marched to Brussels Generals: de Chatillon, de Breze, la Meilleraye SPANISH Troops General: Thomas of Savoy Numbers: 6,000 fantassins; 2,500 horse *BATTLE OF AVINS* (French v. Spanish) Date: May 20 Victor: French; after battle, French marched up Meuse to Maastricht IMPERIAL Troops (Croates) General: Piccolomini Date: November	French enter 30 Years' War Weather: hard winter; hot, dry sum- mer Epidemic: dysentery
1635, *cont.*	Action: wanted winter quarters	

	in Pays de Liège, but left after opposition in a few days	

1636	IMPERIAL Troops (Croates)
	   Generals: Jean de Weert,
	   Piccolomini
	   Number: 4,000 men
	   Locale: Fexhe-Slins
	LORRAINE Troops
	   General: Duke of Lorraine
	   Date: all Imperial troops
	   (including Lorraine) left
	   at end of June
		Weather: hot, dry summer
		Epidemics: plague, dysentery

1637		Weather: hot, dry summer

1638	IMPERIAL Troops
	   General: Piccolomini
	   Action: peaceful crossing
	   of Meuse, June	

1639	SPANISH Troops
	   General: Marquis of Gonzaga
	   Locales: Fosses (between
	   Charleroi and Namur)
	   Thuin (sw of Charleroi)
	   (January)
	   Couvin (sw of Dinant)
	   (April)
	LORRAINE Troops
	   General: Duke of Lorraine
	   Action: winter quarters
	   Locale: Entre-Sambre-Meuse
	   (the region south of
	   Charleroi and Namur)
	DUTCH Troops
	   General: Casimir de Nassau
	   Number: 4,000 fantassins; 49
	   companies cavalry
	   Locale: Pays de Liège
	PRINCE'S Troops
		Weather: late frost

1640	LORRAINE Troops
	   General: Duke of Lorraine
	   Action: winter quarters
	   Date: December
	   Locale: Fosses, Thuin,
	   Entre-Sambre-Meuse
		Weather: hot, dry summer

1641		Weather: early frost
1642	GARRISONS – Dutch at Maastricht	

214

Year	Local Military Events	Other Events
	and Hessian at Calcar — frequently took contributions in Pays de Liège	
1643	*SIEGE OF GRONSVELDT* HESSIAN Troops General: Cauvenberg Date: Retaken by Liégeois militia July 21 LORRAINE Troops Action: winter quarters Locale: Entre-Sambre-Meuse Date: left February 20, 1644	
1644	DUTCH Troops — garrison at Maastricht Action: retook Dalhem Date: 20 June HESSIAN Troops Action: continued local attacks	Weather: late frost
1645	*CIVIL WAR* in Liège Actions of so-called "refugies," resident at Maastricht Commander: Laroque de Boulihar Locale: Herstal Date: February	
1646	*CIVIL WAR* in Liège LORRAINE Troops Action: winter quarters Locale: Entre-Sambre-Meuse	
1647	LORRAINE Troops General: De Housse Action: moved to Marquisate of Franchimont Locale: Jalhay (east of Verviers)	
1648		Treaties of Westphalia end 30 Years' War Weather: cold, wet summer
1649	BAVARIAN (PRINCE'S) Troops 1) General: Spaar Number: 3,000 or 3,500 Locale: Liers 2) Generals: Schroets & Cratz Locale: Visé & Haccourt	Settlement of Liégeois Civil War General European harvest crisis, 1649-1651 Weather: hot, dry summer; late frost
1649, *cont.*	These troops became the German garrison of	

the City of Liège
LORRAINE TROOPS
1) General: Salms
Action: crossed Hesbaye
Date: June; returned November
and December
2) General: Baron de Clinchamps

1650 SWEDISH Troops
General: Otton Steinbuck
Locale: from Visé to Herstal
Date: July 21-August 22
Reason: demand for payment
from Liège in war
settlement
HESSIAN Troops
Date: followed Swedes in August
LORRAINE Troops
Action: winter quarters
Date: November
Locale: Condroz
PRINCE'S (GERMAN) garrison
Action: mutiny for lack of pay
Date: November

Construction begun on Citadel of
Liège
Death of Prince-Bishop Ferdinand of
Bavaria (1612-1650)
Election of Maximilian Henry of
Bavaria as Bishop of Liège
Weather: cold, wet summer

1651 LORRAINE Troops
1) Action: winter quarters
1650-1651
Date: Left at end of July
2) Action: winter quarters
1651-1652
Date: returned later in year
SPANISH Troops
Action: winter quarters 1651-1652
FRENCH Troops
Generals: Rose, Turenne
IRISH Troops
Action: crossed Meuse near
Maastricht

Citadel completed

1652 LORRAINE Troops
Locale: Entre-Sambre-Meuse

1653 VARIOUS Troops in Entre-Sambre-
Meuse (Lorraine, Condé,...)
LORRAINE Troops
Locale: Navagne, Oupeye
Date: May

1653, *cont.* FRENCH Troops
Generals: Comte de Linguieville

Year	Local Military Events	Other Events
	Wilmaer, Bassompierre	
1654	LORRAINE Troops	Treaty of Tirlement; Spanish guarantee Liégeois neutrality
	Locale: Hesbaye	
	Action: arrest of Charles,	
	Duke of Lorraine	
	by the Spanish	
	SPANISH Troops	
	General: Condé	
	FRENCH Troops	
	General: Fabert	
	Number: 8,000 men	
	Purpose: force Lorraine	
	Troops out of	
	Liégeois territory	
1655	VARIOUS Troops in Entre-Sambre-Meuse	Execution of 1546 Treaty giving sovereignty over Herstal to Liège
1656		
1657		Weather: hard winter
		Epidemic: dysentery at Sart
1658		
1659		General European harvest crisis, 1659-1661
1660		Weather: hard winter
1661		Louis XIV assumes personal direction of government of France. Settlement of division of Pays d'Outre Meuse between Spanish and Dutch
1662		
1663		Weather: cold, wet summer
1664		
1665		
1666		
1667		War of Devolution
		Epidemic: Last plague outbreak in the Basse-Meuse, 1667-1670
1668		War of Devolution
1669		
1670		Weather: hard winter
1671		
1672	FRENCH Troops	Beginning of Dutch War
	1) Action: passed by on way up Meuse	Weather: hard winter, hot, dry summer
	Generals, etc.: Duke of Orleans,	
	Viscount Turenne,	
	Chamilly, Condé, Louvois,	
	Rochefort, de Montal	
	Locales: Visé, camp May 17	

1672, *cont.*	Left garrisons at Tongeren, Maaseik 2) Action: winter quarters General: Duras Numbers: 12,000 cavaliers Date: arrived December 25 Locales: Burnt Lixhe, Loen, Nivelle DUTCH Troops General: Prince of Orange Locale: Maastricht, Eysden Date: November	
1673	*SIEGE OF MAASTRICHT* FRENCH Troops Generals: Louis XIV, Lorges Attacking force: 20,000 foot; 12,000 horse; 52 artillery pieces Dates: set siege May 10; successful July 1-2 New Governor: d'Estrades New Garrison: 6,000 foot; 2,000 horse Other action: destruction of walls of Tongeren DUTCH Troops (defending) Commander: Jacques Fariaux Defending force: 5,000 foot *WINTER QUARTERS* (end of December) SPANISH Troops Locale: quarter of Moha (near Huy) IMPERIAL Troops Locale: Condroz FRENCH Troops 1) General: Luxembourg Locale: Hesbaye Number: 1 *corps d'armée* 2) General: de T'Serclaes Locale: Entre-Sambre-Meuse	
1674	FRENCH Troops General: Bellefons Action: demolition of forts at Argenteau and Navagne Date: May	Liège changes sides from France to Allies

218

1674, *cont.*　　Also: gave up all garrisons
　　　　　　won in 1672 except Maastricht
　　　　　　and Grave (which the Dutch
　　　　　　took on October 28)
　　　　　BATTLE OF SENEFFE
　　　　　　Date: August 11
　　　　　　Casualties: 27,000
　　　　　　Winner: French
　　　　　　Losers: Dutch (Prince of Orange)
　　　　　　Imperials (Souches,
　　　　　　Monterey)
　　　　　ALL MAJOR ARMIES except
　　　　　　Dutch wintered in Liégeois ter-
　　　　　　ritory, making heavy demands

1675　　　FRENCH TROOPS　　　　　　New Governor of Spanish Nether-
　　　　　　1) Citadelle of Liège　　　　lands: Villa Hermosa
　　　　　　delivered to French　　　　　Weather: cold, wet summer; late frost
　　　　　　Date: March 27-28　　　　　Serious Grain Shortage
　　　　　　Consequences: this brought out
　　　　　　all the bourgeois and rural
　　　　　　Militia to the City
　　　　　　and Basse-Meuse;
　　　　　　IMPERIAL army offered
　　　　　　to help evict French,
　　　　　　but were refused
　　　　　　2) Demolition of fortifications
　　　　　　of Visé by French force
　　　　　　from Maastricht
　　　　　　Date: January
　　　　　　3) French evacuated Masseik;
　　　　　　military hardware moved
　　　　　　to Maastricht
　　　　　　Date: mid-March
　　　　　　4) *SIEGE OF DINANT*
　　　　　　Date: successful at end of
　　　　　　May
　　　　　　Attacking French general:
　　　　　　Crequi
　　　　　　Defending Imperial general:
　　　　　　Colonel Streif
　　　　　　5) *SIEGE OF HUY*
　　　　　　Date: 3-6 June; successful
　　　　　　Attacking French general:
　　　　　　Marquis de Rochefort
　　　　　　Defending general:
　　　　　　Nigrelli

1675, *cont.*   6) *SIEGE OF LIMBOURG*
Date: 3-21 June; Successful
Attacking French general:
Rochefort, later aided by Condé
and Engien
Consequences for Basse-Meuse:
during the siege of
Limbourg, Louis XIV made
his camp at Lanaye and Navagne
7) Winter quarters
DUTCH Troops
General: Waldeck
Locale: Hasselt
Action: winter quarters
Date: October
Constant demands for con-
tributions
all year from French,
Dutch, Imperial, Spanish
forces

1676   FRENCH Troops
Action: evacuated and
destroyed Citadel of
Liège. Equipment and men (2,300)
taken to Maastricht
Date: March 31
Action: destroyed walls,
fort, and bridge of Huy
Date: April 10-13
DUTCH Troops
1) Action: took Heers
Number: 300 horse & 50 dragons
General: Count of Nassau
Counterattack: French under
d'Estrades set siege and failed
with 4,000 foot soldiers
2) *SIEGE OF MAASTRICHT*
Dates: July 6-August 26 (failed)
Generals: Prince of Orange
Rhysgrave
Defenders: Calvo, with help
from Schomberg

Weather: hot, dry summer
Epidemics: dysentery at Hasselt and
near Maastricht

1677   DUTCH Troops
Garrison at Hasselt
FRENCH Troops (garrison at
Maastricht)

Weather: hard winter

220

Year	Local Military Events	Other Events

1677, *cont.*   General: Calvo
Action: destruction of Tongeren,
Visé, Limbourg
Date: September
BRANDENBURG Troops
Number: 1 *corps de troupes*
General: Baron de Spaen
Place: Reckheim

1678-1679 MAASTRICHT evacuated by French Treaties of Nijmegen, August, 1678.
and returned to Dutch control End of Dutch War
Date: August, 1678 Weather (1679): hard winter
Other garrisons in neighborhood
remained and heavily taxed Basse-
Meuse and whole region of Liège all
through 1678-1679

1680 Weather: mild winter

1681   PRINCE'S (GERMAN) Troops
General: Schaden
1) Action: took Visé (May)
2) Action: attacked city forces
at Visé and Herstal
3) Action: retreated to fortress
of Stockem
4) Later locale: Heer

1682

1683 War of the Reunions

1684 War of the Reunions
Weather: hard winter; hot, dry summer

1685 Weather: cold, wet summer

1686

1687 French intervention to influence
election of new Bishop as Maximilian
Henry aged

1688   FRENCH Troops Death of Maximilian Henry, Bishop
1) Action: occupied Dinant of Liège.
2) Action: various actions in Election of Jean-Louis d'Elderen,
Principality of Liège Bishop of Liège
General: Gournay War of the League of Augsburg
Locale: Huy, Chiney (east begins.
of Dinant),
Duras (near St. Truiden),
Gorsom (near St. Truiden),
Kuringen (near Hasselt)
Date: November
3) Garrison at Huy

Year	Local Military Events	Other Events
1688, *cont.*	Intendant: Bouridal Action: demanded contributions in Hesbaye & Condroz	
1689	FRENCH Troops 1) Action: burnt part of Faubourg Sainte-Marguerite 2) Action: general treatment of Liège as enemy (rather than neutral) territoy 3) *SIEGE OF HUY* Failed (April) Returned and succeeded (May)	Liège along with Empire and "allies" declared war against France Treaty with Dutch Estates-General for protection
1690	LIEGEOIS Troops (only war in which Liège was an *active* belligerent) Action: recruited 5,-6,000 men; formed part of Dutch Gen. Flodroff's force FRENCH Troops Action: threatened city of Liège Date: June *BATTLE OF FLEURUS* Date: end of June DUTCH Troops General: Prince Waldeck Action: winter quarters Locale: Maastricht and nearby places	Weather: hard winter; hot, dry sum- mer
1691	FRENCH Troops General: Boufflers Actions: 1) Attacked Charteuse, defended by Liégeois, led by T'Serclaes Date: June 2-4 2) Attempted to cross Meuse, but were repulsed Locale: Jupille, among others 3) Results of failure: bombardment of city of Liège from Charteuse DUTCH Troops General: Lippe Action: arrival threatened French and convinced them to leave Char- teuse *WINTER QUARTERS* Liège's allies	Rebuilding of City of Liège's for- tifications, 1691-1693 Weather: hot, dry summer

222

Year	Local Military Events	Other Events
1692	WINTER QUARTERS Liège's allies FRENCH Troops Action: tried to take Huy for winter quarters, but failed Date: December 26	Weather: hard winter; hot, dry summer
1693	ALLIED AND LIÉGEOIS Troops General: T'Serclaes Action: 1) Camped between Liège and Tongeren 2) Went to Maastricht to avoid French 3) Stayed in Liège to keep order Date: July and August FRENCH Troops 1) General: Marshal Luxembourg Numbers: 10,000 men Locale: Houtain-St. Simeon to east of Liégeois forces Date: July 18 2) SIEGE OF HUY General: Marechal de Villeroi Date: July 19-23 Successful Defending general: Baron de Renesse After siege of Huy, both French forces threatened Liège 3) BATTLE OF LANDEN-NEERWINDEN (near St. Truiden) Date: July 29 Results: mixed, with French staying at Landen until August 13 Heavy contributions demanded, July 30 to August 13 WINTER QUARTERS 1) Liège's allies 2) French troops at Huy	Epidemic: all through the region after Battle of Landen-Neerwinden
1694	SIEGE OF HUY General: Holstein-	Death of Jean-Louis d'Elderen, Bishop of Liège

Year	Local Military Events	Other Events
1694, *cont.*	Ploen (allies) Dates: September 17-28 Successful Results: allied garrison replaced French FRENCH Troops General: Dauphin Locale: Tongeren *WINTER QUARTERS* Liégeois and allied troops	Election of Joseph Clement of Bavaria, Bishop of Liège (dies 1723) Weather: hot, dry summer
1695	*WINTER QUARTERS* Liégeois troops Allies: Dutch, Brandenburgers	Weather: cold, wet summer
1696	FRENCH Troops Action: threatened city of Liège General: Lacroix Response: repelled by a small Liégeois force, led by T'Serclaes *WINTER QUARTERS* Liégeois troops Foreign troops, but fewer than other years	
1697	Some foreign troops remained after peace DUTCH Troops General: Athlone Action: put Hesbaye to contribution	Peace of Rijswijk, 1697, ends War of the League of Augsburg Weather: cold, wet summer
1698		General European harvest crisis, 1698-1700 Weather: hard winter; cold, wet summer; late frost
1699		
1700		Weather: mild winter
1701	FRENCH Troops 1) General: Marquis de Boufflers Locale: Richelle Date: October 2) Prince of Liège ordered that Citadel be turned over to French troops Date: November	Beginning of War of Spanish Succession Prince of Liège allies with French/ Spanish side Weather: mild winter; hot, dry summer
1702	DUTCH & ENGLISH Troops (unified army)	Power stripped from Prince of Liège by Imperial Diet for supporting

1702, *cont.*	Generals: Marlborough, Athlone	France. Power divided according to allied occupation
	Action: approached city of Liège	Joseph-Clement goes into exile in France
	Date: early October	Weather: mild, winter; hot, dry summer; late frost
	Campsites: Athlone at Grace; Marlborough at Grace; Coehoorn at Herstal	
	City of Liège negotiated a treaty with the Allies, against the Prince of Liège	
	FRENCH Troops	
	Generals: Boufflers, Duke of Maine, T'Serclaes	
	Actions: left city of Liège, went to Tongeren, then rejoined main French army	
1703	FRENCH Troops	Treaties of Contribution between principality of Liège and France
	Generals: Boufflers, Villeroy	(50,000 écus = 180,000 florins/yr.)
	Number: 40,000	and United Province
	Purpose: put siege to Maastricht	Weather: mild winter
	Date: May	
	Action: took Tongeren	
	ALLIED Troops	
	General: Marlborough	
	Actions:	
	1) Were sieging Bonn	
	Date: May	
	2) After success, returned to Liège region and chased French from Maastricht	
	3) Took Limbourg and Huy	
	4) Winter quarters (heavy exactions)	
1704	ALLIED Troops	Weather: mild winter
	Actions:	
	1) At beginning of campaign, Maastricht was the meeting place for the various allied armies	
	2) Winter quarters	
	General: Ouwerkeke	
1705	FRENCH Troops	Contribution Treaty between Liège and United Provinces renewed (Nov.)
	1) *SIEGE OF HUY*	
	General: comte de Gasse	

Year	Local Military Events	Other Events
1705, *cont.*	Successful Dates: May 26-June 1 2) Generals: Elector of Bavaria; Marshal Villeroy; Saint-Maurice Action: taking of city of Liège (not Citadel) Date: June 16-18 ALLIED Troops General: Marlborough 1) Coming via Maastricht, chased French from Liège (French went to Tongeren) Date: June 27 2) Retook Huy Date: July 11 General: Schotten 3) Winter quarters General: Salisch	
1706	*BATTLE OF RAMILLIES* Date: May 23 Consequence: end of heavy military activity in Liège region for War of the Spanish Succession *WINTER QUARTERS* Dutch at Liège and Hasselt; Prussians at Visé (one batallion)	
1707	*WINTER QUARTERS* Hanoverian Troops near Hasselt	Weather: mild winter; cold, wet summer
1708	April: Principality of Liège crossed by Dutch and Prussian Troops Dutch General: Tilly General Allied Commander: Marl- borough *WINTER QUARTERS* Allied and Imperial Troops (beginning Jan., 1709) Places: Liège, Sint Truiden (4 batallions), Kempen region	Weather: mild winter; cold, wet summer
1709	*WINTER QUARTERS* Prussian Troops	Very hard winter 1708-1709 Contribution Treaty between Liège

Year	Local Military Events	Other Events
1709, *cont.*	Number: One regiment Place: County of Horne; Peer, Bree, Hamont Major General: Dorfling Hanoverian Troops One regiment	and United Provinces renewed (Feb.).
1710	*WINTER QUARTERS* Hanoverian and Prussian Troops Places: Sint-Truiden, Hasselt, Beeringen, Stocken, Bilsen, Bree, Hamont	Weather: hot, dry summer
1711	*WINTER QUARTERS* Prussian Troops (Nov. 1, 1711 to April, 1712) Number: One Regiment Commander: Lieutenant-General Panwitz Place: County of Horne, moved to Heer, Bree, and Hamont	Death of Emperor Joseph I, 17 April (Sovereign of Liège in the Absence of Prince-Bishop). Cathedral Chapter takes over government Election of Emperor Charles VI, 12 October
1712	WINTER, 1712-1713 Winter quarters for Imperial Troops avoided by a payment of 100,000 écus.	Weather: hot, dry summer
1713		Treaties of Utrecht (April); Former Spanish Netherlands turned over to Austria Weather: cold, wet summer
1714		Treaties of Rastadt & Broen (Emperor and France-Oct.) discharge Liège of requirement to make contributions to France as of Jan. 1, 1715. Weather: mild winter; hot, dry summer
1715		Third (and final) Treaty of the Barrier. Gave Dutch power to build a line of fortresses across the Austrian Nether- lands. Moved strategic border south of the Basse-Meuse. Return of Prince-Bishop Joseph Cle- ment to Liège Weather: mild winter
1716		Liège reunited diplomatically with the Empire, but reserves the right to stay neutral or pay contributions in case of

Year	Local Military Events	Other Events
1716, *cont.*		war between the Empire and another state
		Prince Eugene of Savoy appointed Governor of the Autrian Netherlands
		Weather: hard winter; hot, dry summer
1717		Weather: mild winter
1718	Dutch Troops occupied Liège and Huy until early this year	Weather: mild winter; hot, dry summer
1719		Weather: mild winter; hot, dry summer
1720		Weather: mild winter
1721		Weather: mild winter; hot, dry summer
1722		Weather: mild winter
1723		Death of Joseph Clement of Bavaria, Prince-Bishop of Liège (12 November).
		Weather: mild winter; hot, dry summer
1724		Mary-Elizabeth of Austria becomes Archduchess of Austrian Netherlands
		Election of Georges-Louis de Berghes as Prince-Bishop of Liège (Feb. 7)
		Weather: mild winter; hot, dry summer
1725		Weather: mild winter; cold, wet summer
1726		Weather: mild winter; hot, dry summer
1727		Weather: hot, dry summer; late frost
1728		
1729		Weather: hard winter
1730		
1731		Weather: hard winter; hot, dry summer; late frost
1732		Lordship over Herstal passes from the House of Nassau to Frederick-William, King of Prussia (Liège is still sovereign)
		Weather; late frost
1733		War of the Polish Succession
1734		War of the Polish Succession
		Weather: hard winter; cold, wet summer
1735		War of the Polish Succession
		Weather: hard winter

Year	Local Military Events	Other Events
1736		
1737		Weather: late frost
		Epidemics: city of Liège
1738		Weather: hard winter
1739		Weather: mild winter
1740		Death of Emperor Charles VI (Oct.); Maria Theresa becomes Empress; Frederick II becomes King of Prussia and forces estates of Liège to buy Herstal for 300,000 florins (20 October)
		Weather: hard winter; cold, wet summer
1741		Death of Archduches Mary Elisabeth
		Outbreak of the War of the Austrian Succession
		Weather: hard winter
1742		
1743		Death of Georges-Louis de Berghes (6 December)
		Weather: hot, dry summer
1744	FRENCH Invade Austrian Netherlands	Charles Alexander of Lorraine becomes Governor of the Austrian Netherlands (March)
		Election of John Theodore of Bavaria as Prince-Bishop of Liège (13 January; dies 1763)
1745		Weather: cold, wet summer
1746	FRENCH Garrisons at Huy and Liège under the Marshal Saxe (August)	Weather: hard winter
	ALLIED Troops on East Bank of Basse-Meuse (Sept. 5)	
	HUNGARIAN, HESSIAN, ENGLISH, DUTCH, HANOVERIAN Camps at Housse and Richelle and north to Maastricht; Moved Sept. 14 to West Bank of Meuse, near Maastricht, 88.000 men at Vlytingen, 14 Sept. to 7 Oct.	
	BATTLE OF ROCOURT (near Voroux Les Liers) Imperial Troops (under Ch. of Lorraine) defeated by France (under Maurice of Saxony) 11 Oct.	
	ALLIED Armies retain Maastricht and Liège	

Year	Local Military Events	Other Events
1746, *cont.*	BATTLE OF HACCOURT	
1747	BATTLE OF LAEFFELT (part of Vlytingen, west of Maastricht) France defeats England	Weather: hot, dry summer Epidemics: dysentery through whole Mosan region
1748	SIEGE OF MAASTRICHT by French AUSTRIAN Troops Place: Dalhem Regiment Troops: Regiment of Curassiers Date: 24 March to 7 April FRENCH Troops Arrive in region (April 7) At Maastricht (April 12) Begin siege (April 15) Capitulation (May 7) FRENCH Troops remained in the Basse-Meuse until late autumn	Treaty of Aix-La-Chapelle (23 Oct.) ends war; Preliminary agreement (April 30) ended hostilities; French reserved right to continue siege of Maastricht Weather: hot, dry summer
1749		Weather: mild winter; hot, dry summer
1750		

Notes

Years are calendar years. Since winter ordinarily spans two calendar years, winter descriptions are as follows: for military activities, winter events come at the end of the given year. Thus, the winter quarters taken by General Tilly's troops in 1628 took place at the end of that year. For weather, winter is considered to be at the beginning of the year. Thus, the hard winter attributed to 1620 probably was worst in January, February, or March, 1620.

Sources. This chronology is drawn from a number of published and manuscript sources, which cannot be reproduced completely here. The principal published sources are: for weather (weather conditions reflect weather for all of Belgium), see E. Vanderlinden, *Chronique des événement méterologiques en Belgique jusqu'en 1834* (Brussels, 1924). [Extract from Mémoires Publiés par la Classe des Sciences de l'Academie Royale de Belgique, Collection in-4°, series 2, vol. 5, 1924.] For epidemics, see E. Hélin, "Les Recherches sur la mortalité dans la region liégeoise (XVe-XIXe siècles)," *Actes du colloque international de démographie historique, Liège, 1963,* ed. by Paul Harsin and Etienne Hélin (Liège, 1965), pp. 115-184. For military and political events, see Joseph Daris, *Histoire du diocèse et de la principauté de Liège pendant le XVIIᵉ siècle,* 2 vols. (Liège: Demarteau, 1877); *id., Histoire du diocèse et de la principauté de Liège (1724-1852),* 4 vols. (Liège, 1868-1873); Théodose Bouille, *Histoire de la ville et pays de Liège,* III (Liège, 1732); and Henri Pirenne, *Histoire de Belgique,* IV-V (Brussels, 1926-1927).

230

Appendix B

An Index of Extreme Behavior

A basic hypothesis of this work has been that war contributed to a broad range of economic and demographic crises in the seventeenth century. Thus it became necessary to identify and classify those crises, unusual movements in long temporal series of demographic and economic data. In the simplest of all cases, that process of identification and classification would be possible by using the data values themselves. An example might be the number of people dying each year in several parishes. Peak values could be used to identify crises, and then the frequency, duration, and, perhaps most interesting, the intensity of the crisis recorded, for comparison with other crises, either caused by war or other unusual external conditions.

Unfortunately, comparison would be hindered if there was a long-term trend in the data, for example if, in the study of deaths just mentioned, the population was growing so that even with a constant rate of mortality, the number of deaths would be expected to rise. Comparing two crises at a fifty-year interval would lead to errors, if we assumed that the "normal" situation – that to which, after all, we are comparing the extreme behavior – was the same. If the two crises reached the same peak level, that is, the same number of deaths in the worst years of each crisis the second would have been less severe than the first, since the "normal" number of deaths would have increased by some unknown amount during the fifty years.

The existence of trend in all the data I studied made necessary the quantification of the relationship between the extreme years and normal for those years – an *index of extreme behavior*.[1] I chose a simple formula for the index:

$$\text{Index value } (x) = \frac{\text{Predicted value } (x)}{\text{Actual value } (x)}$$

where x was the year.

The problem is to obtain a predicted value, which would remove the trend evident in all the data. The simplest of trend lines, long-term moving means or medians, were not particularly useful. That is because, first, accurate computation of long moving means loses data at each end of the series, and because intermediate lacunae (often the case in the data used in this book) add further problems. Furthermore, even long moving means show a relatively short trend, which can include the impact of the crises studied temselves. After a certain amount of experimentation and dissatisfaction with different methods, I chose to use a least-squares regression, to fit a linear equation to the data. While that assumes a single line of development, in one direction, which was not always the case, it seemed in the end simpler and less ambiguous than other methods, and it was relatively resistant to the problems of short time series and missing data.

Some scholars have felt that indexes of this sort should exclude extreme values from the computation of the formula for computing expected values. I experimented with different schemes for eliminating outliers, and found none of them satisfactory. Therefore, I have stayed with the simple computation of a regression line, without eliminating any points.

The formula can then be rewritten as follows:

$$I(x) = \frac{A(x)}{Y(x)},$$

where, $I(x)$ is the index value at year x

$A(x)$ is the actual data value at year x

$Y(x)$ is the predicted value at year x and

$$Y(x) = a + bX$$

where a is the Y-intercept and b is the slope, determined using conventional least squares regression computing formulae.

The index which is the result has the convenient property of a mean roughly equal to one, and a standard deviation approximately equal to the coefficient of variation. This contributes further to ease of comprehension.

When plotting the index, I have used semi-logarithmic forms, since the Y-origin is at one, and the change in index value from 0.5 to 1 reflects the same degree of extreme behavior (although in the opposite direction) as the change from 1 to 2. Logarithmic plotting allows the same degree of change to be represented graphically as the same distance.

Notes

1.   For a discussion of other scholars' ideas on the subject of indices of extreme behavior, see Andre B. Appleby, "Crises of Mortality: Periodicity, Intensity, Chronology and Geographical Extent," Hubert Charbonneau and Andre Larose, eds., *The Great Mortalities: Methodological Studies of Demographic Crises in the Past* (Liège: Ordina Editions, 1979), pp. 283-295.

Index Values for Grain Prices

Year	Liège Spelt	Liège Rye	Maastricht Rye	Amsterdam Rye
1620	0.46 (13.13)*		0.44 (16.5)	0.47 (78.75)
1621	0.66 (18.75)		0.61 (23)	0.68 (115.09)
1622	0.80 (22.5)		0.85 (32)	0.88 (147.41)
1623	0.63 (17.75)		0.67 (25)	1.18 (197.34)
1624	0.59 (16.5)		0.72 (27)	1.01 (168.76)
1625	1.12 (31.38)		1.66 (62)	0.96 (159.83)
1626	0.83 (23.25)		0.73 (27)	0.97 (160.58)
1627	0.76 (21.38)		0.57 (21)	0.96 (159.54)
1628	0.76 (21.38)		1.03 (38)	1.28 (211.46)
1629	0.85 (23.62)		0.87 (32)	1.47 (243.08)
1630	0.87 (24.12)	0.83 (47.5)	1.03 (38)	1.92 (318.46)
1631	0.77 (21.5)	0.76 (43.3)	0.76 (28)	1.05 (172.55)
1632	0.92 (25.5)	0.96 (54.2)	1.09 (40)	0.80 (130.32)
1633	0.75 (20.62)	0.84 (47.5)	1.04 (38)	0.84 (137.43)
1634	0.91 (25.25)	0.85 (48.0)	1.04 (38)	0.92 (150.56)
1635	1.23 (34.0)	0.99 (55.6)	1.26 (46)	0.80 (129.97)
1636	1.34 (37.0)	0.88 (49.5)	0.82 (30)	0.82 (133.23)
1637	1.18 (32.5)	0.88 (49.4)	0.85 (31)	1.01 (163.62)
1638	0.94 (25.75)	0.87 (48.9)	0.83 (30)	0.85 (136.73)
1639	0.96 (26.25)	0.94 (52.5)	0.94 (34)	0.97 (155.88)
1640	0.95 (26.0)	0.89 (49.4)	0.94 (34)	0.89 (143.38)
1641	0.90 (24.44)	0.89 (49.4)	0.91 (33)	0.75 (120.93)
1642	0.87 (23.75)	0.86 (47.5)	0.94 (34)	0.79 (127.05)
1643	0.92 (25.0)	0.86 (47.6)	0.94 (34)	1.00 (159.72)
1644	0.94 (25.38)	0.82 (45.0)	0.84 (30)	0.88 (140.27)
1645	0.80 (21.66)	0.63 (34.6)	0.50 (18)	0.69 (109.84)
1646	0.89 (23.94)	0.53 (29.1)	0.50 (18)	0.72 (114.86)
1647	0.97 (26.25)	0.85 (46.4)	0.98 (35)	0.96 (152.43)
1648	1.45 (38.91)	1.73 (94.2)	1.77 (63)	1.28 (201.97)
1649	1.60 (42.91)	1.85 (100.6)	1.77 (63)	1.44 (226.26)
1650	1.22 (32.72)	1.37 (74.4)	1.75 (62)	1.65 (259.10)
1651	1.44 (38.44)	1.63 (87.8)	1.75 (62)	1.59 (249.32)
1652	1.23 (32.81)	1.05 (56.2)	0.99 (35)	1.18 (184.28)

Year	Liège Spelt	Liège Rye	Maastricht Rye	Amsterdam Rye
1653	0.93 (24.78)	0.79 (42.2)	0.77 (27)	0.93 (144.43)
1654	0.90 (23.88)	0.71 (38.2)	0.85 (30)	0.67 (104.1)
1655	1.13 (30.0)	0.96 (51.2)	1.08 (38)	0.93 (143.97)
1656	1.00 (26.41)	0.74 (39.2)	0.71 (25)	0.96 (148.23)
1657	0.84 (22.34)	0.72 (38.4)	0.86 (30)	0.96 (148.08)
1658	0.90 (23.62)	0.86 (45.5)	0.86 (30)	1.07 (165.38)
1659	1.05 (27.75)	0.88 (46.4)	1.03 (36)	1.13 (173.78)
1660	1.06 (27.88)	0.85 (44.8)	1.18 (41)	1.32 (202.18)
1661	1.63 (42.66)	1.88 (98.8)	2.30 (80)	1.87 (286.48)
1662	1.34 (35.22)	1.26 (65.7)	0.95 (33)	1.69 (257.13)
1663	0.99 (25.94)	0.83 (43.3)	0.87 (30)	1.06 (161.41)
1664	1.71 (44.69)	0.82 (42.8)	0.87 (30)	1.01 (154.29)
1665	1.09 (28.25)	0.83 (43.0)	0.81 (28)	0.99 (149.28)
1666	0.85 (22.06)	0.79 (41.0)	0.76 (26)	0.90 (135.36)
1667	0.86 (22.22)	0.65 (33.4)	0.67 (23)	0.76 (115.12)
1668	0.82 (21.25)	0.70 (36.0)	0.76 (26)	0.58 (86.39)
1669	1.11 (28.75)	0.89 (45.5)	1.00 (34)	0.56 (84.03)
1670	0.97 (25.0)	0.72 (37.0)	0.76 (26)	0.56 (83.81)
1671	1.04 (26.62)	0.81 (41.5)	1.23 (42)	0.83 (124.24)
1672	1.01 (25.94)	0.81 (41.0)	0.88 (30)	0.89 (132.55)
1673	1.06 (27.25)	0.91 (46.0)	1.12 (38)	0.98 (145.89)
1674	0.68 (17.5)	2.28 (115.)	2.37 (80)	1.38 (203.53)
1675	2.00 (51.0)	2.08 (105.)	1.78 (60)	1.39 (204.83)
1676	1.67 (42.5)	1.52 (76.5)	1.63 (55)	1.06 (155.70)
1677	0.89 (22.5)	0.99 (49.5)	0.89 (30)	0.95 (138.83)
1678	1.06 (26.88)	0.89 (44.5)	0.95 (32)	0.69 (100.60)
1679	1.16 (29.38)	0.84 (42.0)	0.78 (26)	0.61 (88.55)
1680	1.04 (26.25)	0.90 (44.5)	0.96 (32)	0.59 (85.95)
1681	1.03 (25.94)	0.88 (43.8)	0.78 (26)	0.65 (93.77)
1682	0.93 (23.44)	0.85 (42.0)	0.81 (27)	0.71 (102.55)
1683	0.92 (23.16)	0.87 (42.8)	1.06 (35)	0.72 (104.27)
1684	1.25 (31.25)	1.43 (70.0)	1.33 (44)	1.02 (146.21)
1685	0.83 (20.75)	0.77 (35.0)	0.55 (18)	0.79 (113.92)
1686	0.86 (21.56)	0.78 (38.0)	0.79 (26)	0.65 (93.45)
1687	0.87 (21.56)	0.72 (35.0)	0.67 (22)	0.58 (82.25)
1688	0.73 (18.12)	0.70 (34.0)	0.73 (24)	0.70 (95.43)
1689	0.73 (18.12)	0.80 (38.8)	0.70 (23)	0.74 (105.29)
1690	0.76 (18.75)	0.80 (38.8)	0.73 (24)	0.79 (112.52)
1691	0.81 (20.0)	0.85 (41.0)	1.20 (39)	0.77 (108.91)
1692	1.04 (25.62)	1.12 (53.5)	1.48 (48)	1.30 (182.58)
1693	1.57 (38.56)	1.68 (80.0)	1.69 (55)	1.37 (192.85)
1694	1.69 (41.56)	1.92 (91.5)	1.02 (33)	1.15 (160.88)
1695	1.42 (34.75)	1.40 (66.2)	0.99 (32)	1.06 (148.75)
1696	1.18 (28.75)	1.60 (75.5)	1.40 (45)	1.21 (168.32)
1697	1.21 (29.38)	1.30 (61.2)	1.55 (50)	1.51 (209.24)

Year	Liège Spelt	Liège Rye	Maastricht Rye	Amsterdam Rye
1698	1.95 (47.5)	2.75 (129.5)	2.34 (75)	2.29 (317.16)
1699	1.15 (27.84)	1.33 (62.2)	1.19 (38)	1.57 (217.63)
1700	0.85 (20.5)	0.87 (40.5)	0.94 (30)	1.05 (145.13)
1701	0.97 (23.5)	0.99 (46.0)	1.13 (36)	0.87 (119.70)
1702	1.07 (25.75)	1.04 (48.0)	0.97 (31)	0.77 (106.05)
1703	1.24 (29.75)	1.16 (53.5)	1.01 (32)	0.90 (123.38)
1704	1.09 (26.25)	0.96 (44.0)	0.98 (31)	0.79 (107.68)
1705	1.12 (26.88)	0.99 (45.5)	0.95 (30)	0.80 (108.51)
1706	0.91 (21.88)	0.79 (36.0)	0.76 (24)	0.75 (101.22)
1707	0.90 (21.44)	0.71 (32.2)	0.70 (22)	0.78 (105.23)
1708	1.51 (35.88)	1.48 (67.2)	2.22 (70)	1.60 (215.83)
1709	1.24 (29.5)	2.06 (93.5)	1.60 (50)	2.01 (269.69)
1710	1.01 (23.97)	1.00 (45.2)	0.93 (29)	1.33 (178.68)
1711	0.88 (20.91)	0.94 (42.2)	0.83 (26)	0.98 (131.31)
1712	0.89 (21.06)	1.01 (45.2)	0.96 (30)	1.01 (134.46)
1713	1.00 (23.5)	1.19 (53.0)	1.22 (38)	1.22 (162.50)
1714	0.86 (20.13)	1.08 (48.2)	0.81 (25)	1.21 (160.59)
1715	0.85 (20.0)	0.73 (32.5)	0.74 (23)	1.06 (140.29)
1716	0.81 (19.03)	0.68 (30.2)	0.65 (20)	0.95 (124.54)
1717	0.80 (18.75)	0.68 (30.0)	0.65 (20)	1.01 (132.15)
1718	0.74 (17.16)	0.67 (29.2)	0.72 (22)	0.91 (119.12)
1719	0.90 (20.88)	0.87 (38.0)	0.91 (28)	1.00 (130.75)
1720	0.78 (18.06)	0.70 (30.8)	0.69 (21)	0.88 (114.45)
1721	0.63 (14.69)	0.70 (30.2)	0.66 (20)	0.73 (95.08)
1722	0.64 (14.75)	0.70 (30.2)	0.82 (25)	0.73 (93.98)
1723	0.80 (18.5)	0.78 (33.5)	0.82 (25)	0.81 (104.18)
1724	1.26 (28.91)	0.75 (32.2)	1.32 (40)	1.05 (135.44)
1725	1.05 (24.0)	1.19 (51.0)	0.79 (24)	1.06 (136.27)
1726	0.90 (20.66)	0.90 (38.5)	0.90 (27)	1.05 (134.87)
1727	0.81 (18.47)	0.97 (41.5)	0.80 (24)	1.04 (133.18)
1728	0.94 (21.44)	1.04 (44.0)	1.33 (40)	0.95 (120.40)
1729	0.85 (19.38)	0.84 (35.8)	0.67 (20)	0.75 (94.98)
1730	0.97 (21.94)	0.85 (36.0)	0.94 (28)	0.70 (88.78)
1731	0.97 (21.94)	0.65 (27.5)	0.74 (22)	0.73 (91.92)
1732	0.77 (17.28)	0.56 (23.5)	0.67 (20)	0.69 (86.19)
1733	0.86 (19.47)	0.74 (30.9)	0.74 (22)	0.87 (108.85)
1734	0.81 (18.12)	0.72 (30.0)	0.68 (20)	0.88 (109.78)
1735	0.70 (15.75)	0.66 (27.2)	0.61 (18)	0.82 (101.73)
1736	0.53 (11.78)	0.56 (23.2)	0.54 (16)	0.92 (113.88)
1737	0.71 (15.94)	0.68 (28.0)	0.72 (21)	0.87 (107.10)
1738	0.87 (19.44)	1.08 (44.2)	1.23 (36)	0.87 (106.92)
1739	1.10 (24.38)	1.26 (51.5)	1.64 (48)	1.23 (150.97)
1740	1.40 (31.06)	1.61 (65.5)	1.17 (34)	1.61 (197.17)
1741	0.99 (21.91)	0.95 (38.5)	0.89 (26)	1.17 (142.8)
1742	0.93 (20.44)	0.82 (33.0)	0.83 (24)	0.87 (105.64)

Year	Liège Spelt	Liège Rye	Maastricht Rye	Amsterdam Rye
1743	0.95 (20.97)	0.75 (30.0)	0.69 (20)	0.78 (95.08)
1744	0.71 (15.62)	0.64 (25.8)	0.62 (18)	0.80 (96.72)
1745	0.67 (14.66)	0.78 (31.3)	0.80 (23)	1.10 (132.79)
1745	1.26 (27.5)	1.41 (56.0)	1.36 (39)	1.27 (152.48)
1746	1.25 (27.28)	1.29 (51.2)	0.98 (28)	1.20 (144.38)
1748	0.83 (18.12)	1.00 (39.6)	0.91 (26)	1.08 (129.50)
1749	1.12 (24.38)	1.24 (48.9)	1.47 (42)	0.94 (112.47)

* Figures in parentheses are annual prices. Liège prices are patards/setier; Maastricht prices are *stuivers/vat;* Amsterdam prices are guilders/last.

Notes

Regression Equations for Price Index Computations:

Liège Spelt: Slope = -.05167
  Y-Intercept = 112.061

Liège Rye: Slope = -.05966
  Y-Intercept = 120.008

Maastricht Rye: Slope = -.07069
  Y-Intercept = 152.132

Amsterdam Rye: Slope = -.38318
  Y-Intercept = 789.259

Sources for Basse-Mosan and Amsterdam Prices

Liège: P. Simenon, *Traite de la reduction des rentes ...* (Liège, 1753), pp. 111-119.

Maastricht: Stadsarchief van Maastricht. Handschriftcollectie. Handschrift No. 201. These prices have been checked against the following sources for the years 1620-1742:
1. RAL Aanwinst 1936, no. 599.
2. RAL Collectianea Collete, vol. 3.

Amsterdam: Nicholaus Wilhelmus Posthumus, *Inquiry into the History of Prices in Holland,* I (Leiden: E. J. Brill, 1946), 569-576. To get the Amsterdam prices recorded in this appendix, I took a harvest year beginning in September and computed annual means from the monthly prices Posthumus gives.

Appendix D

Correlation coefficients for Variables Describing Life in the Basse-Meuse

The table that follows this introduction presents correlation coefficients for a number of annual variables I collected to describe war and other conditions in the Basse-Meuse between 1620 and 1749. All the correlations are based on the Index of Extreme Behavior values except for war and five of six weather variables. Five variables were coded to reflect weather conditions in the Basse-Meuse, based on Vanderlinden's study of historical weather conditions in the Low Countries. They are hard winters; mild winters; hot, dry summers; cold, wet summers; and late or early frosts. The weather conditions during each year from 1620 to 1749 are shown in Appendix A. When a specific weather condition was present in a given year, I coded a value of 1.0 for that variable for that year; otherwise, I gave it a value of zero. I created two variables for war, one indicating all years in which any military activity took place in the Basse-Meuse, and the second indicating those years in which major military activity, such as a siege, battle, or bombardment, took place. The first is referred to as "Normal War" in the accompanying table of coefficients, and I gave a value of 1.0 for the following years: 1622, 1626-1636, 1643-1644, 1649-1651, 1653-1654, 1672-1678, 1681, 1688-1697, 1701-1712, and 1746-1748. The second I called "Major War," and I coded a value of 1.0 for these years: 1632, 1634, 1673, 1691, 1746-1748. The reader will note that the two war variables often produced quite different correlations, a fact that I will discuss in a future, technical paper on the statistical relationships discovered in this work.

The values coded for prices, weather, production, and some of the demography (as marked in the table) are for harvest years. War, and the rest of the demographic variables are for calendar years. The correlations have been computed based on simultaneous interraction, with the exception that production has been lagged one year earlier than the price and demographic variables. This means that it is assumed that a given harvest will affect population and prices in the year that begins immediately following the harvest.

The correlations make use of values for 1620-1749, with the following exceptions:
Liège rye prices: 1630-1749
Maastricht tithe: 1620-1631, 1633-1640, 1657-1671, 1674-1746, 1748-1749
Louwberg farm: 1660-1727, 1729-1749.
Deaths: 1628-1636, 1639-1645, 1649-1749
Births and conceptions: 1665-1749

Correlation Coefficients

	Amsterdam Rye Price	Liège Spelt Price	Liège Rye Price	Maastricht Rye Price	Maastricht Tithe	Louwberg Production (Value)	Louwberg Production (Volume)	Calendar Year Deaths	Harvest Year Deaths
Late Freeze	.0152 (.432)	-.0508 (.284)	.0704 (.223)	.1244 (.080)	-.0901 (.175)	.1250 (.120)	-.0181 (.433)	-.1044 (.132)	-.1187 (.101)
Wet Summer	.1293 (.072)	-.0237 (.395)	.1769 (.027)	.0911 (.152)	.0731 (.224)	.1865 (.039)	.0118 (.456)	-.0184 (.422)	-.1291 (.083)
Dry Summer	.0174 (.422)	-.0417 (.319)	.0348 (.354)	.0395 (.328)	-.3216 (.001)	-.0825 (.220)	-.1329 (.107)	.0942 (.157)	.0215 (.409)
Mild Winter	-.0883 (.160)	-.1639 (.032)	-.1229 (.092)	-.1237 (.081)	-.0315 (.372)	.1067 (.158)	.1311 (.110)	-.1062 (.128)	-.1440 (.061)
Hard Winter	.0229 (.398)	-.0508 (.284)	-.0464 (.308)	.0818 (.178)	-.0728 (.225)	.1040 (.165)	.0301 (.390)	.0556 (.277)	.0720 (.220)
Winter Temp.	.0329 (.365)	-.0404 (.336)	.0307 (.373)	-.0211 (.412)	-.0206 (.421)	-.1932 (.034)	-.1772 (.048)	.0976 (.170)	.0796 (.206)
Normal War	.1424 (.054)	.1671 (.029)	.2813 (.001)	.2700 (.001)	-.2365 (.006)	.0558 (.301)	-.1278 (.116)	.0823 (.189)	.0837 (.185)
Severe War	.0162 (.428)	-.0656 (.230)	-.0268 (.386)	-.0368 (.359)	-.3313 (.001)	-.0923 (.194)	-.2266 (.016)	.2690 (.002)	.3227 (.001)
Har. Yr. Concept.	-.4584 (.001)	-.5528 (.001)	-.5749 (.001)	-.6152 (.001)	.4621 (.001)	-.1873 (.044)	.2311 (.018)	-.1620 (.071)	-.3120 (.002)
Cal. Yr. C.....	-.4160 (.001)	-.5700 (.001)	-.5350 (.001)	-.4224 (.001)	.3712 (.001)	-.0660 (.275)	.1867 (.045)	-.4500 (.001)	-.5449 (.001)

	Amsterdam Rye Price	Liège Spelt Price	Liège Rye Price	Maastricht Rye Price	Maastricht Tithe	Louwberg Production (Value)	Louwberg Production (Volume)	Calendar Year Deaths	Harvest Year Deaths
Har. Yr. Baptisms	-.3864 (.001)	-.5154 (.001)	-.4847 (.001)	-.4019 (.001)	.3268 (.001)	.0146 (.448)	.2412 (.014)	-.4474 (.001)	-.5084 (.001)
Cal. Yr. Baptisms	-.1735 (.056)	-.2827 (.004)	-.2820 (.004)	-.1135 (.150)	.2511 (.011)	.1268 (.124)	.1730 (.058)	-.5280 (.001)	-.3796 (.001)
Har. Yr. Deaths	.0542 (.281)	.2368 (.005)	.1672 (.037)	.1618 (.041)	-.3294 (.001)	-.1043 (.165)	-.2202 (.020)	.7954 (.001)	
Cal. Yr. Deaths	-.0159 (.432)	.1575 (.045)	.1323 (.079)	.0911 (.164)	-.3067 (.001)	-.1594 (.067)	-.2029 (.028)		
Louwberg Volume	.2428 (.011)	-.0267 (.402)	.0716 (.252)	-.0350 (.372)	.3843 (.001)	.7534 (.001)			
Louwberg Value	.6361 (.001)	.3623 (.001)	.5473 (.001)	.5051 (.001)	.0575 (.298)				
Maastr't Tithe	-.0470 (.317)	-.2597 (.004)	-.2401 (.009)	-.3190 (.001)					
Maastr't Rye	.7148 (.001)	.6736 (.001)	.8557 (.001)						
Liège Rye	.7903 (.001)	.7457 (.001)							
Liège Spelt	.5963 (.001)								

Figures in parentheses are significance levels

Correlation Coefficients

	Calendar Year Baptisms	Harvest Year Baptisms	Calendar Year Concept.	Harvest Year Concept.	Normal War	Severe War	Winter Temp	Hard Wint	Mild Wint	Hot, Dry Summers	Cold, Wet Summers
Late Freeze	-.0505 (.324)	-.1420 (.099)	-.1184 (.142)	-.1637 (.068)	-.0226 (.399)	-.0725 (.206)	.1257 (.092)	-.0081 (.464)	-.0734 (.203)	-.0647 (.232)	.0102 (.454)
Wet Summer	-.0717 (.258)	-.0388 (.363)	-.0460 (.339)	.0004 (.499)	.0921 (.149)	-.0168 (.425)	-.1847 (.025)	.0921 (.149)	-.0033 (.485)	-.1814 (.019)	
Dry Summer	.0720 (.258)	.1295 (.120)	.1045 (.172)	-.0660 (.276)	.1770 (.022)	.2394 (.003)	-.0549 (.282)	.0559 (.264)	.2029 (.010)		
Mild Winter	.0052 (.481)	.0927 (.201)	.1073 (.166)	.1583 (.075)	-.1052 (.117)	-.1135 (.099)	.2623 (.003)	.2322 (.004)			
Hard Winter	.1478 (.090)	.0599 (.294)	.0839 (.224)	-.1228 (.133)	-.0398 (.326)	-.0299 (.368)	-.3967 (.001)				
Normal War	-.2449 (.012)	-.2856 (.004)	-.2851 (.004)	-.2591 (.009)							
Winter Temp.	-.0466 (.336)	.0263 (.406)	.0496 (.327)	.0831 (.226)	-.1281 (.088)	-.1510 (.055)					
Severe War	-.1215 (.134)	-.0859 (.219)	-.1165 (.146)	-.1200 (.138)							
Har. Yr. Concept.	.2050 (.031)	.4771 (.001)	.5928 (.001)								
Cal. Yr. Concept.	.5582 (.001)	.9482 (.001)									
Har. Yr.	.6114										

Methods for Correcting Incomplete Parish Register Data

The three methods for correcting incomplete parish register data described below have been used to prepare the data used in Chapters VII and VIII. I chose which method to use when completing data as follows: I always chose Method 1 over the other two, and Method 2 over Method 3.

1. When incomplete data existed for a single parish in only some months of the year, the distribution of births or deaths through the year was assumed to reflect the pattern of all years (Tables 7.3 and 8.3). Then, it was possible to compute likely numbers of births and deaths for each missing month by assuming, first, that the total value of the months known was accurate in the aggregate, and second, that any missing months reflected the "all years" proportion attributed to that month.

2. Sometimes no data existed for a single parish for a whole year. In that case I assumed that the proportion of all events (either births, deaths or conceptions) in all parishes attributed to that parish in that year would equal the events of that parish in all years as a proportion of events in all parishes in all years for which complete data existed.

3. In a few cases, when the first two methods were impossible to use I computed a probable number of births or deaths in a parish in a given year by taking the mean of the five preceding and five following years.

Notes

"Measures and Moneys"

1. Joseph Ruwet, *L'Agriculture et les classes rurales au pays de Herve sous l'ancien régime* (Liège, 1943), pp. 78-79.
2. Hans van Werveke, "Monnaie de compte et monnaie réele," *RBPH*, 13 (1934), 123-152.
3. Hubert Frère, "Numismatique liégeoise: notes sur la monnaie de compte dans la principauté de Liège," *BIAL*, 80 (1967), 91-112.

Introduction

1. Jean Meuvret, "Les Crises de subsistance et la démographie de la France d'Ancien Régime," *Population*, 1 (1946), 643-650.
2. Pierre Goubert, *Beauvais et le Beauvaisis de 1600 à 1730*, 2 vols. (Paris: SEVPEN, 1960).
3. See especially, Pierre Goubert, *L'Ancien Régime*, I, "La Société," (Paris: Armand Colin, 1969), translated as *The Ancien Régime* (New York: Harper, 1973); and Pierre Goubert, "The French Peasantry of the Seventeenth Century: A Regional Example," *Past and Present*, No. 10 (1956), 55-77.
4. Pierre Goubert, "Historical Demography and the Reinterpretation of Early Modern French History: A Research Review," *Journal of Interdisciplinary History*, 1 (1970), 37-48.
5. Claude Bruneel, in his enormous and thorough study of mortality in the Duchy of Brabant, downplays the importance of war for mortality. Although he considers it in terms of his own data, three of the four secondary works on which he relies were published in 1956 or earlier. Claude Bruneel, *La Mortalité dans les campagnes: le duché de Brabant aux XVIIe et XVIIIe siècles* (Louvain, 1977), I, 121.
6. George Clark, *The Seventeenth Century*, second edition (New York: Oxford University Press, 1961), p. 98.
7. For the German situation, see these summaries: Gunther Franz, *Der Dreissigjährige Krieg und das deutsche volk. Unterzuchungen zur Bevölkerungs- und Agrargeschichte*, third edition (Stuttgart: Gustav Fischer Verlag, 1961); Theodore K. Rabb, "The Effects of the Thirty Years' War on the German Economy," *Journal of Modern History*, 34 (1962), 40-51; and Henry Kamen, "The Social and Economic Consequences of the Thirty Years' War," *Past and Present*, No. 39 (1968), 44-61.
8. One of the best recent books on military history is Geoffrey Parker's study of the machinery of the Spanish army in the Low Countries: Geoffrey Parker, *The Army of*

242

Flanders and the Spanish Road, 1567-1659. The Logistics of Spanish Victory and Defeat in the Low Countries Wars (Cambridge: Cambridge University Press, 1972).

9   The territory is now contained within the Dutch province of Limburg, the Belgian province of Liège, and a small part of Belgian Limburg. The name Basse-Meuse (which should not be confused with the French-regime Departement of the *Meuse-Inferieure*, the northern half of the Basse-Meuse) is a Liégeois expression for the river area around Liège. I use the name even though it may misserve the large Dutch-speaking population in the area. For that, I apologize. For a published example of the use of the name, see Etienne Hélin, "Les Antécédents de l'industrialisation de la Basse-Meuse," *Vieux Liège*, 7 (1970), 458-459.

10   Unfortunately, the available data seldom offer the opportunity to draw a systematic or random sample. I have used whatever data are available. There is, therefore, a chance of bias toward including places or people who were untouched by war or touched only lightly by war, but it is only a remote chance. Most of the materials on which I relied have always been deposited in the cities and not in the countryside, and their survival has more to do with the interest of their collectors and owners in record-keeping than with the destructive capacity of war.

11   The prosperity of the Basse-Meuse is discussed further in Chapters I (where I describe the economic regime), II (the available money for loans in the countryside, a sign of prosperity), IV (the productivity of agriculture) and IX (using the prosperity to explain why the region and its population were relatively stable in spite of wars).

Chapter I

1   Godefroid Kurth, *La Frontière linguistique en Belgique et dans la nord de la France*, Mém. Cour., vol. 48, 2 vols. (Brussels, 1895-1898). See especially the list of linguistic border communities, pp. 21-25. J. M. Remouchamps, "Carte systematique de la Wallonie, precedée d'une note sur la frontière linguistique et d'une double nomenclature des communes belges de langue Romane d'après le recensement du 31 décembre 1930," *Bulletin de la Commission Royale de Toponymie et de Dialectologie*, 9 (1935). For the Liégeois dialect, see the three volumes (a volume of rhymes and two dictionaries), Jean Haust, *Le Dialect wallon de Liège*, 3 vols. (Liège: H. Vailant-Carmanne, 1930-1948). G. de Marez, *Le Problème de la colonization franque et du régime agraire en Belgique*, Mémoires de l'Académie Royale de Belgique, Classe des Lettres, in 4°, 2nd series, 9 (1926). Franz Petri, *Germanisches Volkserbe in Wallonien und Nordfrankreich. Die fränkische Landnahme in Frankreich und den Niederlanden und die Bildung der westlichen Sprachgrenze* (Bonn: Ludwig Rohrscheid, 1937). Charles Verlinden, *Les Origines de la frontière linguistique en Belgique et la colonisation franque* (Brussels: La Renaissance du Livre, 1955).

2   For the religious history of the region, see Henri Pirenne, *Histoire de Belgique*, IV (Brussels, 1911), 295-299; Willem Bax, *Het Protestantisme in het bisdom Luik en vooral te Maastricht*, 2 vols. (The Hague, 1941); P. J. H. Ubachs, *Twee heren, twee confessies. De verhouding von Staat en Kerk te Maastricht, 1632-1673* (Assen: Van Gorcum, 1975); and Eugene Hubert, *Les Eglises Protestantes du Duché de Limbourg pendant le XVIIIe siècle. Etude d'histoire politique et religieuse*. Mémoires, published by the Classe de Lettres et des Sciences Morales et Politiques de l'Académie royale de Belgique, 2nd ser., collection in-4°, vol. 4 (Brussels, 1908).

3   Pirenne, *Histoire de Belgique*, IV, 290.

4 We will use the French spelling *Limbourg* to indicate the ancien régime Spanish/ Austrian possession (where the administrative language was French) and the Dutch spelling, *Limburg*, to indicate the Dutch and modern Belgian provinces of that name. There is relatively little overlap between the old Duchy of Limbourg and the modern Belgian province, Limburg.

5 Ubachs, *Twee heren, twee confessies*; Harsin, *Etudes critiques*, III, 441-450; Louis de Crassier, "Maastricht," *Dictionnaire historique du Limbourg neerlandais de la periode féodale à nos jours* (Maastricht, 1941-1944), pp. 267-269. P. F. Neny, *Mémoires historiques et politiques des Pays-Bas autrichiens* (Neuchatel, 1784), pp. 254-257.

6 See the collections published by the Commission Royale Pour la Publication des Anciennes Lois et Ordonnances de la Belgique, especially, Constance Casier and Louis Crahay, *Coutumes du duché de Limbourg et des pays d'Outre Meuse* (Brussels, 1889); and J. Raikem, J. Polain, L. Crahay and St. Bormans, *Coutumes du Pays de Liège*, 3 vols. (Brussels, 1870-1884).

7 For general characteristics of local government, see Georges Hansotte, "Les Institutions locales dans les campagnes du pays de Liège à la fin de l'ancien régime," *Cahiers de Clio*, 1 (1965), 15-19. For individual communities, see the village monographs cited in the Bibliography.

8 Charles Rahlenbeck, *Les Pays d'Outre-Meuse. Etudes historiques sur Dalhem, Fauquemont et Rolduc* (Brussels: P. Weissenbruch, 1888), p. 198. This book, although biased in favor of the Dutch, is a good source on the government of the Pays d'Outre Meuse, and the transition to Dutch rule.

9 Each had a *matricule*, or schedule for dividing taxation. See the following sources: Joseph Daris, "Quartiers et tailles de la principauté," Ch. X of "L'Ancien principauté de Liège," *NOTICES*, IX, 73-83; G. Bigwood, *Les Impôts généraux dans les Pays-Bas autrichiens; étude historique de législation financière* (Paris and Louvain, 1900); G. Bigwood, "Matricules et cadastres. Aperçu sur l'organisation du cadastre en Flandre, Brabant, Limbourg, et Luxembourg avant la domination française," *Annales de la Société d'Archéologie de Bruxelles*, 12 (1898), 388-411; A. Brouwers, "Documents relatifs à la matricule du duché de Limbourg en 1705," *BIAL*, 33 (1903), 69-88.

10 In the seventeenth century, armies did not have the resources to meet frequently in pitched battle. In the eighteenth century, those resources became too valuable to waste. See, among many other possible references on the subject, Michael Howard, *War in European History* (London: Oxford University Press, 1976), pp. 70-71.

11 Pirenne, *Histoire de Belgique*, IV, 290; C. Defrecheux, "Histoire de la neutralité liégeoise," *BIAL*, 37 (1907), 159-286. Paul Harsin, "L'Attitude de l'Empire a l'égard de la neutralité liégeoise," *BIAL*, 51 (1926), 32-61.

12 Such a protectorate led to the eventual incorporation of Utrecht, another major ecclesiastical principality, into the Habsburg succession, in 1527. Pirenne, *Histoire de Belgique*, III, 98-101.

13 Paul Harsin, "Les Origines diplomatiques de la neutralité liégoise (1477-1492)," *RBPH*, 5 (1926), 423-452.

14 Paul Harsin, *Etudes critiques sur l'histoire de la principauté de Liège 1477-1795*, III (Liège, 1958); Paul Harsin, "La Neutralité liégeoise en 1632," *Revue d'Histoire Moderne*, 15 (1940), 13-31.

15 Defrecheux, "Histoire de la neutralité liégeoise," pp. 161-173.

16 For the circumstances of this army, see below, pp. 20.

17 The two armies' losses alone totalled 28,000, four times total Liégeois forces of the

time. See Ernest R. Dupuy and Trevor N. Dupuy, *The Encyclopedia of Military History* (New York: Harper and Row, 1970), p. 548.

18   The historical literature for Liège and the Basse-Meuse is particularly rich. There are two histories in Latin, Fisen, *Historia Ecclesiae Leodiensis* (Liège, 1696), and the continuation of Jean Erard Foullon, *Historia Leodiensis*, III (Liège, 1737). Detailed studies in French include Joseph Daris, *Histoire du diocèse et de la principauté de Liège pendant le XVIIᵉ siècle*, 2 vols. (Liège, 1877), Théodose Bouille, *Histoire de la ville et pays de Liège*, III (Liège, 1732), Paul Harsin, *Les Relations extérieurs de la principauté de Liège sous Jean-Louis d'Elderen et Joseph-Clément de Bavière (1688-1718)* (Liège, 1927); Michel Huisman, *Essai sur le règne du Prince-Evêque de Liège, Maximilien-Henri de Bavière*, Mém. Cour., vol. 59 (Brussels, 1899); Henri Lonchay, *La Rivalité de la France et l'Espagne aux Pays-Bas (1635-1700). Etude d'histoire diplomatique et militaire*, Mém. Cour., vol. 54 (Brussels, 1896); Henri Lonchay, *La Principauté de Liège, la France et les Pays-Bas au XVIIᵉ et au XVIIᵉ siècle*, Mém. Cour., vol. 44 (Brussels, 1890); Albert Waddington, *La Republique des Provinces-Unies, la France et les Pays-Bas espagnols de 1630 à 1650*, 2 vols. (Paris, 1895-1897); and Harsin, *Etudes critiques sur l'histoire de la principauté de Liège*, III. The two most useful surveys are the section on Liège, in the context of all of Belgium, in Pirenne, *Histoire de Belgique*, vols. 4 and 5, and the excellent work of Alberts on the "Limburgs" (including the Pays d'Outre Meuse and Maastricht), W. Jappe Alberts, *Geschiedenis van de beide Limburgen*, 2 vols. (Assen: Van Gorcum, 1972-1974).

19   Pirenne, *Histoire de Belgique*, IV, 317; Lonchay, *La Principauté de Liège*, p. 37.

20   Pirenne, *Histoire de Belgique*, IV, 291-308; Harsin, *Etudes Critiques*, III, 435-437.

21   Pirenne, *Histoire de Belgique*, IV, 313-316.

22   *Ibid.*, IV, 323; Daris, *Histoire du diocèse et de la principauté de Liège, pendant le XVIIe siècle*, I, 56-59; Bouille, *Histoire de la ville et pays de Liège*, III, 173; Lonchay, *La Rivalité*, p. 162.

23   Pirenne, *Histoire de Belgique*, IV, 327; Daris, *Histoire du diocèse et de la principauté de Liège pendant le XVIIᵉ siècle*, I, 271.

24   Pirenne, *Histoire de Belgique*, V, 138-139; Huisman, *Essai sur le règne*, pp. 88-91.

25   Max Braubach, *Die Politik des Kurfursten Joseph Clemens von Köln beim Ausbruch des spanischen Erbfolgekrieges und die Vertreibung der Franzosen vom Niederrhein (1701-1703)* (Bonn, 1925); Pirenne, *Histoire de Belgique*, V, 161-162; Daris, *Histoire du diocèse et de la principauté de Liège pendant le XVIIᵉ siècle*, II, 272.

26   Harsin, *Les Relations exterieurs*; Pirenne, *Histoire de Belgique*, V, 148-157; Daris, *Histoire du diocèse et de la principauté de Liège pendant le XVIIᵉ siècle*, II, 218-228; Lonchay, *La Rivalité*, p. 317.

27   Geoffrey Parker, *The Army of Flanders and the Spanish Road* (Cambridge: Cambridge University Press, 1972), pp. 50-105.

28   Charles Rahlenbeck, *Les Pays d'Outre-Meuse*, p. 244. Philippe de Hurges, *Voyage à Liège et à Maestricht en 1615*, Henri Michelant, ed. (Liège: Société des Bibliophiles Liégeois, 1872), p. 226.

29   Alberts, *Geschiedenis van de beide Limburgen*, II, 2; Daris, *Histoire du diocèse et de la principauté de Liège pendant le XVIIᵉ siècle*, I, 86-95; Frederick Henry, Prince of Orange, *A Iournal of all the principall passages of that late famous siege and taking of the citie of Mastricht by the Prince of Orange . . .* [Pollard-Redgrave Short Title Catalogue, no. 11365]; *id., Articles accordez av magistrat, bovrgeois et habitans de la ville de Maestric . . .* (Paris, 1632); Ubachs, *Twee Heren, Twee Confessies*. For the treaty settlement, see J. Dumont, *Corps universel diplomatique du droit des gens contenent un recueil des traités.* (Amsterdam and La Haye, 1726-1731), VI, pt. I, 430.

30 For discussions of the siege, see the following works: Daris, *Histoire du diocèse et de la principauté de Liège pendant le XVIIe siècle*, II, 56; Lonchay, *La Rivalité*, p. 258; Alberts, *Geschiedenis van de beide Limburgen*, II, 30-33; Josef Habets, "Analects concernant le siège de Maestricht et le sejour des Francais dans les pays d'Outre-Meuse, 1672-1679," *Publications de la Société d'Histoire et d'Archéologie dans le Duché de Limbourg*, 7 (1870), 488-498; *Journal fidelle de tout ce qui s'est passe au siège de Maestricht attaqué par Louis XIV, roy de France, et defendu par M. de Fariauz* . . . (Amsterdam, 1674); P. Lazard, *Vauban* (Paris, 1934), pp. 77, 154-157; and Louis XIV, King of France, *Oeuvres de Louis XIV* (Paris, 1806), III, 326-395.

31 Daris, *Histoire du diocèse et de la principauté de Liège pendant le XVIIe siècle*, II, 77-78; Lonchay, *La Rivalité*, pp. 275-276; "Dagverhaal van 't beleg van Maastricht in 1676," *De Maasgouw* (1881), 489-490, 493-495, 498-499, 502-503, 506-507.

32 Lonchay, *La Rivalité*, p. 289; H. Vast, *Les Grandes traités du règne de Louis XIV*, II (Paris, 1898), 57-58, 83.

33 Pirenne, *Histoire de Belgique*, V, 225-226; Alberts, *Geschiedenis van de beide Limburgen*, II, 79-80.

34 Georges Hansotte, "La Vie quotidienne à Herstal sous le régime francais," *Vieux Liège*, 5 (1959), 361. For the area of Herstal, see Royaume de Belgique, Ministère de l'Intérieur, *Tableau statistique à l'appui du projet d'organisation d'un service médical rural* (Brussels, 1849), p. 140. See, also, André Collart-Sacré, *La Libre Seigneurie de Herstal: Son histoire, ses monuments, ses rues, et ses lieux-dits*, I (Liège: Georges Thone, 1927), 345; and Henri Francotte, "La Vie rurale en Belgique sous l'ancien régime: Le Village de Bombaye," *BSAHL*, 2 (1882), 252.

35 Charles Bihot, *Le Pays de Herve, Etude de géographie humaine* (Antwerp: J. van Hille-de Backer, 1913), pp. 28-29. Joseph Deckers, "Vente de biens meubles à la ferme du Temple (Visé) en 1784," *Vieux Liège*, 8, No. 175 (1971), 75. Jacques Thielens, "La Cense du château d'Argenteau au XVIIe et XVIIIe siècles," *Anciens Pays et Assemblées d'Etats*, 48 (1966), 207.

36 The geographical and cultural characteristics presented in the next few paragraphs are based, for the Hesbaye, on Ivan Delatte, *Les Classes rurales dans la principauté de Liège au XVIIIe siécle* (Liège, 1945), pp. 29-31; for the Pays de Herve, it is based on Bihot, *Le Pays de Herve, passim*, and Joseph Ruwet, *L'Agriculture et les classes rurales au pays de Herve sous l'ancien régime* (Liège, 1943), pp. 39-43. See, also, Cavenne, *Statistique de département de la Meuse-Inférieure* . . . (Maastricht, year-X [1802]), pp. 23-25, for a description of the northern half of the area I call the Basse-Meuse, which was part of the French Regime department of the Meuse-Inférieure. For an overview of these geographic regions, see M. A. Lefevre, "Carte des regions géographiques belges," *Bulletin de la Société Belge d'Études Géographiques*, 10 (1940), 67-68, and map.

37 Grapevines were still planted in the Basse-Meuse in the eighteenth century. See AEL C *de* J, Hermalle-sous-Argenteau, 86, Rapports et mesures de biens, 1750; AEL C *de* J, 20, Richelle, Rapport des biens de la juridiction de Richelle, 1663, and Mesure des terres, 1722. See, also Leon Halkin, "Étude historique sur la culture de la vigne en Belgique," *BSAHL*, 9 (1895); Joseph Dejardin, "Recherches historiques sur la Commune de Cheratte dans l'ancien pays du Limbourg," *Bulletin de la Société Scientifique et Litteraire du Limbourg*, 2 (1854), 184; and Collart-Sacré, *La Libre Seigneurie de Herstal*, I, 84. By the late seventeenth century, with improvements in transportation bringing southern wines, the production of local wines was declining.

38 See Marc Bloch, *French Rural History, An Essay on its Basic Characteristics*, Janet

Sondheimer, trans. (Berkeley: University of California Press, 1970). For traditional Belgian agrarian techniques, see Paul Lindemans, *Geschiedenis van de landbouw in België*, 2 vols., (Antwerp, 1952).

39 Joseph Ruwet, "Prix, production et bénéfices agricoles. Le Pays de Liège au XVIIIe siècle," *Cahiers d'histoire de prix*, 2 (1957), 71. Ernest Piton, "Histoire de Grand-Hallet et de Petit-Hallet," *BIAL*, 60 (1936), 256-257.

40 Ruwet, *Agriculture et les classes rurales au pays de Herve*, p. 58. His figures are based on AEL C*de*J, Bombaye, 57.

41 Ruwet, *L'Agriculture et les classes rurales au pays de Herve*, pp. 58-64.

42 Ruwet attributes the dense population of the Pays de Herve, and the transition to dairying, to the opportunities for industrial employment. He implies, rightly in my opinion, that this made the peasants more, rather than less, prosperous.

43 AEL C*de*J, Richelle, 20 (1722), and Myron P. Gutmann, "War and Rural Life in the Seventeenth Century: The Case of the Basse-Meuse" (diss., Princeton, 1976), pp. 54-61. Measures are explained more fully above, pp. XII-XIII.

44 This is based on an analysis of AEL C*de*J, Eben-Emael, 19. The character of the document, limitations on its use, and methods of analysis are discussed in detail in Gutmann, "War and Rural Life," pp. 54-61, and especially Table 2.2, p. 59. For the subsistence level, see the discussion of income distributions in J. C. G. M. Jansen, "Agrarian Development and Exploitation in South Limburg in the years 1650-1850," *Acta Historiae Neerlandica*, 5 (1970), 260-264, and especially, 263-264.

45 Pierre Goubert, *L'Ancien Régime*, I (Paris: Armand Colin, 1969), pp. 104-11.

46 For a discussion of the non-agricultural activities of the Basse-Meuse, see below and, for more detail, Gutmann, "War and Rural Life in the Seventeenth Century," pp. 63-71, and René Leboutte, "La Population de Dalhem du XVIIe au debut de XXe siècle; étude de démographie historique" (Mémoire de Licence, Liège, 1975).

47 The basic work on Liégeois heavy industry is Jean Yernaux, *La Metallurgie liégeoise et son expansion au XVIIe siècle* (Liège, 1939). Georges Hansotte has also been a prolific writer on this subject. See, especially, his "L'Industrie sidérurgique dans la valée de l'Ourthe liégeoise aux temps modernes," *La Vie Wallone*, 29 (1955), 116-224.

48 Claude Gaier, *Quatre siècles d'armurerie liégeoise* (Liège: Librairie Halbert, 1976).

49 The notarial archives of Liège are full of wartime contracts between gun-smiths and gun-merchants and military officers, agreeing to manufacture or provide arms. For a selection of those contracts, see Paulette Pieyns-Rigo and Claude Gaier, "Fournitures d'armes et vie armurière à Liège vers le milieu de XVIIIe siècle d'après les actes notariaux," *Le Musée d'Armes*, 5 (1977), 13-19.

50 Cecile Douxchamps-Lefevre, "Le Commerce du charbon dans les Pays-Bas autrichiens à la fin du XVIIe siècle," *RBPH*, 46 (1968), 394. The best single study of the coal-mining industry in the Basse-Meuse is J. Renard, "Vie et mort d'une industrie multiséculaire: la houillerie à Wandre," *BIAL*, 81 (1968), 73-280. Also important is the section on mining in André Collart-Sacre, *La Libre Seigneurie de Herstal*, pp. 90-141. See, also, Jean Ceyssens, "A Propos d'engins et d'anciens houillères," *CAPL*, 16 (1925), 86-88; Joseph Dejardin, "Recherches historiques sur la commune de Cheratte," pp. 184-185; and Edouard Poncelet, "La Seigneurie de Saive," *BIAL*, 22 (1891), 394-395.

51 Pirenne, *Histoire de Belgique*, V, 358.

52 *Ibid.*, 356-359; AEL PdD 129, f. 238, 10 Dec. 1675.

53 Collart-Sacré, *La Libre Seigneurie de Herstal*, I, 85-87; Poncelet, "Seigneurie de Saive," pp. 394-395; Dejardin, "Recherches historiques sur la Commune de Cheratte," p. 185.

F. Henaux, "Histoire de la bonne ville de Visé," *BIAL*, 1 (1852), 357. Rahlenbeck, *Les Pays d'Outre Meuse*, p. 267.

54　N. Briavoinne, *Mémoire sur l'état de la population des fabriques, des manufactures et du commerce dans les provinces des Pays-Bas depuis Albert et Isabelle jusqu'à la fin du siècle dernier*, Mémoires in-4° de l'Académie Royale de Belgique, vol. 14 (Brussels, 1840), pp. 60-61, 140-141. Rahlenbeck, *Les Pays d'Outre Meuse*, pp. 266, 274. For perspective on the growth of the Limbourg cloth industry, relative to the older industry at Leiden, see N. W. Posthumus, "De industrieele concurrentie tusschen Noord- en Zuidnederlandsche Nijverheidscentra in de XVIIe en XVIIIe eeuw," *Mélanges d'histoires offerts à Henri Pirenne . . .* (Brussels: Lamertin, 1926), II, 369-378. This article has been summarized in French in Henri Laurent, "La Concurrence entre les centres industriels des Provinces-Unies et de la principauté de Liège aux XVIIᵉ et XVIIIᵉ siècles et les origines de la grande industrie drapière Vertiétoise, d'après les travaux recents de M. Posthumus," *Revue d'Histoire Moderne*, 2 (1927), 216-219. For more on the shift of industry to Verviers, and local industry in the Basse-Meuse, see P. Lebrun, *L'Industrie de la laine à Verviers pendant le XVIIIᵉ et le commencement du XIXᵉ siècle* (Liège, 1948); and Poncelet, "Seigneurie de Saive," pp. 394-395. Also, L. Dechesne, *Industrie drapière de la Vesdre avant 1800* (Paris and Liège, 1926) and J. S. Renier, *Histoire de l'industrie drapière au Pays de Liège* (Liège, 1881).

55　Rahlenbeck, *Les Pays d'Outre Meuse*, pp. 266-267.

56　*Ibid.*, p. 262.

Chapter II

1　Henri de Sonkeux, *La Vie à Verviers il y a trois siècles* (Verviers, n.d. [probably 1946]), p. 37. On de Sonkeux himself, see J. Lejear, "Henri de Sonkeux et ses Mémoires," *Bulletin de la Société Verviétoise d'Archéologie et d'Histoire*, 11 (1910), 61-72.

2　"La déclaration de guerre et ses effets immédiats dans le pays." Chapter 1 of Hubert van Houtte, *Les Occupations étrangères en Belgique sous l'Ancien Régime*, I (Ghent, 1930), 1-29. A. Hansay, "Documents inédits concernant la mise en défense des compagnes lossaines à l'époque moderne," *Bulletin de la Commission Royale d'Histoire*, 95 (1931), 151-222.

3　Geoffrey Parker, *The Army of Flanders and the Spanish Road, 1567-1659* (Cambridge: Cambridge University Press, 1972), pp. 13-16.

4　In part, this is because the scale of armies did not appreciably increase between 1715 and 1789. See Geoffrey Parker, "The Military Revolution, 1560-1660 – a Myth?" *Journal of Modern History*, 48 (1976), 195-214.

5　The following are good examples of complaints: AEL St. Pierre 45-52; AEL Prieuré et Seigneurie d'Aywaille 180; *Tableau de la dévastation du pays de Liège* (Liège, no date [probably 1747]); L. Tassin, "Un document dit la misère de notre région au XVIIᵉ siècle," *L'Antiquaire* (Philippeville), 3, 53-55. Also, Théodose Bouille, *Histoire de la ville et pays de Liège*, III (Liège, 1737), reproduces a number of official complaints.

6　Besides de Sonkeux's chronicle, cited in note 1, see dom Bernard Mehren and Joseph Ruwet, eds., *Journal des abbés de Val-Dieu* (Val-Dieu, Belgium, 1946); Sylv. Balau and Em. Fairon, *Chroniques liégeoises*, 2 vols. (Brussels, 1913-1931); J. Brassine, ed., "Chronique verviétoise de 1746 à 1755," *Bulletin de la Société des Bibliophiles Liégeois*, 14 (1937), 13-147; J. Ceyssens, "Notes du curé Jean Herviannus de Hermalle sous Argenteau," *Leodium*, 5 (1906), 125-132; Charles Piot, "Les Lorrains au pays de Liège,"

Bulletin de Commission Royale d'Histoire, 4th ser., 2 (1875), 361-376; *Rerum Leodiensium status anno M.DC.XLIX*, trans. J. Alexandre (Liège, 1885); Guillaume Simenon, ed., *Chronique de Servais Foullon, abbé de Saint-Trond* (Liège, 1910); Nicolas van Werveke, "Chronique Blanchart," *Publications de la Section Historique de l'Institut Grande Ducal du Luxembourg*, 52 (1903), 53-125; Edm. van Wintershoven, "Chronique tirée des registres paroissiaux d'Emael," *BSSLL*, 22 (1904), 43-106; Melchior F. Crahay, "Fragment de chronique liégeoise et franchimontoise," ed. Ph. de Limbourg, *Bulletin de la Société des Bibliophiles Liégeois*, 2 (1884), 65-109; and Jean Brose, "La Guerre de Hollande (1673-1676) vue par une curé hesbignon. La Chronique de Laurent Chabot, cure de Villers-le-Bouillet," *La Vie Wallone*, 42 (1968), 311-333.

7 See especially Jean Haust, ed., *Quatre dialogues de paysans (1631-1636)* (Liège: H. Vaillant-Carmann, 1939). Also, Guillaume Hennen, "Pamphlets politiques wallons du XVIIᵉ siècle," *Bulletin de la Société Verviétoise d'Archéologie et d'Histoire*, 13 (1913), 171-291.

8 H. J. C. von Grimmelshausen, *The Adventurous Simplicissimus*, tr. A. T. S. Goodrick (Lincoln, Nebraska: The University of Nebraska Press, 1962), original edition, 1669. Gustav Freytag, *Pictures of German Life in the XVth, XVIth and XVIIth Centuries*, tr. Mrs. Malcolm, 2 vols. (London, 1862).

9 References will be to the suite of eighteen etchings by Callot, *Les Misères et les mal-heurs de la guerre* (Paris, 1633). The de Hooghe illustrations are from Lambert van de Bos, *Tooneel des Oorlogs, opgericht in de vereenigde Nederlanden . . .* (Amsterdam, 1675).

10 See the Callot etchings, "La Maraude", "Le Pillage," "Pillage et incendie d'un village," and "Vols sur les grands chemins."

11 Grimmelshausen, *Simplicissimus*, p. 7.

12 "L'Entre-jeux de paysans," verses 140-145, in Haust, ed., *Quatre dialogues de paysans*, pp. 67-68. I am grateful to Etienne Hélin for translating these dialogues for me from Walloon to French. The English translations are my own.

13 See "Salazar liégeois," verses 63-72, in Haust, ed., *Quatre dialogues de paysans*, p. 46. For one of the rare episodes when the peasants were successful, see van Wintershoven, "Chronique tirée des registres paroissaux d'Emael," 65. In 1689, the Visé council received a letter announcing a meeting of "the men of the Condroz," to discuss the problem of occupation. They sent representatives. AEL C*de*J Visé 202, 9 May 1689.

14 Grimmelshausen, *Simplicissimus*, p. 8.

15 "L'Entre-jeux de paysans," verses 146-148.

16 See "Devastation d'un Monastère," and "Pillage et incendie d'un village."

17 "L'Entre-jeux de paysans," verses 162-167.

18 Grimmelshausen, *Simplicissimus*, pp. 9-10.

19 "Desolation des pauvres paysans," verses 23-40, in Haust, ed., *Quatre dialogues de paysans*, p. 81.

20 *List chronologique des édits et ordonnances de la principauté de Liège, de 1507 à 1684* (Brussels: Em. Devroye, 1860), *passim; List chronologique . . . de 1684 à 1794* (Brussels: Em. Devroye, 1851), *passim*. Both were published under the supervision of the Commission Royale pour la Publication des Anciennes Lois et Ordonnances de la Belgique. The word *Harlaque* derives either from the name of a French Marshal, Erlach, who was active in 1649-1650, or Harlak, a leader of a violent peasant band in 1697. Jules Herbillon, "Wallon harlaque et les harlaques," *La Vie Wallone*, 6 (1964), 434-435.

21 Van Wintershoven, "Chronique tirée des registres paroissiaux d'Emael." 59-60; AEL CP 824 Canne and Nedercame, Petition of the Community of Wonck, 21 Dec. 1747.

22 Bouille, *Histoire de la ville et pays de Liège*, III, 409. Most of the rural collegiate churches and monasteries had permanent places of refuge in a walled city, such as Liège or Huy.

23 Jean Ceyssens, "En temps de guerre 1746-1747-1748," *Leodium* (1907), 142. When I did the research for this book in Belgium and the Netherlands, a frequent response to my interest in the seventeenth century was to tell me about the horrors of that century's wars.

24 Van Houtte, *Les Occupations étrangères en Belgique*, I, 86-88.

25 AEL St. Pierre 46, Complaints dated 11 August 1696, and 16 October 1699.

26 Mehren and Ruwet, eds., *Journal des abbés du Val-Dieu*, p. 21. On page 24, the abbot of Val-Dieu reports that a French army of ten to twelve thousand "completely foraged" the territory from Charleroi to Brussels.

27 For the size of the French army, Ernest R. Dupuy and Trevor N. Dupuy, *The Encyclopedia of Military History* (New York: Harper and Row, 1970), p. 563.

28 Van Houtte, *Les Occupations étrangères en Belgique*, I, 9-17, 62-63. Parker, *The Army of Flanders and the Spanish Road*, pp. 166-167. The size of communities, and the number of troops they could support with an infrastructure of buildings, mills, ovens, and granaries, and supplies of firewood, pioneers, and fascines, were important items of military intellegence in the seventeenth and eighteenth centuries. They were often indicated on military maps. See E. Hélin, "Les plans anciens de Liège," *Annuaire d'Histoire Liégeoise*, 6 (1961-1962), 589-736, 1289-1538, but especially 1300 and 1303. Also, see the beautiful series of maps in *Carte de Cabinet des Pays-Bas Autrichiens levée à l'initiative du Comte de Ferraris* (Brussels: Pro Civitate, 1965).

29 De Sonkeux, *La Vie à Verviers*, p. 42. See also Parker, *The Army of Flanders and the Spanish Road*, Appendix I, "The 'Tail' of the Army of Flanders: Women and Servants with the Troops," pp. 288-289.

30 Van Wintershoven, "Chronique tirée des registres paroissiaux d'Emael," 83. There were 57 households in Emael in 1749; AEL Etats 96, Tocage Emael 1749.

31 Van Wintershoven, "Chronique tirée des registres paroissiaux d'Emael," p. 56.

32 Jean Ceyssens, "En temps de guerre," *Leodium*, 5 (1906), 148.

33 *Ibid.*

34 AEL C*de*J, Jupille, Commune de Jupille, 2.

35 RAL LVO 5546, Rapport vor die van St. Gertruyden en Eckelrade over ende wegens twee companien van de densche troupen desen 11 Juny 1736.

36 Van Winterhoven, "Chronique tirée des registres paroissiaux d'Emael," 84. For the size of military units in the seventeenth century, see Parker, *The Army of Flanders and the Spanish Road*, Appendix A, "The Organization of the Army of Flanders," pp. 274-276.

37 G. D. Franquinet, "Les Seigneuries d'Agimont et de Nedercanne, près de Maestricht," *BIAL*, 1 (1852), 73.

38 De Sonkeux, *La Vie à Verviers*, p. 59. Verviers had a population of about 6500 in 1662. Herve Hasquin, et al., *La Wallonie: le pays et les hommes*, I (Brussels: La Renaissance du Livre, 1975), p. 366.

39 De Sonkeux, *La Vie à Verviers*, p. 59.

40 *Ibid.*

41 The numerous villages, nobles, and clergy of the Spanish Netherlands' Province of Limbourg paid 110,000 florins to be freed of lodging in 1672, and about 150,000 to be freed of it in 1671. Was this roughly equivalent to the cost of such lodging? Surely, if it was, it was quite expensive. Mehren and Ruwet, eds., *Journal des abbés du Val-Dieu*, p. 22.

42 The excellent records pertaining to military occupation of the Principality of Liège in the 1740's contain many detailed descriptions of physical destruction of houses. For two examples among many, see: AEL CP 805 Herstal, 4 Oct. 1747; and AEL CP 824, Canne and Nedercanne (1747).

43 Parker, *The Army of Flanders*, pp. 158-161.

44 De Sonkeux, *La Vie à Verviers*, p. 42.

45 *Ibid.*, p. 41.

46 Ceyssens, "En Temps de Guerre," *Leodium*, 5 (1906), 146.

47 RAL LVO 5546, 3 July 1675.

48 See Daniel Berlamont, "Occupations militaires et finances urbaines au XVIIe et XVIIIe siècles: l'example verviétois," *Annuaire d'Histoire Liégeoise*, 13 (1972), 59-106.

49 It went so far as to mean that local residents paid wages and all other expenses of the army. See the excellent discussion of issues surrounding this precept in van Houtte, *Les Occupations étrangères en Belgique*, especially I, 113-114. For the origins of this precept in the Thirty Years' War, see F. Redlich, "Contributions in the Thirty Years' War," *Economic History Review*, 12 (1959-1960), 247-254.

50 Ceyssens, "En Temps de Guerre," *Leodium*, 6 (1907), 139, 141.

51 Berlamont, "Occupations militaires et finances urbaines," p. 67. For another example of the low cost of lodging in the 1740's, see AEL CP 805, Herstal. Herstal provided 16,612 man-days of infantry winter quarters in 1747-1748 for 904 florins, or roughly one patard (= one sous) per man-day.

52 Louis XIV, King of France, *Oeuvres de Louis XIV* (Paris, 1806), III, 346.

53 AEL CP 806.

54 De Sonkeux, *La Vie à Verviers*, pp. 47-48.

55 See the amounts spent on *chariages* in Berlamont, "Occupations militaires et finances urbaines," 84-85. Also, see de Sonkeux, *La Vie à Verviers*, especially p. 80.

56 AEL CP 806.

57 RAL LVO 5546, May, 1675.

58 Ceyssens, "En Temps de Guerre," *Leodium*, 6 (1906), 139.

59 *Ibid.*, p. 138.

60 Van Houtte, *Les Occupations étrangères en Belgique*, chapters 6 and 7, I, 257-572.

61 *Ibid.* Chapters 4 and 5, I, 142-256. I have italicized *contributions* throughout this discussion to distinguish it from the normal English meaning of the word, which is a tax or a voluntary tax. In this I follow Redlich, "Contributions in the Thirty Years' War."

62 Redlich, "Contributions in the Thirty Years' War."

63 Van Houtte, Les Occupations étrangères en Belgique, I, 145-149.

64 Charles Piot, "Les Lorrains au pays de Liège," p. 365. In 1675 the villagers of Flemalle complained that they had to borrow money to ransom men and animals. AEL St. Pierre 46, Supplique des debiteurs de Flemalle, 4 December 1675.

65 De Sonkeux, *La Vie à Verviers*, p. 55.

66 Van Houtte, "L'Exécution militaire," section 1 of Chapter 5, *Les Occupations étrangères en Belgique*, I, 197-212.

67 De Sonkeux, *La Vie à Verviers*, pp. 69, 71.

68 Ceyssens, "En temps de Guerre," *Leodium*, 6 (1906), 146. See also AEL PdD 129, f. 240, 30 Dec. 1675.

69 De Sonkeux, *La Vie à Verviers*, p. 55.

70 There are a number of these forms in RAL LVO 5546. For the process, see the

deliberations of the town council of Visé, in AEL CdeJ Visé, 202-203.

71 AEL CdeJ Visé, 202, 28 June 1689.

72 RAL LVO 5546, 3 July 1675.

73 See the Visé Council minutes, cited above, and the archives of Jupille, in AEL CdeJ Jupille, Commune de Jupille, 2.

74 AEL CdeJ Visé, 202, 20 April 1689.

75 AEL CdeJ Visé, 202, 19 June 1689.

76 AEL CdeJ Visé, 202, 23 April 1690.

77 AEL St. Pierre 46, *Supplique* by the vicaire of Serexhe-Heuseur, 27 May 1675. For another example, see AEL PdD 129, f. 168vo., 17 July 1674, Grace to Badon de Trez.

78 For other examples of safeguards, see RAL LVO 5546, Second copy of 1632 complaint. AEL CdeJ Visé, 203, 22 October 1702.

79 A formal *parti* seeking contributions need consist of only twenty men. Van Houtte, *Les Occupations étrangères en Belgique*, I, 145.

80 The town of Visé regularly received requests for contributions, not only from Liège and Maastricht, but also from Luxemburg and Huy. AEL CdeJ Visé, 202, 3 January 1689.

81 See the narrative histories of Liège, such as Joseph Daris, *Histoire du diocèse et de la principauté de Liège pendant le XVIIe siècle*, 2 vols. (Liège, 1877), and Boulle, *Histoire de la ville et pays de Liège*, III, for wartime years, for evidence of this treatment. See also, de Sonkeux, *La Vie à Verviers*, pp. 35, 38-40.

82 De Sonkeux, *La Vie à Verviers*, p. 37.

83 There are no provisions for managing relations with armies in the formal customs of the Principality of Liège or the Pays d'Outre Meuse. See Constant Casier and Louis Crahay, *Coutumes du duché de Limbourg et des Pays d'Outre Meuse* (Brussels, 1889) and J. Raikem, et al., *Coutumes du pays de Liège*, 3 vols. (Brussels, 1870-1884). Rather, procedures seemed to develop organically in the sixteenth and seventeenth centuries. See also, Robert Jacob, "Les Communautés d'habitants au droit liégeois recént (XVII-XVIIIes siècles)," *Credit Communal de Belgique*, 31 (1977) 84-85. On communal responsibility for lodging, see AEL CdeJ Visé, 202, 17 Nov. 1689, and Archives de l'Etat à Arlon, Famille de Trappe, Chateau de Losenge, documents pertaining to lodging in Jupille.

84 Berlamont, "Occupations militaires et finances urbaines," has a good summary of communal handling of the costs of lodging. See also de Sonkeux, *La Vie à Verviers*, especially pp. 42-43, and the appropriate sections of van Houtte, *Les Occupations étrangères en Belgique*.

85 For the law on this issue, see D. F. de Sohet, *Instituts de droit, ou sommaire de jurisprudence canonique, civile, féodale et criminelle, pour les pays de Liège, de Luxembourg, Namur et autres* (Bouillon, 1772), especially "Traité Préliminaire," title 1, nos. 61-91, pp. 7-9; book 1, title 29, no. 68, p. 106; book 2, title 40, nos. 20-22, p. 110; [for the Pays d'Outre-Meuse] book 2, title 40, nos. 23-32, pp. 115-116. Also, M. G. de Louvrex, *Recueil contenant les édits et règlements faits pour le Pais de Liège et Comte de Looz, par les Evèques et Princes . . .* (Liège, 1751), II, 377-378, 385-387. Even pioneer demands were to be divided up as though they were a personal tax. AEL PdD 132, f. 85, 22 July 1695, Order to grand bailiff Libert.

86 For two examples of such disagreements, see RAL LVO 5558 (Conflict between Eysden and Breust) and AEL CdeJ Jupille, Commune de Jupille, 3, Request to the Prince-Bishop dated 6 May 1751.

252

87   For the personal tax, RAL LVO 5490-5527; for the property taxes, RAL LVO 5451-5480; for the French contributions, RAL LVO 5534-5543. Another good example is the town of Huy, southwest of Liège. See the detailed study of its finances, and the need for wartime expedients, in D. Morsa, "Etude sur les finances de la ville de Huy au XVIIᵉ siècle," *Finances publiques d'ancien régime. Finances publiques contemporaines en Belgique de 1740 à 1840*. Colloque International, Spa, 19-22 December 1972. Collection Histoire Pro Civitate, series in-8°, no. 39 (Brussels: Credit Communal de Belgique, 1975), pp. 137-174. The rapid increase in the amounts of tax raised is also shown in AEL C*de*J Jupille, Commune de Jupille, 3, Tailles 1677-1767.

88   These figures ring true, according to other sources. In 1699, two farmers claimed to have paid 40 florins per bonnier for "contributions, tailles [land taxes] and lodgings," for the three years 1695, 1696 and 1697, or about 13 florins per year. AEL St. Pierre 46, Supplique of Noel le Charlier and Jean Sauvenea, 1699. The village of Housselt paid considerably more, about 32-33 florins, in 1690. AEL PdD 131, ff. 284vo.-285, 22 March 1681, grace to tenants at Housselt.

89   See chapter IV, pp. 98-101.

90   Berlamont, "Occupations militaires et finances urbaines," p. 73.

91   The villages of the *banlieu* contributed to taxes for special purposes and participated in the urban militia which was supposed to guard the city. In return they received an exemption from certain taxes, most notably the duties on goods imported into the city, and increased privileges, such as reciprocal bourgeois status. Robert Ulens, "Les Milices rurales au pays de Liège," *Leodium*, 24 (1931), 37.

92   In wartime, the actions of the estates of Liège were almost exclusively devoted to raising money and keeping foreign troops out of the principality. See Emile Fairon, "Analyses sommaires des journées d'états de la principauté de Liège, 1541-1684," *Annuaire d'Histoire Liégeois*, 5 (1954-1956), 285-412, 469-573, 654-759; and see E. Hélin, "Les Capitations liégeoises," *Anciens Pays et Assemblées d'Etats*, 21 (1961).

93   For the fiscal problems of the estates of the Principality of Liège, see Fairon, "Analyses sommaires des journées d'états de la principauté de Liège," *passim*. In 1639, the Prince still complained that they had not collected and paid him 150,000 patacons in taxes voted in 1631. Fairon, "Analyses sommaires . . .," pp. 87-88.

94   Fairon, "Analyses sommaires des journées d'états de la principauté de Liège," especially p. 533.

95   Berlamont, "Occupations militaires et finances urbaines," 71. RAL LVO 5559, Obligatie van fl 400 tot laste der gemeente tot Eysden (1696).

96   Claude Desama and André Blaise, "Comment les communautés villageoises avaient recourse au credit au XVIIᵉ siècle," *Credit Communal de Belgique*, 21 (1967), 58-60. Claude Desama, "Les Rentes en argent, fournissent-elles un diagnostic de l'activité économique? Enquête dans un protocole liégeois au XVIIᵉ siècle," *Annuaire d'Histoire Liégeoise*, 10 (1967), 27-28. Residents often felt themselves dependent on, and resented, the moneylenders they needed. Like most rural citizens they also resented tax collectors. See Hennen, "Pamphlets politiques wallons."

97   See the introduction and bibliography in, Belgium, Archives de l'Etat, Liège, *Catalogue general des protocoles de notaires conservées dans la province de Liège*, by Jean Pieyns (Brussels, 1972); and *Le Notaire dans la vie namuroise: Catalogue d'un exposition à Namur, 9-19 Octobre, 1975* (Brussels, 1975).

98   Desama, "Les Rentes en argent."

99   The Dutch government conducted a survey of village debts in 1682. Some owed by

Eysden and Herkenrade went back as far as 1672 and 1673. Similar surveys were necessary again in 1695 and 1726. RAL LVO 5563, 5564. Verviers collected a five percent property tax from 1678 to 1698 to amortize a loan. De Sonkeux, *La Vie à Verviers*, p. 54. Dalhem owed 2,800 florins in 1748, and then borrowed an additional 4,000 florins to meet the expenses of a French occupation. They still owed those 6,800 florins in 1762, and had paid off only 3,000 florins by 1787. Ceyssens, "En temps de Guerre," *Leodium*, 6 (1907), 141-142.

100 Pierre-J. Debouhxtay and Floribert Dubois, *Histoire de la seigneurie de Nivelle-sur-Meuse et l'ancien paroisse de Lixhe* (Liège, 1935), pp. 220-221. Also, see the following permissions granted by the Cathedral Chapter of Liège to the residents of their seigneuries to alienate property (usually not permanently) in order to pay off wartime debts: AEL PdD 129; f. 98 vo., 9 June 1673 (Feneur); AEL PdD 129, ff. 148-148 vo., 12 April 1674 (Fize); AEL PdD 129, f. 235, 19 Nov. 1675 (Hexhe); AEL PdD 130; f. 169, 20 March 1681 and ff. 169-169 vo., 24 April 1681 (Boirs); AEL PdD 131, ff. 238 vo.-239, 20 March 1690 and ff. 241-241 vo., 15 April 1690 (Tiffe).

101 See the argument in J. C. G. M. Jansen, "Agrarian Development and Exploitation in South Limburg in the years 1650-1850," *Acta Historiae Neerlandica*, 5 (1970), 247-248. This subject is discussed more fully in Chapter IV, pp. 108-109.

Chapter III

1 This is a widely held point of view. See, among many authors who make this point, George Clark, *The Seventeenth Century*, second ed. (Oxford, 1961), Ch. 7, "Armies," pp. 98-114; Michael Howard, *War and European History* (Oxford, 1976), pp. 54-74.

2 Arnold Toynbee, *A Study of History*, IV (London: Oxford University Press, 1939), p. 144.

3 George Clark, *War and Society in the Seventeenth Century* (Cambridge: Cambridge University Press, 1958), pp. 76-85.

4 The best general summaries of these developments can still be found in Michael Roberts, "Gustav Adolf and the Art of War," and "The Military Revolution, 1560-1660," in *Essays in Swedish History* (London: Weidenfield and Nicholson, 1967), pp. 56-81, 195-225. Recently, Geoffrey Parker has attempted to put Roberts' claims in perspective. Geoffrey Parker, "The 'Military Revolution,' 1560-1660 – a Myth?" *Journal of Modern History*, 48 (1976), 195-214. There are a number of works that consider this question for individual nations, while we still need a fresh general consideration of early modern land war. For Spain, and especially the Spanish armies in the Low Countries, see Geoffrey Parker, *The Army of Flanders and the Spanish Road, 1567-1659: The Logistics of Spanish Victory and Defeat in the Low Countries' Wars* (Cambridge: Cambridge University Press, 1972). For France, the best work is that of Louis André, *Michel le Tellier et Louvois* (Paris, 1942; reprinted Geneva, 1974), especially pp. 307-427; also for France see *id.*, *Michel le Tellier et l'organisation de l'armée monarchique* (Paris, 1906), and Camille Rousset, *Histoire de Louvois et de son administration politique et militaire*, 4 vols. (Paris, 1861-1863); for Sweden, see Michael Roberts, *Gustavus Adolphus, A History of Sweden 1611-1632* (London: Longmans, 1958), II, 169-271.

5 Roberts, "The Military Revolution, 1560-1660," and "Gustav Adolf and the Art of

War"; Parker, *The Army of Flanders*, pp. 3-24; and "The 'Military Revolution,' 1560-1660 – a Myth?"

6   *Rerum Leodiensium status anno M.DC.XLIX*, tr. J. Alexandre (Liège: Société des Bibliophiles Liégeois, 1885), p. 57.

7   Hubert van Houtte, *Les Occupations étrangères en Belgique sous l'Ancien Régime*, I (Ghent, 1930), 80.

8   On civilian control, see André, *Michel le Tellier et l'organisation de l'armée monarchique*, and *Michel le Tellier et Louvois*, pp. 409-427; and John C. Rule, "Louis XIV, Roi-Bureaucrate," in John C. Rule, ed., *Louis XIV and the Craft of Kingship* (Columbus, Ohio: Ohio State University Press, 1969), pp. 48-53.

9   *Règlemens et ordonnances du roy pour les gens de guerre* (Paris: Fréderic Léonard, 1680-1706), 15 vols. Andre Corvisier, *L'Armée Française de la fin du XVIIe siècle au ministère de Choiseul. Le Soldat* (Paris, 1964), II, 880-893. The subject of military discipline is also dealt with in the works by André and Roberts.

10   Lieutenant colonel, baron de Sparre, *Code militaire ou compilation des règlemens et ordonnances de Louis XIV faites pour les gens de guerre depuis 1651 jusqu'à present* (Paris, 1709). Sparre's work was only the first of several published in the eighteenth century. See Corvisier, *L'Armée française*, I, 4. Even small countries, like Liège, with its tiny army, had military regulations in the eighteenth century, designed to moderate the impact of troops on civilians. For such a code established in Liège in 1747, see Eugene Poswick, *Histoire des troupes liégeoises pendant le XVIIIe siècle* (Liège, 1893), pp. 190-199.

11   Clark, *The Seventeenth Century*, pp. 102-103. See also, Fritz Redlich, *The German Military Enterpriser and his Work Force. A Study in European Economic and Social History*, 2 vols. (Wiesbaden: Franz Steiner Verlag, 1964-1965). Published as Beiheften 47 and 48 of the *Vierteljahrschrift für Sozial- und Wirtschaftsgeschichte*.

12   Charles Piot, "Les Lorrains au pays de Liège," *Bulletin de la Commission Royale d'Histoire*, 4th series, 2 (1875), 361-376; and F. Tihon, "Le Duc Charles de Lorraine et la principauté de Liège," *BIAL*, 40 (1910), 235-242; and van Houtte, *Les Occupations étrangères en Belgique*, I, 77.

13   See Daris, *Histoire du diocèse et de la principauté de Liège pendant le XVIIe siècle*, I, 108-290; II, 1-29.

14   Tihon, "Le Duc Charles de Lorraine et la principauté de Liège," 238.

15   Daris, *Histoire du diocèse et de la principauté de Liège pendant le XVIIe siècle*, II, 28-29.

16   Parker, *The Army of Flanders*, p. 166.

17   Frederick Henry, Prince of Orange, *A Iournal of all the principall passages of that late famous siege and taking of the citie of Mastricht by the Prince of Orange . . .* (London. Printed by J. D[awson] for Nathaniel Butter and Nicholas Bourne, 1632) [Pollard-Redgrave *Short Title Catalog* no. 11365], p. 5.

18   Jean Ceyssens, "Notes du curé Jean Hervianus de Hermalle sous Argenteau," *Leodium*, 5 (1906), 128-129.

19   Corvisier, *L'Armée française*, II, 848-850; André, *Michel le Tellier et Louvois*, pp. 358-368.

20   Daniel Berlamont, "Occupations militaires et finances urbaines au XVIIe et XVIIIe siècle: l'exemple verviétois," *Annuaire d'Histoire Liégeoise*, 13 (1972), 74-75, 85.

21   *Ibid*, p. 87.

22   *Ibid.*, pp. 85-86.

23   Parker, *The Army of Flanders and the Spanish Road*, pp. 158-160.

24   *Ibid.*, Chapter 8, "Mutiny," pp. 185-205. Geoffrey Parker, "Mutiny and Discontent in the Spanish Army of Flanders, 1572-1607." *Past and Present*, No. 58 (1973), 38-52. André, *Michel le Tellier et Louvois*, pp. 343-344.

25 Parker, *The Army of Flanders and the Spanish Road*, p. 161. André, *Michel le Tellier et Louvois*, pp. 344-345.

26 For the comparison between western and central Europe, see Toynbee, *A Study of History*, IV, 145, note 2. For the practices and attitudes of Wallenstein regarding the provision of troops in the field, see Golo Mann, *Wallenstein Sein Leben erzählt* (Frankfurt am Main: S. Fischer, 1971).

27 Parker, *The Army of Flanders and the Spanish Road*, pp. 162-164. André, *Michel le Tellier et Louvois*, pp. 368-377. There are numerous contracts in the Liégeois archives describing the arrangements made by armies with provisioners and all sorts of suppliers. Obviously, given Liège's arms business, the production of arms figures strongly in these contracts. On this, see Paulette Pieyns-Rigo and Claude Gaier, "Fournitures d'armes et vie armurière à Liège vers le milieu du XVIIe siècle d'après les actes notariaux," *Le Musée d'Armes* (Liège), 5 (1977), 13-19. See also, AEL Notaire Bidart, 5 October 1747 (various arms): AEL Notaire Xheneumont, F., 1 August 1742 (rations); and AEL Notaire Sprimont, 30 July 1742 (more rations).

28 Henri de Sonkeux, *La Vie à Verviers il y a trois siècles* (Verviers, n.d. [about 1946]), pp. 162-164.

29 *Ibid.*

30 Only Louvois, the master of the French military under Louis XIV, did not hold to this viewpoint. He thought that a terrorized and impoverished enemy population would convince their leaders to give in to French wishes (see van Houtte, *Les Occupations étrangères en Belgique*, I, 472-473). It is hard to understand how this could apply to a presumably neutral Principality such as Liège, especially one that was leaning diplomatically toward France. Nevertheless, French armies treated Liégeois civilians rudely in the period of Louvois' power. See, for example, the discussion of French invasions (especially of 1671-1673), in Daris, *Histoire du diocèse et de la principauté de Liège, pendant le XVIIe siècle.*

31 Van Houtte, *Les Occupations étrangères en Belgique*, I, xi; Clark, *War and Society in the Seventeenth Century*, pp. 77-79.

32 *Rerum Leodiensium status anno M.DC.XLIX*, p. 38.

33 Jean Ceyssens, "Deux documents concernant les guerres de Louis XIV dans notre pays," *Leodium*, 5 (1906), 116-117.

34 Van Houtte, *Les Occupations étrangères en Belgique*, I, 167-168.

35 Hubert van Houtte, "Les Conferences franco-espagnoles de Deynze," *Revue d'Histoire Moderne* (1927), 191-215.

36 *Ibid.*, pp. 198-212.

37 *Ibid.*

38 *Ibid.*, pp. 203-210; and van Houtte, *Les Occupations étrangères en Belgique*, Chapter 4, "L'Exécution militaire et la rupture de contributions," I, 197-256. See the documents pertaining to the *exécution* of Villers St. Simeon, when the mayor and four horses were taken as hostages, and the Seigneur (in this case, the Cathedral Chapter of Liège) attempted to remedy the situation. It is significant that kidnapping and not fire were used here. AEL PdD 132, ff.106vo-107, 3 Jan 1696; f.145vo., 2 May 1696; ff.169-169vo., 21 June 1696. Also, see the safeguard issued in 1702 to Jupille by the Dutch, in return for payment of contributions, Archives de l'Etat à Arlon, Famille de Trappe, Chateau de Losenge.

39 Van Houtte, *Les Occupations étrangères en Belgique*, I, 202-212.

40 AEL CP 703-704.

41 There is only one file, AEL CP 705, for 1641-1688. It contains eight items. There are 5 substantial files for 1689-1718, AEL CP 706-710; there are 7 files for the War of Polish Succession, 1735-1739, AEL CP 711-717; there are 39 files for the War of the Austrian Succession, 1741-1748, AEL CP 718-754; and there are 48 files for the Seven Years' War, AEL CP 757-804. In addition, AEL CP 805-840 deal with the experiences of individual communities. Almost nothing in these files antedates 1690, and virtually everything they contain is after 1740.

42 Berlamont, "Occupations militaires et finances urbaines," pp. 87-88.

43 AEL CP 753.

44 AEL CP 752bis.

45 AEL CP 805 (Oupeye), 808 (Saive), 824 (Eben-Emael), 825 (Haccourt).

46 AEL CP 753. The original payment (1750-1751) reimbursed villagers for 3/20 of their losses for grains, and about 1/40 of their losses for woods. Later payments roughly equalled the original payment. For most of the accounts of payments, see AEL CP 752.

Chapter IV

1 AEL CP 804, Herstal, Petition of Jean Binon, 1747.

2 AEL Cathédrale Secretariat 123-165, Protocoles des Directeurs, 1626-1747. These records are referred to in the notes below as AEL PdD.

3 J. Pacquay, "Le Patrimoine de l'église de Liège, aperçu économique," *Analecta Ecclesiastica Leodiensia*, fasc. 4 (Liège, 1936).

4 Alice Dubois, *Le Chapitre cathédral de Saint-Lambert à Liège au XVIIe siècle* (Liège, 1949), pp. 227-229.

5 Complaints received by the Prince and Estates of Liège are found in the archives of the *Conseil Privé*, described in Chapter III, pp. 64-65.

6 AEL PdD 129, f. 105, 17 July 1673, grace to the widow la Haye; AEL PdD 129, f. 142, 20 Feb. 1674, grace to Jean Scoff; AEL PdD 129, f. 131, 24 Oct. 1673, grace to Valerian de la Croix; AEL PdD 129, f. 130vo., 23 Oct. 1673, grace to Arnold Freson; AEL PdD 131, f. 226, 10 Dec. 1689, grace to Sr. Denys Everards; AEL PdD 129, ff. 95-95vo., 9 May 1673, grace to Hubert Dosin.

7 AEL PdD 130, f. 2vo., 29 Jan. 1678, grace to George Caenen; AEL PdD 130, f. 109, 4 June 1680, grace to the widow la Haye; AEL PdD 132, f. 149, 15 May 1696, grace to Tossaint le Page; AEL PdD 137, f. 122 vo., 15 Nov. 1701, grace to Gillet Marcotti; AEL PdD 132, ff. 17vo.-18, 24 March 1694, grace to Francois and Thibaut Piette.

8 AEL CP 824 Canne and Nedercanne, Petition of the community of Wonck, 21 Dec. 1747.

9 AEL PdD 130, f. 5vo., 2 Oct. 1678 (he received an additional grace on 5 Oct. 1679: AEL PdD 130, f. 68). See also, AEL PdD 129, f. 114vo., 2 Sept. 1673, grace to Gaspar Walthour; AEL PdD 129, f. 176, 10 Sept. 1674, grace to tithe-collectors of Oleye; AEL PdD 131, f. 203vo., 22 March 1689, grace to the widow of Jeane Henry Adile; AEL PdD 137, f. 111vo., 1 Oct. 1701, grace to the widow of Jean Henry Boux; AEL PdD 146, f. 41, 29 May 1714, grace to Wathieu Grosfils.

10 Henri de Sonkeux, *La Vie à Verviers il y a trois siècles* (Verviers, n.d., but probably 1946), p. 48.

11 See *Le Notaire dans la vie namuroise* (catalog of an exposition at Namur, 9-19 Oct., 1975) (Brussels, 1975), pp. 97-98.

12 AEL PdD 132, *passim*, graces granted in 1695-1696.

13   AEL PdD 129, ff. 167-167vo., 12 July 1674.

14   AEL CP 805 Herstal, Complaint of Jacques Conegracht.

15   There are many more examples. See, for example, RAL LVO 5546, 1632 complaint; AEL PdD 129, f. 119, 19 Sept. 1673, grace to delle Mincheste; AEL PdD 129, f. 133vo., 9 Nov. 1673, grace to the Commissaire delle Trappe; AEL St. Pierre 46, petition of the debtors of Flemalle, 4 Dec. 1675; AEL St. Pierre 46, petition of Mathy le Germeau; AEL PdD 131, ff. 249vo.-250, 6 June 1690, grace to the tithe-collectors of Visé; AEL PdD 131, f. 303vo., 6 Nov. 1691, grace to the tithe collectors of Fanthin, Mery and Dolembreux; AEL PdD 131, f. 307vo., 20 Nov. 1691, grace to the Damoiselle de Sprimont; AEL PdD 132, f. 60, 14 April 1695, grace to Pierre delle Creyr; AEL PdD 139, f. 42, 30 Jan. 1703, grace to Arnold le Grand; AEL PdD 139, ff. 42vo.-43, 1 Feb. 1703, grace to Sr. Bettonville; AEL CP 824 Eben-Emael, *Procès-verbal* of the widow of Jean Libert Wirix (1747-1748).

16   AEL CP 824 Canne and Nedercanne, complaint of 1747; RAL LVO 5546, complaint of 1632.

17   AEL St. Pierre 46, Petition of Guilheaume le Febve, 17 June 1678. In Wonck in 1747, soldiers took a large number of sheep and other animals, and then an epizootic killed two-thirds of the few that remained. AEL CP 824 Canne and Nedercanne, Complaint of the community of Wonck, 21 Dec. 1747.

18   AEL PdD 129, 17 July 1673; see also AEL PdD 129, f. 115vo., 14 Sept. 1673.

19   AEL CP 824 Canne and Nedercanne, complaint of 1747.

20   AEL CP 824 Canne and Nedercanne, Petition of the Community of Wonck, 21 Dec. 1747. This must have been a bad year for brewing. The main farmers of Canne and Nedercanne also complained of brewing inadequate amounts. AEL CP 824 Canne and Nedercanne, complaint of 1747.

21   De Sonkeux, *La Vie à Verviers il y a trois siècles*, pp. 47-48.

22   AEL PdD 129, f. 182vo., 30 Oct. 1674, agreement with Simon Beaupre; AEL PdD 129, ff. 146-146vo., 10 April 1674, lease to Jacque Piettre.

23   Problems for fisheries: AEL PdD 130, f. 4vo., 3 Feb. 1678, grace to fishers of Fourchoufosse, because "the fishery had been long deserted"; AEL PdD 131, f. 308vo., 27 Nov. 1691, grace to same. Problems for millers: AEL PdD 140, pp. 235-236, 29 Oct. 1705, grace to Jean Stas, miller at Visé. Problems for ferry operators: AEL PdD 129, f. 124vo., 7 Oct. 1673, grace to ferry-operators of Visé (the barge had been taken by Dutch soldiers at Maastricht for three months, and then "mutilated.") AEL PdD 129, f. 140, 16 Jan. 1674, order to Receiver Warnotte to pay for a new ferry-barge for Tiffe (price: 50 patacons); AEL PdD 140, p. 230, 10 Oct. 1705, grace to the ferry-operator of Visé because his boats had been taken by the armies.

24   AEL PdD 129, 131-132, *passim*; AEL Notaire P. Craheau, 1670-1676. Craheau was a notary who practiced in Cheratte, and worked frequently with a number of miners.

25   De Sonkeux, *La Vie à Verviers*, p. 40.

26   Claude Desama, "Les Rentes en argent, fournissent-elles on diagnostic de l'activité économique? Enquête dans un protocole ligéois au XVIIe siècle," *Annuaire d'Histoire Liégeois*, 10 (1967), 1-32.

27   For the natural causes of damage to crops, see the requests for official visits (tenants could request an inspection by their landlord to see and evaluate damage) in AEL PdD 144, visitations 1711-1712.

28   Pierre Goubert, *The Ancien Régime* (New York, 1973), pp. 38-39.

29   The best discussion of this issue and the problems and sources involved is in Emmanuel

Le Roy Ladurie, *Histoire du climat depuis l'an mil* (Paris, 1967).

30 G. Utterström, "Climatic Fluctuations and Population Problems in Early Modern History," *The Scandinavian Economic History Review*, 3 (1955). Utterström's argument has been more or less effectively demolished by Le Roy Ladurie in his *Histoire du climat* (pp. 14-18), but the article is still valuable for its point of view, the data it presents, and the bibliography.

31 For this paragraph, I rely on Le Roy Ladurie, *Histoire du climat*, pp. 280-286, and B. H. Slicher van Bath, "Les Problèmes fondamentaux de la société pré-industrielle en Europe occidentale. Une Orientation et un programme," *A.A.G. Bijdragen* 12 (1965), 9-11.

32 E. Vanderlinden, *Chronique des événements météorologiques en Belgique jusqu'en 1834* (Brussels, 1924). For some guidelines on using subjective data for the study of weather, see J. Oliver, "The Use of Weather Diaries in the Study of Historical Climates," *Weather*, 13 (1958), 251-256.

33 De Vries discusses his sources and his method in his article, "Histoire du climat et économie: des faits nouveaux, une interpretation differente," *Annales E.S.C.* 32 (1977), 198-226. I am grateful to Professor de Vries for permitting me to use his unpublished data in my analysis.

34 The correlation between winter temperatures and Vanderlinden's "hard winters" is −.3967, at a significance level of 0.001. Between average winter temperatures and "mild winters," the r value was lower, 0.2623, at a significance level of 0.003. In view of the sources involved, these are significant, if not perfect, correlations.

35 The classic example of the use of tithe data to demonstrate changing agricultural patterns is in E. Le Roy Ladurie, *Paysans de Languedoc* (Paris, 1967). For a number of other examples and an introduction to methodology, see Joseph Goy and Emmanuel Le Roy Ladurie, eds., *Les Fluctuations du produit de la dîme* (Paris: Mouton, 1972).

36 For an introduction to the problems of using the tithe for the measurement of short-term agricultural changes, see Myron P. Gutmann, "War the Tithe, and Agricultural Production: The Meuse Basin North of Liège, 1661-1740," in Herman van der Wee and Eddy van Cauwenberghe, eds., *Productivity of Land and Agricultural Innovation in the Low Countries (1250-1800)* (Leuven: Leuven University Press, 1978), pp. 65-76.

37 AEL PdD 130, f. 171, 29 April 1681. The only commodities that may not have been included were dairy products.

38 For the Maastricht tithes, and the source for the data in Table 4.1, see J. C. G. M. Jansen, *Landbouwproduktie en Economische Golfbeweging in Zuid-Limburg, 1250-1800. Een Analyse van de Opbrengst van Tienden* (Assen, The Netherlands: Van Gorcum, 1979). The parishes used are listed in Table 4.1, below.

39 A *par* contained 48 *vats*, of which 24 were always rye and the remaining 24 either all oats or two-thirds oats and one-third barley. *Ibid.*

40 The following are decennial averages for the Maastricht tithe data, expressed in *pares* (the number in parentheses is the number of years included in the computation):

1620-1629 (10)	304.0	1690-1699 (10)	332.3
1630-1639 (9)	197.6	1700-1709 (10)	337.4
1640-1649	no data	1710-1719 (10)	395.0
1650-1659 (3)	351.0	1720-1729 (10)	358.7
1660-1669 (10)	339.7	1730-1739 (10)	343.9
1670-1679 (8)	248.6	1740-1749 (10)	324.0
1680-1689 (10)	342.6		

41   For the principles used in this and other multivariate statistical tests, see Appendix D.

42   The years are 1633-1639, 1674-1679, 1689-1697, 1701-1706, 1746 and 1748.

43   The years are 1631, 1633-1640, 1674-1679, 1693-1694, 1703-1705, 1746, and 1748-1749.

44   The three Liégeois tithe series used are Visé, Vottem, and Milmort. The sources for these series are AEL Cathédrale Compterie du Grenier (for Vottem) 4-13, Registres aux stuits 1617-1749, and 108-235, Comptes des cens et rentes, 1620-1750; and Grande Compterie (for Visé and Milmort) 12-21, Registres aux stuits, 1616-1746, and 237-347, Comptes des cens et rentes, 1621-1750.

45   The collection of the tithe around Liège has been described by Joseph Ruwet, in "Mesure de la production agricole sous l'Ancien Régime: le blé en pays mosan," *Annales: E.S.C.,* 19 (1964), 625-642; and "Prix, production et bénéfices agricoles: le pays de Liège au XVIIIe siècle," *Cahiers d'Histoire de Prix* (Louvain), 2 (1957), 69-108. See also Gutmann, "War, the Tithe and Agricultural Production."

46   For the usefulness of this technique, see Gutmann, "War, the Tithe and Agricultural Production."

47   See these examples of collection agreements in the *Protocoles des Directeurs*: AEL PdD 129, ff. 112-112vo., 8 August. 1673 (Alleur); AEL PdD 129, f. 138vo., 12 Dec. 1673 (Oley); AEL PdD 129, f. 141vo., 13 Feb. 1674 (Alleur); AEL PdD 129, f. 169, 18 July 1674 (Villers and Juprelle), also ff. 173 and 184; AEL PdD 129, f. 215vo., 20 June 1675 (Attenhoven); AEL PdD 130, f. 77vo., 28 June 1678 (Milmort); AEL PdD 130, f. 284-284vo., 28 June 1683 (Milmort and Oleye); AEL PdD 132, f. 150vo.-151, 17 May 1696 (Vottem); and AEL PdD 132, f. 155, 5 June 1696 (Milmort). Such contracts also appear in the registers of leases and contracts maintained by the various Liégeois collegiate churches. See, among many possible examples, AEL Cathedrale Grande Compterie 15, ff. 302vo.-303, contract with Collas Henrice and others (Milmort), 16 June 1695.

48   I am grateful to Dr. J. C. G. M. Jansen, of the Sociaal Historisch Centrum voor Limburg, for providing me with his worksheets for this data. He has written about Louwberg in J. C. G. M. Jansen, "Landbouw rond Maastricht (1610-1865)," *Studies over de Sociaal-Economische Geschiedenis van Limburg*, 13 (1968), 1-98; and "Agrarian Development and Exploitation in South Limburg in the years 1650-1850," *Acta Historiae Neerlandica*, 5 (1971), 243-270.

49   Sharecropping was not widespread around Liège before the eighteenth century. See Ruwet, "Prix, production et bénéfices agricoles," p. 69. For one example, see the case of Renard Jodogne, who farmed the lands in Visé owned by the Collegiate Church of St. Croix from 1690 to 1705 on a sharecropping basis: AEL St. Croix 26, ff. 276vo.-278; Reg. 27, ff. 26-27, 231vo.-234, leases of 4 March, 1690, 1 June 1696 and 11 February 1699.

50   The figures were prepared by computing the value of annual production for each grain (multiplying the price of the grain in the given year by the amount produced), then summing all grains and dividing by the surface area of the farm in that year. When the price of a commodity was unavailable, I used the price of barley in that year. Sources for Maastricht prices are listed in Appendix C.

51   This is in substantial agreement with the conclusions of Jansen, for all of South Limburg, who wrote, "for the farms on a half-yield [sharecrop] and leasehold basis we may therefore estimate the area of land from which the farmer obtained a minimum income at 2 hectares and for self-owned land at 1 hectare." A hectare equals 0.84 *bonnier,* Jansen, "Agrarian Development and Exploitation," p. 263.

52 AEL PdD 130, f. 78-78vo., 30 June 1678.

54 AEL St. Pierre 46, Petition of the children and successors of the late Wathieu delle Haye, 26 June 1697.

55 AEL PdD 129, f. 191, 10 Jan. 1675.

56 For more examples of the handling of abandonment and replacement of tenants, see the following: AEL PdD 129, ff. 112-112vo., 8 August 1673, renunciation of Jean Pasque; AEL PdD 129, ff. 110-110vo., 27 July 1673; AEL PdD 129, f. 174, 13 August 1674, lease granted in Houme and Horpmael; AEL PdD 129, f. 145 vo., 20 March 1674, renunciation of Oger de Boislenache; AEL PdD 129, ff. 234-235, 14 Nov. 1675, lease to Pierre de Vivier of Fexhe-Slins; AEL PdD 129, ff. 237-237vo., 5 Dec. 1675, renunciation of Nicolas Bichart and AEL PdD 129, f. 239vo., 19 Dec. 1675, agreement with Nicolas Bichart; Ael PdD 131, f. 221vo., 17 Nov. 1689, grace to Jean Fraickin; AEL PdD 132, f. 32, 29 Sept. 1694, instructions to Peters Everars; AEL PdD 132, f. 120vo., 1 March 1696, lease to Baron Surlet.

57 AEL PdD 129, f. 219vo.-220, 9 July 1675; AEL PdD 131, ff. 222-222vo., 19 Nov. 1689, order to the Mayor of Schendremael; AEL PdD 132, f. 3vo., 4 Aug. 1693, order to Germeau, Mayor of Visé; AEL PdD 132, ff. 123-124, 3 March 1696, lease to Guilheaume Doupie; AEL PdD 137, ff. 193vo.-194, 25 April 1702, lease to Andre Massar; AEL PdD 139, f. 96, 5 June 1703, lease to Pierre Bouchamps and Baltus Frents; AEL PdD 144, f. 43vo., 10 Sept. 1711, and AEL PdD 144, f. 50vo., 6 Oct. 1711, orders to Coulpin, Priest at Visé.

58 Consider the repairs ordered by the Cathedral Chapter of Liège, in AEL PdD 132, f. 88vo., 22 Sept. 1695, order to the farmer of Mont. St. Andre. In 1680, they ordered a new door for the Granary at Milmort, AEL PdD 130, f. 116, 25 June 1680. This register (AEL PdD 130) shows numerous repairs to churches, farms, and granaries financed by the cathedral in 1680.

59 AEL PdD 129, f. 120, 19 Oct. 1673.

60 Henri Pirenne, *Histoire de Belgique*, V (Brussels, 1926), 57-58.

61 This is evident from de Vries' data, as well as that pertaining to other regions. See, for example, Christian Pfister, "Zum Klima des Raumes Zürich im späten 17. und frühen 18. Jahrhundert," *Vierteljahrschrift der Naturforschenden Gesellschaft in Zürich*, 122 (1977), 447-471.

62 The most recent comprehensive discussion of the crises of the European economy in the seventeenth century is Jan de Vries, *The Economy of Europe in an Age of Crisis, 1600-1750* (Cambridge: Cambridge University Press, 1976). For a good discussion of the idea of crisis, and its applicability as a general theme in the history of Europe in the seventeenth century, see Theodore K. Rabb, *The Struggle for Stability in Early Modern Europe* (New York, 1975).

63 Jean Meuvret, "Les Crises de subsistance et la démographie de la France d'Ancien Régime," *Population* 1 (1946), 643-650. B. H. Slicher van Bath, *The Agrarian History of Western Europe, A.D. 500-1850*, tr. Olive Ordish (London: Edward Arnold, 1963), pp. 206-220. E. J. Hobsbawm, "The Crisis of the Seventeenth Century," *Past & Present*, No. 5 (1954), 33-53, and No. 6 (1954), 44-65; reprinted in T. Aston, ed., *Crisis in Europe, 1560-1660* (New York, 1967), pp. 35-38. Roland Mousnier, *Histoire générale des civilisations*, IV (Paris, 1953), esp. pp. 145-151.

64 See, for example, Charles Wilson, *England's Apprenticeship 1603-1763* (London, 1965), and Joan Thirsk, *English Peasant Farming* (London, 1957).

65 G. E. Mingay, "The Agricultural Depression, 1730-1750," *Economic History Review*, 8 (1956), 323-338.

66   A. M. van der Woude, "Het Noorderkwartier," *A.A.G. Bijdragen*, 16 (1972); and J. A. Faber, "Drie Eeuwen Friesland," *A.A.G. Bijdragen*, 17 (1972).

67   Van der Woude, "Het Noorderkwartier," p. 613.

68   For individual works, see Goy and Le Roy Ladurie, *Les Fluctuations du produit de la dîme*. For a summary of conditions in France and elsewhere in northwest Europe in the seventeenth and eighteenth centuries, see Le Roy Ladurie's summary and, especially, pp. 356-374. Recently, they have added to their analysis and summary. This work is contained in a 1978 report to the Seventh International Conference on Economic History (Edinburgh), entitled, "A.3. Peasant Dues, Tithes and Trends in Agricultural Production in Pre-Industrial Societies."

69   For comparisons from Belgium, the Low Countries, and Northern France, see H. Neveux, "La Production céréalière dans une région frontalière: le Cambrèsis du XVe au XVIIIe siècle. Bilan provisoire," in Goy and Le Roy Ladurie, *Les Fluctuations du produit de la dîme*, pp. 58-66; J. Ruwet, "Pour un indice de la production céréalière à l'époque moderne: la région de Namur," in *ibid.*, pp. 67-82; *id.*, "Mesure de la production agrocole sous l'ancien régime: le blé en pays mosan," *Annales E.S.C.* (19), 1964, 625-642; and the contributions in van der Wee and van Cauwenbergh, *Productivity of Land and Agricultural Innovation in the Low Countries*.

70   A similar pattern of growth stymied in the 1670's by Louis XIV's wars is found in Alsace. See B. Veyrassat-Herren, "Dîmes alsaciennes," in Goy and Le Roy Ladurie, *Les Fluctuations du produit de la dîme*, pp. 83-102.

71   In 1678, the canons ordered their receiver to pay 477 florins for taxes as quickly as possible, to avoid *exécution*. AEL PdD 130, f. 47, 30 August 1678, order to Receiver Rouveroy. Also: AEL PdD 129, f. 183vo., 9 Nov. 1674, order to the tithe collectors of Visé; AEL PdD 129, f. 236, 28 Nov. 1675, order to receiver Salms.

72   Such a clause was a regular part of leases under Liégeois law. See the discussion of leasing techniques in Léonce Deltenré, *Note sur le bail à ferme dans le pays de Thuin au XVIIIe siècle* (Thuin, 1936), p. 17.

73   These conclusions (and those in the next paragraph) were reached after reading through the graces granted in the following registers of *Protocoles des Directeurs*: 129 (1671-1678), 130 (1678-1684), 131 (1685-1693), 132 (1693-1697), 137 (1700-1702), 139 (1702-1704), and 140 (1704-1706).

74   AEL PdD 130, f. 172vo., 8 May 1681; f. 178, 3 July 1681.

75   Dubois, *Le Chapitre cathédral*, pp. 286-289.

76   Consequently, the *Protocoles des Directeurs* usually show a pair of entries at the expiration of each lease. One entry grants a grace, and demands that any balance due be paid immediately, while the second notes the writing of a new lease.

77   This is based on an admittedly small study of eighteen Basse-Mosan farms owned by a number of Liégeois religious institutions. The data are presented in Myron P. Gutmann, "War and Rural Life in the Seventeenth Century: the Case of the Basse-Meuse" (diss., Princeton, 1976), pp. 426-430. The problem of non-renewal is discussed more fully in *ibid.*, pp. 183-190.

78   Jean Jacquart, *La Crise rurale en Ile-de-France, 1550-1670* (Paris: Armand Colin, 1974); Guy Cabourdin, *Terre et hommes en Lorraine du milieu du XVIe siècle à la Guerre de Trente Ans*, 3 vols. (Lille, 1975).

79   Jansen, "Agrarian Development and Exploitation," pp. 244-245.

80   *Ibid.*

81   We see this if we compare data collected by Jansen for the Manor of Eys in 1663 and

1776 with data I have collected for Richelle in 1722 and Emael in 1717-1718. Middle-sized farms, which disappeared in Eys between 1663 and 1776, still existed in Emael and Richelle in the early eighteenth century. Sources: *ibid.*, p. 247; and Gutmann, "War and Rural Life in the Seventeenth Century," p. 59.

82   Jansen, "Agrarian Development and Exploitation," pp. 247-248.

Chapter V

1   For the market structure of the Liégeois region, see Joseph Ruwet, *L'Agriculture et les classes rurales au pays de Herve sous l'Ancien Régime* (Liège, 1943), pp. 171-179; Marie-Louise Fanchamps, *Recherches statistiques sur le problème annonaire dans la principauté de Liège de 1475 à la fin du XVIe siècle. Tendances, cycles, crises* (Liège: Editions de la Commission Communale de l'Histoire de l'Ancien Pays de Liège, 1970); J. de Chestret de Haneffe, "La Police de vivres à Liège, pendant le moyen âge," *BIAL*, 23 (1892), 217-267; and R. van Santbergen, *Les Bons métiers des meuniers, des boulangers, et des brasseurs de la cité de Liège* (Liège, 1949).

2   On diet in nearby Brabant, see Claude Bruneel, *La Mortalité dans les campagnes: le duché de Brabant aux XVIIe et XVIIIe siècles* (Louvain, 1977), I, 154-163. On spelt, see L. Genicot, "La Limite des cultures du froment et de l'épeautre dans le Namurois au bas moyen âge," *Namurcum*, 22 (1947), 17-24.

3   Fanchamps, *Recherches statistiques sur le problème annonaire*, p. 229.

4   *Ibid.* L. Rouhart-Chabot, "Les Pouvoirs publics liégeois devant la disette de 1565-1566," *BIAL*, 67 (1949-1950), 124.

5   Maurice Yans, "La Meuse et nos relations commerciales avec la Hollande," *BIAL*, 63 (1939), 131-140. Th. L. M. Thurlings, *De Maashandel van Venlo en Roermond in de 16e eeuw, 1473-1572* (Amsterdam: H. J. Paris, 1945).

6   See the problems described in Yans, "La Meuse et nos relations commerciales avec la Hollande."

7   RAL LVO 5546, Complaint by the citizens of Eysden, dated 1632.

8   Yans, "La Meuse et nos relations commerciales avec la Hollande," pp. 138-139.

9   *Ibid.*, p. 135. Fanchamps, *Recherches statistiques sur le problème annonaire*, p. 234. Hubert van Houtte, *Les Occupations étrangères en Belgique sous l'Ancien Régime* (Ghent, 1930), I, 2-3.

10   See the discussion in Charles Tilly, "Food Supply and Public Order in Modern Europe," in Charles Tilly (ed.), *The Formation of National States in Western Europe* (Princeton: Princeton University Press, 1975), pp. 380-455.

11   Rouhart-Chabot, "Les Pouvoirs publics liégeois . . .," 122-123.

12   Joseph Daris, *Histoire du diocèse et de la principauté de Liège pendant le XVIIe siècle* (Liège: Demarteau, 1877), I, 26-27, and II, 297.

13   *List chronologique des édits et ordonnances de la principauté de Liège*, 2 vols. (Brussels: Em. Devroye, 1851-1860), *passim.* For some examples, see 28 March 1631, "Edit interdisant la sortie des grains de la cité et de sa franchise et banlieu, et defendant aux recoupeurs, brasseurs, boulangers, porteurs de sacs, botteresses et autres d'aller chez les particuliers pour en acheter," I, 153; 6 September 1631, "Règlement relatif à l'achat des grains dans le cité de Liège, avec défense de les marchander, acheter et recouper, dans la ville et sa banlieu, avant qu'ils soient amenés au marche," I, 155; 26 January 1675, "Règlement relatif à l'achat des grains et à la défense d'en exporter hors du pays," I, 227.

14   For the next three paragraphs, see Hubert van Houtte, *Les Occupations étrangères en Belgique*, I, 2-3, 178-187, 466-469.

15   C. Douxchamps-Lefevre, "Le Traité de Freyr conclu le 25 octobre 1675 entre la France et l'Espagne," *Annales de la Société Archéologique de Namur*, 58 (1977), 47-67.

16   AEL St. Pierre 46, petition of Louis Burton, tithe-collector of Monfrin, 23 April 1675.

17   Henri de Sonkeux, *La Vie à Verviers il y a trois siècles* (Verviers, n.d. but probably 1946), p. 40.

18   There are a variety of sources for prices in the region of Liège. They, and their usefulness, are considered in Myron P. Gutmann, "War and Rural Life in the Seventeenth Century: the Case of the Basse-Meuse" (diss., Princeton, 1976), pp. 404-409. Also, see Joseph Ruwet, "Prix, production et benefices agricoles: le pays de Liège au XVIIIᵉ siècle," *Cahiers d'Histoire des Prix*, 2 (1957), 87-90.

19   The sources for these prices are listed in Appendix C. It should be noted here that, while the annual price for Amsterdam is based on a harvest-year price, the moving means presented in Figure 5.1 are based on calendar-year prices. In the case of Maastricht and Liège prices, the annual prices and long moving mean prices all have the same base.

20   See Fanchamps, *Recherches statistiques sur le problème annonaire*, especially pp. 40, 241.

21   The price level during the depression of the first half of the eighteenth century, it should be noted, is above the price level in the years between 1580 and 1610. In part, this is because the last substantial devaluation of currency in Liège and Brabant took place around 1612. Thus, at least part of the rise in prices in the years from 1610 to 1640 was caused by the devaluation of the currency, and not by market forces. See Ruwet, *L'Agriculture et les classes rurales*, pp. 80-83; and Hubert Frère, "Numismatique liégeoise: notes sur la monnaie de compte dans la principauté de Liège," *BIAL*, 80 (1967), 91-112. On the eighteenth-century depression itself, see also, G. E. Mingay, "The Agricultural Depression, 1730-1750," *Economic History Review*, 8 (1956), 323-338.

22   The Liège and Maastricht correlations reflect the Pearson product-moment correlation coefficient calculated using the index values for the three cities. A full table of correlation coefficients for prices, production and demographic variables pertaining to the Basse-Meuse comprises Appendix D. For Arnhem and Utrecht, my source is Walter Achilles, "Getreidepreise und Getreidehandelsbeziehungen europäischer Räume im 16. und 17. Jahrhundert," *Zeitschrift für Agrargeschichte und Agrarsoziologie*, 7 (1959), 32-53.

23   Another possible cause is a slight methodological difference. Achilles has computed coefficients using the prices themselves. I have used the de-trended index of extreme behavior.

24   The significance level is 0.001. The 10 percent statement is based on the assumption that the simple correlation squared equals the proportion of total variation in the dependent variable explained by the independent variable. See Hubert Blalock, *Social Statistics*, second edition (New York, 1972), p. 392.

25   For the Maastricht tithe and Liège rye, the correlation coefficient is −0.239 (significance level 0.008); for Liège spelt, it is −0.266 (significance level 0.003). The correlations between Louwberg farm production (expressed in grain) and the prices are all less than 0.1, with unstable signs.

26   On the strong relationships between prices in the Low Countries, see the discussion in J. A. Faber, "The Decline of the Baltic Grain Trade in the Second Half of the Seventeenth Century," *Acta Historiae Neerlandica*, 1 (1966), 120, note 2.

27   AEL C*de*J Visé 203, 1 December 1701.

28   The Amsterdam grain prices are for a last, roughly equivalent to 27 *muids*, or 540 *setiers*, or 4,000 pounds. These prices were used to set Amsterdam's official bread price. We are interested here in relative price changes, rather than their absolute level. See Nicolaus Wilhelmus Posthumus, *Inquiry into the History of Prices in Holland*, I (Leiden: E. J. Brill, 1946), 569-571. It is possible that they were subject to manipulation, but it does not seem likely that any manipulation had much of an impact on our analysis here. See Gutmann, "War and Rural Life in the Seventeenth Century," p. 166.

29   De Sonkeux, *La Vie à Verviers il y a trois siècles*, pp. 44-47, 51, 53.

30   The following small table shows the correlation coefficients after the removal of wartime years for the Basse-Meuse.

	Amsterdam Rye With	
	Liège Rye	*Maastricht Rye*
1620-1699		
All Years	0.730	0.692
Without 1632-1638, 1672-1678, 1689-1697	0.771	0.710
1700-1749		
All Years	0.814	0.631
Without 1701-1706, 1746-1748	0.862	0.655

The differences are about five percent. The small differences are all in the same direction, which suggests they are not produced by the normal margin of error in the computation of these coefficients. Achilles found a similar result for the relationship between prices in Danzig and Utrecht, in the second half of the sixteenth century. The coefficient for 1551-1600 was 0.686; when he took out the years of the Dutch Revolt, the coefficient rose to 0.950. Achilles, "Getreidepreise und Getreidehandelsbeziehungen . . .," p. 46.

31   These divisions are confirmed by more precise statistical tests; the standard deviation for the index of extreme behavior for Maastricht and Liège rye prices is 0.382, suggesting that about 95 percent of all years had index values for prices less than 1.75. A value above 1.60 was thus genuinely extreme.

32   In 1708-1709, there were winter quarters, but they would have had little impact on prices. Moreover, there was not even much wartime loss of production in those years. In the records of the Directors of the St. Lambert Chapter of the Cathedral of Liège, there are no complaints of troops damaging crops between 1705 and 1716. AEL Cathédrale Secretariat 140-147, Protocoles des Directeurs 1704-1716.

33   It is comforting to note that extremely high prices in the Basse-Meuse conform to the model of subsistence crises established by Goubert and others. They have not, however, sufficiently emphasized the psychological nature of these price increases, which is what makes them so important to understanding early modern life. See Pierre Goubert, *The Ancien Régime* (New York: Harper, 1973), pp. 36-42. For weather conditions, see Appendix A, below.

34   Posthumus has argued that the price of grain in Amsterdam in the 1670's is unusually low because of manipulation by the authorities (they apparently sold grain from their own reserves to alleviate the price of bread and reduce the burden on their citizens). It is unlikely, however, that they were able to reduce the price of grain by more than 10

percent, if that much. Compare the prices at the Corn Exchange of Amsterdam with those at the Chief Exchange, which should not have been manipulated. Only in 1676 were prices lower at the Corn Exchange, challenging Posthumus' assertion of manipulation. See Posthumus, *Inquiry into the History of Prices of Holland*, I, 20, 569, 574.

35 Faber, "The Decline of the Baltic Grain Trade."

36 AEL Notaire P. Craheau, 1670-1676, f. 107, agreement dated 15 May 1675. It should be noted that the 30 *dallers* he should have received is a rather small amount. We can compare it with the wages of a miner in one of the area's numerous coal mines, working three days a week, at a minimum salary of 15 patards a day. Such a miner would earn slightly more than 100 florins a year. The 30 *dallers*, on the other hand, converts in the seventeenth century to only about 50 florins. For salaries and total employment of miners, I rely on an oral presentation made by M. Pierre Guerin at the Institut Archéologique Liégeois, 24 June 1977. I am indebted to Proffessor E. Hélin for transmitting his notes on this presentation to me.

Chapter VI

1 Herman van der Wee, *The Growth of the Antwerp Market and the European Economy*, (The Hague, 1963), II, 269.

2 H. J. C. von Grimmelshausen, *The Adventurous Simpliccissimus*, trans. A.T.S. Goodrick (Lincoln, Nebraska: The University of Negraska Press, 1962), pp. 5-26.

3 Gustav Freytag, *Pictures of German Life in the XVth, XVIth and XVIIth Centurues*, tr., Mrs. Malcolm (London: Chapman and Hall, 1862), II.

4 Gunther Fransz, *Der Dreissigjährige Krieg und das deutsche Volk* (Stuttgart: Gustav Fischer Verlag, 1961), part I. For a more general discussion of war and population, see Roger Mols, *Introduction à la démographie historique des villes d'Europe du XVIe au XVIIIe siècle* (Louvain, 1955), II, 463-473.

5 Karl F. Helleiner, "The Population of Europe from the Black Death to the Eve of the Vital Revolution", *The Cambridge Economic History*, IV (Cambridge: Cambridge University Press, 1967), pp. 42-43.

6 Jean Meuvret, "Les Crises de subsistance et la démographie de la France d'Ancien Régime," *Population,* 1 (1946), 643-650.

7 Philip Benedict, "Catholics and Hugenots in Sixteenth Century Rouen: The Demographic Effects of the Religious Wars," *French Historical Studies,* 9 (1975), 209-234; Alain Croix, "La Démographie du pays nantais au XVIe siècle," *Annales de Démographie Historique* (1967), 63-90. For the effect of the Fronde on the region of Paris, see Jean Jacquart, "La Fronde des princes dans la region parisienne et ses consequences materielles," *Revue d'Histoire Moderne et Contemporaine* (1960), 257-290; and *id, La Crise rurale en Ile-de-France, 1550-1670* (Paris: Armand Colin, 1974).

8 Geoffrey Parker, "War and Economic Change: the Economic Costs of the Dutch Revolt," in J. M. Winter, ed., *War and Economic Development* (Cambridge: Cambridge University Press, 1975), pp. 50-52.

9 Gaston Roupnel, *La Ville et la campagne au XVIIe siècle: étude sur les populations du pays dijonais* (Paris, 1922), pp. 19-50.

10 Andre Humm, *Villages et hameaux disparus en Basse-Alsace* (Strasbourg, 1971), pp. 32-36.

11 Fernand Pirotte, *La Terre de Durbuy au XVIIe et XVIIIe siècles. Les Institutions, l'économie, et les hommes* (Liège: Centre Belge d'Histoire Rurale, 1974), pp. 17-18. Guy Cabourdin, *Terre et Hommes en Lorraine du milieu du XVIe siècle à la Guerre de Trente Ans* (Lille, 1975), I, 86-107.

12 L. Tassin, "Un document dit la misère de notre region au XVIIe siècle," *L'Antiquaire* (Philippeville), III, 53-55; AEL Prieuré et Seigneurie d'Aywaille, 110.

13 The 75 percent comes from a study of the city of Liège, and is probably accurate. Etienne Hélin, *La Démographie de Liège aux XVIIe et XVIIIe siècles,* Academie Royale de Belgique, Classe des Lettres et des Sciences Morales et Politiques, Mémoires in-8°, 56 (1963), 70-77. The 60 percent comes from a report made by the Curé of Herstal in 1759, in which he said the parish had 5,000 residents and 3,000 communicants. Archives de l'Evéché de Liège, Inspections, Herstal, 1757.

14 For most of the parishes of the Basse-Meuse, the records of ecclesiastical visitations have been published in Guillaume Simenon, ed., *Visitationes Archidiaconales Archidiaconatus Hesbanaie in Dioecesi Leodiensi ab anno 1613 ad annum 1763* (Liège: H. Dessain, 1939). The two volumes are arranged in an alphabetic format, with an entry for each parish or chapel. Some parishes could not be included in the computation of the index because they did not have two or more visitations giving the number of communicants. Parishes not included in Simenon (the Council of St. Remacle, near Liège) were unpublished when I did the research for this book, but should appear soon under the editorship of Andre Deblon, archivist of the Episcopal Archives of Liège, in the *BSAHL*. Mr. Deblon was very courteous and permitted me to examine his manuscript prior to publication, so that I could obtain the data I needed. See also his, "Une source capitale pour l'histoire paroissiale de l'Ancien Régime: les visites archidiaconales de Condroz," pp. 55-104, and "Les Rapports des visites archidiaconales de Condroz," *BSAHL*, 50 (1970), 105-239.

15 Emmanuel Le Roy Ladurie, *Les Paysans de Languedoc* (Paris: SEVPEN, 1966), I, 541-545.

16 In 1806, the communes of Herstal and Wandre had a combined population of 6,600. Louis Francois Thomassin, *Mémoire statistique du département de l'Ourte* (Liège, 1879), pp. 37-41.

17 Archives de l'Evêché de Liège, Inspections, 1757.

18 Their rights also included reciprocal bourgeois status in the city of Liège, an important privilege. For this and other information below on the customs of the Herstal bourgeois, see André Collart-Sacré, *La Libre seigneurie de Herstal: son histoire, ses monuments, ses rues et ses lieux-dits,* I (Liège: Georges Thone, 1927), 51-61.

19 Lists for 59 years between 1620 and 1750 still exist. They are to be found in certain of the registers titled *Comptes de la seigneurie de Herstal,* in the *fonds* Etats (of Liège) at the AEL. The records are to be found in this group because the estates of Liège purchased the seigneurie of Herstal from the King of Prussia in 1740; his archives from the earlier period became part of the archives of the estates as part of the sales agreement. There are two different kinds of accounts, and as a result two kinds of lists. The registers titled *Revenus de la seigneurie* (Regs. 534-546 cover the period 1612-1704) are a sort of preliminary register. The *Comptes des recettes et dépenses* (Regs. 553-578 for the period 1648-1740) are a more final accounting prepared for presentation to authorities in the Hague or Berlin, and include a certification of accuracy signed by the echevins of the seigneurie of Herstal. For an example of such a certification, see AEL Etats (de Liège) 558, f. 82 (1673). On the assumption that the final certified accounts were more

accurate than the preliminary accounts, I have chosen to rely on them whenever there was coverage for a given year in both series. In addition, a problem with the *Revenus de la Seigneurie* – the preliminary accounts – must be mentioned. This lists of bourgeois in these accounts are often presented in groups of three years: a list of names was given and then three columns to indicate payment for three years. Unfortunately, while certain people whose names are listed were shown as not paying the second or third year, they rarely show additions to the bourgeois of the seigneurie in the second or third year. Since bourgeois could be added during any year, I have taken the list of bourgeoisie (rather than the payment indications) for the first year to be accurate for that year (with the exceptions based on customary exemptions noted in the text), and disregarded the rest of the information from those registers. After the purchase of the seigneurie by the Estates of Liège in 1740, only simple statements of the number of bourgeois are available. They are found in AEL Etats, Greffe de l'Etat Tiers, 305, 307; and AEL Etats, Greffe de l'Etat Noble, 313-321.

20 A Basse-Mosan coal miner earned between fifteen and twenty patards a day, and worked between three and four days a week in normal times. For the source, see Chapter V, note 36. A seven-pound loaf of bread in Verviers normally cost seven or eight patards. Henri de Sonkeux, *La Vie à Verviers il y a trois siècles,* (Verviers, n.d., but probabaly 1946), pp. 44-47, 51, 53.

21 The Wandre reconstitution is used in Chapters VII and VIII for certain demographic measurements. Here, it permits us to understand the Herstal-Wandre bourgeoisie, although only impressionistically, since the findings apply to only a small number of individuals. For a discussion of data and methods, see Myron P. Gutmann, "War and Rural Life in the Seventeenth Century: the Case of the Basse-Meuse," (diss., Princeton, 1976), pp. 337-380; and *id.* "Reconstituting Wandre: An Approach to Semi-Automatic Family Reconstotution," *Annales de Démographie Historique* (1977), 315-341. Although the Herstal chronology in the 1690's is surprising, the same pattern appears on a much smaller scale in the "population" of the nearby abbey of Val-Dieu. No new monks joined the abbey in 1672-1680, and the monks dispersed to various places. The recovery of the abbey took place in the 1690's. In place of one new monk each year, six monks joined in 1690. Like the nearby communities, the first two-thirds of the eighteenth century were a period of dramatic growth. Bruno Dumont, "La Population de l'Abbaye du Val-Dieu sous l'ancien régime," *Citeaux-Commentarii Cisterciences,* 27 (1976), 249-253.

22 The seigneur of Argenteau was owed one-half capon for each of his *surceants* or *manants* (landholders.) The year given is an accounting year, beginning on St. Andre's day (November 30) of the year specified, and ending November 29 of the following year. The number of landholders actually reflects the number on October 1 of the second calendar year covered by the accounts. AEL Mercy-Argenteau, Comptes Generaux, 2510-2576, covering the years 1619-1751.

23 The economic growth of Liège did not result in much growth in the city's population. Rather, the faubourgs and parishes outside the old walls grew dramatically, pushed by the same forces that acted on Herstal and Wandre. Etienne Hélin, *La Population des paroisses liégeoises aux XVIIe et XVIIIe siècle* (Liège: Editions de la Commission Communale de l'Histoire de l'Ancien Pays de Liège, 1959), especially pp. 271-274, 377-379.

24 RAL LVO 5490-5504, 5507-5527, 5570, 5571, 5583.

25   Claude Bruneel, *La Mortalité dans les campagnes: le duché de Brabant aux XVIIᵉ et XVIIIᵉ siècles* (Louvain, 1977), esp. I, 125-131.

26   See A. M. van der Woude, "Het Noorderkwartier," *A.A.G. Bijdragen,* 16 (1972); J. A. Faber, "Drie Eeuwen Friesland," *A.A.G. Bijdragen,* 17 (1972); and J. A. Faber, *et al.,* "Population Changes and Economic Developments in the Netherlands: a Historical Survey." *A.A.G. Bijdragen,* 12 (1965), 50-72.

27   Faber, et al., "Population Changes ... in the Netherlands," pp. 72-113.

28   H. J. van Xanten and A. M. van der Woude, "Het Hoofdgeld en de Bevolking van de Meierij van 's-Hertogenbosch omstreeks 1700," *A.A.G. Bijdragen,* 13 (1965), 3-96.

29   Georges Duby and Armand Wallon, eds., *Histoire de la France rurale,* II (Paris, 1975), 359-372.

30   Mols, *Introduction à la démographie historique,* II, 472.

31   Humm, *Villages et hameaux disparus,* p. 32.

32   Parker, "War and Economic Change," pp. 51-54, van der Wee, *The Growth of the Antwerp Market,* II, 269-272.

Chapter VII

1   The parishes are Herstal, Wandre, Vivegnis, Hermalle-sous-Argenteau, Cheratte, Dalhem, Harcourt, Heure-le-Romain, and Saive. All are Catholic parishes, from all-Catholic villages, except Dalhem. The number of baptism and deaths entries in the Reformed Church registers for Dalhem were so few as to make them worthless for the purposes of this study. The parish registers used can all be found in the collection of parish registers located in the AEL. For the monthly and yearly totals for each of the parishes, see Myron P. Gutmann, "War and Rural Life in the Seventeenth Century: the Case of the Basse-Meuse," (diss., Princeton, 1976), pp. 436-495.

2   This process of aggregation also solves some of the statistical problems imposed by attempting to study extreme behavior in demographic variables. Births, marriages, and deaths are rare events and statistically this brings their occurrence under the controls of the Poisson distribution. With the sort of data considered in this chapter and in Chapter VIII, one of the properties of the Poisson distribution is that the standard deviation is equal to the square root of the number of events happening. In other (and very simplified) words, we might say that for about two-thirds of the years studied, the number of deaths per year would be within a range equal to the mean of all years plus or minus the square root of the mean number of deaths each year. For a small number of deaths per year, the standard deviation would thus be relatively large in proportion to the actual number of deaths: for ten deaths per year, the range would be ± 30 percent. To prove that the number of events in a given year was "extreme" the number would have to skyrocket or plummet. Yet, extreme behavior is the object of this study. By increasing the number of deaths through the aggregation of a number of parishes, the standard deviation becomes a progressively smaller proportion of the mean. At 100 deaths each year, the standard deviation is only 10 percent of the mean, a much more manageable proportion. See Murray R. Speigel, *Shawn's Outline Series Theory and Problems of Statistics* (New York: McGraw-Hill Book Co., 1961), pp. 124, 348, and Frank A. Haight, *Handbook of the Poisson Distribution* (New York: John Wiley & Sons, Inc., 1967). For the methods used to correct incomplete data, see Appendix E.

3   Calendar years are used here because they are more easily understood. One should

recall, however, that food supply conditions are geared much more closely to a harvest year. Harvest years are used in most of the multivariate statistical tests.

4   For the chronology of and some sources for epidemics in the Low Countries, see Etienne Hélin, "Les Recherches sur la mortalité dans la region liégeoise (XVe - XIXe siècles)," in Paul Harsin and Etienne Hélin, eds., *Actes du collogue international de démographie historique. Problèmes de mortalité, Liège, 1963* (Liège, 1965), pp. 155-184. The 1634-1636 epidemic, variously described in the sources as plague and dysentery, is probably the best-documented modern epidemic in the Low Countries, and possibly, thus, the most severe. On that epidemic, see, among many sources, J. Schoetter, "Etat du duché de Luxembourg et du comté de Chiny pendant la guerre de Trente Ans," *Annales de l'Academie d'Archéologie de Belgique,* 33 (1876), 325-459, and especially 338-340 and 398-399; and Melchior F. Crahay, "Fragment de chonique liégeois et franchimontoise," ed. by Ph. de Limbourg, *Bulletin de la Société des Bibliophiles Liégeois,* 2 (1884), 68-69. For the chronology of epidemics in the Duchy of Brabant, not far from the Basse-Meuse, see Claude Bruneel, *La Mortalité dans les campagnes: le duché de Brabant aux XVIIe et XVIIIe siècles* (Louvain, 1977), I, 213-317.

5   See the discussion of the situation in the city of Liège, where even in the second half of the eighteenth century, registration of children's deaths was rare, in Etienne Hélin, *La Démographie de Liège aux XVIIe et XVIIIe siècles,* Academie Royale de Belgique. Classe des Lettres et des Sciences Morales et Politiques. Mémoires. Collection in-8°, vol. 56 (Brussels, 1963) pt. 4, p. 216.

6   For information on weather, see E. Vanderlinden, *Chronique des événements metéorologiques en Belgique jusqu'en 1834* (Brussels, 1924). Extract from Mémoires publiés par la Classe des Sciences de l'Academie Royale de Belgique, Collection in-4°, series 2, vol. 5, 1924. The meteorological events of 1676 are recorded on pp. 162-164. Weather is summarized, along with other events, in the Chronological Table, Appendix A. For the problems caused by a wet fall and a subsequent dry summer (which makes germination difficult and leaches certain valuable nutrients out of the soil, as well as making harvesting and storage difficult), and a subsequent dry summer, see E. Le Roy Ladurie, *Histoire du climat depuis l'an mil* (Paris, 1967, especially pp. 284-285). Bruneel has noticed the role of a wet summer and fall, followed by a dry summer, in dysentery outbreaks in Brabant. *La Mortalité dans les campagnes,* I, 521. He also presents this interesting idea of why dry summers were so disastrous, on p. 522.

7   Vanderlinden, *Chronique des événements metéorologiques,* pp. 152-154. The peak in prices was not reached until the harvest year, September 1635 to August 1636.

8   On the plague epidemic of 1667-1670, see Jacques Revel, "Autour d'une épidémie ancienne: la peste de 1666-1670," *Revue d'Histoire Moderne et Contemporaine,* 17 (1970), 953-983; Marie Delcourt and Jean Hoyoux, "Quatre ans de la vie à Liège d'un diplomate italien (1666-1670). Les ephemerides du Nonce Agostino Franciotti," *Vieux Liège,* 7 (1974), 381-389: Crahay, "Fragment de Chronique," pp. 93-94; Henri de Sonkeux, *La Vie à Verviers il y a trois siècles* (Verviers, n.d., but probably 1946), p. 28; AEL Cathedrale Secrétariat 52, Conclusions Capitulares, 13 Oct. 1668; and AEL Etats Nobles 17, f. 139, Récés de 3 April 1674.

9   The evidence to support this conclusion is not presented here. For the figures, see Gutmann, "War and Rural Life in the Seventeenth Century," p. 239.

10   See Pierre Guillaume and Jean-Pierre Poussou, *Démographie Historique* (Paris, 1970), pp. 142-144.

11   Totals were computed by aggregating all monthly death counts for all nine parishes by

year. A month's total was included only if all the months for that harvest year for that parish were available (none missing).

12 Bruneel, *La Mortalité dans les campagnes,* I, 482, 528.

13 See, for example. Etienne Gautier and Louis Henry, *La Population de Crulai, paroisse normande,* Institute National d'Etudes Démographiques, Travaux et Documents, Cahier no. 33 (Paris: Presses Universitaires de France, 1958), pp. 63-66. Crulai presents the modern pattern, where the maximum is in March and April. Bruneel, in his *La Mortalité dans les campagnes,* actually charts the evolution of the modern pattern over time. By examining each half-century from 1601-1650 until 1751-1795, he shows the emergence of the modern pattern (vol. I, p. 325). The problem in his analysis is that he does not extract extreme mortality. Had he done so, he would have seen that the real difference between the old and the new regime of mortality is the presence of epidemics. When epidemics are frequent, the peak number of deaths, even for a period of time as long as a half-century, will be in the fall. When epidemics are infrequent, as they were in the eighteenth century, or have changed from plague to influenza and smallpox (dysentery seems to be a constant), the peak is in the winter or spring, when non-epidemic mortality (which primarily took the very old and the very young) was greatest.

14 AEL PR Hermalle-sous-Argenteau 2, pp. 198-236 (June-August, 1630).

15 AEL PR Hermalle-sous-Argenteau 2, pp. 191-198 (April, 1623).

16 Edmund van Wintershoven, "Chronique tirée des registres paroissiaux d'Emael," *BSSLL,* 22 (1904), 58.

17 AEL PR Wandre 5, pp. 39-44.

18 AEL PR Dalhem 2, p. 135.

19 They were: Jean-Francois Haultonsen, of the parish of St. Catherine in Liège; Jean-Pierre Berhembosse, a young man from Maseyck; Elisabeth, the young daughter of Lambert Gaty of the parish of St. Foi at the border between Liège and Herstal; J.-H. Bex, an officer of the militia of Liege; and Jean du Berny, a citizen of Dinant and valet of a Canon of the Cathedral. AEL PR Herstal 11, p. 93. For another example, see de Sonkeux, *La Vie à Verviers il y a trois siècles,* p. 63.

20 Joseph Daris, *Histoire du diocèse et de la principauté de Liège pendant le XVIIᵉ siècle* (Liège: Demarteau, 1877), II, 56. Théodose Bouille, *Histoire de la ville et pays de Liège* (Liège, 1732), III, 414. AEL PR Herstal 11, p. 104. Maurice Yans, "Le Destin diplomatique de Herstal-Wandre terre des Nassau en banlieu liégeois," *Annuaire d'Histoire Liégeoise,* 6 (1960), 531. For more examples, see *Rerum Leodiensium status anno M.DC.XLIX,* ed., tr., J. Alexandre (Liège: Société des Bibliophiles Liégeois, 1885), especially pp. 41-42.

21 Two good examples of the uses of peasant militia are presented in Wintershoven, "Chronique ... d'Emael," p. 65, and Crahay, "Fragment de Chronique," pp. 75-81.

22 When visited by ecclesiastical authorities in 1658, the parish priest of Sint Pieters near Maastrict reported that there may have been Catholic soldiers in the adjacent garrison of Maastrict, but he did not know them. Guillaume Simenon, ed. *Visitationes Archidiaconales Archidiaconatus Hesbanaie in Dioecesi Leodiensi ab anno 1613 ad annum 1763* (Liège: H. Dessain, 1939), p. 623. See also, F. Jacquet-Ladrier, "Soldats blessés à Namur au XVIIᵉ siècle (1635-1643)," *Annales de la Société Archéologique de Namur,* 58 (1977), 25-46.

23 AEL PR Dalhem 1, f. 28-34vo.; Reg. 2, pp. 130-137.

24 *Fastes Militaires du Pays de Liège* (Catalog of an exhibition at the Musee d'Art Wallon, Liège, October-November, 1970), (Liège, 1970).

25   Examples of home-grown soldiers dying elsewhere are numerous in the Basse-Meuse. See especially AEL PR Wandre 5, *passim.*

26   The best source for understanding these diseases in the Low Countries is now Bruneel, *La Mortalité dans les campagnes.* For other works (almost all now superseded by Bruneel), see the primitive and incomplete, but still useful, narrative by C. Bamps, "Epidemies et disettes qui ont anciennement règné dans la province de Limbourg," *Bulletin de la Commission Centrale de Statistique* (Brussels), 6 (1855), 597-615. More interesting, but still primitive, is Louis Torfs, *Fastes des calamités publiques survenues dans les Pays Bas,* 2 vols. (Paris-Tournai, 1859). For an attribution of all these diseases in a single year (1636), see Leon Lahaye, "Carnets de comptes de Jean Lintermans, chanoine de Saint Jean l'Evangeliste à Liège," *Leodium,* 32 (1939), 60. The material Lahaye cites can be found in AEL St. Jean 941, Cahiers de Jean Lintermans. In general terms, the best recent description of causes of death during early modern crises can be found in Andrew B. Appleby, *Famine in Tudor and Stuart England* (Stanford: Stanford University Press, 1978), pp. 97-108, 118-121.

27   AEL PR Herstal 11, pp. 1-16.

28   AEL PR Haccourt 1, pp. 27-30.

29   AEL PR Hermalle-sous-Argenteau 2, pp. 198-236.

30   Crahay, "Fragment de chronique," pp. 68-69.

31   AEL PR Cheratte 1, pp. 282-292.

32   Diarrhea is an acknowledged symptom of malnutrition. Ancel Keys, *et al., The Biology of Human Starvation* (Minneapolis: The University of Minnesota Press, 1950), I, 587-590.

33   Between the Maastricht Tithe results discussed in Chapter IV and harvest-year deaths (lagged so that the autumn harvest is related to deaths in the year that begins with that harvest and runs for a year), the Pearson correlation coefficient is -0.329, at a significance level of .001. For the relationship between Liège rye prices and harvest-year deaths (using a similar harvest year), the coefficient is 0.167, at a significance level of 0.037. On the relationship between food supply and epidemic diseases, see Andrew B. Appleby, "Nutrition and Disease: the Case of London, 1550-1750," *Journal of Interdisciplinary History,* 6 (1975), 1-22.

34   De Sonkeux, *La Vie à Verviers il y a trois siècles,* p. 53.

35   *Ibid.,* p. 54.

36   Josef Habets, "Analectes concernant le siège de Maestricht et le sejour des Francais dans les pays d'Outre-Meuse, 1672-1679," *Publications de la Société d'Histoire et d'Archéologie dans le Duché de Limbourg,* 9 (1870), 494.

37   Bouille, *Histoire de la ville et pays de Liège,* III, 500; Bamps, "Epidemies et disettes ...," 604.

38   J. Daris, *Histoire du diocèse et de la principauté de Liège pendant le XVIIᵉ siècle,* II, 231. Joseph Daris, "L'Ancienne principauté de Liège," Chapter X: "Quartiers et tailles de la principauté," in *NOTICES,* IX, 73-83, for the communities that made up the quarter of Montenacken.

39   AEL CP 824, Kanne and Nedercanne.

40   AEL PR Wandre 5, p. 210.

41   "Ordonnance prescivant la suspension pour l'annee 1630 la foire libre de Saint-Trond ...," 17 August 1630, at Liège, *Liste Chronologique des Edits et Ordonnances de la Principauté de Liège, 1507 à 1684,* Commission Royale pour la Publication des Anciennes Lois et Ordonnances de la Belgique (Brussels: Emm. Devroye, 1860), p. 153.

42   Edicts and *mandemants* on the following dates: 13 and 16 November 1629, 12 January
      (2), 30 March, 4 April, 19 April, 8 May, 10 May 1630. *List Chronologique des Edits et
      Ordonances de la Principauté de Liège, 1507 à 1684,* pp. 150-153. On the plague epidemic
      of 1630, see AEL PR Hermalle-sous-Argenteau 2, pp. 198-236 (June-July-August,
      1630); see also the discussion of the crisis of 1629-1631 in Switzerland in Helleiner,
      "The Population of Europe," p. 44. One of the great 30-yearly crises identified by
      Goubert in his *L'Ancien Régime* took place in 1630. Pierre Goubert, *L'Ancien Régime,* I
      (Paris: Armand Colin, 1969), p. 43.

43   *Rerum Leodiensium status anno M.DC.XLIX,* p. 64. W. Jappe Alberts, *Geschiedenis van de
      beide Limburgen,* II (Assen, Netherlands: Van Gorcum, 1974), 30. Garrisons could be
      ridiculously small. In 1683-1684 (The War of the Reunions), Diksmuide was defended
      by seventeen calvalry. Henri Pirenne, *Histoire de Belgique,* 2nd ed., V (Brussels, 1926),
      38. In 1702, the fort of Navagne, in the Basse-Meuse, was defended from attack by only
      13 soldiers. It fell in 15 minutes. Edm van Wintershoven, "Chronique tirée des
      registres paroissiaux d'Emael," p. 86.

44   For general issues of the cost of seventeenth-century war, see these two works: Karl F.
      Helleiner, "The Population of Europe;" and Roger Mols, *Introduction à la démographie
      historique des villes d'Europe du XIVe au XVIIe siècles* (Louvain, 1955), II, 466-473. For a
      full introduction to the literature on mortality crises, see. J. Dupaquier, T. H. Hol-
      lingsworth, W. Kollmann and N. Sanchez-Albornoz, "Bibliographie Internationale
      sur les Crises de Mortalité," in Hubert Charbonneau and André la Rose, eds., *The Great
      Mortalities: Methodological Studies of Demographic Crises in the Past* (Liège: Ordina
      Editions, 1979), pp. 257-270. For disease among soldiers, see Andre Corvisier, *L'Armée
      française de la fin du XVIIe siècle au Ministère de Choiseul. Le Soldat* (Paris: Presses
      Universitaires de France, 1964), II, 654-681. For the general spread of disease and evil
      from camp to village, see Gustav Freytag, *Pictures of German Life in the XVth, XVIth
      and XVIIth Centuries,* tr. Mrs. Malcolm (London: Chapman and Hall, 1862), II, 81-87.
      In this vein we should not neglect Simplicissimus' smallpox. See H. J. C. von
      Grimmelshausen, *The Adventurous Simplicissimus,* tr. A. T. S. Goodrick (Lincoln: The
      University of Nebraska Press, 1962), pp. 247-251.

45   For the age distribution of deaths in Brabant (the registers of the Basse-Meuse are
      inadequate for this analysis), see Bruneel, *La Mortalité dans les campagnes,* I, 355-424,
      546-567, and 592-597; and Michel Meeus, "La Mortalité à Meerhout-en-Campine de
      1686 à 1815," *Population et Famille,* 33 (1974), 131-184.

46   De Sonkeux, *La Vie à Verviers il y a trois siècles,* p. 82.

47   AEL Fonds Lefort, Part III, s.v. Gordinne. Those members of the clergy who had the
      regular care of souls and who cared for the plague-stricken also died in large numbers.
      See Alfred Poncelet, *Nécrologe des jésuites de la province Flandro belge,* (Wetteren, 1931),
      pp. cviii-cix and note 1.

48   See, for example, the level 6 West model life table. For females, under the $1(x)$ column,
      40,847 died by age 15 (59,153 survived). Of those 40,847, 23,398 would have died in
      the first year (57.3 percent) and 35,730 (87.4 percent) in the first five years of life.
      Ansley J. Coale and Paul Demeny, *Regional Model Life Tables and Stable Populations*
      (Princeton: Princeton University Press, 1966), p. 7.

49   The raw data on which this analysis is based can be found in Gutmann, "War and
      Rural Life in the Seventeenth Century," p. 276. To have survived, for the purposes of
      calculating these proportions, the individual had to have died over age ten, to have
      married, or been confirmed, or have participated in a secondary role at someone else's

baptism, confirmation, or marriage, so that the Wandre parish register recorded his survival. This secondary participation might have been as a godparent or as a witness to a marriage. This test permits the inclusion of a number of individuals who survived, but who left the parish before their marriage, never married, or somehow otherwise escaped inclusion in the death register, an understandable phenomenon, given the quality of registration.

It is possible that some individuals survived but are not counted as surviving. Some left the parish before their marriage. In addition, there must have been individuals who never married, and who lived their entire lives without once being entered in the parish register after their baptisms. While this last group is small, there is no way that one can account for them. They are simply lost to the measure of survival, and reinforce the fact that the proportions surviving are minima. In cases where the families of children born in Wandre moved before those children reappeared as adolescents or adults in the register, the children who survived are lost to our measure of survival, just like the people who stayed in Wandre but never reappear in the register. Again, however, this group does not seem to have been large, and helps us to concentrate on the minimal nature of the proportions surviving. It is unlikely that children left the parish to serve as servants or apprentices elsewhere, which would potentially be a much more disruptive influence. Indicative of this are the records of confirmations in Wandre. Rarely were children confirmed in Wandre who were baptised elsewhere; almost all the confirmations are those of children whose baptism can be found in the Wandre register. This suggests that even if children did move around while their families stayed in one place, they did so after confirmation (or were confirmed in their parents' parish) thus negating the possibility of that sort of migration influencing rates of survival.

The possibility that some Wandre residents married in other parishes is not a major concern because of the character of the Wandre register. Problems exist in all seventeenth-century Basse-Mosan marriage registers (for a discussion of that problem, see *ibid.,* pp. 431-433). In Wandre, these problems work to our advantage. Virtually all marriages, whether or not they took place in Wandre, were recorded there. As a result, we know which children born in Wandre survived long enough to get married, so long as they did not marry in a parish so far distant that they did not even bother to obtain an attestation of baptism and good character.

50 One very recent statement of the rethinking of this problem, with the appropriate citations to the work of others, is in Bruneel, *La Mortalité dans les campagnes,* I, 577-609. Even Bruneel, I think, however, has not gone far enough in minimizing the role of famine in mortality. The classic statement in English of the new thinking on subsistence crises can be found in Pierre Goubert, "Historical Demography and the Reinterpretation of Early Modern French History: A Research Review," *Journal of Interdisciplinary History,* 1 (1970), 37-48. The most recent view, which attempts to revive the influence of starvation on mortality, is found in Appleby, *Famine in Tudor and Stuart England,* Chapters 7-9, pp. 95-154. Appleby discusses a region less well supplied than the Basse-Meuse, thus making his conclusions less than fully applicable here.

1   The seven parishes are Herstal, Wandre, Vivegnis, Hermalle-sous-Argenteau, Dalhem, Haccourt, and Heure-le-Romain. The original registers are all located in the collection of parish registers at the AEL. For the unaggregated monthly and yearly totals, see Myron P. Gutmann, "War and Rural Life in the Seventeenth Century: the Case of the Basse-Meuse" (diss., Princeton, 1976), Appendix E, pp. 436-465. The procedures for correcting any incomplete data are discussed in Appendix E, below.

2   Gutmann, "War and Rural Life in the Seventeenth Century," p. 341.

3   AEL PR Haccourt 2, p. 92. Also, see the discussion of the quality of baptism registration in the Basse-Meuse, in Gutmann, "War and Rural Life in the Seventeenth Century," pp. 340-342.

4   Another way to show that deaths were subject to wider fluctuations than baptisms is to look at the coefficient of variation, which is the result of dividing the standard deviation by the mean. The coefficient of variation for the index of extreme behavior values are as follows:

Calendar-year deaths	0.322
Harvest-year deaths	0.344
Calendar-year baptisms	0.122
Harvest-year baptisms	0.129

5   Harvest-year totals for the demographic variables are used in these computations. For demographic purposes, the harvest year goes from August 1 to July 31. For prices, the harvest year begins and ends later, sometime in September. For production, the harvest year ends in the beginning of the demographic and price-year, so we see the impact of one year's harvest on demographic conditions for the twelve months following the harvest.

6   These are not real conceptions, of course, because it is impossible to discover the number of pregnancies lost between conception and birth. But by transposing the number of baptisms back by nine months, and then re-adding them into harvest year totals, we can get useful information.

7   For the normal pattern in the ancien régime, see Pierre Guillaume and Jean-Pierre Poussou, *Démographie Historique* (Paris, 1970), pp. 171-172.

8   These are all years for which the index value falls below 0.86.

9   The family reconstitution is discussed in detail in Gutmann, "War and Rural Life in the Seventeenth Century," pp. 337-380, and Myron P. Gutmann "Reconstituting Wandre: An Approach to Semi-Automatic Family Reconstitution," *Annales de Démographie Historique* (1977), 325-341.

10   This is, of course, somewhat oversimplified. Birth intervals are never constant for all a couple's children. Rather, they tend to become longer as parity increases.

11   The standard deviation for all years is 1.19 years.

12   The 25 years are 1673-1680, 1693-1696, 1699-1706, 1741-1742, and 1747-1749.

13   The standard deviation for the 25 years is 1.23 years.

14   The standard deviation for the 65 years is 1.17 years.

15   It is sometimes wise to exclude a family's last birth from such calculations since the intervals leading to those last births are unusually long and display unusual characteristics. Eliminating last intervals leaves 1,744 later intervals in the period 1670-1759, of which 417 occurred in the 25 years of reduced childbearing. Not surprisingly, eliminating last intervals decreases the length of all intervals: for all 90 years from 1670

to 1759, the mean length of interval was 2.45 years, or 29.4 months. The standard deviation for these intervals is 1.04 years. The 25 years of low childbearing had an interval of 2.61 years, or 31.3 months, 2.5 months longer than the 2.40 years or 28.8 month mean for the remaining 65 years. The standard deviation for the 25 years is 1.09 years; for the remaining 65 years it is 1.07 years.

16 See the very suggestive article by Emmanuel Le Roy Ladurie, "L'Amenorrhée de famine (XVII^c-XX^c siècles)," *Annales E.S.C.* (1969), 1589-1601. There is a growing scientific literature on nutrition and various components of fertility. The following items are only a few: Ancel Keys, *et. al., The Biology of Human Starvation* (Minneapolis: University of Minnesota Press, 1950), I, 749-752; Rose E. Frisch and Janet W. McArthur, "Menstrual Cycles: Fatness as a Determinant of Minimum Weight for Height Necessary for their Maintenance or Onset," *Science,* 185 (1974), 949-951; Rose E. Frisch, "Demographic Implications of the Biological Determinants of Female Fecundity," paper presented to the annual meeting of the Population Association of America, April, 1974, research paper No. 6, Center for Population Studies, Harvard University, July, 1974; C. Gopolan and A. Nadamuni Naidu, "Nutrition and Fertility," *The Lancet,* 1972, ii, 1,077-1,079. Rose E. Frisch and Roger Revelle, "Height and Weight at Menarche and a Hypothesis of Menarche," *Archives of Disease in Childhood,* 46 (1971), 695-701; and Rose E. Frisch and Roger Revelle, "Height and Weight and Menarche and a Hypothesis of Critical Body Weights and Adolescent Events," *Science,* 169 (1970), 397-399.

17 Gopolan and Nadamuni Naidu, "Nutrition and Fertility," p. 1,078.

18 For the spread of contraceptive practices in Europe, see A. J. Coale, "The Decline of Fertility in Europe from the French Revolution to World War II," in S. J. Behrman, L. Corsa, and R. Freedman, eds., *Fertility and Family Planning* (Ann Arbor: University of Michigan Press, 1969), pp. 3-24; E. A. Wrigley, "Family Limitation in Pre-Industrial England," *Economic History Review,* 2nd series, 29 (1966), 82-109. See also, Philippe Ariès, "On the Origins of Contraception in France," and "An Interpretation to be Used for a History of Mentalities," translated and reprinted in Orest and Patricia Ranum, eds., *Popular Attitudes Toward Birth Control in Pre-Industrial France and England* (New York: Harper & Row, 1972), pp. 10-20, 100-125.

19 Historians have been increasingly concerned recently with childhood and the role of children in family and society. The best-known work, and a useful introduction for the early modern period, is Philippe Ariès, *Centuries of Childhood* (New York: Random House, 1962). Some other recent works that deal with families and children are Lawrence Stone, *The Family, Sex and Marriage in England, 1500-1800* (New York: Harper and Row, 1977); David Hunt, *Parents and Children in History* (New York: Basic Books, 1970); and Edward Shorter, *The Making of the Modern Family* (New York: Basic Books, 1975). For a bibliographic starting point, see John Sommerville, "Bibliographic Note: Toward a History of Childhood and Youth," *Journal of Interdisciplinary History,* 3 (1972); reprinted in Theodore K. Rabb and Robert I. Rotberg, *The Family in History* (New York: Harper and Row, 1973), pp. 227-235.

20 See the suggestive discussion of the relationship between mortality and fertility in Ronald Demos Lee, "Methods and Models for Analyzing Historical Series of Births, Deaths and Marriages," in Ronald Demos Lee, ed., *Population Patterns in the Past* (New York: Academic Press, 1977), pp. 355-363.

21 For five parishes (Herstal, Wandre, Vivegnis, Hermalle and Dalhem) the seasonal distribution of deaths and conceptions is as follows:

Harvest Year	Aug.-Nov.	Dec.-March	April-July	Total
1667				
Deaths	23	27	24	74
Conceptions	62	50	78	190
1668				
Deaths	82	44	26	152
Conceptions	55	80	88	223

The greatest increase in deaths (Aug.-Nov., 1668) does coincide with a small decline in conceptions. However, the decline in conceptions in no way equals the increase in deaths. Moreover, the figures show that the conceptions lost in those months were made up in the next period, December, 1668 to March, 1669.

22 Because the baptism registers begin only in 1666, we would expect the ages at marriage in the 1690's to be lower than those of the 1700's because of truncation (no one born before 1666 can provide a known date of marriage, so no one married in the 1690's could be more than 33 years old; in the 1700's people as old as 43 could marry for the first time). The higher ages in the 1690's are therefore even more conclusive evidence than they would otherwise seem.

23 The breakdown by parity of the 3226 children born to complete families is as follows:

Parity	%	Parity	%
1	21.4	6	8.2
2	18.5	7	5.4
3	15.9	8	3.2
4	13.6	9	1.5
5	10.8	10-14	1.5

24 The years are 1678-1680, 1693-1696, and 1699-1706.

25 The years are 1678-1680, 1693-1696, 1699-1706, 1741-1742, and 1747-1749.

26 Jean Meuvret, "Les Crises de subsistance et la démographie de la France d'Ancien Régime," *Population*, 1 (1946), 643-650.

27 Bruneel, in *La Mortalité dans les campagnes*, I, 351, calculates a minimum crude death rate of 25-29 per thousand for Brabant, an area with demographic characteristics close to those of the Basse-Meuse. He puts that in context by finding others of about the same level.

Chapter IX

1 Edm. van Wintershoven, "Cronique tirée des registres paroissiaux d'Emael," *BSSLL*, 22 (1904), 58-59.

2 Pierre Goubert, *The Ancien Régime*, (New York: Harper and Row, 1973), p. 38.

3 It should be noted that the Basse-Meuse never took as long to recover from any catastrophe as did some English communities in the eighteenth century. See J. D. Chambers, *Population, Economy and Society in Pre-Industrial England* (London: Oxford University Press, 1972), p. 66.

4   Gunther Franz, *Der Dreissigjährige Krieg und das deutsche Volk: Untersuchungen zur Bevölkerung- und Agrargeschichte,* third edition (Stuttgart: Gustav Fischer Verlag, 1961), p. 8. The nearby principalities of Jülich and Köln were each in the 20-30 percent loss category, according to Fransz.

5   On Louvois, see Chapter III, note 30.

6   For the Herstal-Wandre bourgeois, see Chapter VI, note 19. For Maastricht, the documents are to be found at the Stadsarchief te Maastricht, in the Collection of Court Documents, registers 197-198, 201-202, 204.

7   Jerome Blum, *The End of the Old Order in Rural Europe* (Princeton, 1978), especially pp. 11-115.

Bibliography

I. Manuscript Sources

Archives de l'Etat à Liège (AEL)

Cathédrale. Compterie du Grenier
    4-13   Registres aux stuits, 1617-1749 (leases and contracts)
    108-235   Comptes des cens et rentes, 1620-1750 (receipts)
Cathédrale. Grande Comperie
    12-21   Registres aux stuits, 1616-1746
    237-347   Comptes des cens et rentes, 1621-1750
Cathédrale. Secrétariat
    123-165, 184   Protocoles des directeurs, 1626-1742. (AEL PdD)
Conseil Privé (AEL CP)
    703-04   Commissariat General
    705-56   Passages of Troops (1690-1790)
    805-40   Dossiers of individual communities pertaining to the costs of war
Cours de Justice (AEL C*de*J)
    Eben-Emael
        19   Etat des biens fonciers, 1717
    Hermalle-sous-Argenteau
        86   Rapports et mesures de biens, 1750
    Jupille. Communauté de Jupille
        2   Comptes, 1663-1765
           Emprunts, 1704-1745
           Requisitions Militaires, 1697-1762
        3   Tailles, 1677-1767
    Richelle
        20   Rapport des biens de la juridiction de Richelle, 1663
           Mesure des terres, 1722
    Visé
     · 202-203 Récés de la Ville, 1681-1692, 1698-1707
Etats (de Liège)
    82   List of Bonniers and List of Afforains,
        Seigneurie of Vivegnis, 1743
    96   Tocage, Emael, 1749
    97   Capitation, Hermée, 1674

Denombrement de feu, Haccourt and Hallembaye, 1748

Denombrement de feu, Heure-le-Romain, 1748

98 Capitation, Jupille, 1674, 1740

100 Tocage, Nedercanne, 1748

Tocage, Nivelle, 1748

102 Capitation, Wonck, 1674

534-547 Herstal: revenues de la seigneurie, 1612-1753

553-579 Herstal: comptes de recettes et depenses, 1648-1741

Greffe de l'Etat Tiers

305,307 Comptes du domaine de Herstal, 1741-1743, 1745

Greffe de l'Etat Noble

313-321 Comptes du domaine de Herstal, 1744-1752

Fonds Francais. Ventes des biens nationaux

2010-2054 Registres de procès-verbaux d'adjudication definitive de ventes de biens nationaux, en vertu de la loi du 16 Brumaire an V

2055-2069 Registres des ventes des biens nationaux cédés à la Caisse d'Amortissement, Nos. 1 à 1294, affiches Nos. 1 à 100 – 9 avril 1807 au 23 septembre 1813

Mercy-Argenteau

2510-2576 Comptes Generaux, 1619-1751

Notaire Craheau, P.

Registers for years: 1670-1676, 1676-1682, 1682-1695

Parish Registers (AEL PR)

Cheratte Regs. 1-2

Dalhem Regs. 1, 2, 4, 7, 12 (Catholic)

Regs. 3, 5, 10 (Protestant)

Haccourt Regs. 1-2

Hermalle-sous-Argenteau Regs. 1-5

Herstal Regs. 2-6, 11-13, 16-19

Heure-le-Romain Regs. 1-4

Saive Regs. 1-2, 5-6

Vivegnis Regs. 1-2

Wandre Regs. 1-3, 5, 9

Prieuré et Seigneurie d'Aywaille

180 Procès entre les jesuites de Luxembourg ... et la communauté

St. Croix

23-26 Registres aux stuits, 1620-1749

St. Denis

15-22 Registres aux baux ou stuits, 1565-1752 (leases).

24-25 Registres aux baux des dîmes, 1656-1776 (tithe contracts)

311-337, 98, 99, 101 Accounts of receipts, 1674-1743

St. Pierre

16-24 Registres aux stuits, etc., 1559-1749

45-52 Liasses de supplices envoyées au chapitre pour des nominations, procès, delais de payement, etc.

Archives de l'Etat à Arlon

Famille de Trappe. Chateau de Losenge. Documents pertaining to Jupille

Archives de l'Evêché de Liège

P.V.11 Effractions du Clergé (prices)

Rijksarchief in Limburg (Maastricht)

Aanwinst 1936
    599   Prijzen der granen te Maastricht
Collectianea Collette
    3   Prices
Land van Overmaas (RAL LVO) (All documents pertain to Eysden)
    5451-5459 Real Tax records
    5461-5465
    5469-5471
    5473-5480
    5490-5504 Personal tax records
    5507-5527
    5533-5544 French contributions
    5546, 5556, 5558 Military matters
    5559, 5563, 5564 Loans
    5570, 5571 Population
    5583-5585 Agriculture

Rijksarchief Hasselt

Munsterbilzen Stiff
    125-137   Documents pertaining to the Seigneurie of Haccourt and Hellembaye

Sociaal Historisch Centrum voor Limburg

Source materials for the Louwberg Farm

Stadsarchief en -bibliotheek te Maastricht

Handschriftencollectie
    201   Manuscript with chronology of Maastricht and list of effractions of the Chapter of
        St. Servais
Collection of Court Documents
    197-198   Register of new bourgeois, kept by the Burgermasters, 1482-1777
    201-202   Registers of new bourgeois, kept by the Brabancon court
    204   Registers of new bourgeois, kept by the Liégeois court

II. Published Sources

Balau, Sylv. and Fairon, Em. *Chroniques liégeoises.* 2 vols. Brussels, 1913-1931.

Belgium. Archives de l'Etat, Liège. *Catalogue général des protocols de notaires conservés dans la province de liège.* Prepared by Jean Pieyns. Brussels: Archives Generaux du Royaume, 1972.

Belgium. Ministère de l'Interieur. *Tableau statistique a l'appui du projet d'organisation d'un service médical rural.* Brussels, 1849.

Bergeron, Pierre. *Voyage de Pierre Bergeron ès Ardennes, Liège et Pays-Bas en 1619.* Ed. Henri Michelant. Liège: Société des Bibliophiles Liégeois, 1875.

Bos, Lambert van den. *Tooneel des Oorlogs, Opgericht in de Vereenigde Nederlanden ...* Amsterdam, 1675.

Brassine, J., ed. "Chronique verviétoise de 1746 à 1755." *Bulletin de la Société des Bibliophiles Liégeois,* 14 (1937), 13-147.

Brose, Jean. "La Guerre de Hollande (1673-1676) vue par un curé hesbignon. La Chronique de Laurent Chabot, curé de Villers le Bouillet." *La Vie Wallonne,* 42 (1968), 311-333.

Callot, Jacques. *Les Misères et les mal-heurs de la guerre.* Paris, 1633.

Casier, Constant, and Crahay, Louis. *Coutumes du duché de Limbourg et des Pays d'Outre Meuse.* Brussels, 1889.

Ceyssens, J. "Deux documents concernent les guerres de Louis XIV dans notre pays." *Leodium,* 5 (1906), 116-118.

−. "Notes du curé Jean Hervianus de Hermallé-sous-Argenteau." *Leodium,* 5 (1906), 125-132.

Crayhay, Melchior F. "Fragment de chronique liégeoise et franchimontoise." *Bulletin de la Société des Bibliophiles Liégeois,* 2 (1884), 65-109.

"Dagverhaal van 't beleg van Maastricht in 1676." *De Maasgouw* (1881), 489-490, 493-495, 498-499, 502-503, 506-507.

Deblon, Andre. "Les Rapports des visites archidiaconales du Condroz." *BSAHL,* 50 (1970), 105-239.

Debouxhtay, Pierre. *Documents inédits relatifs à l'ancien ban de Cheratte.* Visé, 1925.

Delatte, I. *La Vente des biens du clergé dans le département de l'Ourthe, 1797-1810.* Typescript, AEL, reading room, 1951.

Dumont, J. *Corps universel diplomatique du droit des gens contenant un recueil des traités.* 8 vols. Amsterdam-La Haye, 1726-1731.

Fairon, Emile. "Analyses sommaires des journées d'états de la principauté de Liège, 1541-1689." *Annuaire d'Histoire Liégeoise,* 5 (1954-1956), 285-412, 469-573, 659-759.

Fisen, *Historia Ecclesiae Leodiensis.* Liège, 1696.

Foullon, Jean Erard. *Historia Leodiensis.* Vol. III. Liège, 1737.

Frederick Henry, Prince of Orange. *Articles accordez av magistrat, bovrgeois, et habitans de la ville de Maestric...* Paris, 1632.

−. *A Iournal of all the principall passages of that late famous siege and taking of the citie of Mastricht by the Prince of Orange.* London: Printed by J. D.[awson] for Nathaniel Butter and Nicolas Bourne, 1632. (Pollard-Redgrave Short-Title Catalogue #11365).

−. *Mémoires de Frédéric-Henri.* Amsterdam, 1733.

Freytag, Gustav. *Pictures of German Life in the XVth, XVIth and XVIIth Centuries.* Trans. Mrs. Malcolm. London: Chapman and Hall, 1862.

Goosens, Godefroy. *Etude sur les états du Limbourg et des pays d'Outremeuse pendant le premier tiers du XVIIIᵉ siècle, suivie du texte de la Notitia de rebus statuum provinciae Limburgensis de l'abbé Nicolas Heyendal.* Université de Louvain. Recueil de Travaux publiés par les membres des conferences d'histoire et de philologie, 26 (1910).

Grimmelshausen, H. J. C. von. *The Adventurous Simplicissimus: Being the Description of the Life of a Strange Vagabond named Melchior Sternfels von Fuchsair.* Trans. A. T. S. Goodrick. Lincoln, Nebraska: University of Nebraska Press, 1962.

Haust, Jean, ed. *Quatre Dialogues de Paysans (1631-1636).* Le Dialecte liégeois au XVIIᵉ siècle, No. 2. Collection "Nos Dialectes," No. 9. Liège: H. Vaillant Carmanne, 1939.

Hennen, Guillaume. "Pamphlets politiques wallons du XVIIᵉ siècle." *Bulletin de la Société Verviétoise d'Archéologie et d'Histoire,* 13 (1913), 171-291.

Huisman, M., Dhondt, J., and van Meerbeeck, L., eds. *Les Relations militaires des années 1634 et 1635, redigées par Jean-Antoine Vincart, Secretaire des avis secrets de guerre aux Pays-Bas.* Academic Royale de Belgique. Commission Royale d'Histoire. Publication 71. Brussels, 1958.

Hurges, Philippe de. *Voyage à Liège et à Maestricht en 1615.* Ed. Henri Michelant. Liège: Société des Bibliophiles Ligeois, 1872.

Journal fidelle de tout ce qui s'est passe au siège de Mastricht, attaqué par Louis XIV, roy de France et defendu par Mr. de Fariaux, ... Amsterdam: P. Wanaer and F. Lamminga, 1674.

List chronologique des édits et ordonnances de la principauté de Liège, 1507-1794. 2 vols. Brussels: Em. Devroye, 1851-1860.

Louis XIV, King of France. *Oeuvres de Louis XIV.* 6 vols. Paris-Strasbourg, 1806.

Louvrex. *Recueil contenant les edits et reglements faits pour le pays de Liège et comté de Looz, par les évêques et princes, ...* 4 vols. Liège, 1751.

Mehren, dom Bernard, and Ruwet, Joseph, eds. *Journal des abbés du Val-Dieu.* Val-Dieu, 1946.

Montglat, Francois de Poule de Clermont, marquis de. *Mémoires.* Collection des mémoires relatifs à l'histoire de France ... par Petitot, 2nd series, vols. 49-51. Paris, 1825.

Polain, L. *Recueil des ordonnances de la principauté de Liège.* 2nd ser. (1507-1684). 3 vols. Brussels, 1869-1872. 3rd ser. (1684-1794). 2 vols. Brussels, 1855.

Piot, Charles. "Les Lorrains au pays de Liège." *Bulletin de la Commission Royale d'Histoire,* 4th ser., 2 (1875), 361-376.

Poncelet, E. "Trois documents relatifs à la paroisse de Wandre." *BSAHL,* 13 (1902), 97-107.

Posthumus, Nicolaas Wilhelmus. *Inquiry into the History of Prices in Holland.* 2 vols. Leiden: E. J. Brill, 1946-1964.

Raikem, J., Polain, L., Crahay, L. and Bormans, St. *Coutumes du pays de Liège.* 3 vols. Brussels, 1870-1884.

Règlemens et ordonnances du roy pour les gens de guerre. 15 vols. Paris: Fréderic Léonard, 1680-1706.

Rerum Leodiensium status anno M.DC.XLIX. Trans. J. Alexandre. Liège: Société des Bibliophiles Ligeois, 1885.

Richelieu. *Mémoires du Cardinal de Richelieu, sur le règne de Louis XIII, depuis 1610 jusqu'à 1638.* Ed. Petitot. 10 vols. Paris: Foucault, 1823.

Simenon, Guillaume. *Chronique de Servais Foullon, Abbé de Saint-Trond.* Liège: Société des Bibliophiles Ligeois, 1910.

—. *Visitationes Archidiaconales Archidiaconatus Hesbanaie in Dioecesi Leodiensi ab anno 1613 ad annum 1763.* 2 vols. Liège: H. Dessain, 1939.

Simonon, P. *Nouveau traité des rentes et des monnoies...* Liège, 1765.

—. *Traité de la reduction des rentes ...* Liège, 1753.

—. *Traité historique et methodique, sur l'usage et la nature des anciennes monnoies d'or et d'argent...* Liège, 1758.

Sohet, D. F. de. *Instituts de droit, ou sommaire de jurisprudence canonique, civile, féodale et*

criminelle, pour les pays de Liège, de Luxembourg, Namur et autres. 3 vols. Bouillon, 1772.

Sonkeux, Henri de. *La Vie à Verviers il y a trois siècles.* Verviers, n.d. (about 1946).

Sparre, Lieutenant Colonel, baron de. *Code militaire ou compilation des règlemens et ordonnances de Louis XIV faites pour les gens de guerre depuis 1651 jusqu'à present.* Paris, 1709.

Tableau de la dévastation du pays de Liège. Liège, n.d. (probably 1747).

Tassin, L. "Un document dit la misère de notre region au XVIIe siècle." *L'Antiquaire* (Philippeville), III, 53-55.

Vanderlinden, E. *Cronique des événements météorologiques en Belgiques jusqu'en 1834.* Brussels, 1924. Extract from Mémoires publiés par la Classe des Sciences de l'Academie Royale de Belgique. Collection in-4°. 2nd series, vol. 5.

Vast, H. *Les Grandes traités du règne de Louis XIV.* 3 vols. Paris, 1893-1899.

Werveke, Nicolas, "Chronique Blanchart." *Publications de la Section Historique de l'Institut Grande Ducal du Luxembourg,* 52 (1903), 53-125.

Wintershoeven, Edm. van, "Chronique tirée des registers paroissiaux d'Emael," *BSSLL,* 22 (1904), 43-106.

III. Secondary Works

A. Bibliographical guides
B. General works, including political and diplomatic history
C. Organization of communities and states
D. Military history and organization
E. Economy and geography
    1. Agriculture, geography, and climate
        a. The Basse-Meuse
        b. Other regions
    2. Mining and Industry
        a. The Basse-Meuse
        b. Other regions
    3. Prices, trade, and measurement
F. Demography
    1. The Basse-Meuse
    2 Other regions
G. Local Studies
    1. The Basse-Meuse
    2. Other regions
H. Religion and religious organization
I. Language
J. Printed maps

A. Bibliographical Guides

The eastern Low Countries have been remarkably well studied by an able group of amateur and professional local historians. Anyone interested in this area will do well to examine the major series of local history journals listed below, or to look at one of these two series of bibliographical articles on Liégeois history:

Debouxhtay, Pierre. "Chronique d'histoire liégeoise des origines à 1795." *RBPH,* 7 (1928), 8 (1929), 10 (1931), and 13 (1934).

"Bulletin bibliographique d'histoire liégeoise." *Annuaire d'Histoire Liégeoise* (every volume).

Local History Journals for the Basse-Meuse and Neighboring Regions:

Anciens Pays et Assemblées d'Etats

Annuaire d'Histoire Liégeoise

Bulletin de l'Institut Archéologique Liégeois (BIAL)

Bulletin de la Société d'Art et d'Histoire du Diocèse de Liège (BSAHL)

Bulletin de la Société des Bibliophiles Liégeois

Bulletin de la Société Royale "Le Vieux Liège" (Vieux Liège)

Bulletin de la Société Scientifique et Litteraire du Limbourg (BSSLL)

Bulletin de la Société Verviétoise d'Archéologie et d'Histoire

Chronique Archéologique du Pays de Liège (CAPL)

Leodium

Publications de la Société Historique et Archéologique dans le Duché de Limbourg

Revue Belge de Philologie et d'Histoire (RBPH)

Studies over de Sociaal-Economische Geschiedenis van Limburg

La Vie Wallone

Further Bibliographical Guides to the History of the Basse-Meuse:

Arnould, Maurice A. "Les Registres paroissiaux en Belgique." *Bulletin de Statistique,* 34 (1948), 1,313-1,324.

Baillien, Henry. *Systematische Inhoudstafel op het Bulletin de la Société Scientifique et Litteraire du Limbourg.* Tongeren, 1967.

Brassine, J. "Jean Ceyssens." *Leodium,* 27 (1934), 42-54.

—. "Registres de l'état civil de Liège sous l'Ancien Régime." *Leodium,* 34 (1947), 16-24.

Brouette, Emile and Forgeur, Richard. *Leodium. Table des cinquante premiers volumes de la revue (1902-1963).* Liège: Société d'Art et d'Histoire, 1964.

Ceyssens, Jean. "Les Anciens records civil et ecclésiastiques comme sources pour l'histoire." *Leodium,* 14 (1921), 74-91.

Dejardin, A. "Cartes de l'ancien duché de Limbourg." *BIAL,* 17 (1883), 315-361.

Dupaquier, J., Hollingsworth, T. H., Köllmann, W., and Sanchez-Albornoz, N. "Bibliographie Internationale sur les Crises de mortalité." Hubert Charbonneau and Andre Larose, eds. *The Great Mortalities: Methodological Studies of Demographic Crises in the Past.* Liège: Ordina Editions, 1979, pp. 257-270.

Forgeur, Richard. "Table des 'Notices sur les églises du diocèse de Liège' du chanoine Daris." *Leodium,* 43 (1956), 21-30.

Halkin, Leon E. "Introduction à l'histoire paroissiale de l'ancien diocèse de Liège." *BIAL,* 59 (1935), 137-231.

—. "Supplement de l'introduction à l'histoire paroissiale de l'ancien diocèse de Liège." *BIAL,* 61 (1937), 261-271.

Hansotte, Georges. *Tables generales des tomes 1 à 20 (1882-1959) du Bulletin de la Société des Bibliophiles Liégeois.* Liège, 1968.

Hélin, Etienne. "Les Plans anciens de Liège." *Annuaire d'Histoire Liégeois,* 6 (1961-1962), 589-736, 1289-1538.

Magnette, F. *Table de matières des années 1906 à 1939 (I à XXX) de Chronique Archéologique du Pays de Liège.* Liège, n.d.

Monchamp, Georges. "Le Chanoine Daris." *Leodium,* 4 (1905), 129-152.

Sabbe, E. "Les Registres paroissiaux et leur conservation en Belgique." *Archivum,* 9 (1959), 3-14.

Stekke, Joseph. "Les Capitations paroissiales de la ville et du pays de Liège, aux XVIIᵉ et XVIIIᵉ siècles." *Annuaire d'Histoire Liégeoise,* 4 (1951), 527-545.

Verbeemen, J. "Liste des registres aux admissions de nouveaux bourgeois existant en Belgique." *Tablettes du Brabant.* (Hombeek), 4 (1960), 229-246.

Yans, Maurice. "Les Archives de Dordrecht et l'histoire liégeoise." *Annuaire d'Histoire Liégeoise* (1939), 133-144.

B. *General Works, Including Political and Diplomatic History*

Alberts, W. Jappe. *Geschiedenis van de beide Limburgen.* 2 vols. Assen, Netherlands: Van Gorcum, 1972-1974.

Blum, Jerome. *The End of the Old Order in Rural Europe.* Princeton: Princeton University Press, 1978.

Bouille, Théodose. *Histoire de la ville et pays de Liège.* 3 vols. Liège, 1732.

Braubach, Max. *Die Politik des Kurfürsten Joseph Clemens von Köln beim Ausbruch des spanischen Erbfolgekrieges und die Vertreibung der Franzosen vom Niederrhein (1701-1703).* Bonn-Leipzig, 1925.

Brouwers, D. "Relations entre la Prusse et le pays de Liège au XVIIIᵉ siècle: recruitement d'ouvriers armuriers et de soldats." *BIAL,* 35 (1905), 75-116.

Clark, George N. *The Seventeenth Century.* Second edition. New York: Oxford University Press, 1961.

–. *War and Society in the Seventeenth Century.* Cambridge: Cambridge University Press, 1958.

Daris, Joseph. *Histoire du diocèse et de la principauté de Liège (1724-1852).* 4 vols. Liège, 1868-1873.

–. *Histoire du diocèse et de la principauté de Liège pendant le XVIIᵉ siècle.* 2 vols. Liège, 1877.

–. *Notices sur les églises du diocèse de Liège.* 17 vols. Liège, 1867-1899.

Defrecheux, C. "Histoire de la neutralité liégeoise." *BIAL,* 37 (1907), 159-286.

Delcourt, Marie, and Hoyoux, Jean. "Quatre ans de la vie à Liège d'un diplomate italien (1666-1670). Les Ephemerides du Nonce Agostino Franciotti." *Vieux Liège,* 7 (1974), 381-389.

Douxchamps-Lefevre, Cecile. "Le Traité de Freyr conclu le 25 octobre 1675 entre la France et l'Espagne." *Annales de la Société Archéologique de Namur,* 58 (1977), 47-67.

Ernst, S. P. *Histoire du Duché de Limbourg.* 7 vols. Liège, 1837-1852.

Franz, Gunther. *Der Dreissigjahrige Krieg und das deutsche Volk. Untersuchungen zur Bevölkerungs- und Agrargeschichte.* Third edition. Stuttgart: Gustav Fischer Verlag, 1961.

Gachard, Louis Prosper. *Histoire de la Belgique au commencement du XVIIIᵉ siècle.* Brussels, 1880.

Genicot, Léopold, ed. *Histoire de la Wallonie.* Toulouse: Privat, 1973.

Gobert, Théodore. "Le Rôle de la France au pays de Liège durant le second quart du XVIIIᵉ siècle. Recit d'un ambassadeur français de l'époque." *BIAL,* 41 (1911), 1-61.

Goubert, Pierre. *L'Ancien Régime.* Vol. I. Paris: Librarie Armand Colin, 1969. Translated to English as *The Ancien Régime.* New York: Harper and Row, 1973.

Habets, A. "Geschiedenis van de Landen van Overmaas, sedert den Vrede van Munster tot aan het Partage-Tractaat, 1648-1662." *Publications de la Société Historique et Archólogique dans le Duché de Limbourg,* 33 (1896-1897), 135-214.

286

Hasquin, Hervé, ed. *La Wallonie: le pays et les hommes.* Vol. I. Brussels: La Renaissance du Livre, 1975.

Gutmann, Myron P. "War and Rural Life in the Seventeenth Century: the Case of the Basse-Meuse." Diss., Princeton, 1976.

Harsin, P. "L'Attitude de l'Empire à l'égard de la neutralité liégeoise." *BIAL,* 51 (1926), 32-61.

—. *Etudes critiques sur l'histoire de la principauté de Liège, 1477-1795.* Liège, 1958.

—. "La Neutralité liégeoise en 1632." *Revue d'Histoire Moderne,* 15 (1940), 13-31.

—. "Les Origines diplomatiques de la neutralité liégeoise." *RBPH,* 5 (1926), 423-452.

—. *Les Relations extérieures de la principauté de Liège sous Jean-Louis d'Elderen et Joseph-Clément de Bavière (1688-1718).* Liège-Paris, 1927.

Helbig, J. (ed.) *Mémoires concernant les negotiations de la France relatives à la neutralité du pays de Liège en 1630.* Liège, 1875.

Henaux, Ferd. *Histoire du pays de Liège.* Third ed. 2 vols. Liège, 1874.

Hobsbawn, E. J. "The Crisis of the Seventeenth Century." *Past & Present.* No. 5 (1954), 33-53, and No. 6 (1954), 44-65. Reprinted in T. Aston, ed. *Crisis in Europe, 1560-1660.* New York, 1967, pp. 5-62.

Houtte, Hubert van. "Les Conférences franco-espagnoles de Deynz." *Revue d'Histoire Moderne,* 2 (1927), 191-215.

Huisman, Michel. *Essai sur le règne du Prince-Evêque de Liège, Maximilien-Henri de Bavière.* Mém. Cour., vol. 59. Brussels, 1889.

Kamen, Henry. "The Social and Economic Consequences of the Thirty Years' War." *Past and Present,* No. 39 (1968), 44-61.

Lejeune, Jean. *La Principauté de Liège.* Liège, 1948.

Lonchay, Henri. *La Principauté de Liège, la France et les Pays-Bas au XVIIe et au XVIIIe siècle.* Mém. Cour., vol. 44. Brussels, 1890.

—. *La Rivalité de la France et de l'Espagne aux Pays-Bas (1635-1700). Etude d'histoire diplomatique et militaire.* Mém. Cour., vol. 54. Brussels, 1896.

Lottin, Alain. *Vie et mentalité d'un lillois sous Louis XIV.* Lille, 1968.

Maelen, Ph. van der. *Dictionnaire Géographique de la Province de Liège.* Brussels, 1831.

Mousnier, Roland. *Histoire generale des civilisations.* Vol. IV. Paris, 1953.

Nef. J. U. "Limited Warfare and the Progress of European Civilization, 1640-1740." *Review of Politics,* 6 (1944), 275-314.

—. "Wars and the Rise of Industrial Civilization, 1640-1740." *Canadian Journal of Economics and Politics,* 10 (1944), 36-78.

Neny, P. F. *Mémoires historiques et politiques des pays-bas Autrichiens.* Neuchatel, 1784.

Le Notaire dans la vie namuroise. Catalogue d'un exposition à Namur, 9-19 Octobre, 1975. Brussels, 1975.

Pirenne, Henri. *Histoire de Belgique.* 7 vols. Brussels, 1900-1932.

Rabb, Theodore K. "The Effects of the Thirty Years' War on the German Economy." *Journal of Modern History,* 34 (1962), 40-51.

—. *The Struggle for Stability in Early Modern Europe.* New York: Oxford University Press, 1975.

Ryckel, Amedée de. *Les Communes de la Province de Liège.* Liège, 1892.

Seyn, Eugene de. *Dictionnaire historique et géographique des communes belges.* Third ed. 2 vols. Turnhout, 1947.

Thomassin, Louis Francois. *Mémoire statistique du département de l'Ourte.* Liège, 1879.

Toynbee, Arnold J. *A Study of History.* Vol. 4. London: Oxford University Press, 1939.

Waddington, Albert. *La République des Provinces-Unies, la France et les Pays-Bas espagnols de 1630 à 1650.* 2 vols. Paris, 1895-1897.

C. Organization of Communities and States

Berlamont, Daniel, "Occupations militaires et finances urbaines au XVIIe et XVIIIe siècle: l'exemple verviétois." *Annuaire d'Histoire Liégeoise,* 13 (1972), 59-106.

Bigwood, G. *Les Impôts généraux dans les Pays-Bas autrichiens; étude historique de législation financière.* Paris-Louvain, 1900.

—. "Matricules et cadastres. Aperçu sur l'organisation du cadastre en Flandre, Brabant, Limbourg et Luxembourg avant la domination francaise." *Annales de la Société d'Archéologie de Bruxelles,* 12 (1898), 388-411.

Blum, Jerome. "The Internal Structure and Polity of the European Village Community from the Fifteenth to the Nineteenth Century." *Journal of Modern History,* 43 (1971), 541-576.

Brouwers, A. "Contribution à l'histoire des états du duché de Limbourg au XVIIIe siècle." *BIAL,* 34 (1904), 339-365.

—. "Documents relatifs à la matricule du duché de Limbourg en 1705." *BIAL,* 33 (1903), 69-88.

Corswarem, Guil-Jos. *Mémoire historique sur les anciens limites et circonscriptions de la province de Limbourg.* Brussels, 1857.

Crassier, Louis de. "Dictionnaire historique du Limbourg néerlandais de la période féodale à nos jours." *Publications de la Société Historique et Archéologique dans le Duché de Limbourg,* 69 (1937).

Daris, Joseph. "Les Cours de justice de l'ancien principauté de Liège." *BIAL,* 16 (1881), 1-46.

Desama, Claude. "Les Rentes en argent fournissent-elles un diagnostic de l'activité économique? Enquête dans un protocole liégeois au XVIIe siècle." *Annuaire d'Histoire Liégeoise,* 10 (1967), 1-32.

Desama, Claude, and Blaise, André. "Comment les communautés villageoises avaient recours au crédit au XVIIe siècle." *Credit Communal de Belgique,* 21 (1967), 55-65.

Finances publiques d'ancien régime. Finances publiques contemporaines en Belgique de 1740 à 1860. Collection Histoire Pro Civitate, in-8°, No. 39. Brussels: Credit Communal de Belgique, 1975.

Hansotte, Georges. "Les Institutions locales dans les compagnes du Pays de Liège à la fin de l'ancien régime." *Cahiers de Clio,* 2 (1965), 15-19.

Jacob, Robert. "Les Communautés d'habitants au droit liégeois recent (XVII-XVIIIes siècles)." *Credit Communal de Belgique,* 31 (1977), 71-89.

Poullet, Edmond. *Les Constitutions nationales belges de l'ancien régime à l'époque de l'invasion française de 1794.* Mém. Cour., vol. 26, Brussels, 1875.

Rule, John C. "Louis XIV , Roi-Bureaucrate." John C. Rule, ed. *Louis XIV and the Craft of Kingship.* Columbus: Ohio State University Press, 1969. Pp. 3-101.

Tilly, Charles, ed. *The Formation of National States in Western Europe.* Princeton, 1975.

Yans, Maurice. "Les Tribunaux liégeois de l'ancien régime et leurs archives." *Vieux Liège* (1948), 257-261.

Andre, Louis. *Michel le Tellier et Louvois.* Paris, 1942. Reprinted, Geneva, 1974.

—. *Michel le Tellier et l'organisation de l'armée monarchique.* Paris, 1906.

Bourelly, Jules. *Le Marechal de Fabert (1599-1662).* 2 vols. Paris, 1881.

Brouwers, A. "A Propose des recrutements au pays de Liège." *CAPL,* 1 (1906), 67-69.

Buchet, Arsene. "Les Deux premiers campagnes de John Churchill, duc de Marlborough aux Pays-Bas lors de la Guerre de Succesion d'Espagne. Le Siège de Huy (1702). Les Sièges de Bonn, Huy et Limbourg (1703)." *Bulletin des Archives Verviétoises,* 8 (1972).

Ceyssens, Jean. "En temps de guerre 1746-1747-1748." *Leodium,* 5 (1906), 144-148, 6 (1907), 137-142.

Corvisier, Andre. *L'Armée francaise de la fin de XVII* siècle au Ministère de Choiseul. Le Soldat. 2 vols. Paris: Presses Universitaires de France, 1964.

Dupuy, R. Ernest, and Dupuy, Trevor N. *The Encyclopedia of Military History.* New York: Harper and Row, 1970.

Fastes militaires du pays de Liège (Catalogue of an exhibition at the Musée d'Art Wallon, Oct. 24 to Nov. 29, 1970). Liège, 1970.

Gaier, Claude. *Art et organisation militaires dans la principauté de Liège.* Academie Royale de Belgique, Classe de Lettres, Mémoires, vol. 44. Brussels, 1968.

Habets, Josef. "Analectes concernant le siège de Maestricht et le sejour des Francais dans les pays d'Outre-Meuse, 1672-1679." *Publications de la Société d'Histoire et d'Archéologie dans le Duché de Limbourg,* 7 (1870), 488-498.

Hansay, A. "Documents inédits concernant la mise en defense des campagnes lossaines à l'époque moderne." *Bulletin de la Commission Royale d'Histoire,* 95 (1931), 151-222.

Hélin, Etienne. "Les Fortifications de Liège pendant les guerres de Louis XIV." *Vieux Liège,* 5 (1959), 258-361.

Heuse, H. "L'Armée des Princes-Evêques de Liège, en 1715." *La Vie Wallone,* 20 (1940), 156-157.

Houtte, Hubert van. *Les Occupations étrangères en Belgique sous l'ancien régime.* Recueil de Travaux Publiés par la Faculté de Philosophie et Lettres de l'Université de Gand, 62-64 (1930).

Howard, Michael. *War in European History.* London: Oxford University Press, 1976.

Hubert, Eugene Ernest. *Les Garnisons de la Barrière dans les Pays-Bas autrichiens.* Mémoires couronnes et mémoires des savants etrangers, publiés par l'Academie Royale des Sciences, des Lettres et des Beaux-Arts de Belgique, vol. 59. Brussels, 1902.

Lazard, P. *Vauban, 1633-1707.* Paris, 1934.

Leur, L. van der. "Het beleg van Maastricht in 1673." *Publications de la Société d'Histoire et d'Archéologie dans le Duché de Limbourg,* 45 (1909), 131-438.

Maas, P.-J. "Marlborough dans la Campine limbourgeoise." *L'Ancien Pays de Looz,* 7-8 (1903-1904), 5-9, 17-29.

Mann, Golo. *Wallenstein. Sein Leben erzählt.* Frankfurt am Mein: S. Fischer, 1971.

Nève, Joseph E. *Gand sous l'occupation de Louis XIV (1678-1679, 1701-1707, 1708).* Ghent, 1929.

Paquay, Jean. "Relation de ce qui s'est passé pendant le siège de Maestricht." *BSSLL,* 41 (1927), 42-45.

Parker, Geoffrey. *The Army of Flanders and the Spanish Road, 1567-1659.* Cambridge: Cambridge University Press, 1972.

—. "The Military Revolution, 1560-1660 — a Myth?" *Journal of Modern History,* 48 (1976), 195-214.

—. "Mutiny and Discontent in the Spanish Army of Flanders, 1572-1607." *Past and Present*, No. 58 (1973), 38-52.

—. "War and Economic Change: the Economic Costs of the Dutch Revolt." J. M. Winter, ed. *War and Economic Development*. Cambridge: Cambridge University Press, 1975. Pp. 49-72.

Poswick, Eugene. *Histoire des troupes liégeoises pendant le XVIIIe siècle*. Liège, 1893.

Redlich, F. "Contributions in the Thirty Years' War." *Economic History Review*, 12 (1959-1960), 247-254.

—. *The German Military Enterpriser and his Work Force. A Study in European Economic and Social History*. 2 vols. Beihefte 47 and 48 of *Vierteljahrschrift für sozial und wirtschaftsgeschichte*. Wiesbaden 1964-1965.

Roberts, Michael. "Gustav Adolf and the Art of War." *Essays in Swedish History*. London: Weidenfield and Nicolson, 1967. Pp. 56-81.

—. *Gustavus Adolphus, A History of Sweden 1611-1632*. 2 vols. London: Longmans, 1958.

—. "The Military Revolution, 1560-1660." *Essays in Swedish History*. London: Weidenfield and Nicolson, 1967. Pp. 195-225.

Rousset, Camille. *Histoire de Louvois et de son administration politique et militaire*. 4 vols. Paris, 1861-1863.

Schaepkens, Arnaud. "Relation du siège et du bombardement de la ville de Maestricht." *Annales de la Société Historique et Archéologique dans le Duché de Limbourg* (1857).

Thihon, F. "Le Duc Charles de Lorraine et la Principauté de Liège." *BIAL*, 40 (1910), 235-242.

Ulens, Robert. "Les Milices rurales au pays de Liège." *Leodium*, 24 (1931), 36-42.

Vigier, Octave. "Une invasion en France sous Louis XIII." *Revue des Questions Historiques*, 56 (1894), 440-492.

Wouters, H. H. E. "Rond een Onuitgegeven Journaal van Vauban over het Beleg van Maastricht in 1673." *De Maasgouw*, 74 (1955), 161-170.

E. Economy and Geography

1. Agriculture, Geography, and Climate

a. The Basse-Meuse

Baar, Armand. "Au bon temps du vignoble liégeois." *La Vie Wallonne*, 20 (1940), 209-214.

Bihot, Charles. *Le Pays de Herve. Etude de géographie humaine*. Antwerp, 1913. Extract from the *Bulletin de la Société Royale de Géographie d'Anvers*, 1913.

Deckers, Joseph. "Vente de biens meubles à la Ferme du Temple (Visé) en 1784." *Vieux Liège*, 8 (1971), 65-76.

—. "La Vie quotidienne dans la principauté de Liège à la fin de XVIIe et au debut de XVIIIe siècle. Un exemple d'utilisation des archives liégeoises." *Federation Archéologoque et Historique de Belgique, Annales du XLIe Congrès, Malines, 1970*. Malines, 1971. Vol. II, pp. 374-382.

Delatte, Ivan, *Les Classes rurales dans la principauté de Liège au XVIIIe siècle*. Bibliothèque de la Faculté de Philosophie et Lettres de l'Université de Liège. No. 105. Liège, 1945.

—. "Considérations sur l'évolution des exploitations agricoles dans l'ouest de la Hesbaye liégeoise de 1750 à 1850." *Vieux Liège*, 3 (1946), 165-167.

—. "L'Evolution de la structure agraire en Belgique de 1575 à 1850." *Annales de la Federation*

Archéologique et Historique de Belgique. Tournai, 1951. Vol. II, pp. 480-488.

—. "Introduction a l'étude du régime seigneurial dans la principauté de Liège du XIVe au XVIIIe siècle." *Vieux Liège,* 3 (1948), 275-280.

—. "La Vente des biens du clergé dans le département de l'Ourte." *Vieux Liège,* 3 (1949), 391-402.

Deltenre, Léonce. *Note sur le bail à ferme dans le pays de Thuin au XVIIIe siècle.* Thuin, 1936.

Gutmann, Myron P. "War, the Tithe and Agricultural Production. The Meuse Basin North of Liège, 1661-1740." Herman van der Wee and Eddy van Cauwenberghe, eds. *Productivity of Land and Agricultural Innovation in the Low Countries (1250-1800).* Leuven, Belgium: Leuven University Press, 1978. Pp. 65-76.

Habets, J. "Over de Wynbouw in nederlandsch en belgisch Limburg gedurende vroegere eeuwen." *Publications de la Société Historique et Archéologique dans le Duché du Limbourg,* 3 (1866), 380-394.

Halkin, Leon. "Etude historique sur la culture de la vigne en Belgique." *BSAHL,* 9 (1895), 1-146.

Halkin, Leon-E. "Description inédite du duché de Limbourg." Premier Congrès International de Géographie Historique. *Mémoires.* Vol. 2. Brussels, 1931. Pp. 135-139.

Jansen, J. C. G. M. "Agrarian Development and Exploitation in South Limburg in the Years 1650-1850." *Acta Historiae Neerlandica,* 5 (1970), 243-270.

—. "Landbouw rond Maastricht (1610-1865). Een analyse van de exploitatieuitkomsten van enige lossbedrijven in halfwinning." *Studies over de Sociaal-economische geschiedenis van Limburg,* 13 (1968), 1-98.

—. *Landbouwproduktie en Economische Golfbeweging in Zuid-Limburg, 1250-1800. Een Analyse van de Opbrengst van Tienden.* Assen, The Netherlands: Van Gorcum, 1979.

Jansen, J. C. G. M., and Bauduin, H. O. J. H. "Aspecten van de Limburgse landbouwgeschiedenis." *Studies over de Sociaal-Economische Geschiedenis van Limburg,* 14 (1969), 1-102.

Leclercq, Jean, "La Réaction seigneuriale du XVIIIe siècle et les corvées à Argenteau." *Vieux Liège,* 4 (1953), 237-238.

Philips, J. F. R., Jansen, J. C. G. M., Claessens, Th. J. A. H. *Geschiedenis van de Landbouw in Limburg, 1750-1914.* Assen, The Netherlands: Van Gorcum, 1965.

Pirotte, Fernand. *La Pomme de Terre en Wallonie au XVIIIe siècle.* Collection d'études publiée par le Musée de la Vie Wallonne, no. 4. Liège, 1976.

Ruwet, Joseph. *L'Agriculture et les classes rurals au Pays de Herve sous l'ancien régime.* Bibliothèque de la Faculté de Philosophie et Lettres de l'Université de Liège. No. 100. Liège, 1943.

—. "Mesure de la production agricole sous l'ancien régime: le blé en pays mosan." *Annales E. S. C.,* 19 (1964), 625-643.

—. "Prix, production et bénéfices agricoles: le pays de Liège au XVIIIe siècle." *Cahiers d'Histoire de Prix* (Louvain), 2 (1957), 69-108.

Thielens, Jacques. "Le Cense du château d'Argenteau aux XVIIe et XVIIIe siècles." *Anciens Pays et Assemblées d'Etats,* 48 (1969), 203-237.

Yans, Maurice. "Note sur la vie rurale. Contrats de circonstance." *Leodium,* 57 (1970), 61-65.

Ylieff, Yvan. "Une exploitation agricole: la grande cense d'Ourdoumont à Saive." Unpublished Mémoire de License, University of Liège, 1963.

b. Other Regions

Bloch, Marc. *French Rural History. An Essay on its Basic Characteristics.* Trans. Janet Sondheimer. Berkeley: University of California Press, 1970.

Duby, Georges, and Wallon, Armand, eds. *Histoire de la France rurale.* Vol. 2. *L'Age classique des paysans, 1340-1789.* Paris: Seuil, 1975.

Genicot, Leopold. "La Limite des cultures du froment et de l'épeautre dans le Namurois au Bas Moyen âge." *Namurcum.* 22 (1947), 17-24.

Goy, Joseph, and Le Roy Ladurie, Emmanuel, eds. *Les Fluctuations du produit de la dîme.* Cahiers des Etudes Rurales, No. 2. Paris: Mouton, 1972.

Labeau, R. "Organisation de la dîme dans les Pays-Bas à la fin de l'Ancien Régime." *Annuaire de l'Université de Louvain* (1914), 453-461.

Laenen, J. "La Dîme ecclésiastique dans le droit local de Brabant." *Vie Diocésiane* (Malines), 5 (1911), 56-67, 284-297, 305-317.

Le Roy Ladurie, Emmanuel. *Histoire du climat depuis l'an mil.* Paris: Flammarion, 1967.

Lindemans, Paul. *Geschiedenis van de landbouw in België.* 2 vols. Antwerp, 1952.

Mingay, G. E. "The Agricultural Depression 1730-1750." *Economic History Review,* 8 (1956), 323-338.

Neveux, Hughes. "La Production céréalière dans un région frontalière: le Cambrésis du XVe au XVIIIe siècle. Bilan provisoire." J. Goy and E. Le Roy Ladurie, eds. *Les Fluctiations du produit de la dîme.* Paris, 1972. Pp. 58-66.

Olivier, J. "The Use of Weather Diaries in the Study of Historical Climates." *Weather,* 13 (1958), 251-256.

Pfister, Christian. "Zum Klima des Raumes Zurich im späten 17. und Frühen 18. Jahrhundert." *Vierteljahrschrift der Naturforschenden besellschaft in Zürich,* 122 (1977), 447-471.

Roland, Joseph. "La Revolution agricole au XVIIIe siècle, specialement dans la province de Namur." *Annales de la Federation Archéologique et Historique de Belgique, Namur, 1938.* Namur, 1939. Pp. 356-370.

Ruwet, Joseph. "Pour un indice de la production céréalière à l'époque moderne; le région de Namur." J. Goy and E. Le Roy Ladurie, eds. *Les Fluctuations du produit de la dîme.* Paris, 1972. Pp. 67-82.

Slicher van Bath, B. H. *The Agrarian History of Western Europe, A. D. 500-1850.* Trans. Olive Ordish. London, 1963.

–. "Les Problèmes fondamentaux de la société pre-industrielle en Europe occidentale. Une orientation et un programme." *A.A.G. Bijdragen,* 12 (1965), 3-46.

–. "The Rise of Intensive Husbandry in the Low Countries." *Britain and the Netherlands, Papers Delivered to the Oxford-Netherlands Conference.* London, 1960. Pp. 130-153.

Thirsk, Joan. *English Peasant Farming: the Agrarian History of Lincolnshire from Tudor to Recent Times.* London: Routledge & Kegan Paul, 1957.

Utterstrom, Gustav. "Climatic Fluctuations and Population Problems in Early Modern Europe." *Scandinavian Economic History Review,* 3 (1955), 3-47.

Vandervelde, Emile. *La Propriété foncière en Belgique.* Paris, 1900.

Verhulst, A. "Les Types differents de l'organisation domainiale et structures agraires en Belgiques au moyen âge." *Annales E.S.C.,* 11 (1956), 61-70.

Veyrassat-Herren, B. "Dîmes alsaciennes." J. Goy and E. Le Roy Ladurie, eds. *Les Fluctuations du produit de la dîme.* Paris, 1972. Pp. 83-102.

Vries, Jan de. *The Dutch Rural Economy in the Golden Age,* 1500-1700. New Haven: Yale University Press, 1974.

–. *The Economy of Europe in an Age of Crisis, 1600-1750.* Cambridge: Cambridge University Press, 1976.

–. "Histoire du climat et économie: des faits nouveaux et une interpretation differente." *Annales E.S.C.,* 32 (1977), 198-226.

292

Wee, Herman van der, and Cauwenberghe, Eddy van, eds. *Productivity of Land and Agricultural Innovation in the Low Countries (1250-1800)*. Leuven, Belgium: Leuven University Press, 1978.

Wilson, Charles. *England's Apprenticeship 1603-1783*. London. 1965.

2. Mining and Industry

a. The Basse-Meuse

Berck, Franz. "Notes sur l'industrie extractive de la pierre à Flemalle-Grande." *BIAL*, 67 (1949-50), 347-361.

Bourgignon, M. "La Sidérurgie, industrie commune des pays d'Entre-Meuse-et-Rhin." *Anciens Pays et Assemblées d'Etats,* 28 (1963), 81-120.

Briavoinne, N. *Mémoire sur l'état de la population des fabriques, des manufactures et du commerce dans les provinces des Pays-Bas depuis Albert et Isabelle jusqu'à la fin du siècle dernier*. Mém. Cour. in-4°, vol. 14. Brussels, 1840.

Ceyssens, Jean. "A propos d'engins et d'anciennes houillères." *CAPL,* 16 (1925), 84-89.

Collart-Sacré, André. "Dallage et pilotis dans le lit de la Meuse, au lieu-dit 'à l'Inghin' à Wandre." *CAPL,* 13 (1922), 98-104.

Dechesne, L. *Industrie drapière de la Vesdre avant 1800*. Paris, 1926.

Gaier, Claude. *Quatre siècles d'armurerie liégeoise*. Liège: Eugène Wahle, éditeur, 1976.

Hansotte, Georges. "La Clouterie liégeoise et la question ouvrière au XVIIIᵉ siècle." *Anciens Pays et Assemblées d'Etats,* 55 (1972), 1-119.

—. "L'Industrie sidérurgique dans la vallée de l'Ourthe liégeoise aux temps modernes." *La Vie Wallonne,* 29 (1955), 116-224.

—. "L'Introduction de la machine à vapeur à Liège, 1720." *La Vie Wallonne,* 24 (1950), 47-56.

—. "La Métallurgie wallonne au XVIᵉ et dans la première moitie du XVIIᵉ siècle. Essai de synthèse." *BIAL,* 84 (1972), 21-42.

—. "La Révolution industrielle dans la métallurgie du bassin de Liège." *Cahiers de Clio,* 17 (1966), 23-32.

Harsin, Paul. "Etudes sur l'histoire économique de la principauté de Liège, particulièrement au XVIIᵉ siècle," *BIAL,* 52 (1928), 100-161.

Hélin, Etienne. "Les Antécédents de l'industrialisation de la Basse-Meuse." *Vieux Liège,* 7 (1970), 458-459.

Houtte, H. van. *Histoire économique de la Belgique à la fin de l'ancien régime*. Ghent, 1920.

Jaer, L. de "De l'épuisement des eaux dans les mines de houille au Pays de Liège, avant le XIXᵉ siècle." *La Vie Wallonne,* 8 (1927), 95-109.

Lahaye, Leon. "Une curieux accident de houillère au XVIIᵉ siècle." *Leodium,* 12 (1913), 139-140.

Laurent, Henri. "La Concurrence entre les centres industriels des provinces unies et de la principauté de Liège aux XVIIᵉ et XVIIIᵉ siècles et les origines de la grande industrie drapière Verviétoise, d'après les travaux recents de M. Posthumous." *Revue d'Histoire Modern,* 2 (1927), 216-219.

Lebrun, P. *L'Industrie de la laine à Verviers pendant le XVIIIᵉ et le commencement du XIXᵉ siècle*. Bibliothèque de la Faculté de Philosophie et Lettres de l'Université de Liège, No. 114. Liège, 1948.

Malherbe, Renier. *Historique de l'exploitation de la houille au pays de Liège*. Liège, 1863.

Panhuysen, G. W. A. "Het mijnreglement voor het staatsland van Dalhem van 1668 en

enige toelichtende stukken." *Publications de la Société Historique et Archéologique dans le Duché de Limbourg,* 85 (1949), 530-572.

Pieyns-Rigo, Paulette, and Gaier, Claude. "Fournitures d'armes et vie armurière à Liège vers le milieu du XVIIIe siècle d'après les actes notariaux." *Le Musée d'Armes,* 5 (1977), 13-19.

Posthumus, N. W. "De industrieele concurrentie tusschen Noord- en Zuidnederlandsche Nijverheidscentra in de XVIIe en XVIIIe eeuw." *Mélanges d'histoire offerts à Henri Pirenne...* Brussels, 1926. Vol. II. pp. 369-378.

Renard, J. "Vie et mort d'une industrie multiseculaire. La Houillerie à Wandre." *BIAL,* 81 (1968), 73-280.

Renier, J. S. *Histoire de l'industrie drapière de Liège.* Liège, 1881.

Yans, Maurice. "L'engin' de Wandre vu de la Haye." *La Vie Wallonne,* 25 (1951), 222-224.

–. "Histoire de nos charbonnages. Les Planchar, charbonniers de la banlieu liégeoise." *CAPL,* 38 (1947), 5-16.

–. *Histoire économique du duché de Limbourg sous la Maison de Bourgogne. Les Forêts et les mînes.* Mémoires courronnés par l'Academie royale de Belgique, Lettres, No. 38. Brussels, 1937.

Yernaux, Jean. "Les Carrières du pays wallon." *La Vie Wallonne,* 22 (1948), 71-86.

–. *Contrats de travail liégeois du XVIIe siècle.* Academie Royale de Belgique. Commission Royale d'Histoire, No. 53. Brussels, 1941.

–. *La Metallurgie liégeoise et son expansion au XVIIe siècle.* Liège, 1939.

b. Other Regions

Ashton, T. S., and Sykes, J. *The Coal Industry in the Eighteenth Century.* Second ed. Manchester, 1964.

Decamps, G. "Mémoire historique sur l'origine et des développements de l'industrie houillère dans le bassin du Couchant de Mons." *Mémoires et Publications de la Sociéte des Sciences, des Arts et des Lettres du Hainaut,* Series 5, 5 (1889).

Douxchamps-Lefevre, Cecile. "Le Commerce du charbon dans les Pays-Bas autrichiens à la fin du XVIIe siècle." *RBPH,* 46 (1968), 393-421.

–. "Notes sur l'industrie houillère dans la région de Charleroi au XVIIIe siècle." *Documents et Rapports de la Société Royale d'Archéologie et de Paléontologie de Charleroi,* 52 (1966), 131-158.

Nef, J. U. *The Rise of the British Coal Industry.* 2 vols. London, 1932.

Rouff, Marcel. *Les Mines de charbon en France au XVIIIe siècle, 1744-1791. Etude d'histoire économique et sociale.* Paris, 1922.

3. Prices, Trade and Measurement

Achilles, Walter. "Getreidepreise und Getreidehandelsbeziehungen europäischer Räume im 16. und 17. Jahrhundert." *Zeitschrift für Agrargeschichte und Agrarsoziologie,* 7 (1959), 32-53.

Bigwood, G. "Gand et la circulation des grains en Flandre au XIVe au XVIIIe siècle." *Vierteljährschrift fur Sozial- und Wirtschaftsgeschichte,* 4 (1906), 397-460.

Braudel, F. and Spooner, F. "Prices in Europe from 1450 to 1750." *The Cambridge Economic History,* IV, 378-486. Cambridge, Cambridge University Press, 1967.

Bruyne, P. de. "Les Anciennes mesures liégeoises." *BIAL,* 40 (1936), 287-316.

Ceyssens, Jean. "Les Anciennes mesures des grains surtout par rapport au pays de Dalhem." *Leodium,* 13 (1914), 18-21.

Chestret de Haneffe, J. de. "La Police de vivres à Liège pendant le moyen âge." *BIAL,* 23 (1892), 217-267.

Faber, J. A. "The Decline of the Baltic Grain-Trade in the Second Half of the Seventeenth Century." *Acta Historiae Neerlandica,* 1 (1966), 108-131.

Fanchamps, Marie-Louise. *Recherches statistiques sur le problème annonnaire dans la principauté de Liège de 1475 à la fin du XVIe siècle. Tendances, cycles, crises.* Liège: Editions de la Commission Communale de l'Histoire de l'Ancien Pays de Liège, 1970.

Frère. Hubert. "Numismatique liégeoise. Notes sur la monnaie de compte dans la principauté de Liège." *BIAL,* 80 (1967), 91-112.

Goffinet, H. "Notice sur l'ancien Chemin-Neuf de Sedan à Liège." *Annales de l'Institut Archéologique du Luxembourg,* 14 (1882), 163-198.

Knaepen, J. "La Route d'Aix-la-Chapelle à Visé." *BIAL,* 68 (1951), 6-37.

Lambert, E. "La Signification économique des différends territoriaux entre Liège et les Pays-Bas à la fin du XVIIIe siècle." *RBPH,* 31 (1953), 448-489.

Laport, George. "Moyens de transport d'autrefois." *La Vie Wallonne,* 8 (1927-1928), 229-239, 258-262, 296-306.

Rouhart-Chabot, Juliette. "Les Pouvoirs publics liégeois devant la disette de 1565-1566." *BIAL,* 67 (1949-1950), 121-139.

Ruhl, Gustave, "Le Pied de Saint Lambert." *Leodium,* 7 (1908), 66-67.

Santbergen, R. van. *Les Bons metiers de meuniers, des boulangers, et des brasseurs de la cité de Liège.* Bibliothèque de la Faculté de Philosophie er Lettres de l'Université de Liège. No. 115. Liège, 1949.

Thurlings, Th. L. M. *De Maashandel van Venlo en Roermond in de 16e eeuw, 1473-1572.* Amsterdam, 1945.

Wee, Herman van der. *The Growth of the Antwerp Market and the European Economy.* 3 vols. The Hague, 1963.

Werveke, Hans van. "Monnaie de compte et monnaie réelle." *RBPH,* 13 (1934), 123-152.

Yans, Maurice. "La Meuse et nos relations commerciales avec la Hollande." *BIAL,* 63 (1939), 131-140.

—. "La Rente en droit privé liégeois." *Leodium,* 56 (1969), 36-48.

F. Demography

1. The Basse-Meuse

Bamps, C. "Epidémies et disettes qui ont anciennement régné dans la province de Limbourg." *Bulletin de la Commission Centrale de Statistique,* 6 (1855), 597-615.

Brassinne, Joseph. "La Population de Liège en 1650." *BIAL,* 33 (1903), 232-250.

Dumont, Bruno, "La Population de l'Abbaye du Val-Dieu sous l'ancien régime." *Citeaux-Commentarii Cistercienses,* 27 (1976), 226-266.

Gutmann, Myron P. "Putting Crises in Perspective: the Impact of War on Civilian Populations in the Seventeenth Century." *Annales de Démographie Historique* (1977), 101-128.

—. "Reconstituting Wandre: an Approach to Semi-Automatic Family Reconstitution." *Annales de Démographie Historique* (1977), 315-341.

—. "Why They Stayed: the Problem of Wartime Population Loss." *Tijdschrift voor Geschiedenis.* 91 (1978), 407-428.

Hélin, Etienne. "Les Capitations Liégeoises." *Ancien Pays et Assemblées d'Etats,* 21 (1961).

—. *La Démographie de Liège aux XVIIe et XVIIIe siècles.* Academie Royale de Belgique. Classe des Lettres et des Sciences Morales et Politiques. Mémoires. Collection in-8°. Vol. 56, pt. 4. Brussels, 1963.

—. "Le Déroulement de trois crises à Liège au XVIIIe siècle." *Actes du Colloque International de Démographie Historique, Liège, 1963.* Ed. Paul Harsin and Etienne Hélin. Liège, 1965. Pp. 483-497.

—. "La Disette et le recensement de 1740." *Annuaire d'Histoire Liégeoise,* 6 (1959), 443-477.

—. "L'Impôt sur les fenêtres à Liège au XVIIe siècle." *BIAL,* 75 (1962), 153-163.

—. "Migrations d'ouvriers avant la révolution industrielle." *Federation Archéologique et Historique de Belgique. Annales du Congrès de Liège.* Liège, 1969. Vol. I, pp. 167-179.

—. *La Population des paroisses liégeoises aux XVIIe et XVIIIe siècles.* Liège: Editions de la Commission Communale de l'Histoire de l'Ancien Pays de Liège, 1959.

—. "Les Recherches sur la mortalité dans la region liégeoise (XVe-XIXe siècles)." *Actes du Colloque International de Démographie Historique, Liège, 1963.* Paul Harsin and Etienne Hélin, eds. Liège, 1965. Pp. 155-184.

—. "Une approche de la pauvrété: Qui recevait les aumônes distribuées par les curés liégeois?" *Leodium,* 58 (1971), 64-83.

Herbillon, Jules. "Wallon Harlaque et les 'Herlaques'." *Vieux Liège,* 6 (1964), 434-435.

Kemp, A. G. H. "Het Verloop van de bevolkingscurve van Maastricht tot 1830." *Werken uitgegeven door Limburgs geschied- en oudheidkundig genootschap gevestigd te Maastricht,* 4 (1962), 339-362.

Leboutte, René. "La Population de Dalhem du XVIIe au debut du XXe siècle. Etude de démographie historique." Unpublished Mémoire de Licence, University of Liège, 1975.

Meeus, Michel. "La Mortalité à Meerhout-en-Campine de 1686 à 1815." *Population et Famille,* 33 (1974), 131-189.

Polain, M. L. "Population de l'ancien pays de Liège, au XVIIIe siècle." *BIAL,* 3 (1857), 345-350.

Ruwet, Joseph. "Crises démographiques, problèmes économiques ou crises morales? Le Pays de Liège sous l'ancien régime." *Population,* 9 (1954), 451-476.

Torfs, Louis. *Fastes des calamités publiques survenues dans les Pays-Bas et particulièrement en Belgique, depuis les temps les plus reculés jusqu'à nos jours,* 2 vols. Paris-Tournai, 1859.

Turney-High, Harry Holbert. *Château-Gerard: The Life and Times of a Walloon Village.* Columbia, S. C.: University of South Carolina Press, 1953.

2. Other Regions

Appleby, Andrew B. "Crises of Mortality: Periodicity, Intensity, Chronology and Geographical Extent." Hubert Charbonneau and Andre Larose, eds. *The Great Mortalities: Methodological Studies of Demographic Crises in the Past.* Liège: Ordina Editions, 1979.

—. *Famine in Tudor and Stuart England.* Stanford: Stanford University Press, 1978.

—. "Nutrition and Disease: the Case of London, 1550-1750." *Journal of Interdisciplinary History,* 6 (1975), 1-22.

Ariès, Philippe. *Centuries of Childhood.* New York: Random House, 1962.

—. "Interprétation pour une histoire des mentalités." Hélène Bergues, et al. *La Prevention des naissances dans la famille.* Institut National d'Etudes Démographiques. Travaux et Documents, cahier 35. Paris, 1960. Pp. 311-327. Translated in Orest Ranum and Patricia

Ranum, eds. *Popular Attitudes Toward Birth Control in Pre-Industrial France and England.* New York: Harper and Row, 1972. Pp. 100-125.

—. "Sur les origines de la contraception en France." *Population,* 3 (1953), 465-472. Translated in Ranum and Ranum (above), pp. 10-20.

Benedict, Philip. "Catholics and Huguenots in Sixteenth-Century Rouen: The Demographic Effects of the Religious Wars." *French Historical Studies,* 9 (1975), 209-234.

Boumans, R. "Le Dépeuplement d'Anvers dans le dernier quart du XVIᵉ siècle." *Revue du Nord,* 29 (1947), 181-194.

—. "L'Evolution démographique d'Anvers (XVᵉ-XVIIIᵉ siècle)." *Bulletin de Statistique,* 34 (1948), 1683-1693.

Bruneel, Claude. *La Mortalité dans les campagne: le duché de Brabant aux XVIIᵉ et XVIIIᵉ siècles,* 2 vols. University de Louvain. Recueil de Travaux d'Histoire et de Philologie, 6th series, no. 10. Louvain, 1977.

Coale, A. J. "The Decline of Fertility in Europe from the French Revolution to World War II." S. J. Behren, L. Corso and R. Freedman, eds. *Fertility and Family Planning.* Ann Arbor, Michigan: The University of Michigan Press, 1969. Pp. 3-24.

Coale, A. J., and Demeny, Paul. *Regional Model Life Tables and Stable Populations.* Princeton: Princeton University Press, 1966.

Croix, Alain. "La Démographie du pays nantais au XVIᵉ siècle." *Annales de Démographie Historique* (1967), 63-90.

Faber, J. A., et al. "Population Changes and Economic Developments in the Netherlands: a historical survey." *A. A. G. Bijdragen,* 12 (1965), 47-112.

Frisch, Rose E. "Demographic Implications of the Biological Determinants of Female Fecundity." Research Paper No. 6, Center for Population Studies, Harvard University. July, 1974.

Frisch, Rose E., and McArthur, Janet W. "Menstrual Cycles: Fatness as a Determinant of Minimum Weight for Height Necessary for Their Maintenance or Onset." *Science,* 185 (1974), 949-951.

Frisch, Rose E., and Revelle, Roger. "Height and Weight at Menarche and a Hypothesis of Critical Body Weights and Adolescent Events." *Science,* 169 (1970), 397-399.

—. "Height and Weight at Menarche and a Hypothesis of Menarche." *Archives of Disease in Childhood,* 46 (1971), 695-701.

Gautier, Etienne, and Henry, Louis. *La Population de Crulai, paroisse normande. Etude historique.* Institut National d'Etudes Démographiques, Travaux et Documents, cahier No. 33. Paris, 1958.

Gopolan, C., and Naidu, A. Nadamuni. "Nutrition and Fertility". *The Lancet,* 1972, ii, 1077-1079.

Goubert, Pierre. "Historical Demography and the Reinterpretation of Early Modern French History: A Research Review." *Journal of Interdisciplinary History,* 1 (1970), 37-48. Reprinted in Theodore K. Rabb and Robert I. Rotberg, eds. *The Family in History: Interdisciplinary Essays.* New York: Harper and Row, 1973. Pp. 16-27.

Helleiner, Karl F. "The Population of Europe from the Black Death to the Eve of the Vital Revolution." E. E. Rich and C. H. Wilson, eds. *The Cambridge Economic History,* IV. Cambridge: Cambridge University Press, 1967. Pp. 1-95.

Humm, Andre. *Villages et hameaux disparus en Basse-Alsace.* Strasbourg, 1971.

Jacquart, Jean. "La Fronde des princes dans la région parisienne et ses conséquences matérielles." *Revue d'Histoire Moderne et Contemporaine,* 7 (1960), 257-290.

Jacquet-Ladrier, F. "Soldats blessés à Namur au XVIIᵉ siècle (1635-1643)." *Annales de la*

Société Archéologique de Namur, 58 (1977), 25-46.

Keys, Ancel, et al. *The Biology of Human Starvation.* 2 vols. Minneapolis, 1950.

Le Roy Laduri, Emmanuel. "L'Aménorrhée de famine (XVIIᵉ-XXᵉ siècle)." *Annales E. S. C.,* 24 (1969), 1589-1601. Translated and reprinted in Robert Forster and Orest Ranum, eds. *Biology of Man in History.* Baltimore: The Johns Hopkins University Press, 1975. Pp. 163-178.

Lee, Ronald Demos. "Methods and Models for Analyzing Historical Series of Births, Deaths and Marriages." R. D. Lee, ed. *Population Patterns in the Past.* New York: Academic Press, 1977. Pp. 337-370.

Meuvret, Jean. "Les Crises de subsistance et la démographie de la France d'Ancien Régime." *Population,* 1 (1946), 643-650. Translated and reprinted in D. V. Glass and D. E. C. Eversley, eds. *Population in History.* Chicago: Aldine, 1965. Pp. 507-522.

Mols, Roger. *Introduction à la démographie historique des villes d'Europe du XIVᵉ au XVIIIᵉ siècle.* 3 vols. Louvain, 1955.

Poncelet, Alfred. *Nécrologe des jesuites de la province Flandro-Belge.* Wetteren, 1931.

Revel, Jacques. "Autour d'une épidémie ancienne: la peste de 1666-1670." *Revue d'Histoire Moderne et Contemporaine,* 17 (1970), 953-983.

Roupnel, Gaston. *La Ville et la campagne au XVIIᵉ siècle. Etude sur les populations du pays dijonais.* Paris, 1922.

Ruwet, Joseph. "Crises de mortalité et mortalité de crise à Aix-la-Chapelle (XVIIᵉ-debut du XVIIIᵉ siècle)." *Actes du Colloque International de Démographie Historique, Liège, 1963.* Paul Harsin and Etienne Helin, eds. Liège, 1965. Pp. 379-408.

Villages desertés et histoire économique, XIᵉ-XVIIIᵉ siècles. Paris: SEVPEN, 1965.

Wrigley, E. A. "Family Limitation in Pre-Industrial England." *Economic History Review,* 2nd series, 29 (1966), 82-109.

Xanten, H. J. van, and Woude, A. M. van der. "Het Hoofdgeld en de Bevolking van de Meierij van 's-Hertogenbosch omstreeks 1700." *A.A.G. Bijdragen,* 13 (1965), 3-96.

G. Local Studies

1. The Basse-Meuse

Bayer-Lothe, J., and Demoulin, L. "Recherches sur la fortune de patriciens liégeois au XVIIᵉ siècle." *Vieux Liège,* 6 (1967), 145-156, 345-360.

Bonfond, Louis, and Thonnart, Matthieu. *Histoire de la Commune de Jupille-sur-Meuse.* Liège, 1938.

Cavenne. *Statistique du département de la Meuse-Inférieure, par le Citoyen Cavenne, Ingenieur des ponts et chaussées.* Maastricht, an X-1802.

Ceyssens, Jean. *Les Bans, seigneuries laiques et immunités ecclesiastiques du pays de Dalhem, specialement au XVᵉ siècle.* Liège, 1929.

–. "Dalhem, son château et son église jusqu'à l'érection de la paroisse en 1618." *Leodium,* 25 (1932), 69-77.

–. "La Droit de banalité." *BIAL,* 25 (1896), 33-98.

–. "Feneur, la seigneurie. Un prétendant comte en 1550." *Leodium,* 2 (1903), 93-100.

–. "Housse. Comment l'abbaye de Val-Dieu devint propriétaire de la ferme de Leval." *Leodium,* 2 (1903), 20-24.

–. "Paroisse de Visé." *BSAHL,* 6 (1890), 13-227.

–. "Les Privileges de la bonne ville et franchise de Dalhem d'après un document de 1516." *Leodium,* 1 (1902), 49-56.

–. "Val-Dieu et la grange de Froidmont à Haccourt." *Leodium,* 9 (1910), 100-108.

–. "Val-Dieu et la Seigneurie de Housse." *Leodium,* 2 (1903), 119-124.

Charles, H. A. "A Propos de Berneau et ses 'thours.'" *CAPL,* 41 (1950), 40-49.

Chestret de Haneffe, J. de "Histoire de la seigneurie imperiale de Gronsveld." *Publications de la Société historique et Archéologique dans le Duché de Limbourg,* 12 (1875), 3-126.

Collart, A. "A Oupeye." *CAPL,* 17 (1926), 75-76.

Collart-Sacré, André. *La Haute cour et justice souverain de Herstal.* Herstal, 1924.

–. *La Libre seigneurie de Herstal. Son histoire, ses monuments, ses rues et ses lieux-dits.* 2 vols. Liège, 1927-1930.

–. *La Seigneurie de Herstal sous les Hancellets (1568-1604).* Herstal, 1923.

Colleye, Maximilien. *Argenteau et les environs. Notice historique sur la Basse-Meuse.* Liège, 1921.

Debouxhtay, Pierre-J., and Dubois, Floribert. *Histoire de la seigneurie de Nivelle-sur-Meuse et de l'ancien paroisse de Lixhe.* Liège, 1935.

Dejardin, Jos. "Recherches historiques sur la commune de Cheratte dans l'ancien pays du Limbourg." *BSSLL,* 2 (1854), 181-200.

Dodémont, Urban J.-C. *Histoire politique et administrative de la bonne ville de Visé-sur-Meuse depuis ses origines jusqu'après la Revolution Français.* Visé, 1922.

Franchotte, Henri. "La Vie rurale en Belgique sous l'ancien régime. Le Village de Bombaye." *BSAHL,* 2 (1882), 243-307.

Franquinet, G.-D. "Les Seigneuries d'Agimont et de Nedercanne près de Maestricht." *BIAL,* 1 (1852), 71-90.

Granville, Francois. "Histoire d'Ans et Glain sous l'ancien régime." *BIAL,* 74 (1961), 5-252.

Habets, Josef. *Geschiedenis van het leenhof en de leenen van Valkenburg.* Roermond, 1884.

Hansotte, Georges. "La Vie quotidienne à Herstal sous le régime française." *Vieux Liège,* 5 (1959), 361-364.

Henaux, F. "Histoire de la bonne ville de Visé." *BIAL,* 1 (1852), 349-400.

Kanepen, John. *Visé, place forte, les anciennes portes.* Publication de la Société Archéo-Historique de Visé et la Region, No. 1 Visé, 1958.

Krains, Hubert. "La Hesbaye." *La Vie Wallonne,* 9 (1928), 99-103.

Lahaye, Leon. "Carnets de comptes de Jean Lintermans, chanoine de Saint Jean l'Evangeliste à Liège." *Leodium,* 32 (1939), 51-63.

–. "Les Paroisses de Liège." *BIAL,* 46 (1921), 1-208.

Laumont-Marechal, Michele. "Recherches sur Jean-Mathieu de Saroléa, sa fortune, sa bibliothèque." *Annuaire d'Histoire Liégeoise,* 14 (1973), 129-155.

Lejear, J. "Henri de Sonkeux et ses mémoires." *Bulletin de la Société Verviétoise d'Archéologie et d'Histoire,* 11 (1910), 61-72.

Lequarré, D. "La Terre franche de Herstal et sa cour de justice." *BIAL.* 29 (1900), 75-166.

Lequare, N., Jacquemotte, E., and Lejeune, J. "Histoire de la commune de Jupille." *Vieux Jupille,* 1 (1909-10), 6-12, 49-55, 73-78, 115-117, 129-133.

Linotte, Leon. "Histoire de l'ancien ban de Cheratte." Unpublished Mémoire de Licence, University of Liège, 1958.

Lurkin, Jean. "Au Pays de Herve." *La Vie Wallonne,* 10 (1929), 5-8.

Made, Raoul van der. "L'Abbaye de Vivegnis et le paiement des tailles de la communauté de Herstal." *BIAL,* 77 (1964), 157-169.

Matthieu, G. "Les Arbalétriers et les arquebusiers de Visé." *BIAL,* 10 (1870), 243-284.

Ô-Kelly, C. "A Propos de Navaigne." *Leodium,* 35 (1948), 50-54.

—. "L'Ancien fief Ter Droyen ou de Loye (Mouland)." *Leodium,* 32 (1939), 29-32.

—. "Les Archives de Berneau." *Leodium,* 25 (1932), 22-23.

—. "Berneau-Bombaye au XVIIIᵉ siècle." *Leodium,* 33 (1946), 41-42.

—. "Feneur Ancien." *Leodium,* 33 (1946), 23-30.

—. "La Poudrerie de Curtius à Dalhem." *Leodium,* 35 (1948), 44-46.

—. "Secouses sismiques à Dalhem au XVIIIᵉ siècle." *Leodium,* 34 (1947), 40-42.

—. "Les Seigneurs de Berneau au XVIᵉ siècle." *Leodium,* 35 (1948), 54.

Otte, Marcel. "Etude archéologique et historique sur le château medieval de Saive." *BIAL,* 83 (1971), 176-275.

Pelerin. *Essais historiques et critiques sur le département de la Meuse-Inferieure en general, et la ville de Maestricht, chef-lieu, en particulier.* Paris, 1805.

Pety de Thozée, J. "Le Cresus liégeois Jean Curtius, seigneur d'Oupeye, et sa famille, 1200-1851." *BIAL,* 40 (1910), 65-97.

Pirotte, Fernand. *La Terre de Durbuy au XVIIᵉ et XVIIIᵉ siècles. Les Institutions, l'économie et les hommes.* Centre Belge d'Histoire Rurale. Publication No. 35. Liège-Louvain, 1974.

Piton, Ernest. "Histoire Grand-Hallet et de Petit-Hallet." *BIAL,* 60 (1936), 191-265.

Poncelet, Edouard. "L'Abbaye de Vivegnis." *BSAHL,* 10 (1896), 1-141.

—. "Le Comté de Beaurieux." *BIAL,* 24 (1895), 385-486.

—. *Paysages Mosans du XVIᵉ siècle: le quai sur Meuse à Liège en 1553; la Meuse à Leuth en 1561; la terre libre de Leuth.* Liège: Société des Bibliphiles Liégeois, 1939.

—. "La Seigneurie de Saive." *BIAL,* 22 (1891), 251-433.

—. "La Seigneurie de Tignée." *BIAL,* 23 (1893), 115-190.

Poswick, Eugene. *Histoire de la seigneurie libre et imperiale d'Argenteau et de la maison de ce nom, aujourdhui Mercy-Argenteau.* Brussels, 1905.

Poumon, Emile. "Petites villes liégeoise (Visé, Herve, Eupen, Limburg, Spa, Stavelot, Malmedy)." *La Revue Nationale,* 35 (1963), 231-239.

Rahlenbeck, Charles A. *Histoire de la ville et du comté de Dalhem depuis les temps les plus reculés jusqu'à nos jours.* Brussels, 1852.

—. *Les Pays d'Outre-Meuse. Etudes historiques sur Dalhem, Fauquemont, et Rolduc.* Brussels, 1888.

Renardy, Christine, and Wegnez, Anne-Marie. "Pascase Foullon (1615-1678). La Vie d'un patricien liégeois révélée par la gestion de ses biens." *Vieux Liège,* 7 (1970), 472-491.

Rouhart-Chabot, Juliette, and Hélin, Etienne, *Admissions à la bourgeoisie de la cité de Liège, 1273-1794.* Liège: Société des Bibliophiles Liégeois, 1962.

—. "Comment devenait-on bourgeois de la cité de Liège?" *BIAL,* 76 (1963), 91-114.

Ruhl, Gustave. "L'Ancien couvent des carmes et l'église de Devant le Pont près Visé." *Leodium,* 6 (1907), 45-49.

—. "Coup d'oeil archéologique sur la ville de Visé, en 1902." *Leodium,* 2 (1903), 25-33.

Ryckel, Amédée de. "La Cour féodale dans l'ancien duché de Limbourg." *BSAHL,* 9 (1895), 273-455.

—. "Les Fiefs du Comté de Dalhem." *BSAHL,* 18 (1908), 272-384.

—. "Notice sur la libre seigneurie de Breust." *Publications de la Société Historique et Archéologique dans le Duché de Limbourg,* 27 (1890), 3-22.

—. "Rivières et ruisseaux de la province de Liège." *BSAHL,* 21 (1923), 27-111.

Schnackers, Joseph. "Le Comté de Dalhem et son drossard hodimontois Franquinel." *Bulletin de la Société Verviétoise d'Archéologie et d'Histoire,* 44 (1957), 319-320.

—. "Un Conflit aux états de Dalhem au XVIIIᵉ siècle." *CAPL,* 50 (1959), 10-26.

—. *Dalhem, ancienne franchise et capitale du comté.* Brussels, 1965.

—. *Le Pays de Dalhem au XVIIIᵉ siècle.* Brussels, 1955.

Vandekerkhove, Antoine. *Histoire de l'abbaye de Val-Dieu à travers les siècles.* Second ed. Liège, 1954.

Veldman, J.-C. *Nivellae Supra Mosam in Valle Obituarium. Notices historiques sur les inhumations dans les églises de Lixhe et de Lanaye.* Lixhe, 1967.

Yans, Maurice. "Le destin diplomatique de Herstal-Wandre terre des Nassau, en banlieu liégoise." *Annuaire d'Histoire Liégeoise,* 6 (1960), 487-562.

—. "Textes relatifs à la reconstruction de Liège après le bombardement de 1691." *Leodium,* 58 (1971), 5-19.

—. "Urbanisme et vie religieuse à Visé au XIVᵉ siècle." *Leodium,* 42 (1951), 29-36.

2. Other Regions

Baehrel, Rene. *Une Croissance: la Basse-Provence rurale (fin du XVIᵉ siècle-1789).* Paris: SEVPEN, 1961.

Cabourdin, Guy. *Terre et Hommes en Lorraine du milieu du XVIᵉ siècle à la Guerre de Trente Ans.* 3 vols. Lille: Service de Reproduction des Thèses de l'Université de Lille III, 1975.

Faber, J. A. "Drie Eeuwen Friesland." *A.A.G. Bijdragen* 17 (1972).

Goubert, Pierre. *Beauvais et le Beauvasis de 1600 à 1730.* Paris: SEVPEN, 1960.

—. "The French Peasantry of the Seventeenth Century: a Regional Example." *Past and Present,* No. 10 (1956), 55-77.

Jacquart, Jean. *La Crise rurale en Ile-de-France, 1550-1670.* Paris: Librarie Armand Colin, 1974.

Le Roy Ladurie, Emmanuel. *Les Paysans de Languedoc.* 2 vols. Paris: SEVPEN, 1966.

Schotter, J. "Etat du duché de Luxemburg et du comté de Chiny pendant la guerre de trente ans." *Annales de l'Academie Archéologique de Belgique,* 33 (1876), 325-459.

Woude, A. M. van der. "Het Noorderkwartier." *A.A.G. Bijdragen,* 16 (1972).

H. Religion and Religious Organization

Bas, Willem. *Het Protestantisme in het bisdom Luik en vooral te Maastricht.* 's Gravenhage, 1941.

Bragard, Rene. "Le Legislation sur la mainmorte et les couvents à Liège specialement au XVIIᵉ siècle." *BIAL,* 70 (1953-1954), 285-368.

Brassine, J. "Les Paroisses de l'ancien concile de Saint-Remacle." *BSAHL,* 14 (1903), 267-277.

Ceyssens, Jean. "Les Curés de Dalhem." *Leodium,* 26 (1933), 14-32.

—. "Les Doyens ruraux dans l'ancien diocèse de Liège." *BSAHL,* 9 (1895), 159-224.

—. "Etude historique sur l'origine des paroisses." *BSAHL,* 14 (1903), 161-221.

—. "Val-Dieu et la paroisse de Saint-Remy." *Leodium,* 10 (1911), 66-73.

Daniels, P. "Document touchant les charges des decimateurs." *Leodium,* 5 (1906), 78-80.

Danthinne, P. "Incidents de divorce au XVIIᵉ siècle." *CAPL,* 42-44 (1953), 112-118.

Deblon, André. "Les Rapports des visites archidiaconales de Condroz." *BSAHL,* 50 (1970), 105-239.

—. "Une source capitale pour l'histoire paroissiale de l'ancien régime; les visites archidiaconales de Condroz." *BSAHL,* 50 (1970), 55-104.

Dubois, Alice. *Le Chapitre cathédral de Saint-Lambert à Liège au XVIIᵉ siècle.* Liège, 1949.

Dupont, Léopold. *La Condition des enfants nes hors mariage en droit liégeois.* Liège, 1960.

Forgeur, Richard. "Les Paroisses du diocèse de Liège desservies par des religieux à fin du XVIIIe siècle." *Leodium,* 41 (1954), 35-36.

Halkin, Leon-Ernest. "La Competence criminelle des tribunaux ecclésiastiques liégeois au debut du XVIIIe siècle." *Annuaire d'Histoire Liégeoise,* 5 (1956), 761-801.

Hélin, Etienne. "Le Sort des enfants trouvés au XVIIIe siècle." *Vieux Liège,* 6 (1953), 203-206.

Hubert, Eugène. *Les Eglises protestantes du duché de Limbourg pendant le XVIIe siècle. Etude d'histoire politique et religieuse.* Mémoires publies par la Classe des Lettres et des Sciences Morales et Politiques de l'Academie Royale de Belgique, series in-4°. New series, vol. 4. Brussels, 1908.

Made, Raoul van der. "La Jurisprudence pénale de l'officialité liégeois au XVIIe et XVIIIe siècles." *Annuaire d'Histoire Liégeoise,* 5 (1955), 575-640.

—. "La Publicité du mariage en droit liégeois." *BIAL,* 67 (1949-1950), 363-378.

Moreau, Edouard de, S. J., et al. *Histoire de l'Eglise en Belgique.* 5 vols. and 2 complementary vols. Brussels, 1946-1952.

Ô-Kelly, C. "Auxiliaires des curés de Dalhem (1645-1796)." *Leodium,* 34 (1947), 30-32.

—. "Coup d'oeil sur le protestantisme au comté de Dalhem avant et au temps de la retrocession du pays à l'Autriche le 5 novembre 1785." *Leodium,* 28 (1935), 57-66, 70-76.

Paquay, J. "Le Patrimoine de l'Eglise de Liège, aperçu économique." *Analecta Ecclesiastica Leodensia,* 4 (1936).

Pasture, A. *Les Anciennes dîmes dans l'administration paroissiale.* Wetteren, 1938.

Rahlenbeck, Charles. "Le Protestantisme dans les pays de Limbourg et d'Outre-Meuse." *Revue Trimestrielle,* 11 (1856), 86-120.

Ubachs, P. J. H. *Twee heren, twee confessies. De verhouding van Staat en Kerk te Maastricht, 1632-1673.* Assen, The Netherlands: Van Gorcum, 1975.

Yans, Maurice. "Contributions à l'étude du droit matrimonial liégeois." *Annuaire d'Histoire Liégeoise,* 4 (1951), 301-344.

—. "Textes liégeois relatifs au rapt et au consentement paternal." *Annuaire d'Histoire Liégeoise,* 4 (1948), 23-49.

I. Language

Haust, Jean. *Le Dialect wallon de Liège.* 3 vols. Liège, 1930-1948.

Kurth, Godefroid. *La Frontière linguistique en Belgique et dans la Nord de la France.* 2 vols. Mém. Cour., vol. 48. Brussels, 1895-1898.

Marez, G. de. *La Problème de la colonisation franque et du régime agraire en Belgique.* Mémoires de l'Academie Royale de Belgique, Classe des Lettres, in-4°, second series, vol. 9. Brussels, 1926.

Petri, Franz. *Germanisches Volkserbe in Wallonien und Nordfrankreich. Die fränkische Landnahme in Frankreich und den Niederlanden und die Bildung der westlichen Sprachgrenze.* Bonn, 1937.

Verlinden, Charles. *Les Origines de la frontière linguistique en Belgique et la colonisation franque.* Brussels: La Renaissance du Livre, 1955.

Carte de Cabinet de Pays-Bas autrichiens de Ferraris (1771-1778). Manuscript map in the collection of the Bibliothèque Royal Albert Ier, Brussels. Reproduced and Published by the Credit Communal de Belgique, Brussels, 1965. Sections 189, 190 and 191 include much of the Basse-Meuse.

Essen, Léon van der. *Atlas de géographie historique de la Belgique.* Brussels-Paris, 1919-1927

Lefevre, M. A. "Carte des regions géographiques belges." *Bulletin de la Société Belge d'Etudes Géographiques,* 10 (1940), 49-80.

Remouchamps, J. M. "Carte systematique de la Wallonie, précédée d'une note sur la frontière linguistique et d'une double nomenclature des communes belges de langue Romane d'après le recensement du 31 decembre 1930." *Bulletin de la Commission Royale de Toponymie et de Dialectologie,* 9 (1935).

Ruwet, Joseph. *La Principauté de Liège en 1789, carte de géographie historique.* Brussels, 1958.

Index

Place names are in italics

Aachen, 40, 113
Abandoned Farms, 101-102
Achilles, Walter, 116
Aix-la-Chapelle, Treaty of (1748), 230
Amenorrhea of famine, 185-186
Amsterdam, 111, 113; prices at, 115-130
Argenteau, 22, 58, 153, 213, 218; coal mining, 26; population, 143-145, 148
Armament industry, 26
Armies: civilian control of, 64-66; private, 57-58; of various countries, *see* names of individual countries
Arnhem, 116, 119
Athlone, Godard van Reede, 1st Earl of, 224, 225
Augsburg, War of the League of (1688-1697), 16, 18, 20, 56, 64, 69, 76, 78, 89, 98, 102, 107, 108, 110, 138, 148, 178, 199, 203, 222, 224
Austrian Succession, War of the (1741-1748), 6, 16, 22, 39, 59, 66, 69-71, 75, 78, 89-90, 98, 110, 148, 158, 178, 195, 229
Avins, Battle of (1635), 213
Aytona, Don Francisco de Moncada, Marquis of (1586-1635), 196, 213
Banlieu (of the city of Liège), 50, 212
Barracks, 36, 58-59
Barrier, Treaties of (1709-1715), 227
Basse-Meuse: definition of, 6; terrain and agriculture, 23-25
Bassompiere, General, 217
Battles, impact of, 16, 69
Beeringen, 227
Bellefons, Bernadin Gigault de (d. 1694), 218

Berg, 87
Berg, Henry van den (1573-1638), 212
Berghes, Georges-Louis de, Prince-Bishop of Lièges (1724-1743), 228, 229
Berlamont, Daniel, 59, 66
Belsen, 227
Blanckart, General, 212
Bois-le-Duc: population of, 147
Bolder, 87
Bombaye, 24
Borders, and military action in the Basse-Meuse, 9, 13
Borrowing, 50-52; farmers, after wartime losses, 100-101, 108, 206
Boufflers, Louis François, Duke of (1644-1711), 222, 224, 225
Boulihar, Laroque de, 215
Bouridal, General, 222
Brabant, Duchy of, 11; population, 146
Brandenburg army, 221, 224, 226, 227
Bree, 227
Breze, General de, 213
Bribery, 44-45
Bridges across the Meuse, 22
Brussels, 213
Bubonic Plague, 152, 158-159, 161, 162, 164, 178, 187, 217
Burgundy, Circle of, 11
Burgundy, Duchy of, and Liégeois neutrality, 17
Cabourdin, Guy, 108
Cadier, 87
Calcar, 215
Callot, Jacques (1592-1687), 33, 34, 199
Calvo, Jean Sauveur de (1625-1690), 220, 221

310

Library of Congress Cataloging in Publication Data

Gutmann, Myron P.   1949-
    War and rural life in the early modern Low Countries.

    Based on the author's thesis, Princeton University, 1976.
    Bibliography: p. 279
    Includes index.
1. Liège (Province) - Rural conditions. 2. Liège (Province) - History. 3. Limburg, Belgium
(Province) - History. 4. Limburg, Belgium (Province) - Rural conditions. 5, Maastricht
region, Netherlands - History. 6. Maastricht region, Netherlands - Rural conditions. I. Title.
HN493.G87   1980   949.3'2   79-23502